The Pacific Northwest's Best Bed & Breakfasts

Delightful Places to Stay

Great Things to Do When You Get There

4th Edition

FODOR'S TRAVEL PUBLICATIONS, INC.

NEW YORK • TORONTO • LONDON • SYDNEY • AUCKLAND

THE PACIFIC NORTHWEST'S BEST BED & BREAKFASTS

Editor: Caragh Rockwood

Editorial Contributors: Brian Clark, Julie Fay, Sue Kernaghan, Christina Knight, Jena MacPherson, James McQuillen, Donald S. Olson, Martha Paulsen, Dianna Schmid, Peggy Stafford

Editorial Production: Linda K. Schmidt

Maps: David Lindroth, *cartographer*; Robert Blake, Steven Amsterdam, *map editors*

Design: Guido Caroti

Illustrations: Kayley LeFaiver

Cover Photograph: © Randy Wells

ISBN 0–679–00178–6

Fourth Edition

SPECIAL SALES

Fodor's Travel Publications are available at special discounts for bulk purchases for sales promotions or premiums. Special editions, including personalized covers, excerpts of existing guides, and corporate imprints, can be created in large quantities for special needs. For more information contact your local bookseller or write to Special Markets, Fodor's Travel Publications, 201 East 50th Street, New York, NY 10022. Inquiries from Canada should be directed to your local Canadian bookseller or sent to Random House of Canada, Ltd., Marketing Department, 2775 Matheson Boulevard East, Mississauga, Ontario L4W 4P7. Inquiries from the United Kingdom should be sent to Fodor's Travel Publications, 20 Vauxhall Bridge Road, London SW1V 2SA, England.

PRINTED IN THE UNITED STATES OF AMERICA

10 9 8 7 6 5 4 3 2 1

CONTENTS

Foreword *iv*

Introduction *v*

Oregon 1

South Coast *4*

Southern Oregon *16*

Including Ashland

Willamette Valley *29*

Including Eugene

Wine Country *38*

Including Salem

Portland *49*

North Coast *61*

Columbia River Gorge and Mt. Hood *73*

Central and Eastern Oregon *84*

Including Bend

Washington 97

Columbia River and Long Beach Peninsula *100*

Olympic Peninsula *115*

Seattle and Environs *127*

Whidbey Island *139*

San Juan Islands *150*

Whatcom and Skagit Counties *165*

Including Anacortes, Bellingham, and La Conner

Cascade Mountains and Foothills *178*

Spokane and Environs *189*

Including Coeur d'Alene

The Palouse *198*

British Columbia 205

Vancouver and Environs *208*

Whistler *216*

Vancouver Island *221*

Victoria *231*

The Gulf Islands *239*

Alphabetical Directory 251

Geographical Directory 255

FOREWORD

While every care has been taken to ensure the accuracy of the information in this guide, the passage of time will always bring change, and, consequently, Fodor's cannot accept responsibility for errors that may occur.

All prices and listings are based on information available to us at press time. Details may change, however, and the prudent traveler will avoid inconvenience by calling ahead.

Fodor's wants to hear about your travel experiences, both pleasant and unpleasant. When an inn or B&B fails to live up to its billing, let us know and we will investigate the complaint and revise our entries where the facts warrant it.

Send your letters to the Pacific Northwest's Best Bed & Breakfasts editor at Fodor's Travel Publications, 201 East 50th Street, New York, NY 10022, or e-mail us at editors@fodors.com.

INTRODUCTION

You'll find bed-and-breakfasts in big houses with turrets and little houses with decks, in mansions by the water and cabins in the forest, not to mention structures of many sizes and shapes in between. B&Bs are run by people who were once lawyers and writers, homemakers and artists, nurses and architects, singers and businesspeople. Some B&Bs are just a room or two in a hospitable local's home; others are more like small inns. So there's an element of serendipity to every stay in an inn or B&B. But while that's part of the pleasure of visiting these establishments, it's also an excellent reason to plan your travels with a good B&B guide. The one you hold in your hands serves the purpose neatly. We think it's the best of its kind.

All the establishments we've included promise a unique experience, a distinctive sense of time and place. Each is a destination in itself, not just a place to rest your head at night but an integral part of a weekend escape, with the owners providing endless thoughtful touches—binoculars for bird-watching or pancakes bursting with local huckleberries at breakfast. We'll tell you just what to expect both at the B&B and in the area, everything from historic sites and parks to antiques shops, boutiques, and the area's niftiest restaurants and nightspots. What are the must-sees and what's not worth your time? You'll hear it all from us.

To create this guide and keep it up to date, we've handpicked a team of professional writers who are also confirmed B&B lovers: people who adore the many manifestations of the Victorian era; who go wild over wicker and brass beds, four-posters and fireplaces; and who know a well-run operation when they see it and are only too eager to communicate their knowledge to you. For all the premier inns and B&Bs in the areas they cover, they've inspected the premises and checked out every corner, and in these pages they report critically on only the best in every price range—what's good, what's bad, and what could be better.

CONTRIBUTORS

As a feature writer for The Olympian *newspaper in Olympia,* **Brian Clark** *has reported about travel in the Northwest for the past six years. When not surveying B&Bs on the Olympic Peninsula, Brian pursues his other great passions: skiing, climbing, kayaking, scuba diving, bicycling, and trekking around the West. As for his recent relocation to Las Vegas after a decade in the Northwest, he's looking forward to exploring the Southwest and its extreme outdoor opportunities.*

Freelance writer and former caterer **Julie Fay**—*a native Seattleite and fifth-generation Washingtonian—lives with her daughter and husband in Seattle. Since retiring her toque, she has worked on several Fodor's projects, including reporting on the Seattle bed-and-breakfast scene. She spends much of every summer at her family's cabin in the San Juan Islands.*

Vancouverite **Sue Kernaghan,** *who upturned many a bed-and-breakfast for the British Columbia chapter, is a fourth-generation British Columbian. "The family's been in B.C. so long we've had a swamp named after us," she claims. Her work has appeared in the* Times of London *and Vancouver's own* Georgia Straight. *Between Fodor's assignments, she writes management books, the latest* Doing it Different, the Method in Mad Companies.

Because her grandfather collected automobiles and her English mother wouldn't fly, **Jena MacPherson**'s *earliest memories are of driving the back-roads of Washington and of taking trans-Atlantic cruise ship journeys. Jena's ancestors were pioneers in the San Juan Islands and the Yakima Valley, where she grew up. She has reported on the Northwest for more than 10 years for* Sunset *magazine—among other travel magazines—and her first travel book,* Pacific Northwest Travel Smart, *by John Muir Publishing, will be out in April, 1999. Her pioneering spirit and travel savvy came in handy for her work on the Cascade Mountains section, which brought her to many a mountain lodge and B&B. She lives in Seattle with her husband, Jim, and their dog, Molly the Magnificent.*

James McQuillen, *who covered hundreds of miles in Oregon for this book (South and North coasts, Willamette Valley, Wine Country, Central and Eastern Oregon, and the Columbia River and Long Beach Peninsula in Washington), left Vermont at age 17 and, after a sojourn in Oregon for school, kept heading west. In two circuits of the world and many shorter* *trips, his accommodations included hammocks, yurts, and train station floors, as well as countless small inns and B&Bs. He now lives in Portland where he is a writer and editor at the news and arts weekly* Willamette Week.

Martha Paulsen, *our B&B sleuth for Southern Oregon, Columbia River Gorge and Mt. Hood, Spokane, and the Palouse, has lived in London, the Dominican Republic, and around the United States. Her traveling nature came in handy for her vast assignment, which had her behind the wheel on the Washington and Oregon B&B circuit for weeks. A native Oregonian who spent her childhood in the Rogue Valley, she resides in Portland, where she is a marketing communications specialist and a freelance writer.*

Novelist and playwright **Donald S. Olson** *put nearly 5,000 miles on his car working on* Fodor's Oregon, *but for this book stayed closer to home, revising the Portland section. His travel writing on Oregon and the Pacific Northwest has appeared in* The New York Times *and* Travel & Leisure. *His last novel,* The Confessions of Aubrey Beardsley, *was published by Bantam Press in London.*

A native of Missoula, Montana, **Dianna Schmid** *has worked in print and broadcast media and more recently as an independent marketing communications consultant in Portland. Personal and business travel in the past couple of years alone has taken her throughout the United States as well as to Canada, Europe, and the South Seas. Closer to home, she enjoyed one of her favorite pursuits in visiting the B&Bs and small inns of Whidbey Island and Whatcom and Skagit Counties: getting acquainted with a variety of fascinating people and discovering how they've come to know and follow their bliss.*

Peggy Stafford *lives in Seattle. For her revision of the San Juan Island section, she tended to every last detail—checked out nearly every curtain, side table, and hot tub—to make your B&B experience a happy one. Peggy is a freelance writer and new mother who also spends her time writing children's educational software, including the award-winning "Sky Island Mysteries" from the Edmark Corporation. Her other passion is writing plays; her productions include* Sometimes a Trapeze Artist *and* Fire Down Below.

SOME NOTES ON HOW TO USE THIS BOOK

*Reviews are organized by state, and, within each state, by region. At the
beginning of every review is the address and telephone, with a mailing address if there is one; we list URLs of Web sites where you can find out
more about the inn, and the e-mail address when there's no Web site. A
pineapple highlights properties that are especially recommended. At the
end of the review, in italicized service information, what we describe as
a double room is for two people, regardless of the size or type of its beds.
Unless otherwise noted, rooms don't have phones or TVs; they may not have
a private bath, even some of the most stunning homes and mansions. Rates
are for two, excluding tax, in high season, and include breakfast unless
otherwise noted. Ask about special packages and midweek or off-season
discounts.*

*What we call a restaurant serves meals other than breakfast and is usu-
ally open to the public.*

*The following credit card abbreviations are used throughout this guide:
AE, American Express; D, Discover; DC, Diners Club; MC, MasterCard;
V, Visa.*

*Where applicable, we note seasonal and other restrictions. Although we
abhor discrimination, we have conveyed information about innkeepers'
restrictive practices so that you will be aware of the prevailing attitudes.
Such discriminatory practices are most often applied to parents who are
traveling with small children and who may not, in any case, feel comfortable
having their offspring toddle amid breakable bric-a-brac and near pre-
cipitous stairways.*

*In case you're inspired to seek out additional properties on your own, we
include names and addresses of B&B reservation services.*

OUR BEST TIP

*When traveling the B&B way, always call ahead. You can use this book
confident that all prices and opening times are based on information supplied to us at press time. However, time inevitably brings changes, so always
confirm information when it matters; Fodor's cannot accept responsibility for errors. If you're traveling to an inn because of a specific feature, make
sure that it will be available when you get there and not closed for renovation. The same goes if you're making a detour to take advantage of*

specific sights or attractions. And if you are traveling with children, if you prefer a private bath or a certain type of bed, or if you have mobility problems, specific dietary needs, or any other concerns, discuss them with the innkeeper.

A POINT OF PRIDE

It's a sad commentary on other B&B guides today that we feel obliged to tell you that our writers did, in fact, visit every property in person, and that it is they, not the innkeepers, who wrote the reviews. No one paid a fee or promised to sell or promote the book in order to be included in it. (In fact, one of the most challenging parts of the work of a Fodor's writer is to persuade innkeepers and B&B owners that he or she wants nothing more than a tour of the premises and the answers to a few questions!) Fodor's has no stake in anything but the truth. So trust us, the way you'd trust a knowledgeable, well-traveled friend. Let us hear from you about your travels, whether you found that the B&Bs you visited surpassed their descriptions or the other way around. If you've discovered a special place that we haven't included, we'll have our B&B correspondents check it out. So send us your feedback, positive and negative: email us at editors@fodors.com (specifying Pacific Northwest's Best Bed & Breakfasts *on the subject line) or write* Pacific Northwest's Best Bed & Breakfasts *editor at Fodor's, 201 East 50th Street, New York, New York 10022. And have a wonderful trip!*

Karen Cure
Editorial Director

Pacific Northwest

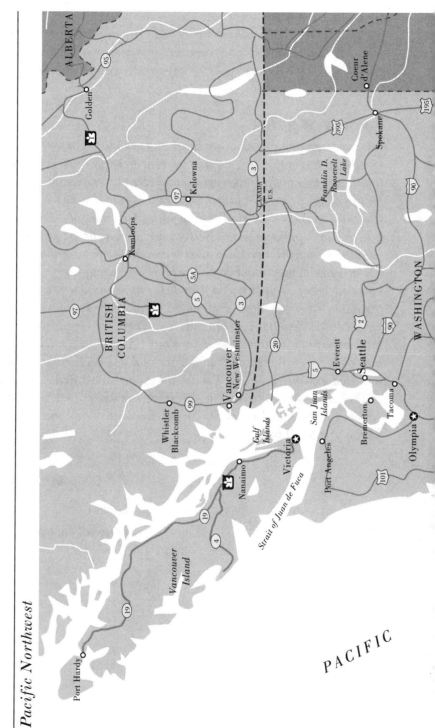

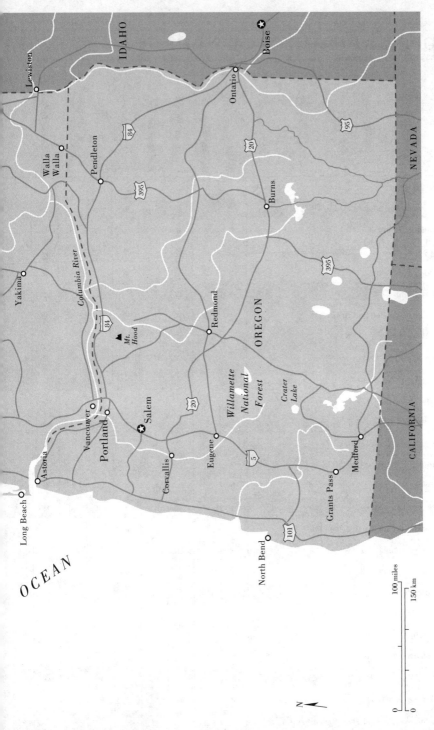

Special Features at a Glance ↩

	Antiques	Car Not Necessary	Conference Facilities	Full Meal Service	Good for Families	Historic Building	Luxurious	No Smoking Indoors	
OREGON									
Anderson's Boarding House	✳		✳		✳	✳		✳	
Antique Rose Inn	✳		✳			✳	✳	✳	
Apple Inn Bed & Breakfast			✳		✳			✳	
Arden Forest Inn		✳			✳			✳	
Astoria Inn	✳		✳			✳		✳	
Bayberry Inn Bed and Breakfast	✳	✳			✳			✳	
Beckley House	✳		✳		✳	✳		✳	
Bed-and-Breakfast by the River					✳			✳	
Benjamin Young Inn	✳		✳			✳	✳	✳	
Beryl House	✳							✳	
Bridal Veil Lodge	✳				✳	✳		✳	
Brightwood Guest House				✳				✳	
Brookside Bed and Breakfast	✳				✳			✳	
Campbell House	✳		✳			✳	✳	✳	
Chamberlain House	✳							✳	
Chandlers Bed, Bread & Trail Inn					✳			✳	
Channel House			✳						
Chanticleer Inn	✳	✳						✳	
Chetco River Inn	✳			✳				✳	
Clear Creek Farm Bed-and-Breakfast			✳		✳			✳	
Cliff House	✳					✳	✳	✳	
Clinkerbrick House	✳	✳			✳			✳	
Columbia Gorge Hotel	✳		✳	✳		✳	✳	✳	
Coos Bay Manor	✳		✳			✳			
Country Willows Bed and Breakfast Inn	✳		✳	✳		✳	✳	✳	

On the Water	Pets Allowed	Romantic Hideaway	Beach Nearby	Boating Nearby	Cross-Country Skiing Nearby	Fishing Nearby	Golf Nearby	Hiking Nearby	Horseback Riding Nearby	Skiing Nearby	Swimming	Tennis Court	Wineries Nearby	Fitness Facilities
❀			❀			❀	❀		❀					
		❀			❀	❀	❀	❀		❀			❀	
				❀		❀		❀					❀	
					❀	❀	❀	❀		❀			❀	
		❀				❀	❀							
					❀	❀	❀	❀		❀			❀	
						❀	❀						❀	
❀					❀	❀		❀	❀				❀	
		❀				❀	❀							
						❀		❀	❀		❀			❀	
		❀						❀					❀	
					❀	❀	❀	❀		❀			❀	
					❀	❀	❀	❀		❀			❀	
		❀					❀							
								❀						
						❀	❀		❀		❀			
❀		❀	❀	❀		❀	❀							
					❀	❀	❀	❀		❀			❀	
❀		❀	❀	❀		❀		❀			❀			
					❀	❀		❀	❀	❀				
❀		❀	❀				❀	❀	❀					
							❀							
❀		❀						❀	❀				❀	
❀	❀							❀					❀	
		❀				❀	❀	❀	❀		❀			

Special Features at a Glance ←

	Antiques	Car Not Necessary	Conference Facilities	Full Meal Service	Good for Families	Historic Building	Luxurious	No Smoking Indoors
Doublegate Inn	✽							✽
Elliott House	✽					✽	✽	✽
Excelsior Inn			✽	✽			✽	✽
Falcon's Crest Inn	✽		✽	✽				✽
Fernwood at Alder Creek	✽					✽		✽
Flery Manor	✽							✽
Floras Lake House by the Sea	✽				✽			✽
Flying M Ranch			✽	✽	✽			✽
Franklin St. Station	✽		✽			✽		✽
Frenchglen Hotel				✽		✽		✽
Geiser Grand Hotel			✽	✽	✽	✽	✽	✽
General Hooker's B&B		✽				✽		
Georgian House	✽	✽						✽
Gilbert Inn	✽		✽			✽		✽
Grandview Bed & Breakfast	✽		✽		✽	✽		✽
Hanson Country Inn	✽		✽		✽	✽		✽
Harrison House	✽		✽		✽	✽		✽
Heceta Lighthouse Bed and Breakfast	✽					✽		✽
Heron Haus	✽	✽	✽			✽	✽	✽
Home by the Sea			✽		✽			✽
Hood River Hotel			✽	✽	✽	✽		✽
Hotel Diamond				✽		✽		
Hotel Vintage Plaza			✽	✽	✽			
House of Hunter	✽		✽		✽	✽		✽
Howell House	✽					✽		✽
Hudson House	✽		✽		✽	✽		✽

On the Water	Pets Allowed	Romantic Hideaway	Beach Nearby	Boating Nearby	Cross-Country Skiing Nearby	Fishing Nearby	Golf Nearby	Hiking Nearby	Horseback Riding Nearby	Skiing Nearby	Swimming	Tennis Court	Wineries Nearby	Fitness Facilities
	❋	❋			❋	❋	❋	❋		❋			❋	
		❋				❋	❋	❋						
							❋							
		❋			❋			❋		❋				
❋						❋	❋	❋		❋			❋	
				❋		❋		❋						
❋		❋	❋	❋			❋		❋		❋			
❋	❋	❋				❋		❋	❋		❋	❋	❋	
						❋	❋							
		❋						❋						
		❋			❋	❋		❋	❋					❋
	❋	❋	❋				❋							❋
							❋							
		❋	❋			❋	❋		❋					
		❋				❋	❋							
		❋		❋		❋	❋	❋					❋	
				❋			❋	❋	❋				❋	
❋		❋	❋			❋		❋						
		❋					❋					❋		
❋			❋					❋						
	❋		❋	❋	❋		❋	❋			❋		❋	❋
								❋						
		❋						❋						
				❋		❋	❋	❋					❋	
		❋											❋	
				❋										

Special Features at a Glance

	Antiques	*Car Not Necessary*	*Conference Facilities*	*Full Meal Service*	*Good for Families*	*Historic Building*	*Luxurious*	*No Smoking Indoors*
Inn at Manzanita			✽					✽
Inn at Nesika Beach	✽							✽
Ivy House	✽				✽	✽		✽
Jacksonville Inn	✽	✽	✽	✽		✽	✽	✽
Johnson House	✽					✽		✽
Kelty Estate	✽					✽		✽
Kittiwake								✽
Lakecliff Estate Bed & Breakfast	✽					✽	✽	✽
Lara House	✽		✽			✽		✽
The Lighthouse			✽		✽			✽
Lion and the Rose	✽	✽	✽		✽		✽	✽
Lithia Springs Inn	✽				✽			✽
MacMaster House		✽	✽					✽
Main Street Bed & Breakfast								✽
Maple River			✽				✽	✽
Marquee House	✽							✽
Mattey House	✽					✽	✽	✽
McGillivray's Log Home Bed and Breakfast					✽			✽
McMenamins Edgefield				✽	✽	✽		✽
Morical House Garden Inn	✽							✽
Mt. Ashland Inn	✽		✽	✽	✽		✽	✽
Nye Beach Hotel					✽	✽		
Old Welches Inn	✽		✽			✽		✽
Orchard View Inn	✽		✽					✽
Oval Door Bed and Breakfast	✽		✽		✽			✽
Parker House Bed and Breakfast	✽					✽	✽	✽

On the Water	Pets Allowed	Romantic Hideaway	Beach Nearby	Boating Nearby	Cross-Country Skiing Nearby	Fishing Nearby	Golf Nearby	Hiking Nearby	Horseback Riding Nearby	Skiing Nearby	Swimming	Tennis Court	Wineries Nearby	Fitness Facilities
		❀	❀				❀	❀						
❀		❀	❀											
				❀	❀	❀	❀	❀		❀			❀	
		❀		❀	❀	❀	❀			❀			❀	
			❀	❀		❀	❀	❀	❀					
							❀						❀	
❀		❀	❀					❀						
❀		❀		❀	❀		❀	❀		❀			❀	
		❀		❀		❀		❀						
❀		❀	❀				❀							
		❀					❀		❀				❀	
					❀	❀	❀	❀		❀			❀	
		❀					❀							
													❀	
❀		❀			❀	❀	❀	❀		❀			❀	
❀							❀						❀	
		❀					❀		❀				❀	
		❀		❀		❀		❀						
			❀				❀	❀					❀	
		❀			❀	❀	❀	❀		❀			❀	
		❀		❀	❀	❀	❀	❀		❀			❀	
❀		❀	❀	❀		❀	❀	❀						
❀		❀			❀	❀	❀	❀		❀			❀	
		❀			❀								❀	
							❀							
		❀				❀		❀	❀					

Special Features at a Glance ←

	Antiques	Car Not Necessary	Conference Facilities	Full Meal Service	Good for Families	Historic Building	Luxurious	No Smoking Indoors
Partridge Farm	✽					✽		✽
Peerless Hotel	✽	✽	✽	✽		✽	✽	✽
Pine Meadow Inn Bed and Breakfast	✽							✽
Pine Valley Lodge and Halfway Supper Club			✽	✽		✽		✽
Portland Guest House	✽	✽			✽		✽	
Portland's White House	✽	✽			✽	✽	✽	✽
RiverPlace Hotel		✽		✽			✽	✽
Romeo Inn	✽			✽				✽
St. Bernards	✽						✽	
Sandlake Country Inn	✽		✽			✽		✽
The Sather House Bed-and-Breakfast	✽					✽		✽
Sea Quest	✽							✽
Serenity	✽							✽
Shaniko Hotel				✽	✽	✽		✽
Springbrook Hazelnut Farm	✽					✽	✽	✽
Stang Manor	✽		✽		✽	✽		✽
State House					✽			✽
Steamboat Inn			✽	✽	✽		✽	✽
Steens Mountain Inn	✽		✽	✽		✽	✽	✽
Steiger Haus			✽		✽			✽
Stephanie Inn				✽	✽			✽
Suite River Bed and Breakfast	✽							✽
Sylvia Beach Hotel	✽		✽	✽				
Touvelle House	✽			✽		✽		
Tudor House	✽				✽	✽		✽
Tu Tu Tun Lodge			✽	✽	✽		✽	

On the Water	Pets Allowed	Romantic Hideaway	Beach Nearby	Boating Nearby	Cross-Country Skiing Nearby	Fishing Nearby	Golf Nearby	Hiking Nearby	Horseback Riding Nearby	Skiing Nearby	Swimming	Tennis Court	Wineries Nearby	Fitness Facilities
		❀					❀	❀					❀	
		❀		❀	❀	❀	❀	❀		❀			❀	
				❀										
	❀	❀			❀					❀				
		❀					❀					❀	❀	
		❀					❀		❀					
		❀	❀				❀	❀						❀
					❀	❀	❀	❀		❀	❀		❀	
❀		❀	❀						❀					❀
		❀	❀				❀	❀						
		❀			❀			❀						
❀		❀	❀					❀						
		❀		❀		❀		❀						
		❀					❀	❀			❀	❀	❀	
					❀	❀	❀							
	❀	❀					❀	❀			❀	❀	❀	
❀	❀	❀				❀		❀			❀			
		❀						❀						
❀							❀	❀					❀	
❀		❀	❀						❀					
❀		❀	❀			❀	❀	❀		❀			❀	
			❀	❀		❀	❀	❀						
	❀				❀	❀		❀	❀	❀		❀	❀	❀
❀		❀	❀	❀			❀	❀	❀		❀			

Special Features at a Glance ←

	Antiques	Car Not Necessary	Conference Facilities	Full Meal Service	Good for Families	Historic Building	Luxurious	No Smoking Indoors	
Tyee Lodge	✿							✿	
Westfir Lodge	✿					✿		✿	
Whiskey Creek Bed & Breakfast			✿		✿			✿	
Winchester Country Inn	✿	✿		✿	✿	✿		✿	
Woods House	✿	✿			✿			✿	
Youngberg Hill Vineyard	✿			✿	✿		✿	✿	
Ziggurat			✿					✿	
WASHINGTON (including Idaho)									
Abendblume Pension	✿						✿	✿	
Albatross	✿				✿	✿			
Alexander's Country Inn	✿			✿		✿			
All Seasons River Inn Bed & Breakfast	✿						✿		
Anchorage Inn	✿						✿	✿	
Annapurna Inn Massage and Retreat Center	✿		✿		✿	✿	✿	✿	
Ann Starrett Mansion	✿			✿		✿	✿	✿	
Bacon Mansion/Broadway Guest House	✿	✿	✿		✿	✿	✿	✿	
Big Trees Bed & Breakfast	✿	✿				✿	✿	✿	
Bingen Haus	✿				✿	✿		✿	
Birchfield Manor	✿		✿	✿		✿	✿	✿	
Bombay House	✿		✿	✿	✿	✿		✿	
Borea's Bed & Breakfast Inn	✿							✿	
Bradley House Bed & Breakfast	✿					✿		✿	
Captain Whidbey Inn	✿	✿	✿	✿	✿	✿		✿	
Caswell's on the Bay	✿		✿				✿	✿	
Chambered Nautilus	✿	✿		✿		✿		✿	
Channel House	✿	✿	✿	✿		✿		✿	

Oregon/Washington (including Idaho)

On the Water	Pets Allowed	Romantic Hideaway	Beach Nearby	Boating Nearby	Cross-Country Skiing Nearby	Fishing Nearby	Golf Nearby	Hiking Nearby	Horseback Riding Nearby	Skiing Nearby	Swimming	Tennis Court	Wineries Nearby	Fitness Facilities
		✻	✻	✻			✻	✻	✻					
		✻			✻	✻		✻						
✻	✻	✻	✻					✻						
				✻	✻	✻	✻	✻		✻	✻		✻	
				✻	✻	✻	✻	✻		✻			✻	
		✻				✻	✻	✻					✻	
✻		✻	✻					✻						
		✻		✻	✻	✻	✻	✻	✻	✻				
✻	✻	✻	✻	✻		✻	✻	✻				✻	✻		✻
					✻	✻		✻						
✻		✻		✻	✻	✻	✻	✻		✻				
		✻	✻	✻		✻	✻	✻	✻			✻	✻	
	✻	✻	✻	✻		✻	✻	✻				✻	✻	✻
		✻	✻	✻		✻	✻	✻				✻	✻	
		✻												
		✻	✻	✻	✻	✻	✻	✻	✻	✻	✻	✻	✻	✻
		✻		✻		✻	✻	✻					✻	
		✻					✻						✻	
			✻		✻			✻				✻		
		✻	✻							✻				
		✻		✻		✻		✻						
✻		✻	✻	✻		✻	✻	✻	✻				✻	
✻		✻	✻	✻		✻	✻							
							✻							
		✻	✻	✻		✻	✻	✻				✻	✻		✻

Special Features at a Glance ⬱

	Antiques	Car Not Necessary	Conference Facilities	Full Meal Service	Good for Families	Historic Building	Luxurious	No Smoking Indoors
Chestnut Hill Inn	※						※	※
Chick-a-Dee Inn at Ilwaco	※					※		※
Clark House on Hayden Lake	※		※	※	※	※	※	※
Cliff House and Sea Cliff Cottage		※			※		※	※
Coast Watch Bed & Breakfast			※					※
Colonel Crockett Farm	※	※				※	※	
Compass Rose Bed and Breakfast	※					※	※	※
Country Bed & Breakfast								※
Country Cottage of Langley	※	※					※	※
Cricket on the Hearth Bed and Breakfast Inn			※					※
Deer Harbor Inn						※		※
Domaine Madeleine	※		※				※	※
Duffy House	※							※
Eagles Nest Inn	※	※					※	※
Edenwild Inn	※		※					※
Farm Bed and Breakfast	※				※	※		※
Flying L Ranch								※
Fort Casey Inn	※	※	※		※	※		※
Fotheringham House	※		※			※		※
Freestone Inn			※	※	※		※	※
Friday Harbor House		※	※		※		※	※
Gaslight Inn	※	※				※	※	※
Green Gables Inn	※					※	※	※
Gregory's McFarland House	※					※		※
Guest House Cottages	※	※				※	※	※
Harbinger Inn	※					※	※	※

Washington (including Idaho)

On the Water	Pets Allowed	Romantic Hideaway	Beach Nearby	Boating Nearby	Cross-Country Skiing Nearby	Fishing Nearby	Golf Nearby	Hiking Nearby	Horseback Riding Nearby	Skiing Nearby	Swimming	Tennis Court	Wineries Nearby	Fitness Facilities
		✽	✽	✽			✽	✽						
		✽	✽	✽			✽							
✽		✽	✽	✽			✽	✽						
✽		✽	✽	✽		✽	✽	✽	✽				✽	
✽		✽	✽				✽							
	✽	✽	✽				✽	✽					✽	
			✽	✽		✽	✽	✽	✽			✽	✽	
	✽						✽							
		✽	✽	✽		✽	✽	✽			✽	✽	✽	
			✽				✽							
		✽	✽	✽			✽	✽						
✽			✽	✽		✽		✽	✽		✽			
			✽	✽		✽	✽	✽					✽	
		✽	✽	✽		✽	✽	✽	✽		✽	✽	✽	✽
		✽	✽	✽		✽	✽	✽					✽	
		✽			✽	✽		✽						
	✽				✽	✽		✽	✽					
		✽	✽	✽		✽	✽	✽					✽	
		✽					✽							
✽		✽		✽	✽	✽		✽	✽	✽	✽			✽
	✽		✽	✽		✽	✽	✽					✽	
		✽										✽		
		✽					✽			✽			✽	
							✽							
		✽	✽	✽		✽	✽	✽	✽			✽	✽	✽
✽		✽	✽	✽		✽	✽	✽						

Special Features at a Glance ←

	Antiques	Car Not Necessary	Conference Facilities	Full Meal Service	Good for Families	Historic Building	Luxurious	No Smoking Indoors
Hasty Pudding House	✱					✱	✱	✱
Haus Lorelei	✱				✱			
Haus Rohrbach Pension					✱			
Heron Inn	✱	✱	✱	✱	✱		✱	✱
Hill House	✱							
Hillside House		✱						✱
Home by the Sea Cottages	✱	✱			✱	✱	✱	✱
Hotel Planter			✱			✱	✱	✱
Inn at Harbor Steps		✱	✱	✱	✱		✱	✱
Inn at Langley		✱	✱				✱	✱
The Inn at the Market	✱	✱	✱	✱	✱		✱	✱
Inn at Penn Cove	✱				✱	✱		✱
Inn at Swifts Bay	✱						✱	✱
Inn at White Salmon	✱		✱		✱	✱		
James House	✱					✱	✱	✱
Kangaroo House	✱				✱	✱		✱
Kola House Bed & Breakfast			✱		✱	✱		✱
La Conner Channel Lodge			✱	✱	✱		✱	✱
La Conner Country Inn			✱	✱	✱			
Lake Crescent Lodge	✱	✱	✱	✱	✱	✱		✱
Lake Quinault Lodge	✱	✱	✱	✱	✱	✱		✱
Land's End	✱		✱					✱
Lizzie's Victorian Bed & Breakfast	✱					✱		✱
Log Castle Bed & Breakfast	✱	✱	✱					✱
Lone Lake Cottage and Breakfast		✱						✱
Lopez Farm Cottages								✱

Washington (including Idaho)

On the Water	Pets Allowed	Romantic Hideaway	Beach Nearby	Boating Nearby	Cross-Country Skiing Nearby	Fishing Nearby	Golf Nearby	Hiking Nearby	Horseback Riding Nearby	Skiing Nearby	Swimming	Tennis Court	Wineries Nearby	Fitness Facilities
		✽	✽		✽	✽	✽	✽			✽	✽		✽
✽		✽	✽	✽	✽	✽	✽	✽		✽		✽		
		✽			✽	✽	✽	✽			✽	✽		
		✽		✽		✽	✽	✽						
		✽		✽										
			✽	✽		✽	✽	✽	✽				✽	
✽	✽	✽	✽	✽		✽	✽	✽	✽				✽	
		✽	✽	✽		✽	✽	✽						
											✽			✽
✽		✽	✽	✽		✽	✽	✽	✽			✽	✽	
	✽	✽										✽	✽	✽
		✽	✽	✽		✽	✽	✽	✽				✽	
			✽			✽	✽						✽	✽
	✽			✽		✽	✽	✽					✽	
		✽	✽	✽		✽	✽	✽				✽	✽	
			✽	✽		✽	✽	✽	✽					
			✽	✽		✽	✽							
✽		✽		✽		✽	✽	✽						
	✽	✽		✽		✽	✽	✽						
✽	✽	✽	✽	✽	✽	✽		✽		✽				
✽	✽	✽	✽	✽		✽		✽				✽	✽	
✽		✽	✽				✽							
		✽	✽	✽		✽	✽	✽					✽	✽
✽		✽	✽	✽		✽	✽	✽	✽				✽	✽	✽
✽		✽	✽	✽		✽	✽	✽	✽			✽	✽	✽	✽
		✽	✽	✽		✽	✽	✽					✽	

Special Features at a Glance ❖

	Antiques	Car Not Necessary	Conference Facilities	Full Meal Service	Good for Families	Historic Building	Luxurious	No Smoking Indoors
Love's Victorian Bed and Breakfast	✿		✿					✿
MacKaye Harbor Inn	✿				✿	✿		✿
Majestic Hotel	✿	✿	✿	✿	✿	✿	✿	✿
Manor Farm Inn	✿					✿	✿	✿
Maple Valley Bed & Breakfast					✿			
Marianna Stoltz House	✿		✿			✿		✿
Mariella Inn & Cottages	✿						✿	✿
Mazama Country Inn			✿	✿	✿			✿
Moby Dick Hotel and Oyster Farm			✿	✿		✿		✿
Moore House Bed & Breakfast	✿					✿	✿	✿
Mountain Home Lodge				✿				
Mountain Meadows Inn Bed & Breakfast	✿					✿	✿	✿
M. V. Challenger				✿	✿	✿		✿
North Garden Inn	✿		✿			✿	✿	✿
Old Consulate Inn	✿		✿	✿		✿	✿	✿
Old Trout Inn	✿				✿			✿
Olympic Lights							✿	
Orcas Hotel	✿	✿	✿	✿		✿		✿
The Portico	✿					✿		✿
Purple House Bed and Breakfast	✿			✿		✿	✿	✿
Quimper Inn	✿					✿	✿	✿
Ravenscroft Inn	✿						✿	✿
Ridgeway Farm	✿		✿			✿	✿	✿
Roberta's Bed & Breakfast	✿	✿		✿	✿	✿		✿
Run of the River Inn							✿	✿
Salisbury House	✿	✿		✿	✿	✿		✿

Washington (including Idaho)

On the Water	Pets Allowed	Romantic Hideaway	Beach Nearby	Boating Nearby	Cross-Country Skiing Nearby	Fishing Nearby	Golf Nearby	Hiking Nearby	Horseback Riding Nearby	Skiing Nearby	Swimming	Tennis Court	Wineries Nearby	Fitness Facilities
	✿	✿			✿									
✿		✿	✿	✿		✿	✿	✿						
		✿	✿	✿	✿	✿	✿	✿	✿	✿	✿	✿	✿	✿
		✿	✿	✿		✿			✿			✿	✿	
		✿			✿	✿	✿	✿						
							✿							
✿		✿	✿	✿		✿	✿					✿	✿	
		✿		✿	✿	✿	✿	✿	✿	✿		✿		
✿		✿	✿	✿		✿	✿							
			✿	✿	✿		✿	✿	✿					
					✿	✿	✿			✿	✿			
	✿	✿		✿	✿	✿		✿	✿					
✿				✿							✿			
			✿	✿	✿	✿	✿	✿	✿	✿	✿	✿	✿	✿
		✿	✿	✿		✿	✿	✿	✿			✿	✿	✿
✿		✿	✿	✿		✿	✿	✿	✿					
✿			✿	✿		✿	✿	✿						
✿			✿	✿		✿	✿	✿						
		✿					✿							
	✿				✿		✿						✿	
	✿		✿		✿			✿		✿				
	✿		✿		✿	✿		✿		✿		✿	✿	
		✿	✿	✿	✿	✿	✿	✿	✿	✿	✿	✿	✿	✿
							✿							
✿			✿	✿	✿	✿	✿	✿		✿				
												✿		

Special Features at a Glance ↵

	Antiques	Car Not Necessary	Conference Facilities	Full Meal Service	Good for Families	Historic Building	Luxurious	No Smoking Indoors	
Salish Lodge	✿		✿	✿		✿	✿		
Sand Dollar Inn	✿							✿	
San Juan Inn	✿	✿				✿			
Saratoga Inn		✿	✿				✿	✿	
Scandinavian Gardens Inn					✿			✿	
Schnauzer Crossing		✿	✿		✿		✿	✿	
Shannon House	✿	✿				✿	✿	✿	
Shelburne Inn	✿		✿	✿		✿		✿	
Silver Bay Lodging	✿	✿					✿	✿	
Simone's Groveland Cottage	✿					✿		✿	
Sleeping Lady			✿	✿	✿				
Sorrento Hotel	✿	✿	✿	✿	✿	✿	✿	✿	
South Bay Bed & Breakfast	✿	✿	✿			✿	✿	✿	
Sou'wester Lodge	✿		✿		✿	✿		✿	
Spring Bay Inn					✿			✿	
States Inn			✿			✿		✿	
Stone Creek Inn	✿					✿		✿	
Storyville	✿	✿	✿			✿	✿	✿	
Stratford Manor Bed & Breakfast		✿	✿				✿	✿	
Sun Mountain Lodge			✿	✿	✿		✿	✿	
Sunnyside Inn					✿			✿	
Swantown Inn	✿					✿		✿	
Touch of Europe Bed & Breakfast	✿		✿	✿		✿		✿	
Trout Lake Country Inn	✿			✿		✿		✿	
Trumpeter Inn	✿							✿	
Tudor Inn	✿					✿		✿	

Washington (including Idaho)

	On the Water	Pets Allowed	Romantic Hideaway	Beach Nearby	Boating Nearby	Cross-Country Skiing Nearby	Fishing Nearby	Golf Nearby	Hiking Nearby	Horseback Riding Nearby	Skiing Nearby	Swimming	Tennis Court	Wineries Nearby	Fitness Facilities
	✹	✹	✹		✹	✹		✹	✹		✹				✹
	✹		✹	✹	✹										
					✹		✹	✹	✹					✹	
			✹	✹	✹		✹	✹	✹	✹				✹	✹
			✹	✹			✹	✹		✹					✹
			✹	✹	✹	✹	✹	✹	✹	✹	✹	✹	✹	✹	✹
			✹		✹		✹	✹	✹						✹
			✹	✹			✹	✹		✹					
		✹			✹				✹				✹	✹	
		✹	✹	✹	✹		✹	✹	✹	✹		✹			
	✹		✹		✹	✹	✹	✹			✹	✹			
		✹	✹												✹
			✹	✹	✹	✹	✹	✹	✹	✹	✹	✹	✹	✹	
			✹	✹			✹	✹		✹					
	✹		✹	✹	✹		✹		✹						
				✹	✹		✹		✹	✹				✹	
			✹					✹				✹		✹	
			✹	✹	✹	✹	✹	✹	✹	✹	✹				✹
			✹			✹	✹	✹	✹	✹	✹			✹	✹
			✹		✹	✹	✹	✹	✹	✹	✹	✹	✹		✹
			✹	✹	✹		✹	✹	✹						
			✹					✹						✹	
			✹		✹		✹	✹	✹						
	✹			✹	✹		✹	✹	✹	✹				✹	
			✹	✹	✹	✹	✹	✹	✹	✹		✹	✹		

Special Features at a Glance ⬸

	Antiques	Car Not Necessary	Conference Facilities	Full Meal Service	Good for Families	Historic Building	Luxurious	No Smoking Indoors
Turtleback Farm Inn	❁		❁	❁		❁	❁	❁
Villa Heidelberg	❁				❁	❁		❁
Wall Street Inn		❁			❁	❁		❁
Waverly Place	❁	❁				❁		❁
Wharfside Bed & Breakfast	❁	❁			❁			❁
White Swan Guest House	❁	❁			❁	❁		❁
Wild Iris	❁	❁	❁	❁	❁		❁	❁
Windsong			❁			❁		❁
Wine Country Inn	❁			❁				❁
BRITISH COLUMBIA								
Abigail's Hotel	❁	❁					❁	❁
The Aerie	❁		❁	❁			❁	
Anne's Oceanfront Hideaway							❁	❁
April Point Lodge and Fishing Resort			❁	❁	❁			
Beach House on Sunset, a Bed & Breakfast							❁	❁
The Beaconsfield	❁	❁				❁	❁	❁
Bird Song Cottage	❁	❁				❁	❁	❁
Borthwick Country Manor	❁							❁
Carberry Gardens	❁					❁	❁	❁
Cedar Springs Lodge		❁		❁	❁			❁
Chalet Luise		❁		❁				❁
Chesterman's Beach Bed and Breakfast					❁			❁
Clayoquot Wilderness Resort			❁	❁	❁			❁
Cliffside Inn		❁			❁			❁
Corbett House Heritage Bed and Breakfast	❁	❁		❁		❁		❁
Durlacher Hof		❁	❁	❁				❁

Washington (including Idaho)/British Columbia

On the Water	Pets Allowed	Romantic Hideaway	Beach Nearby	Boating Nearby	Cross-Country Skiing Nearby	Fishing Nearby	Golf Nearby	Hiking Nearby	Horseback Riding Nearby	Skiing Nearby	Swimming	Tennis Court	Wineries Nearby	Fitness Facilities
		✳	✳	✳		✳	✳	✳	✳				✳	
		✳	✳											
			✳	✳		✳								
							✳				✳			
✳	✳		✳	✳		✳	✳	✳					✳	
		✳			✳	✳	✳	✳	✳	✳			✳	✳
		✳		✳		✳	✳	✳						
			✳	✳		✳	✳	✳	✳					
✳		✳											✳	
		✳					✳							
		✳						✳			✳	✳		✳
✳		✳	✳	✳		✳	✳	✳	✳					✳
✳				✳		✳		✳						
✳		✳	✳	✳		✳	✳	✳	✳		✳			
		✳					✳							
		✳	✳	✳		✳								
		✳					✳							
			✳	✳	✳	✳	✳	✳	✳	✳				
		✳	✳	✳	✳	✳	✳	✳	✳	✳			✳	
✳		✳	✳	✳		✳	✳	✳						
✳				✳		✳		✳			✳			✳
✳		✳	✳	✳		✳	✳	✳			✳			
			✳	✳		✳	✳	✳						
		✳	✳	✳	✳	✳	✳	✳	✳	✳			✳	✳

Special Features at a Glance ❖

	Antiques	Car Not Necessary	Conference Facilities	Full Meal Service	Good for Families	Historic Building	Luxurious	No Smoking Indoors
Eaglenook Ocean Wilderness Resort			✳	✳	✳		✳	✳
Edgewater		✳	✳	✳				✳
English Bay Inn	✳	✳					✳	✳
Fernhill Lodge	✳	✳		✳				✳
Greystone Manor	✳					✳		✳
Hastings House	✳	✳	✳	✳			✳	✳
Haterleigh Heritage Inn	✳	✳				✳	✳	✳
Holland House Inn	✳	✳				✳	✳	✳
Humboldt House	✳	✳				✳	✳	✳
Joan Brown's Bed and Breakfast	✳					✳	✳	✳
Johnson Heritage House	✳	✳				✳		✳
Laburnum Cottage	✳				✳		✳	✳
Le Chamois		✳	✳	✳	✳		✳	
Locarno Beach Bed & Breakfast		✳						✳
Mulberry Manor	✳					✳	✳	✳
O Canada House	✳	✳				✳	✳	✳
Ocean Wilderness Inn and Spa Retreat	✳		✳	✳	✳			✳
Oceanwood Country Inn		✳	✳	✳			✳	✳
Old Farmhouse Bed and Breakfast	✳	✳				✳	✳	✳
Penny Farthing	✳	✳						✳
Prior House Bed & Breakfast Inn	✳					✳	✳	✳
Red Crow Guest House								✳
River Run			✳					✳
Ships Point Beach House	✳		✳	✳			✳	✳
Sky Valley Place								✳
Snug Harbor Inn							✳	✳

British Columbia

On the Water	Pets Allowed	Romantic Hideaway	Beach Nearby	Boating Nearby	Cross-Country Skiing Nearby	Fishing Nearby	Golf Nearby	Hiking Nearby	Horseback Riding Nearby	Skiing Nearby	Swimming	Tennis Court	Wineries Nearby	Fitness Facilities
✽		✽	✽	✽		✽		✽						✽
✽		✽	✽	✽	✽	✽	✽	✽	✽	✽				
		✽	✽	✽			✽							
		✽	✽	✽				✽					✽	
		✽				✽	✽	✽	✽	✽				
✽		✽	✽	✽		✽	✽	✽	✽					
		✽					✽							
		✽					✽							
		✽					✽							
		✽					✽							
		✽	✽	✽			✽							
		✽			✽		✽	✽	✽	✽				
			✽	✽	✽	✽	✽	✽	✽	✽	✽			✽
✽		✽	✽	✽			✽	✽			✽			
		✽	✽				✽							
		✽	✽	✽			✽							
✽	✽	✽	✽	✽		✽		✽						
✽		✽	✽	✽				✽						
		✽	✽	✽		✽	✽	✽	✽					
		✽	✽	✽			✽							
		✽					✽							
✽		✽	✽	✽		✽	✽	✽						
✽	✽	✽		✽		✽	✽	✽	✽					
✽		✽	✽	✽		✽	✽	✽		✽				✽
		✽	✽	✽		✽	✽	✽	✽		✽			
✽		✽	✽	✽		✽		✽						

Special Features at a Glance ⬅

	Antiques	Car Not Necessary	Conference Facilities	Full Meal Service	Good for Families	Historic Building	Luxurious	No Smoking Indoors	
Sooke Harbour House			✻	✻			✻	✻	
Sutil Lodge		✻				✻		✻	
Swans		✻		✻	✻				
Thistledown House	✻						✻	✻	
Tsa-Kwa-Luten Lodge			✻	✻	✻				
West End Guest House	✻	✻				✻	✻	✻	
Weston Lake Inn	✻							✻	
Wickaninnish Inn			✻	✻			✻	✻	
Woodstone Country Inn	✻	✻	✻	✻			✻	✻	
Yellow Point Lodge			✻	✻				✻	

British Columbia

On the Water	Pets Allowed	Romantic Hideaway	Beach Nearby	Boating Nearby	Cross-Country Skiing Nearby	Fishing Nearby	Golf Nearby	Hiking Nearby	Horseback Riding Nearby	Skiing Nearby	Swimming	Tennis Court	Wineries Nearby	Fitness Facilities
❋		❋	❋	❋		❋		❋						
❋				❋		❋	❋	❋	❋		❋			
							❋							
		❋			❋		❋	❋	❋	❋				
❋				❋		❋		❋					❋	
		❋	❋	❋			❋							
		❋	❋	❋		❋	❋	❋	❋					
❋		❋	❋	❋		❋	❋	❋						❋
		❋	❋	❋		❋	❋	❋	❋					
❋			❋	❋		❋	❋	❋			❋	❋		

Oregon

Oregon

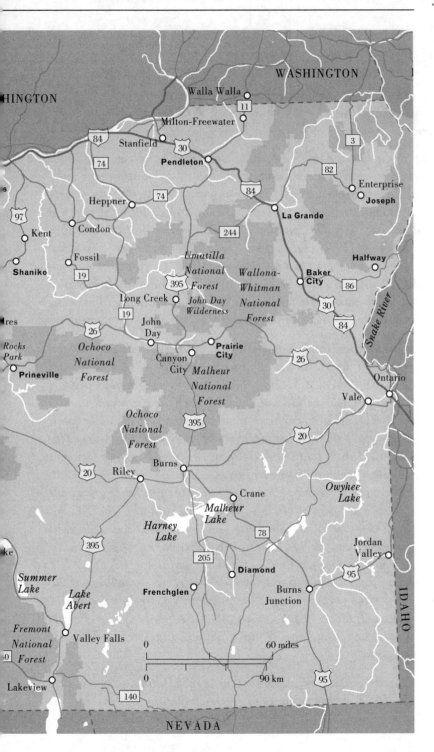

SOUTH COAST

Thanks to the foresight of the state legislature, Oregon's nearly 300-mi coastline is preserved for "free and uninterrupted use" by the public, preventing commercial corruption of its awe-inspiring beauty. Only the mighty Pacific has changed its profile, leaving it looking as untamed as it did a hundred years ago. The southern part of the coast—from points south of Newport down to Brookings on the Oregon-California border—is a kaleidoscopic landscape of rugged offshore monoliths, sweeping dunes, towering cliffs, and quiet coves dotted with bay-front communities. An extensive network of state parks is connected by Highway 101, often said to be the most scenic highway in the United States.

Winter is the time for storm- and whale-watching here; spring is cool and breezy enough for kite festivals; summer brings sunny beach days; and autumn is dependably warm and calm, perfect for viewing blazing fall foliage. Photographers will have a field day with the many old (though presently either automated or defunct) lighthouses that watch over the coast, including Heceta Head Lighthouse (Devil's Elbow State Park north of Florence); Coquille River Lighthouse (Bullards Beach in Bandon); Umpqua River Lighthouse (south of Winchester Bay); Yaquina Bay Lighthouse (south of Newport); and Cape Blanco Lighthouse (north of Port Orford), Oregon's tallest. Also picture-perfect are the offshore seal rookeries, favorite sea lion sunning spots, rocky bird hatcheries, and numerous tidal pools. Avid bicyclers probably won't mind the many steep hills and cliff-hugging passes of the well-marked Oregon Coast Bike Trail, parallel to Highway 101 and running from Astoria in the north all the way to Brookings at the opposite end of the Oregon coast. They'll certainly appreciate the special campgrounds in Bullards Beach, Cape Arago, Cape Blanco, Samuel Boardman, Harris Beach, Humbug Mountain, William Tugman, and Umpqua River state parks.

As on the north coast, the economy concentrates on fishing, shipping, and lumber, though tourism continues to grow in importance. Small coastal towns such as Bandon, cranberry capital of Oregon, and Gold Beach have blossomed into resort communities, with year-round activities and festivals to entertain visitors.

The tiny burg of Yachats has acquired a reputation disproportionate to its size, offering all the coastal pleasures in microcosm: outstanding bed-and-breakfasts, good restaurants, small galleries showcasing the work of local artists, deserted beaches, surf-pounded crags, and fishing and crabbing. It is also one of the few places in the world where the silver smelts come inland, celebrated by a community smelt fry each July.

Just past Heceta Head, Highway 101 jogs inland, and as you head south, you'll notice that the headlands and cliffs give way to the endless beaches and rolling dunes of the Oregon Dunes National Recreation Area. Nearby is Florence, a popular destination for both tourists and retirees. The picturesque Old Town has restaurants, antiques stores, fish markets, and other wet-weather diversions. The largest metropolitan area on the Oregon coast, Coos Bay is also the world's largest lumber-shipping port. But the glory days of the timber industry are over, and Coos Bay has begun to look in other directions, such as tourism—the town has added a boardwalk and interpretive displays along the waterfront, and the Golden and Silver Falls State Park is close by.

Starting at Gold Beach, where the Rogue River, renowned among anglers, meets the ocean, is Oregon's banana belt. From here to Brookings, mild Californialike temperatures encourage a blossoming trade in lilies and daffodils, and you'll even see a few (alright, very few) palm trees. Brookings is equally famous as a commercial and sportfishing port of the incredibly clear, startlingly turquoise-blue Chetco River, and it is (arguably) more highly esteemed among lovers of fishing and the wilderness than is the Rogue.

PLACES TO GO, SIGHTS TO SEE

Beaches. Virtually the entire coastline of Oregon is a clean, quiet white-sand beach, publicly owned and accessible to all. A word of caution: The Pacific off the Oregon coast is 45°–55°F year-round, temperatures that can be described as brisk at best and numbing at worst. Tides and undertows are strong, and swimming is not advised. When fishing from the rocks, always watch for sneaker or rogue waves, and never play on logs near the water—they roll into the surf without warning and have cost numerous lives over the years. Above all, watch children closely while they play in or near the ocean. Everyone has a favorite beach, but Bandon's *Face Rock Beach* is justly renowned as perhaps the state's loveliest for walking. The beach at *Sunset Bay State Park* on Cape Arago, with its protective reefs and encircling cliffs, is probably the safest for swimming. Nearby, *Oregon Dunes*

National Recreation Area adds extra cachet to Florence's beaches. In Gold Beach, the Ophir State Wayside, a day-use area off Hwy. 101, offers access to miles of sandy beach, including serene *Nesika Beach.*

Cape Perpetua. The lookout at the summit of this basalt cape, 3 mi south of Yachats, is the highest point along the Oregon coast, affording a panoramic view of the dramatic shoreline. Forestry service naturalists lead summer hikes along trails from the visitor center, on the east side of the highway, to quiet, sandy coves and fascinating tide pools. During winter storms and high tide, water shoots up at the rear of the steadily worn chasm known as Devil's Churn, just before the entry to the Cape loop drive.

Darlingtonia Botanical Wayside (Mercer Lake Rd.). Immediately east of Highway 101, 6 mi north of Florence, a paved ½-mi trail with interpretive signs leads through clumps of rare, carnivorous, insect-catching cobra lilies (*Darlingtonia californica*), so named because they look like spotted cobras ready to strike. The park is most attractive in May, when the lilies are in bloom.

Mt. Emily. This mountain northeast of Brookings was the only spot in the continental United States to be attacked from the air during World War II. According to local accounts, a single Japanese pilot, using a small plane assembled aboard a submarine offshore, dropped an incendiary bomb here on September 9, 1942. (You can get to the Bomb Site Trail via forestry service road 1205.) Decades later the pilot presented his sword to the town as a gesture of goodwill; it is displayed at the Brookings city hall. Recently the Japanese contributed $2,000 to the town library to promote intercultural understanding.

Oregon Dunes National Recreation Area (tel. 541/271–3611). Stretching between Reedsport and North Bend are 32,000 acres of shifting sand dunes, said to be the largest oceanside dunes in the world. This enormous park encompasses beaches, trails, campgrounds, lakes, marshes, and forested areas. Even though forestry service regulations require mufflers on all vehicles, the screeching of dune buggies, four-wheel-drives, and other all-terrain vehicles careening through the dunes can be overwhelming in some areas. The quietest spot from which to see the dunes is the Dunes Overlook, off Highway 101 about 30 mi north of Coos Bay.

Redwood Grove Nature Trail. This mile-long hiking trail on the north bank of the Chetco River in Brookings (8½ mi inland off Hwy. 101) takes you along paths shaded by an immense canopy of giant redwoods ranging in age from 300 to 800 years. This is the northernmost stand of Coastal redwoods.

Rogue River Tours. You might see bald eagles fishing for salmon, ospreys perched atop high trees, or black bears and deer roaming the banks of the Rogue on the half- and full-day wilderness trips offered by *Jerry's Rogue Jets* (tel. 541/247–4571 or 800/451–3645) or *Mail Boat Hydro-jets* (tel. 541/247–7033 or 800/458–3511), both of which leave from Gold Beach.

Sea Gulch (east side of Hwy. 101 in Seal Rock, tel. 541/563–2727) is a full-size ghost town inhabited by more than 300 fancifully carved wood figures. Ray Kowalski, a master of chain-saw carving—a peculiar Oregon art form—wields his Stihl chain saw with virtuosity to create his cowboys, Native Americans, and hillbillies and his trolls, gnomes, and other mythical figures. You can watch him work in his adjoining studio.

Sea Lion Caves (91560 Hwy. 101, Florence, tel. 541/547–3111). In fall and winter, hundreds of wild Steller sea lions gather in the warm amphitheater of this huge, multihue sea cavern, 208 ft below the highway and about a mile south of Heceta Head. You ride an elevator down to the floor of the cavern, near sea level, to watch from above the antics of the fuzzy pups and their parents. In spring and early summer, the sea lions move to the rocky sun-warmed ledges of the rookery outside the cave.

Shore Acres Arboretum and State Park (Cape Arago Hwy., Charleston, tel. 541/888–3732). Shore Acres, 15 mi south of Coos Bay just outside Charleston, was once the summer estate of a powerful Coos Bay lumber baron. All that remains today are the grounds, which include a Japanese garden and lily pond, rose garden, and formal box-hedged gardens of azaleas, rhododendrons, and flowering annuals and perennials, modeled after those at Versailles. The glass-enclosed gazebo on the sea cliff is a warm and protected spot for whale-watching.

South Slough National Estuarine Research Reserve (Seven Devils Rd., tel. 541/888–5558). Bobcats, raccoons, bears, bald eagles, cormorants, and great blue herons are only a few of the species living in the varied ecosystems (tidal flats, salt marshes, open channels, and uplands) of this 4,000-acre reserve 4 mi south of Charleston. More than 300 species of birds have been sighted here. South Slough, the first estuary reserve in the nation, has well-marked nature trails, guided walks, and an informative interpretive center.

Strawberry Hill. A few miles south of Yachats on Highway 101 is one of the best spots along the Oregon coast from which to view harbor seals at rest on small rocky islands just offshore, and peer at the starfish, anemones, and sea urchins living in the tide pools and exposed at low tide.

RESTAURANTS

Truly good dining options are somewhat limited in Gold Beach; your best bet is to reserve a seat for dinner at **Tu Tu Tun Lodge** (tel. 541/247–6664 or 800/864–6357); the one-seating-per-night dinner of Northwestern fare might include delicious salmon or steak. Otherwise, try the **Nor'wester** (tel. 541/247–2333) for seafood served in a comfortable waterfront setting. If you're craving Norwegian meatballs, schnitzel, fish cakes, and potato dumplings, try **Café Synnøve** (tel. 541/902–9142) on Hwy 101 in Florence. Also in Florence, on Hwy 101 just south of the bridge, the English pub and tearoom at **Lovejoy's at the Pier Point** (tel. 541/902–0502) offers that rare coastal combination—good food and an outstanding view. In Bandon, **Keefer's Old Town Cafe** (tel. 541/347–1133) offers pastas and Northwest seafood dishes with a Pacific Rim influence. Yachats boasts the much-touted **La Serre** (tel. 541/547–3420); clam puffs in fluffy phyllo pastry are front-runners on the seafood, soup, and salad menu. **Yuzen** (tel. 541/563–4766) in Seal Rock (near Waldport) is overpriced and understaffed, but it offers the only authentic Japanese cuisine on the south coast.

TOURIST INFORMATION

Bandon Chamber of Commerce (350 E. 2nd St., Box 1515, Bandon, OR 97411, tel. 541/347–9616). **Bay Area Chamber of Commerce** (50 E. Central, Box 210, Coos Bay, OR 97420, tel. 541/269–0215 or 800/824–8486). **Brookings-Harbor Chamber of Commerce** (16330 Lower Harbor Rd., Box 940, Brookings, OR 97415, tel. 541/469–3181 or 800/535–9469). **Gold Beach Chamber of Commerce** (29279 Ellensburg Ave., No. 3, Gold Beach, OR 97444, tel. 541/247–7526 or 800/525–2334). **Oregon Coast Visitors Association** (Box 74, 609 S.W. Hurbert, Suite B, Newport, OR 97365, tel. 541/574–2679 or 888/628–2101). **Port Orford Chamber of Commerce** (Box 637, Port Orford, OR 97465, tel. 541/332–8055). **Waldport Chamber of Commerce** (620 N.W. Spring St., Box 669, Waldport, OR 97394, tel. 541/563–2133). **Yachats Area Chamber of Commerce** (441 Hwy. 101, Box 174, Yachats, OR 97498, tel. 541/547–3530).

RESERVATION SERVICES

Northwest Bed and Breakfast (1067 Hanover Ct. S, Salem, OR 97302, tel. 503/243–7616, fax 503/316–9118).

CHETCO RIVER INN 🐚

21202 High Prairie Rd., Brookings, OR 97415, tel. 541/670–1645 or 800/327–2688; www.chetcoriverinn.com

Seventeen slow miles inland from Brookings, the Chetco River Inn lies beyond the reach of pavement and utility lines. Propane-generated electricity, gas lighting, and a cell phone provide the necessary modern comforts, and the contemporary design of the structure is anything but rough-and-ready. Long popular with fishermen—the crystal-clear Chetco, just outside the front door, is noted for its steelhead and Chinook salmon runs—the sublimely peaceful setting recommends itself to birders, hikers, and stressed city dwellers looking for a place to unwind.

Broad covered porches, cross-ventilating windows, and deep-green marble floors keep the inn cool during those occasional hot days of summer, when you can lounge in shaded hammocks or bob in the river in inner tubes. During the evenings, everyone gathers to talk in the airy, vaulted-ceiling common room furnished with Oriental rugs, leather couch, caned captain's chairs, and Chippendale dining ensemble.

Upstairs are tall shelves of books and games on the banistered landing outside the guest rooms. The rooms themselves, named after the most common of the many trees outside, are furnished with an eclectic mix of antiques, wicker, fishing creels, duck decoys, and reproduction brass and iron bedsteads. Myrtle and Oak look out onto the surrounding woods, and Alder and Willow overlook the river. An overflow room that opens onto a private bath can be used by families or a group of friends.

Your best dining option is Sandra's multicourse dinners, which are available by advance notice. Featuring fresh local ingredients, the menu might include smoked salmon pâté, orange-carrot soup with Grand Marnier, grilled game hen, and homemade ice cream. It's a good bet that you'll want to skip lunch after indulging in the ample breakfast (included in the tariff), but Sandra can also pack a lunch for your outing if you prefer. ♙ *4 double rooms with baths. Badminton, darts, horseshoes, swimming holes, nature trails, deep-sea charters or fishing guides by arrangement, fishing packages. $115–$135; full breakfast, afternoon refreshments, lunch and dinner available. MC, V. No smoking.*

CLIFF HOUSE 🐚

Yaquina John Point, Adahi Rd., Box 436, Waldport, OR 97394, tel. 541/563–2506, fax 541/563–4393

This 1932 gable-on-hip-roof house, on Yaquina John Point in the coastal town of Waldport, is perhaps the closest you'll come on the Oregon coast to the Smithsonian's attic, with pieces by Steuben, Lalique, Tiffany, Dresden, and Rosenthal among the amazing abundance of objects here. Elaborate lead-glass chandeliers contrast—not unpleasantly—with knotty pine and cedar paneling, modern skylights, and an enormous river-rock fireplace. The setting is spectacular: the Alsea River winds from the graceful Alsea Bay Bridge to the Pacific just below the point, giving way to rolling green surf along endless white beaches.

Each of the four guest rooms reflects the romantic whims of owner Gabrielle Duvall. In the bedrooms, you will find potbellied wood-burning stoves; a profusion of fresh-cut flowers; trays of sherry and chocolates; fluffy down comforters; and mounds of pillows on brass, sleigh, or four-poster rice beds. The Bridal Suite, with a positively royal Louis XV gilt and ice-blue velvet bedroom set, and mirrored bathroom with two-person shower and whirlpool tub overlooking the ocean, is by far the most opulent chamber. In the Alsea, an extra-high bed gives a view of the water even when your head is on the pillow. Terry robes and sandals are supplied for the short trip from your room to the large hot tub or sauna on the broad sundeck overlooking the ocean.

A run on the beach below or a vigorous game of croquet is a good way to work off the large morning meal, an elegant affair served at the black lacquer table on fine china with silver or gold flatware and plenty of fresh flowers. Gabby is happy to arrange a variety of romantic interludes—including catered dinners, sunset horseback rides, or champagne limousine drives into the nearby mountains. ⚓ *4 double rooms with baths. Cable TV, VCR, individual heat control in rooms, wood-burning stoves in some rooms, whirlpool bath in suite. Masseuse, hot tub, sauna. $120–$245; full breakfast, catered meals available. D, MC, V. No smoking, 2-night minimum on weekends, 3-night minimum on holidays, closed Nov.–Jan.*

COOS BAY MANOR 🐚
955 S. 5th St., Coos Bay, OR 97420, tel. 541/269–1224 or 800/269–1224

This 15-room Colonial Revival manor house, built in 1912 and listed on the National Register of Historic Places, is now a charming bed-and-breakfast, thanks to the efforts of transplanted Californian and former banker Patricia Williams. You enter through a formal English garden and imposing, wisteria-draped portico to find such original features as glowing hardwood floors and painted wainscoting, and a tasteful mixture of antiques and period reproductions (although the red-and-gold flocked wallpaper suggests a Victorian bordello). A wraparound balcony lends an open, lofty feel. The star of the living room is an 1878 Weber box baby grand piano with ornate lions' heads adorning the legs.

The guest rooms are theme oriented, such as the frilly Victorian Room, with lace-canopy bed; the Colonial Room, with velvet curtains and four-poster beds; and the Garden Room with white wicker furniture and blue silk wallpaper. All rooms have cozy feather beds and come with robes and coffeemakers. Families will feel right at home in this child-friendly house, but guests allergic to cats are forewarned that there are three friendly felines in residence.

The wharf and waterfront boardwalk are only a short walk away; other sights of interest nearby include Shore Acres Arboretum and the South Slough Estuary. ⚓ *3 double rooms with baths, 2 doubles share bath. Featherbed, robes, and coffeemaker in rooms. Bicycles. $75–$100; full breakfast. D, MC, V. No smoking, well-behaved pets welcome.*

FLORAS LAKE HOUSE BY THE SEA 🐚
92870 Boice Cope Rd., Langlois, OR 97450, tel. and fax 541/348–2573; www.floraslake.com

When the property overlooking Floras Lake, a small body of fresh water only a few feet from the ocean, went up for sale, Will Brady and his wife, Liz, decided that a bed-and-breakfast would be the perfect extension for the windsurfing school they had established here. With a sandy bottom and warm water, the lake is ideal for windsurfing and swimming, but even those who don't indulge in water sports will enjoy the natural setting and the contemporary (1991) board-and-batten cedar home. The inn's location, on a loop road well off the highway, is ideal for exploring the area by bicycle or on foot.

The interior is light and airy, with picture windows, exposed beams, and classic furnishings. Though the contemporary couches and wood stove in the high-ceiling great room are inviting, you are more likely to spend time outside on the decks, in the garden, roaming the beach, or in the sauna at the lake's edge.

One of the two larger guest rooms has an Early American atmosphere; the other is more feminine, with wildflower wallpaper, lace curtains, and white wicker furniture; both offer fireplaces. Nautical and garden themes dominate in the two smaller rooms. ♦ *4 double rooms with baths. Sauna, windsurfing classes and equipment, boats, bicycles. $100–$130; Continental-plus breakfast. D, MC, V. No smoking, closed mid-Nov.–mid-Feb.*

HECETA LIGHTHOUSE BED AND BREAKFAST 🌿

92072 Hwy. 101 S, Yachats, OR 97498, tel. 541/547–3696;
www.hecetalighthouse.com

Visitors to Heceta Head, a windswept cape south of Yachats, have a rare opportunity to encounter Pacific Northwest history face-to-face: Mike Korgan, who operates the Heceta Lighthouse Bed and Breakfast with his wife, Carol, is the former disc jockey who produced the Kingsmen's legendary "Louie, Louie." The two main attractions here, however, are the light station, one of the Oregon coast's most photogenic landmarks, and the inn, an 1893 Queen Anne that once housed the assistant keepers. Back when the light needed intensive maintenance and Florence, the nearest town, was a day's journey away, there was a small community living in two houses on the cape; one has since been torn down, and the other houses the Korgans and their three guest rooms.

The rooms, sparely and tastefully furnished with antiques, are quiet and well lit, and have terrific views—but there is ample reason to spend as little time in them as possible. Trails lead over the cape and down to Devil's Elbow State Park on the water, and park volunteers give tours of the lighthouse. Guests can sit on the spacious, south-facing porch and watch storms and birds (including the half-dozen species of hummingbirds that visit the feeder), or just take in the unbeatable view. Nearby are abundant opportunities to explore tide pools and observe sea lions and harbor seals.

Breakfast is a major event, with up to nine courses, including exotic fruits, homemade bread, local salmon, fruit crepes, asparagus frittata, and roasted-garlic-and-artichoke sausages. For many years before they came to run the inn for the U.S. Forest Service, the Korgans, certified executive chefs, operated a popular Portland restaurant called the Strudel House, and they've brought its reputation for hearty and filling fare with them. At night, some say, a long-time guest comes calling: There have been many reports of a resident ghost, who goes by the name of Rue. ♦ *1 double room with bath, 2 doubles share bath. $115–$145; full breakfast. MC, V. No smoking.*

HOME BY THE SEA 🌿

444 Jackson, Box 606-F, Port Orford, OR 97465, tel. 541/332–2855;
www.homebythesea.com

This quirky little B&B sits on a headland above Battle Rock Park in Port Orford, which offers a spectacular and unique view of the southern Oregon coast:

Jutting south into the Pacific, the point is one of the few places on the West Coast where you can watch the sun rise over the ocean. Built by owners Alan and Brenda Mitchell in 1985, the three-story shingle house is decorated with stained-glass hangings and Brenda's handmade quilts (all for sale). The mix-and-match Americana furnishings are comfortable and low-key; the rare myrtle-wood bedsteads in both ocean-view bedrooms were specially commissioned. Bathrooms are cramped, but tidy and functional; a washer and dryer (which are available for your use) take up space in one bathroom.

Breakfast is served in the lower-level solarium, which offers a conversation-stopping ocean view. This is a prime spot for watching whales (Oct.–May), winter storms, and birds; the Oregon Islands National Wildlife Refuge is just offshore, and the Mitchells can give you information about nighttime lighthouse tours at Cape Blanco. The Wooden Nickel (Hwy. 101, Port Orford, tel. 541/332–5201), a nearby myrtle-wood factory with weekday tours, is a good spot for picking up souvenirs of the area. △ *2 double rooms with baths. Cable TV in rooms. $85–$95; full breakfast. MC, V. No smoking.*

INN AT NESIKA BEACH ☞

33026 Nesika Rd., Gold Beach, OR 97444, tel. 541/247–6434

A large Victorian on a low bluff 6 mi north of the Rogue River, the stately Inn at Nesika Beach looks as though it might been built long ago, back when gold and then salmon fueled the economy of the area. With its period ambience and attention to detail, right down to the pocket doors and wood trim, it's hard to believe that the house is only a few years old.

The spacious interior of the adult-oriented B&B is furnished with well-chosen antiques, and along with the traditional details are some very modern amenities, including whirlpool tubs with panoramic ocean views. Three of the four guest rooms have fireplaces and sitting areas, and two have private decks.

Guests can choose between solitude and socializing downstairs in the two common rooms. One is formal and quiet, perfect for settling down with a book after a day's beachcombing or traveling. The other, where owner and innkeeper Ann Arsenault serves afternoon snacks, has a large stone fireplace and contemporary decor; equipped with games and music, it provides a casual atmosphere for mingling. Breakfast is served in the light-filled, ocean-view dining room, and features entrées such as eggs Benedict with artichoke sauce prepared with Ann's distinctive touch, as well as homemade breads and seasonal fruit. △ *4 double rooms with baths. Fireplace and whirlpool bath in 3 rooms. $100–$130; full breakfast. No credit cards. No smoking.*

JOHNSON HOUSE ☞

216 Maple St., Florence, OR 97439, tel. 541/997–8000 or 800/768–9488;
fax 541/997–2364; www.touroregon.com/thejohnsonhouse

Entering Ron and Jayne Fraese's simple Italianate Victorian (dating from 1892) in Old Town Florence, you will pass into a different era. Antique sepia photographs and political cartoons adorn the walls, and vintage hats hang from the entryway coat tree. Furnishings throughout the house date from the 1890s to the mid-1930s, and include marble-top tables and dressers, Chippendale- and Queen Anne–style chairs, walnut armoires, cast-iron beds, and a sprinkling of ornate Victorian pieces.

The guest bedrooms have lace curtains, crocheted doilies, and eyelet-lace-trimmed percale duvet covers on goose-down comforters and pillows. Sadly, the old hardwood floors have long been covered over in brown and blue paint. The best room in the house isn't actually in the house but in the tiny garden cottage, with a claw-foot tub in the sunny bedroom. Although the porch, with white-washed Adirondack chairs out front, is billed as private, you'll probably find yourself sharing the porch with a friendly cat or two napping in the sun.

Jayne's green thumb is evident in the delightful gardens surrounding the cottage, producing the fresh herbs, fruits, and edible flowers that garnish her bountiful, beautifully presented breakfasts. Among the more popular main courses she serves are wild mushroom and cheese soufflé, Swedish sour cream waffles with lingonberries, and salmon crepes in a mushroom sauce.

The Johnson House is a 5- to 10-minute drive from ocean beaches and only a short walk from the antiques shops, crafts boutiques, and eateries on the bay dock. If you want to reside smack on the ocean, the Fraeses have a romantic vacation rental 9 mi north on Highway 101. Moonset, a stunning octagonal cedar cabin for two, sits on a high meadow with a spectacular view of the coastline. ⚠ *2 double rooms with baths, 3 doubles share 2 baths, 1 cottage suite. Individual heat control in rooms. Croquet, boccie. $95–$125; full breakfast. D, MC, V. No smoking.*

KITTIWAKE 🕊
95368 Hwy. 101, Yachats, OR 97498, tel. 541/547–4470; jszewc@orednet.org

Joseph and Brigette Sweze swapped one coast for another when they moved from Miami to Yachats to build their contemporary oceanfront bed-and-breakfast in 1993. Brigette, a German-born former fashion designer, grew up in Europe, and visited pensions when she traveled the countryside. Someday, she dreamt, she would own an inn of her own. When Joseph retired from the Air Force and from teaching business management, they resolved to fulfill her dream, and the pair were off and running.

This very sweet couple built their guest rooms with comfort and scenic views in mind, and they strive to accommodate both guests who want privacy and those who prefer to gather and chat at the picture windows in the airy common room. Firm beds with carved wooden headboards face windows and glazed doors that open onto decks overlooking the pounding surf; big bathrooms have whirlpool baths to further encourage relaxation. The 2½-acre grounds have been left in a natural state to attract deer, birds, and butterflies, and there are tide pools to explore just below the bluff behind the house. Rubber boots, windbreakers, kites, beach chairs, coolers, and more are provided so that you can really enjoy the setting. Spectacular scenery aside, some guests have been known to return just for Brigette's ample German breakfasts. ⚠ *3 double rooms with baths. Beach and rain gear, beach trail. $125–$140; full or Continental breakfast, complimentary coffee, tea, and cookies. AE, D, MC, V. No smoking, 2-night minimum on weekends and holidays.*

THE LIGHTHOUSE 🕊
650 Jetty Rd., Box 24, Bandon, OR 97411, tel. 541/347–9316;
www.moriah.com/lighthouse

This 1980 contemporary cedar home on the waterfront in Bandon is named for its view of the Coquille River Lighthouse across the estuary. Wide windows in the large sunken living room and a porch off the raised dining room take advantage of the view, with a spotting scope for birders. The simple, eclectic furnishings throughout—from family antiques to contemporary pieces—are brightened by a rainbow painted on the wall, colorful Guatemalan masks, whimsical prints, family photos, huge plants, and battered, neon-color fishnet floats hanging from the ceiling. Owner Shirley Chalupa worked for Hyatt hotels for years before purchasing the bed-and-breakfast as a working retirement.

Two guest rooms on the west side of the home have great views of the ocean, river, lighthouse, and sunsets. The room on the northeast corner of the house lacks the tremendous view but is equipped with a whirlpool tub, a fireplace, and a television. The most recent addition is the Gray Whale, a loft room with skylights, glass-enclosed whirlpool tub, and a big bay window to frame the fabulous sunsets.

The Lighthouse is a great spot from which to watch the timber-rattling storms that draw tourists to the coast in winter. The Bandon Storm Watchers (Box 1693, Bandon, OR 97411) can provide information on storm-watching, whale-watching, and tide-pool exploring in Bandon. △ *5 double rooms with baths. Cable TV in two rooms and common room, whirlpool bath in loft room. $90–$145; full breakfast. MC, V. No smoking, closed July 4.*

SEA QUEST ℘

95354 Hwy. 101, Yachats, OR 97498, tel. 541/547–3782 or 800/341–4878, fax 541/547–3719; www.seaq.com

When Elaine Ireland and George Rozsa bought this contemporary cedar-shingle-and-glass home on a low coastal bluff outside Yachats, they remodeled it to create a romantic seaside retreat. They installed five guest rooms, a lounge, and a rounded entry on the ground floor, with a roomy kitchen open to the main living area above. A round gravel driveway was added to the property, but otherwise the grounds have been left in their natural state, preserving the habitat for the many birds in this area.

Elaine describes the decor as "eclectic, early garage sale," but her treasure trove of fine antique furniture and accent pieces would be the envy of any antiques hound. A pair of wooden skis and a weathered snowshoe hang over the driftwood mantel of the massive fireplace, competing for attention with the intriguing geodes, coral, and polished stones used as accents in the brickwork.

Wall colors coordinate with valances, bed linens, and mounds of pillows on queen-size beds in the guest rooms, each equipped with a whirlpool bath and a private entrance. The hosts are friendly and cheerful. Their L-shape kitchen island becomes a buffet each morning, filled with platters of seasonal fruit, fresh-baked goods, hot entrées such as sautéed apples and sausages and fluffy quiches, and a large bowl of Elaine's homemade granola. You can dine out on the deck or at smartly set tables in the great room, protected from ocean breezes.

Both the deck and the large picture windows inside the house are excellent vantage points from which to experience one of this inn's special attractions: It's not at all unusual to see whales pass by fairly close to shore during their twice-yearly migrations between Baja California and Alaska. △ *4 double rooms with baths. $140–$175; full breakfast, evening snacks and beverages. D, MC, V. No smoking, 2-night minimum on weekends, 3-night minimum on holidays.*

SERENITY ℘

5985 Yachats River Rd., Yachats, OR 97498, tel. 541/547–3813

Baerbel Morgan, originally from Bavaria, was stationed throughout Europe with her husband Sam, an executive in the Boy Scouts organization, before the two retired to 10 peaceful acres a few miles inland from the coastal city of Yachats. During their stay in Europe, they collected the antiques now used in their three enormous guest rooms. The inn is aptly named, situated as it is in utterly peaceful surroundings above the Yachats River, a stone's throw from the Siuslaw National Forest.

Bavaria features pine furniture and wainscoting, as well as ceiling panels that Baerbel has hand-decorated with *bauermalerei*, the German counterpart of Scandinavian rosemaling. But the most romantic choice is Italia, a detached second-floor suite outfitted with a netting-draped canopy bed, a big whirlpool bathtub for two, a wood-trimmed antique settee, and windows overlooking rolling lawns where a herd of deer often congregate. The other rooms also have whirlpool baths, as well as stereos, refrigerators, and plush eiderdown comforters; two are wheelchair accessible.

On warm, sunny days, Baerbel serves her hearty German breakfast alfresco on the large front deck. Afterward, you can stretch out in a hammock strung beneath the trees to soak in the solitude of the setting. German and Italian are spoken.
△ *3 suites. Refrigerator and whirlpool bath in rooms. Nature trails. $99–$145; full breakfast. MC, V. No smoking.*

TU TU TUN LODGE 🦜

96550 N. Bank Rogue, Gold Beach, OR 97444, tel. 541/247–6664 or 800/864–6357, fax 541/247–0672; www.tututun.com

Fine-dining options in the tiny coastal town of Gold Beach are few, but follow the Rogue River 7 mi inland and your culinary prayers will be answered at Tu Tu Tun (pronounced "too tootin") Lodge. Owners Dirk and Laurie Van Zante, two of Oregon's most gracious innkeepers, preside over cocktails and hors d'oeuvres as you relax on the piazza, enjoying the breathtaking river scenery. Then it's on to a multicourse, fixed-price dinner that often features barbecued Chinook salmon or prime rib accompanied by a superior selection of wines. During the busy high season (May–Oct.), there are only four spaces at the table for nonguests at breakfast and dinner (lunch is for guests only), so reservations are essential.

Named after the local riverbank-dwelling tribe, and surrounded by an abundance of wildlife dwelling in the old-growth timber and the rugged river, Tu Tu Tun is an ideal retreat. In the evenings, you might sit near the big stone fireplace in the modern, open-beam cedar inn watching for the pair of bald eagles that fly down over the river at sunset. At "O'dark hundred" (the Van Zantes' expression for daybreak), avid anglers are down at the dock seeking the Rogue's mighty steelhead and salmon.

The two-story wing of riverside guest rooms is motel-like in structure only. Named after favorite fishing holes on the Rogue River, each room features individual artwork and appointments; some have fireplaces, other have outdoor soaking tubs, and all have wonderful river views from a balcony or patio and thoughtful touches such as binoculars for wildlife viewing, fine toiletries, and fresh flowers. The cedar-lined, two-bedroom River House shares the great view and is equipped with a kitchen, as are the spacious suites in the main lodge and the charming, three-bedroom Garden House next to the orchard. △ *16 double rooms with baths, 2 housekeeping suites, 1 2-bedroom housekeeping unit, 1 3-bedroom housekeeping unit. TV in suites. Restaurant, bar, conference facilities, heated lap pool, 4-hole pitch-and-putt, horseshoe court, nature trails, jet-boat tour pickup from dock, guided fishing, complimentary use of fishing gear. $130–$310, with deeply discounted low-season rates; breakfast extra, dinner available May–Oct. MC, V. No smoking, main lodge and restaurant closed last Sun. in Oct.–last Fri. in Apr.*

ZIGGURAT ✇

95330 Hwy. 101, Yachats, OR 97498, tel. 541/547–3925; www.newportnet.com/ziggurat

An ancient architectural form in a thoroughly modern incarnation, Ziggurat rises out of the tidal grasslands of the Siuslaw River 7 mi south of Yachats. This terraced, step-pyramid-shape inn, hand-built with native salt-silvered cedar siding, is without question the most unusual member of Oregon's B&B fraternity. Owner Mary Lou Cavendish soon realized that the interest the pyramid generated would bring a steady stream of visitors and that she and partner Irving Tebor had more than enough room to share, so she opened her amazing home as a bed-and-breakfast after construction was completed in 1987. Come here for the uniqueness of the structure, not for the company of the innkeepers who prefer to leave guests to themselves.

Inside, an eclectic collection of original artwork—from Indonesian *wayang* puppets to Buddhist paintings from Nepal—and specially commissioned wooden furniture complement the house's sleek, ultramodern lines, stainless-steel trim, black carpeting, slatelike tiles, smooth white walls, and tinted triangular windows. On the ground floor, a narrow solarium surrounds two guest suites that share a living room–library, complete with microwave, sink, and refrigerator. The East Room has a modern canopy bed in elm and a sauna in the bathroom. The West Room has a 27-ft-long glass wall, slate tile floor, mirrored ceiling above the bed, and a glass-block shower separating the bedroom from the bathroom. A library nook, living room with grand piano and wood-burning stove, and dining room, kitchen, and bathroom with steam shower share space on the second floor.

A brisk walk to the beach below the house is a good follow-up to the large breakfast served on one of the two glass-enclosed sunporches. Ziggurat is within easy reach of the area's many coastal pleasures, including Cape Perpetua, Sea Lion Caves, Strawberry Hill Wayside, and the boutiques and restaurants of tiny Yachats. ⚴ *1 double room with detached bath, 2 suites. Piano, library. $125–$140; full breakfast. No credit cards. No smoking, 2-night minimum on holidays.*

SOUTHERN OREGON
Including Ashland

Protected by the Klamath and Siskiyou mountain ranges from the extreme weather patterns of the Pacific Ocean, southern Oregon—from points south of Roseburg to Ashland and the Oregon-California border—enjoys a much warmer, drier climate than the Willamette Valley to the north and the coastline to the west. As in the valley, the economy hinges on farming and ranching, with an additional boost from tourists, lured by the area's many historic sites, natural attractions, and cultural events.

With more than its fair share of national parks and challenging rivers, southern Oregon is a paradise for outdoors enthusiasts. At the Mt. Ashland Ski Area there are plenty of cross-country and downhill courses (four lifts and 23 runs at 1,150 vertical ft) to keep skiers busy from Thanksgiving through April. There are also cross-country trails in the heights around Crater Lake and snowmobile trails around Diamond Lake. The Pacific Crest National Scenic Trail and the Siskiyou National Forest offer the best hiking and camping in the region. Water adventurers turn to the Klamath or Rogue rivers for recreation.

The Rogue River, one of Oregon's most scenic waterways, bores through the verdant Siskiyou National Forest and the coastal mountains, rushing full force to meet the ocean. It is a favorite for jet-boat and rafting tours out of Grants Pass, an old stagecoach stop along the Portland–San Francisco route named in 1865 to honor Grant's capture of Vicksburg. Approximately 20 mi north of Grants Pass off busy I–5 is Wolf Creek, another vintage way station, and Golden, an entertaining gold-mining ghost town 3 mi farther east, up Coyote Creek. When gold was discovered in 1851 in Jacksonville, just southeast of Grants Pass, a wave of saloons, gambling houses, and brothels opened to coax the shiny dust from the hordes of miners; today it remains a good example of a Gold Rush boomtown, with more than 75 historic buildings, many dating from the late 19th century.

Southeast on Highway 99 and one of the state's chief tourist destinations, Ashland is home to the renowned Oregon Shakespeare Festival ("festival" is somewhat of a misnomer, since it runs for nine months out of the year). Its immense popularity has provided fertile ground for a flourishing arts community and profusion of boutiques, galleries, taverns, fine restaurants, and exceptional bed-and-breakfasts.

PLACES TO GO, SIGHTS TO SEE

Actors' Theater (101 Talent Ave., Talent, tel. 541/535–5250). Comprising local actors and directors, the Actors' Theater operates year-round and features a season of plays for adults and children alike.

Butte Creek Mill (402 Royal North Ave., Eagle Point, tel. 541/826–3531). This historic mill on the banks of the Little Butte Creek at Eagle Point has been in operation since 1872. You can watch enormous French-quarried millstones hard at work making flour. In the mill is an old-fashioned country store selling a variety of fresh-ground grains and bulk spices, teas, granolas, and raw honey.

Crater Lake National Park (Box 7, Crater Lake, OR 97604, tel. 541/594–2211). Crystal-clear blue waters fill this caldera at the crest of the Cascade Range, formed 7,400 years ago when Mt. Mazama decapitated itself in a volcanic explosion. You can drive, bicycle, or hike the 33-mi rim road. Boat tours leaving from Cleetwood Cove, on the lake's north side, go to Wizard Island, a miniature cinder cone protruding above the surface (at press time, tours were suspended due to construction).

Jacksonville. This 1850s Gold Rush town, on the National Register of Historic Places, has dozens of historic homes and buildings, a fascinating cemetery, a schoolhouse, several saloons, and numerous shops and antiques stores. The *Jacksonville Museum* (206 N. 5th St., tel. 541/773–6536), in the old Jackson County Courthouse, houses an intriguing collection of Gold Rush–era artifacts and outlines the rich local history. Jacksonville is also home to the popular *Peter Britt Festival* (Peter Britt Gardens, tel. 541/773–6077 or 800/882–7488), a weekly series of outdoor concerts and theater lasting from late June to early September that features classical music, jazz, bluegrass, and folk music.

Klamath Basin National Wildlife Refuge (1800 Miller Island Rd. W, Klamath Falls, tel. 541/883–5734). There are many viewing sites around this protected 80,000-acre habitat of marshland and shallow lakes, home to a wide variety of birds and waterfowl. You can observe hundreds of bald eagles that nest here over the winter or watch the endless legions of ducks and geese fly over during spring and fall migrations.

Old Ashland Walking Tours (tel. 541/552–9159) offers reasonably priced, informative walking tours of Old Town Ashland; Monday through Saturday throughout the summer, the tour departs daily at 10 from the plaza information booth across from Lithia Park.

Oregon Caves National Monument (Hwy. 46, 50 mi southwest of Grants Pass, tel. 541/592–2100). Known as the Marble Halls of Oregon, Oregon Caves National Monument, high in the Siskiyou Mountains, entrances with prehistoric limestone and marble formations. Dress warmly and wear sturdy shoes for the chilly, mildly strenuous 75-minute, ½-mi subterranean tour. Call ahead for information as times and price may vary. The rustic *Oregon Caves Chateau* (Box 128, Cave Junction, OR 97523, tel. 541/592–3400) offers food and lodging at the monument from June through September.

Oregon Shakespeare Festival (15 S. Pioneer St., Box 158, Ashland, 97520, tel. 541/482–4331). A Tony Award–winning repertory company presents 11 different Shakespearean, classic, and contemporary plays on three different stages during a season that stretches from February through October. The informative "Festival Tour," led by company members, goes behind the scenes of the festival's three theaters, including the Elizabethan, a re-creation of Shakespeare's Fortune Theatre that operates only from June through October. The cost of the tour includes admission to the *Shakespeare Festival Exhibit Center* (Main and Pioneer Sts.), where you can explore the festival's history in costumes, props, set designs, and photographs. In the Fantasy Gallery, you can don elaborate robes, gowns, and crowns and pose for pictures on set props such as an Elizabethan throne. *The Feast of Will,* held in mid-June in the lovely neighboring Lithia Park—designed by Scotsman John McLaren, who was responsible for San Francisco's Golden Gate Park—kicks off the opening of the outdoor theater's summer season. Lectures, concerts, play readings, and other events are part of the festival activities; some are free, others are ticketed (call for schedule of events and admissions).
River Rafting. Wet-knuckle enthusiasts flock to the challenging Rogue River, near the California border. Many parts of the river flow through true wilderness, with no road access. Deer, bears, eagles, and other wild creatures are abundant here. Outfitters based in Grants Pass and nearby Merlin include *Hellgate Excursions* (966 S.W. 6th St., tel. 541/479–7204 or 800/648–4874) and *Rogue Wilderness, Inc.* (325 Galice Rd., tel. 541/479–9554 or 800/336–1647; www.wildrogue.com).
Wineries and Brewery. Top wineries in the region include *Bridgeview Vineyards* (4210 Holland Loop Rd., Cave Junction, tel. 541/592–4688), which also offers B&B-style accommodations; *Valley View Winery* (1000 Upper Applegate Rd., tel. 541/899–8468) just south of Jacksonville in Ruch; and *Weisinger's* (3150 Siskiyou Blvd., tel. 541/488–5989 or 800/551–9463) in Ashland. The *Siskyou Micro Pub* (31 Water St., tel. 541/482–7718), a pub serving local brews in Ashland, is also worth a visit.

RESTAURANTS

Just as southern Oregon has an abundance of B&Bs, so, too, is there an ample crop of restaurants to choose from throughout the valley. The **Winchester Country Inn** (*see below*) is a longtime favorite for pre-theater dinner. **Chateaulin** (tel. 541/482–2264) serves fine French cuisine in charming ivy-and-brickwork surroundings; after-theater crowds come here for the extensive wine list and bistro menu. **The Peerless Restaurant** (tel. 541/488–6067), an upscale bistro, has Chef Daniel Durfort serving up his own distinct blend of European and pan-Pacific cuisines. Not only do the young chefs at **Firefly** (tel. 541/488–3212) do a masterful job with creative international cuisine (they call it "world fare"), they also manage to rack up high marks for beautiful presentation. For fine Italian fare, the best bet is intimate **Cucina Biazzi** (tel. 541/488–3739). Vegetarians and non-vegetarians will find something to their liking at **Plaza Café** (tel. 541/488–2233). Just north of Ashland in Talent, the **Arbor House** (tel. 541/535–6817) features an eclectic international menu that includes jambalaya, curries, braised lamb, charbroiled steaks, and seafood. The much touted **New Sammy's Bistro** (tel. 541/535–2779), also in Talent, is a pricey, reservations-only diner offering trendy Oregon cuisine that's strictly organic; it's open Thursday–Sunday, and tables are typically booked months in advance. Jacksonville's **McCulley House Inn** (tel. 541/899–1942) serves nouvelle Californian cuisine; just down the street try **Mediterranean Market Place** (tel. 541/899–3995), featuring Mediterranean cuisine and an impressive list of daily specials. Best bets in Grants Pass are **Matsukaze** (tel.

541/479–2961), for reasonably priced Japanese fare, and **Legrand's** (tel. 541/471–1554), for French, Italian, and Continental dishes.

TOURIST INFORMATION

Ashland Chamber of Commerce (110 E. Main St., Box 1360, Ashland, OR 97520, tel. 541/482–3486). **Grants Pass Visitor Center** (1995 N.W. Vine St., Box 970, Grants Pass, OR 97526, tel. 800/547–5927). **Jacksonville Chamber of Commerce** (185 N. Oregon St., Box 33, Jacksonville, OR 97530, tel. 541/899–8118). **Medford Visitors and Convention Bureau** (101 E. 8th St., Medford, OR 97501, tel. 541/779–4847 or 800/469–6307).

RESERVATION SERVICES

Ashland's Bed and Breakfast Network (Box 1051, Ashland, OR 97520, tel. 800/944–0329). **Ashland/Jacksonville B&B Guild Reservations** (tel. 800/983–4667). **Northwest Bed and Breakfast** (1067 Hanover Ct. S, Salem, OR 97302, tel. 503/243–7616, fax 503/316–9118).

ANTIQUE ROSE INN 🦜

91 Gresham St., Ashland, OR 97520, tel. 541/482–6285 or 888/282–6285; antiquebnb@aol.com

Listed on the National Historic Register, this three-story Queen Anne Victorian encrusted with gingerbread trim was a catalog home shipped by rail car from Philadelphia and constructed on a high hill in Ashland in 1888. Built by Henry Carter, who established the first electric company in the region, this dream house was one of the first homes in Ashland to have electric lights. Notice the original fixtures and switches, the amazing built-in hutch in the dining room, and the numerous stained-glass windows throughout.

Lovingly restored by native Oregonian Kathy Buffington, the home features three guest rooms furnished in period antiques and reproductions. Mahogany, named for its paneling, has an old tin ceiling and a claw-foot tub in the bathroom. Rose has a large four-poster bed, a fireplace, and a cozy balcony. Kathy recently refurbished a two-bedroom cottage next door, adding lots of romantic amenities (including a whirlpool bath, a fireplace, and a cedar sauna). All come with terry robes, fresh flowers, and down comforters.

Hearty breakfasts often feature lemon puffs with raspberry sauce, gingerbread pancakes with lemon sauce, or asparagus crab quiche. But nothing beats Kathy's melt-in-your-mouth cinnamon rolls. △ *3 double rooms with baths, 1 2-bedroom housekeeping cottage. Fireplace in 1 room; kitchen, fireplace, whirlpool bath, and sauna in cottage. $117–$159; full breakfast, afternoon refreshments. AE, MC, V. No smoking; 2-night minimum weekends June–Sept. and holidays.*

ARDEN FOREST INN 🦜

261 W. Hersey St., Ashland, OR 97520, tel. 541/488–1496 or 800/460–3912; www.jeffnet.org/aforest

This early 20th-century cross-gabled farmhouse sits on a small plot of land in Ashland's historic district, within walking distance (5 blocks) of the Festival theaters but well removed from busy streets.

Its eclectically decorated interior reflects the interests of owners Bill Faiia and Corbet Unmack, longtime friends and fellow corporate refugees. Bill is now an artist and master gardener, Corbet is a writer and "sit-down comic" (when he tells a joke, everyone insists he sit down). They've redone the house and outbuilding from top to bottom, choosing bold colors and light pine furnishings punctuated by a whimsical collection of fantasy art (wizards, gargoyles, faeries, and such) and a prodigious library of current novels, best-sellers, sci-fi, and fantasy books. This bed-and-breakfast is family-friendly (roll-away bed, high chair, and crib are available), and it is also the only inn in Ashland that is completely accessible to guests with wheelchairs.

The garden, an ongoing project for Bill and Corbet, is in its infancy. The tedious and reportedly militant removal of a snarled mess of blackberry vines was necessary in order to proceed. Now a very pleasant space, there is a large lawn along with some shade trees and new paths. Specimen and rare plants and garden rooms will be added as the landscape develops.

Breakfast, served at 8:30, is family-style with Bill and Corbet. The meal typically begins with a fresh fruit platter and often includes such specialties as a hearty crustless quiche, Arden's breakfast pie, or pecan-studded southern scones. △ *4 double rooms with baths, 1 2-bedroom suite. Air-conditioning in rooms. Horseshoe court. $95–$130; full breakfast. AE, MC, V. No smoking.*

BAYBERRY INN BED AND BREAKFAST ☙
438 N. Main St., Ashland, OR 97520, tel. 541/488–1252 or 800/795–1252; www.bayberryinn.com

Innkeeper Harriet Maher devotes the entire first floor of this white-trimmed, gray clapboard 1925 Craftsman—once a busy restaurant—on Ashland's Main Street to a comfortable living area for her guests. The living room has plenty of snug, book-reading seating, while the large marble fireplace adds a touch of formality. The room is also surprisingly quiet considering it faces one of Ashland's busiest streets. The dining room, lighter and brighter than the living room, doubles as a second common area. There you may find chess, backgammon, and other games.

The decor of this small inn is primarily English country, with deep green carpeting and mauve floral wallpaper. Each room contains family heirlooms and fresh flowers from Harriet's garden. The cozy Sheffield Room upstairs features floral swagged draperies, rose-color carpet, candlestick lamps, and graceful Louis XV–style chairs. Two other second-floor rooms are bright and spacious, with broad window seats beneath wide, lace-swathed dormer windows; these two have detached private baths down the hall. Two rooms on the main floor feature garden themes and private entrances.

Early risers gathering for coffee on the sunny back deck may be joined by the inn's two resident cats. Breakfast, served at 9, includes fresh fruit, baked goods, and a hot entrée. Special emphasis is placed on healthy food from local or organic sources. This is not a good pick for families with children under 12. △ *3 double rooms with baths, 2 rooms with private baths down the hall. Air-conditioning. $100; full breakfast, afternoon refreshments. MC, V. No smoking.*

CHANTICLEER INN ☙
120 Gresham St., Ashland, OR 97520, tel. and fax 541/482–1919 or 800/898–1950

Named after a strutting rooster in Chaucer's *Canterbury Tales*, this tri-level 1920 Craftsman is built into a hill surrounded by cheerful gardens and a long river-rock porch. The inn is tidy and extremely well run, although it lacks a certain home-away-from-home ambience. Nonetheless, owner Pebby Kuan pays attention to detail—including a stuffed cookie jar and a selection of teas and coffees left out for you.

The country French decor in the rooms seems fresh and new, from the thick carpets and soft-colored paint and paper on the walls to the shiny Pierre Deux fabrics covering the cushions and pressed white percale-and-lace pillowcases and duvets on the beds. Reproduction pieces are interspersed with antiques, and carved pine armoires function as closets. Fluffy down comforters cover antique brass and wrought-iron beds in the various guest chambers. Scripts of the current Oregon Shakespeare Festival plays are stacked on the bureaus. Other special touches include fresh flowers, sewing baskets, alarm clocks, telephones, and individual climate control.

Pebby's garden, which includes a fish pond, is a beautiful oasis. She has also created cozy individual patios for some guest rooms, most notably the Jardin Room. Fresh herbs from the garden are used daily in exotic breakfast dishes such as scrambled eggs in puff pastry with smoked salmon and Parmesan sauce, or artichoke heart strata. The bright dining room has a beautiful view of trees, the garden, and the surrounding mountains. ▲ *6 double rooms with baths. Phone and climate control in rooms. Stocked refrigerator, TV. $85–$170; full breakfast, evening refreshments. AE, MC, V. No smoking, 2-night minimum on weekends June–Sept.*

COUNTRY WILLOWS BED AND BREAKFAST INN ☞
1313 Clay St., Ashland, OR 97520, tel. 541/488–1590 or 800/945–5697, fax 541/488–1611; www.willowsinn.com

Two miles south of downtown Ashland, this restored blue clapboard 1896 farmhouse sits on 5 acres with willow trees and a brook, overlooking the Cascade and Siskiyou mountains. Here you can enjoy nestling into willow furniture on the two-tier front porch and soaking in the scenery and the antics of all the creatures—cats, ducks, geese, goats, horses, and rabbits—that live on the property.

Gracious hosts Dan Durant and David Newton have taken great care in decorating each luxurious space. Guest rooms are appointed with period reproductions and modern pieces and have air-conditioning and small private baths. No small detail is forgotten; thick Turkish cotton robes and fluffy terry towels are even provided by the outside door leading to the hot tub and heated swimming pool. Dan and David will also encourage you to harvest what you like from the inn's bountiful vegetable gardens.

The Sunrise Suite, in the renovated barn, is a romantic choice, with skylights, a two-person oak-frame tub, and a large stone fireplace and private deck with mountain views. The Cottage by the pool includes a sitting area, refrigerator, microwave, and queen and twin beds. The enormous Pine Ridge Suite has open beam ceilings and skylights, a custom-made lodgepole pine king-size bed, a seating area in front of a large fireplace, and a dreamy garden bathroom with slate floors and an oval whirlpool bathtub. The suite is also wheelchair accessible.

Breakfasts are served in the sunroom or on the front porch, and include gourmet twists on egg dishes, pancakes, or waffles. Fresh fruit, sausage, and homemade breads or muffins are also on the menu. ▲ *5 double rooms with baths, 3 housekeeping suites, 1 2-bedroom housekeeping cottage. Air-conditioning, phone, TV/VCR, and robes in rooms; fireplace in 2 rooms; whirlpool bath in 1 room. Pool, hot tub, mountain and road bicycles, video library, gift shop. $90–$175; full breakfast, evening refreshments. AE, MC, V. No smoking.*

FLERY MANOR ☙

*2000 Jumpoff Joe Creek Rd., Grants Pass, OR 97526, tel. 541/476–3591,
fax 541/371–2303; www.flerymanor.com*

On 7 lush acres in the scenic Rogue Valley, this sprawling 5,000-square-ft manor house showcases the combined decorating talents of innkeepers Marla and John Vidrinskas. Marla is a fine seamstress, evident in the tasteful window treatments throughout the house and romantic canopies over the beds in the three main guest rooms. John studied the art of 17th century faux finishes as a youngster in Lithuania, and his deft touch is seen in the gold leafing, marbling, and murals that adorn the house and furnishings.

One side of the house has panoramic mountain views and a great deal of wildlife. The Vidrinskas keep several pairs of binoculars on hand for bird-watching guests, one of whom recorded the names of 50 species. Even without the aid of binoculars, the abundant pheasant and quail on the property are easy to spot.

European tapestries, fine antiques, and oil paintings set the tone in the interior. The rooms have triple-sheeted beds, air-conditioning, and ceiling fans, plus turn-down service; phones and TVs are available upon request

The elegance is carried through to breakfast, which is served on china and crystal in the grand formal dining room. Specialties of the house include baked apple stuffed with fresh berries and Grand Marnier cream, Scottish shortbread, beignets, frittatas, stratas, and Lithuanian potato pancakes. After breakfast there are hammocks for relaxing under the trees, a gazebo, and streams, waterfalls, and gardens for exploring. ♙ *2 double rooms with baths, 1 suite. Air-conditioning and robes in rooms. Nature trails, croquet, horseshoes, turn-down service. $75–$125; full breakfast, afternoon refreshments. MC, V. No smoking.*

IVY HOUSE ☙

139 S.W. I St., Grants Pass, OR 97526, tel. 541/474–7363

In Grants Pass, the midpoint of the Rogue River, this English Arts and Crafts brick home—originally operated as a small restaurant and tea house—was built almost 90 years ago by Herbert Smith, a general store owner. According to Josephine County Historical Society records, the Ivy House is one of only two brick houses in the original town boundary. Today the appeal is its good value and proximity to the Rogue, where you can hike, raft, and fish.

British innkeeper Doreen Pontius, a friendly and down-to-earth host, has lovingly restored the interior of the home, and is now concentrating on offering comfort and value to her overnight guests. Once you see the sparsely outfitted rooms, you'll see she does not run a frilly establishment. The bathrooms have been rebuilt to today's standards, with new sinks, countertops, and fixtures, although there are touches of the past in each. The bedrooms are equipped with eiderdown quilts, antiques, and—a plus for families—many offer great sleeping options for up to four people.

Guests are offered morning tea and biscuits in bed. A full English breakfast is also served, complete with bangers if desired. The inn's close proximity to downtown Grants Pass and the Rogue River are added bonuses for outdoor fun. ♙ *1 double room with bath, 4 double rooms share 2 baths. Air-conditioning, TV in parlor. $55–$75; full breakfast. MC, V. No smoking.*

JACKSONVILLE INN 🌿

175 E. California St., Box 359, Jacksonville, OR 97530, tel. 541/899–1900
or 800/321–9344, fax 541/899–1373; www.jacksonvilleinn.com

Gold flecks still sparkle in the mortar of the locally made bricks and quarried sandstone used to construct this two-story building in 1863. On the main street of Jacksonville, this historic building has served as a general store, bank, hardware store, office complex, and furniture repair shop. Purchased in 1976 by Jerry and Linda Evans, it is now an inn and dinner house, with a well-deserved reputation for the best wining and dining around. Ashland and its Oregon Shakespeare Festival activities are about 20 minutes away by car.

Of the eight guest rooms on the top floor, the best and largest is the Peter Britt room, with a whirlpool tub, canopy bed, antique desk, and comfy wing chairs. All the rooms have wood trim salvaged from buildings of the same period, and frontier American antiques including bedsteads, dressers, and chairs. Telephones, mini-refrigerators, computer hookups, and TVs hidden away in specially constructed armoires that match the period furnishings are standard features. Tall brass-and-oak bedsteads have been lengthened to accommodate queen-size mattresses. Seven of the rooms feature cheerful floral wallpapers and linens, upgraded bathroom fixtures, and double-pane windows.

Three one-room wood-frame Honeymoon Cottages two blocks away have canopied pencil-post beds, marble fireplaces, stereos complete with CDs, whirlpool tubs, and sauna showers. These are truly romantic and luxurious little hideaways.

For breakfast, you choose from a gourmet menu; entrées might include a chef's choice omelet, spinach and mushroom *gâteau* in Mornay sauce (scrambled eggs with cream cheese and sherry in a puff-pastry cup), or brioche French toast with maple butter and cinnamon sugar, preceded by fresh-squeezed orange juice and a fruit platter. The dining room is open to inn guests and the general public for breakfast, lunch, dinner, and Sunday brunch. There's also a quiet bar-lounge and a bistro in the basement that features a lighter and less formal menu. △ *8 double rooms with baths, 3 housekeeping cottages. Air-conditioning, mini-refrigerator, phone, and TV in rooms; whirlpool bath in 1 room; kitchenette, steam sauna, and whirlpool bath in cottages. Restaurant, bar, bicycles, wine shop, conference facilities. $115–$245; full breakfast. AE, D, DC, MC, V. No smoking.*

LITHIA SPRINGS INN 🌿

2165 W. Jackson Rd., Ashland, OR 97520, tel. 541/482–7128 or 800/482–7128,
fax 541/488–1645; www.ashlandinn.com

Off the first highway exit for Ashland, 1½ mi north of downtown, this sprawling, gray, Cape Cod–style inn offers an alternative to the froufrou, fancy B&Bs typical of this southern Oregon town. As the name suggests, the focus here is on the hot spring on the 8-acre property, which supplies the inn's water. The pungent, hot mineral water is piped into whirlpool baths in all but two of the large, comfortably furnished rooms.

Innkeeper Duane Smith's sense of humor is evident on the painted walls in the common areas; playful touches here and there suddenly appear to the eye and bring a smile and a laugh. These trompe l'oeil touches are echoed throughout the rooms, too.

The house, constructed in 1993, is still a work in progress, showing signs of newness and continued growth everywhere. Newly landscaped gardens, ponds, and meandering paths surround the inn. Twelve of the 14 rooms and suites have whirlpool baths, and several also include electric fireplaces. The Emperor's Room has one wall covered with an antique Chinese screen and a faux-finish bathroom called the Throne Room. One of the room's first guests interpreted the screen's story; Duane keeps a written copy in the room for other guests to enjoy.

Breakfast is served in the common room/dining room and features Starbucks coffee, papaya scones, fresh poppy-seed bread, and a full country breakfast. △ *10 double rooms with baths, 4 suites. Mini-refrigerator, wet bar, CD player, fireplace, and whirlpool bath in suites and some rooms. Bicycle storage, bicycle trail. $85–$195; full breakfast. AE, D, MC, V. No smoking, 2-night minimum on weekends.*

MORICAL HOUSE GARDEN INN 🐦

668 N. Main St., Ashland, OR 97520, tel. 541/482–2254 or 800/208–9869, fax 541/482–1775; www.garden-inn.com

One and a half acres of trees, tall shrubs, and lush flower gardens surround this charming 1880s Victorian farmhouse. Owners Gary and Sandye Moore added a duck pond, waterfall, and stream to the gardens, as well as a deck overlooking the bucolic valley. The gardens are prime bird habitat, so viewing the many feathered visitors is an integral part of a stay here.

The gardens serve another purpose, for Morical House's front is bordered by Ashland's busy Main Street, and the back by the railroad tracks. Despite the obvious potential for noise out of doors, the serenity of the gardens is imposing; it is easy to forget the outside world within the property's confines.

Inside the main house, period antiques and family heirlooms fit well with the original red-fir floors, leaded- and stained-glass windows, and elaborate woodwork of the wide-entry staircase, paneling, and moldings. Guest rooms, outfitted with antique bedsteads and dressers, are brightened by sun streaming through double-sash windows and little reading lamps on bedside tables. The attic room is a favorite because of its garden views. The Moores also have two luxurious garden suites—Aspen Grove, in a floral motif, and Quail Run, done up in denim—each outfitted with romantic accoutrements such as a fireplace across from a king-size bed and a spacious bathroom with a two-person whirlpool tub and twin-head shower. These rooms are both wheelchair accessible and can also be good for people with sight impairments.

Generous breakfasts of fresh seasonal fruits, homemade baked goods, smoothies, and a main course are served in the dining room or out on the cheery sunporch. In late summer, you can pick blackberries and raspberries and add them to the breakfast menu. △ *5 double rooms with baths, 2 housekeeping suites. Air-conditioning and phone in rooms. Badminton, croquet. $110–$160; full breakfast, afternoon refreshments. MC, V. No smoking, 2-night minimum on weekends Mar.–Oct.*

MT. ASHLAND INN 🐦

505 Mt. Ashland Rd., Ashland, OR 97520, tel. and fax 541/482–8707 or tel. 800/830–8707; www.mtashlandinn.com

It's just not possible to get closer to the cross-country and downhill skiing on Mt. Ashland or the hiking on the Pacific Crest Trail than the Mt. Ashland Inn, a contemporary cedar-log chalet. A crackling fire in the large stone fireplace in the living room provides a welcome hearth for all who enter this cozy mountain retreat 14 mi south of Ashland in the cool heights of the Siskiyou Mountains.

Decorative details exist throughout the inn, from the stained-glass entryway panels, the handmade cedar dining table, the Windsor chairs, and the high-relief carving on the guest room doors to the hand-stitched quilts and the selection of quality Eastlake pieces. The attic is a spacious suite with a waterfall filling its whirlpool tub and a river-rock fireplace facing the bed. The gigantic McLoughlin Suite, with windows on two sides overlooking the various peaks surrounding the lodge, is a favorite. Owners Chuck and Laurel Biegert—and their affable golden retrievers, Aspen and Whistler—do a fine job of making you feel right at home, right down to supplying slippers for the short walk down to the new hot tub and sauna. ♨ *2 double rooms with baths, 3 suites. Whirlpool bath and fireplace in 2 suites. TV/VCR and wet bar in meeting room, ski storage room, snowshoes, sleds, mountain bikes, cross-country skis. $99–$190; full breakfast. AE, D, MC, V. No smoking, 2-night minimum on weekends June–Oct. and holidays.*

PEERLESS HOTEL ☞

243 Fourth St., Ashland, OR 97520, tel. 541/488–1082 or 800/460–8758; www.mind.net/peerless

It took the creative eye of proprietress Crissy Barnett to envision a classic little hotel when looking at an abandoned brick boarding house in the heart of Ashland's railroad district. The rail workers who lived in the building at the turn of the century would be stunned by Crissy's extensive restoration and loving revitalization.

The building, "almost" condemned, had been vacant for years when Crissy bought it in 1991. After more than two years of restoration work, the structure was placed on the National Register of Historic Places.

Six intimate suites are filled with luxurious antiques, hand-painted murals, and rich bedding, draperies, and Oriental rugs. Stand-out rooms are Suite 7, draped in cotton damask and chenille and furnished with West Indies–style furniture, and Suite 3, with its Aesthetics Movement bedroom suite and his and her's claw-foot tubs in the oversize bathroom.

The full breakfast served in the parlor or in the back garden sometimes features such tasty dishes as marionberry crepes. Crissy recently opened The Peerless Restaurant (*see* Restaurants, *above*), luring executive chef Daniel Durfort away from Michel's at the Colony Surf at Diamond Head in Honolulu. With all the wonderful things Crissy has done here, it's a safe bet that her incredible little hotel is fast becoming one of the ultimate addresses in Ashland. ♨ *4 double rooms with baths, 2 suites. Air-conditioning, phone, and TV (on request) in rooms; whirlpool bath in 3 rooms. Health club access. $95–$175; full breakfast, evening refreshments. AE, MC, V. No smoking.*

PINE MEADOW INN BED AND BREAKFAST ☞

1000 Crow Rd., Merlin, OR 97532, tel. and fax 541/471–6277 or tel. 800/554–0806; www.cpros.com/~pmi

Picture a large Midwestern farmhouse in a rural setting, far enough removed from the bustle of major towns in the Rogue Valley to promote an atmosphere of respite and renewal, and you see the charm of Pine Meadow Inn. Innkeepers Nancy and Maloy Murdock came to Oregon from the San Francisco Bay area in 1991 with the express desire of having their own bed-and-breakfast inn. Together they cleared the land and built Pine Meadow. The inn, the evident testimony of a true investment of heart and soul, opened in 1993.

The country-quaint rooms are furnished with turn-of-the-century antiques that are comfortable rather than formal. Homey, hand-stitched quilts and fresh flowers add a warm touch. Two rooms—Willow and Laurel—have cozy built-in window seats.

There are plenty of comfortable chairs on the wraparound porch and terraced garden deck, the perfect places to watch the shenanigans of bunnies, squirrels, deer, and birds parading through the property. There are also nature trails winding through the conifer forest, lovely gardens, and a koi pond to explore after enjoying a hearty breakfast featuring home-baked breads and the herbs, vegetables, and fruits the Murdocks grow themselves. △ *4 double rooms with baths. Air-conditioning and turn-down service. $80–$110; full breakfast. D, MC, V. No smoking.*

ROMEO INN ☙
295 Idaho St., Ashland, OR 97520, tel. 541/488–0884 or 800/915–8899, fax 541/488–0817

This sprawling 1930s Cape Cod–style inn, purchased in 1996 by Don and Deana Politis, features family heirlooms that blend well with the contemporary decor. An L-shape living room has a large fireplace and a sliding door opening onto the patio pool area and garden.

All of the rooms at the inn have king beds and private baths and are supplied with robes and alarm clocks. Amish quilts stand out in the functionally furnished guest rooms, several of which have private entrances and fireplaces. Canterbury features an oak bedstead and nightstands. The Stratford Suite, above the detached garage, enjoys complete privacy and a view of a pastoral valley to the south from the double whirlpool tub.

The kitchen opens into the dining area, creating a warm, at-home feeling as breakfast is prepared and served. The Politises have a large repertoire of breakfast entrées, offering something sweet one morning, something savory the next; by keeping computerized records, they insure that you are served something new and different on every visit. They also stock a refreshment center with snacks and beverages, so there's little chance of leaving this inn hungry. Families are asked to bring only children 12 years of age or older. △ *4 double rooms with baths, 1 suite, 1 housekeeping suite. Air-conditioning and phone in rooms. Library, pool, hot tub. $130–$180; full breakfast, afternoon refreshments, bedtime treats. MC, V. No smoking, 2-night minimum June–Oct. and weekends Mar.–Oct.*

TOUVELLE HOUSE ☙
455 N. Oregon St., Box 1891, Jacksonville, OR 97530, tel. 541/899–8938 or 800/846–8422, fax 541/899–8938; www.wave.net/upg/touvelle

This carefully restored 1916 Craftsman, with its broad covered porches and shingle exterior, is on a peaceful street next to a historic cemetery, just two blocks from the sights, shopping, and dining of downtown Jacksonville. The quick humor and "welcome-home-y'all" attitude of owners Dennis and Carolee Casey make this inn a true charmer, as do the striking architectural features of the house: 14-ft box-beam ceilings in the massive living room, shelf-lined walls in the library, and numerous built-ins, including a beautiful hutch in the dining room.

Favorite rooms are Prairie West, with wicker-and-pine furniture, claw-foot tub, holster, bridles, bear traps, and period photographs, and Granny's Attic, tucked under the gables. Americana, done up in red, white, and blue is another fun choice. All guest rooms have modern bathrooms.

In the evening you might play card games or charades with the hosts; Callie, the calico house cat, is equally happy to entertain. Outside are gardens and a small orchard, and a hot tub and swimming pool. Breakfast specialties include Greek soufflés, tarragon-egg croissants with mushroom sauce, and waffles with pear-pecan sauce. **△** *6 double rooms with baths. Cable TV in library, conference facilities, pool, hot tub, bicycles. $80–$155; full breakfast. AE, D, DC, MC, V. No smoking.*

WINCHESTER COUNTRY INN ☙
35 S. 2nd St., Ashland, OR 97520, tel. 541/488–1113 or 800/972–4991, fax 541/488–4604

Of the many Victorian bed-and-breakfasts in Ashland, this 1886 Queen Anne is the only one with a restaurant, and it's the closest to the Shakespeare Festival theaters as well. Painstakingly renovated by Michael and Laurie Gibbs during the early 1980s and listed on the National Register of Historic Places, the Winchester has established a reputation as one of the finer dining spots in Ashland.

The decor of the guest rooms maintains the period style of the house without Victorian clutter. A mixture of American Colonial reproductions and antiques, as well as Rococo Revival and Eastlake reproductions, including tall-mirrored wardrobes and brass-and-iron or heavy, carved wooden bedsteads, add distinction, while contemporary cushioned chairs and wall-to-wall carpeting make it comfortable. There are many nice touches in the main house, such as a hand-painted porcelain sink set into an antique dresser, which serves as a vanity in the bedrooms, and scented salts in the attached bathroom for luxurious soaking in the deep claw-foot tub. A crystal decanter of sherry and sinfully rich truffles on a tray on the dresser make a late-night snack irresistible.

Favorite rooms include the Sylvan Room, in sunny shades of peach, and the creamy blue Garden Room, both of which have delightful bay sitting areas overlooking the terraced gardens. The Sunset Room has its own balcony view of the treetops of downtown Ashland. Rooms at the basement level have garden patios or small decks as compensation. The private cottage has two beautiful luxury suites, and the Victorian and its carriage house next door have a large guest library, four more suites, and five double rooms (one of which is accessible to wheelchair users), to add to Winchester's array of accommodations.

In winter and spring the Gibbses offer a variety of special packages, from murder-mystery weekends to a popular Dickens Christmas Festival tie-in. **△** *12 double rooms with baths, 6 suites. Air-conditioning in rooms; phone, TV/VCR, fireplace, whirlpool bath, and stereo in suites. Restaurant, library, gift shop. $95–$200; full breakfast. AE, D, MC, V. No smoking.*

WOODS HOUSE ☙
333 N. Main St., Ashland, OR 97520, tel. 541/488–1598 or 800/435–8260, fax 541/482–8027; www.mind.net/woodshouse

Named for one of the founding families of Ashland, this 1908 Craftsman rests on noisy Main Street in the historic district, just blocks from the festival theaters. Lace curtains, dried-flower arrangements, reproduction Early American pieces, and polished fir floors and staircase furnish this rose-scented home owned by Françoise and Lester Roddy.

Original pastel watercolors by Françoise's sister hang throughout the house. The guest rooms are appointed with antique bedsteads (some with lace canopies), floral comforters, and lace curtains and doilies. Robes, hair dryers, and bathroom scales are among the amenities. Phone jacks for Internet access and small baskets filled with everything from emery boards to shoe-shine cloths are also found in each room. Behind the house, the lovely English garden, which has a grape arbor, over 100 rosebushes, and several interesting sculptures, is a good spot to unwind.

Breakfasts are served at the large oak dining table set with fine china and crystal, and might start with Françoise's delicious chocolate-orange or almond–poppy seed scones. Main dishes such as Ms. Jasmine's Sweet Onion Pie (named for the Roddy's friendly Newfie dog) or lemon cloud pancakes follow. Françoise also bakes sinfully delicious cookies for you to munch on later in the day. △ *6 double rooms with baths. Air-conditioning. $110–$120; full breakfast, afternoon refreshments. MC, V. No smoking, 2-night minimum June–Oct.*

WILLAMETTE VALLEY
Including Eugene

Cradled between the Cascade Mountain range to the east and the Coast Range and Pacific Ocean to the west is the serene green expanse of land known as the Willamette Valley. Cloud-shrouded craggy bluffs and sheep-dotted, pastoral meadows line I–5 and Highways 99W and 99E, the major arteries through this lush north–south corridor. Historic stagecoach stops and gold-mining boomtowns, culture-rich college towns, and small farming communities dot the valley between Salem, Oregon's state capital in the north, and Roseburg in the south. For the most part, industry here revolves around what the fertile land and mild climate provides: rich, moist soil for hundreds of thriving farms, orchards, and nurseries; rolling meadows of pastureland for ranching; and stands of timber for the logging trade. During harvest season, highways and byways are lined with roadside stands overflowing with colorful fresh fruits and vegetables, nuts, jams, and flowers. Vineyards abound as well, producing mainly such cool-climate varietals as Pinot Noir, Chardonnay, and Riesling.

Many of Oregon's rivers and streams—including the Santiam, McKenzie, North Umpqua, and Willamette rivers—cut through this valley, providing thrilling whitewater rafting and outstanding fishing for steelhead, sockeye, trout, and bass. About a dozen of Oregon's remaining 54 covered bridges, dating from the turn of the century, are scattered throughout the Willamette Valley.

Colleges and universities in the valley, including Oregon State University in Corvallis and the University of Oregon in Eugene, provide academic and cultural life to the entire region. With its own ballet, opera, symphony, and theater companies, Eugene, Oregon's second-largest metropolitan area, is host to the valley's strongest arts programs.

PLACES TO GO, SIGHTS TO SEE

Albany. There are three distinct historic districts in this vintage Victorian town, each with numerous commercial and residential buildings representing scores of architectural styles and periods.

Cottage Grove. "Tour the Golden Past," a pamphlet available at the ranger station on Row River Road, is a good guide to the abandoned mines, historical buildings, and covered bridges (six in this area) of this nostalgic Gold Rush boomtown. The rangers can also direct you to public gold-panning areas. The Bohemian Mining Days festival in July celebrates Cottage Grove's mining tradition.

Covered Bridges. There are many covered bridges in the Willamette Valley, most of which are clustered in and around Cottage Grove and in Linn County. Contact the Albany Convention and Visitors Commission (*see* Tourist Information, *below*) for a touring map. The *Covered Bridge Society of Oregon* (Box 1804, Newport, OR 97365, tel. 541/265–2934) can also provide historical information.

Euphoria Chocolate Company (6 W. 17th Ave., tel. 541/343–9223). This little company a few blocks south of the heart of downtown Eugene makes some of the best-loved chocolate in Oregon.

Finley National Wildlife Refuge (26208 Finley Refuge Rd., Corvallis, tel. 541/757–7236). This refuge is a bird-watcher's paradise, with large fields of grasses and grains that attract Canada geese, grouse, pheasants, quail, wood ducks, and other varieties of birds. The refuge is also home to numerous deer.

Hult Center for the Performing Arts (1 Eugene Center, Eugene, tel. 541/687–5000). This world-class arts complex in Eugene is an airy structure of glass and native wood, containing two of the most acoustically perfect theaters on the West Coast. It hosts everything from heavy-metal concerts to classical ballets and is the home of Eugene's symphony, ballet, and opera companies. It is also the site of the renowned two-week Oregon Bach Festival that takes place in June and July.

Museums. The top museums in the valley include the *University of Oregon Museum of Art* (1430 Johnson La., Eugene, tel. 541/346– 3027), best known for its Asian collection; the *Horner Museum* (Gill Coliseum, Oregon State University, Corvallis, tel. 541/754- -2951), featuring artifacts from Oregon's natural and cultural history; and the children-friendly *Wistec*, the *Willamette Science and Technology Center* (2300 Leo Harris Pkwy., Eugene, tel. 541/682–3020).

Oakland. The citizens of this small community on the old stage line between San Francisco and Portland have done a lot to restore their 19th-century pioneer town, which is on the National Register of Historic Places. Blocks of refurbished buildings representing styles dating from 1860 include several saloons, the gristmill, livery stable, general mercantile, opera house, icehouse/butcher shop, and pioneer post office, once the distribution center for the West Coast.

Saturday Market (8th and Oak Sts.). This bustling art, craft, and food market in Eugene attracts big crowds each Saturday from April through December, when farmers sell fresh produce and flowers, chefs create ethnic fare, and entertainers perform in the streets.

Wineries. There are nearly two dozen wineries in the valley, offering tours, tastings, and gorgeous scenery. The *Oregon Winegrowers' Association* (1200 Naito Pkwy., Suite 400, Portland, OR 97209, tel. 503/228–8403) can provide information and brochures on the region's wineries.

RESTAURANTS

Chef Rolph Schmidt's **Chanterelle** (tel. 541/484–4065) in Eugene offers hearty French and other European cuisines and delicious pastries in intimate surroundings. Other top restaurants in Eugene include **Ambrosia** (tel. 541/342–4141) for Italian cuisine; **Excelsior Café** (tel. 541/342–6963) for Continental dishes prepared from fresh, local ingredients; and **Cafe Zenon** (tel. 541/343–3005), an eclectic, multiethnic restaurant frequently picked as Eugene's finest by local reviewers. **Tolly's** (tel. 541/459–3796), a combination soda fountain/wine library/restaurant/antiques shop/art gallery in Oakland, offers the best dining in town, with bistro fare, standard American favorites, and a dash of Scandinavian influence. The authentic spaetzle, schnitzel, and sausages make **Teske's Germania Restaurant** (tel. 541/672–5401) a favorite in Roseburg.

TOURIST INFORMATION

Albany Convention and Visitors Association (300 2nd Ave. SW, Box 965, Albany, OR 97321, tel. 541/928–0911 or 800/526–2256). **Convention and Visitors Association of Lane County, Oregon** (115 W. 8th Ave., Suite 190, Box 10286, Eugene, OR 97440, tel. 541/484–5307 or 800/547–5445). **Corvallis Convention and Visitors Bureau** (420 N.W. 2nd St., Corvallis, OR 97330, tel. 541/757–1544 or 800/334–8118). **Cottage Grove Chamber of Commerce** (330 Hwy. 99 S, Suite B, Cottage Grove, OR 97424, tel. 541/942–2411). **Roseburg Visitors and Convention Bureau** (410 S.E. Spruce St., Box 1262, Roseburg, OR 97470, tel. 541/672–9731 or 800/444–9584).

RESERVATION SERVICES

Northwest Bed and Breakfast (1067 Hanover Ct. S, Salem, OR 97302, tel. 503/243–7616, fax 503/316–9118).

APPLE INN BED & BREAKFAST ☞

30697 Kenady La., Cottage Grove, OR 97424, tel. 541/942–2393 or 800/942–2393, fax 541/767–0402; www.pond.net/~bnbassoc/appleinn.html

One recent visitor to this modern ranch house with stunning views wanted to tour the area's renowned covered bridges, but didn't know where to go. So innkeeper Harry McIntire asked the woman, in her sixties, to jump onto the back of his motorcycle and let him show her the sights—and she did.

Harry, a forester, and Kathe McIntire, a middle-school teacher, make you feel at home in their small inn just out of Cottage Grove. Amid 190 gently sloping forested acres, the Apple Inn is a great place to rest between bouts of covered bridge touring and antiques shopping.

The Apple Orchard room, equipped with a wood stove, has a private entrance and an excellent view of the valley. The Treehouse room offers a claw-foot tub and a whimsical collection of miniature trees. Both feature Kathe's handmade quilts and lodge-style furnishings. If you can't get comfortable around country kitsch, it's not the place for you—the guest room decor makes Holly Hobby look like Coco Chanel—but the hospitality and setting are top-notch.

Breakfasts are hearty, with everything from German potato cakes to a rich French toast casserole with apples and sour cream sauce, and evenings often bring freshly made ginger snaps or apples in caramel sauce. ♨ *2 double rooms with baths. TV in rooms. Hot tub, RV parking. $65–$75; full breakfast, afternoon snacks. No credit cards. No smoking.*

BECKLEY HOUSE ☞

338 S.E. 2nd St., Oakland, OR 97462, tel. and fax 541/459–9320; www.makewebs.com/beckley

The entire town of Oakland is on the National Register of Historic Places, and this clapboard 1898 Italianate Victorian fits right in. The large, bright living room features diamond-pane windows, oak floors, whitewashed walls, and high ceilings.

Dark cedar wainscoting, shiny wall sconces, and a large central fireplace give a formal feel to the dining room.

Oil paintings and intricately carved wardrobes and bedsteads fill the roomy second-floor guest rooms. The radiantly sunny suite, a converted sunporch, has a white iron bed topped with a canopylike drapery and a colorful quilt.

Karene and Rich Neuharth bought the inn in late 1994 and have brought their own touches to the old house. Karene, a caterer, serves breakfasts featuring fresh fruit and a variety of egg dishes. Rich, a former software engineer who now runs a camera repair business in town, is able to give you a hand if your f-stop stops.

The Neuharths can provide you with a historical brochure about Oakland, the second town settled in Oregon, and its rich architectural heritage, most dating from the late 19th century. It relates, among other things, Oakland's notable but obscure contribution to American gastronomy: "It was here that the turkey was developed into the broad breasted turkey that we know today." △ *2 doubles with baths, adjoining twin room also available. $65–$85; full breakfast. AE, MC, V. No smoking.*

CAMPBELL HOUSE ☙
252 Pearl St., Eugene, OR 97401, tel. 541/343–1119 or 800/264–2519, fax 541/343–2258; www.campbellhouse.com

Innkeepers Myra and Roger Plant first saw this 8,000-square-ft 1892 Victorian mansion, one of the oldest buildings in Eugene, on a bike ride. Then vacant, it was almost totally obscured by shrubs, trees, and blackberry vines. After years of working to convince the heirs of the original owner to sell, they remade the place from the inside out, adding new oak floors, brass fittings, and turn-of-the-century–style moldings. The dining room and the library were refurbished and the corner sinks in bathrooms saved.

A long drive brings you past green grounds dotted with rhododendrons, to the entrance, at the back of the house. The back patio and gazebo, where local wine is served in the afternoon, is lined with hanging, flowering plants. It's a lovely spot, although the scene deserves better than the white plastic lawn furniture provided. The guest rooms, though, make you quickly forget about lawn furniture. Each of the rooms is unique, although most have a vaguely English country look; some have views of the city and the Cascade Mountains. A new outbuilding, designed to match the style of the house, features luxury rooms and suites with fireplaces and whirlpool baths.

One drawback of the Campbell House is its proximity to the train tracks, which are a few blocks downhill. Evenings can be a bit noisy, but the Plants provide earplugs.

Mornings begin with coffee on a tray outside your room and evolve into a full meal downstairs. Favorite entrées include Belgian waffles and crustless quiches. If possible, sit in the sunny library overlooking town. △ *16 double rooms with baths, 2 suites. Phone, data port, TV/VCR in rooms. Fax and photocopy service, conference facilities. $79–$379; full breakfast. AE, D, MC, V. No smoking.*

EXCELSIOR INN ☙
754 E. 13th Ave., Eugene, OR 97401, tel. 541/342–6963 or 800/321–6963, fax 541/342–1417; www.excelsiorinn.com

Built in 1912, the Excelsior building spent most of this century as home to a campus fraternity, but its ambience these days is a far cry from *Animal House.*

What was to become the Excelsior Inn began as a small café, which with increasing popularity gradually took over the entire ground floor. The upper floors followed in 1995, when they were changed from student housing into guest accommodations. Chef and innkeeper Maurizio Paparo cut no corners in outfitting the rooms along the lines of a sophisticated European inn; marble-and-tile bathrooms and cherry-wood doors, moldings, and furniture are throughout, and some rooms have hardwood floors, arched windows, and vaulted ceilings.

Guest rooms, named after European composers, range from the small, quiet Schumann, with a wood floor, shower, and queen bed, to Bach, a large corner room with high ceilings, sitting area, whirlpool bath, and courtyard view. All rooms are equipped to serve the visiting professor or businessperson as well as the casual traveler, with writing desks and modem lines.

The modest café that started it all is now one of Eugene's best dining establishments, with a full-scale restaurant and bar. The use of fresh local ingredients makes for seasonal changes in the menu, which is inflected with the forms and flavors of Paparo's native Italy: pastas, gnocchi, or grilled fish with *puttanesca* sauce (a spicy combination of tomatoes, onions, olives, capers, and oregano) are good choices. The wine list is excellent, and European-trained pastry chef Milka Babich prepares exquisite pastries and other desserts. When the rain abates in the spring, the front terrace allows for alfresco dining. △ *14 double rooms with baths. Phone, data port, TV/VCR in rooms; whirlpool bath in 2 rooms. Conference facilities. $69–$180; full breakfast. AE, D, DC, MC, V. No smoking.*

HANSON COUNTRY INN ℘

795 S.W. Hanson St., Corvallis, OR 97333, tel. 541/752–2919; pcovey7081@aol.com

In 1928 Jeff Hanson built this rotund Dutch Colonial on a high knoll overlooking the rolling Willamette Valley as the headquarters for his prospering poultry-breeding ranch. Here, in the egg house opposite the main house, he developed his world-famous strain of White Leghorn chickens. After Hanson died, the house stood empty for 13 years. In 1987 it was purchased by Patricia Covey, a friendly Californian looking for escape from the Bay area. With plenty of polish and elbow grease, Patricia was able to restore the grandeur of the house's unique features, including the carefully laid honeycomb tile work in the bathrooms and the spindle room divider and banister, both made of New Zealand gumwood carved by local craftsmen.

A baby grand piano, assorted sculptures, and a selection of Patricia's own paintings bring understated elegance to the great living room with its massive central fireplace. Sun pours through tall windowpanes, brightening the cozy reading nook where a plump easy chair sits beside floor-to-ceiling bookcases. The sunporch, with sparkling stained-glass windows and casual rattan furniture, looks onto a terraced garden with a stone fountain and a white vine arbor.

One suite has a lovingly polished four-poster bed, an attached sitting room, and a private veranda overlooking a gentle slope to the valley below. The largest room, a favorite of wedding couples for its romantic box-canopy bed, has a sitting alcove and windows on three sides—providing views of the valley, the terraced garden, and the quiet pasture behind the house. All rooms are appointed with 1920s American furniture and bed linens imported from England. The two-bedroom cottage with hardwood floors, iron bedsteads, and down comforters is perfect for families needing space and privacy.

Patricia reveals her cooking talent with her abundant breakfast, which starts out with teas and coffee, juice, fresh fruit, and freshly baked bite-size muffins.

From there, move on to such treats as apple crepes, French toast, or "Elliott's pancakes", with cottage cheese and marionberry preserves, recently featured in *Bon Appétit.* ♙ *3 suites, 1 2-bedroom housekeeping cottage. Phone and cable TV in rooms. $75–$125; full breakfast. AE, D, DC, MC, V. No smoking.*

HARRISON HOUSE 🍍

*2310 N.W. Harrison Blvd., Corvallis, OR 97330, tel. 541/752–6248
or 800/233–6248; www.proaxis.com/~harrisonhouse*

Maria and Charlie Tomlinson are refugees from Connecticut corporate culture who moved to Corvallis to take over the 1939 Dutch Colonial inn that for 50 years was home to noted geologist I. S. Allison and his family. The move was a good one, not only for them but also for their guests, as they have proven to be consummate innkeepers.

From the welcome announcement to the thank-you note that follows your stay, the Tomlinsons provide a rare level of hospitality and service. Amenities include fruit and snacks available throughout the day, tastings of local wines, stationery, a butler's basket of toiletries, morning newspapers and evening turn-down service. The immaculately clean house is furnished with Chippendale- and Williamsburg-style antiques, and the four guest rooms come with extra pillows, blankets, and towels. Breakfasts, which feature regional and seasonal ingredients, include a fruit dish and any one of a wide range of entrées, from French toast and Belgian waffles to frittatas and souflées.

Harrison House's location, just a few blocks from the Oregon State University campus, makes it a favorite with visiting parents and professors. Maria and Charlie provide bicycles for touring campus or downtown. Nearby attractions include wineries, Peavy Arboretum, and Mary's Peak, the highest mountain in the Coast Range and a favorite with day hikers. ♙ *2 doubles with bath, 2 doubles share bath. Phone and data port in rooms. Piano, conference facilities, bicycles, turn-down service. $60–$80; full breakfast, afternoon refreshments. AE, D, MC, V. No smoking.*

HOUSE OF HUNTER 🍃

*813 S.E. Kane, Roseburg, OR 97470, tel. 541/672–2335 or 800/540–7704;
www.wizzards.net/hunter*

A path of roses beside two giant tulip trees leads to the bright red door of this Italianate Victorian overlooking downtown Roseburg. Walt Hunter and his wife, Jean, have done an admirable job of renovating the house they bought in 1989. The two-year restoration included completely replacing the plumbing and wiring, so guests can experience old-house charm without having to endure some typical old-house inconveniences.

The interior is mostly formal, especially in the front dining room, where massive cabinets display fine family china and cut glass. The living room, furnished with early 20th-century American chairs and couches, is less stiff and more inviting. Second-floor guest rooms, named after the Hunters' daughters, have small vanities, tall armoires, frilly curtains, ruffled bedspreads, fringed lamp shades, and lacy pillows made by Jean.

Each morning trays of steaming coffee and freshly baked breads and muffins await early risers, followed by a large full breakfast. A back porch looks out onto Walt's English flower garden.

You can wander Roseburg's Mill-Pine neighborhood, 15 blocks worth of late-19th century houses on the National Register, or get acquainted with local history at the Douglas County Museum (tel. 541/440–4507). There's good fishing nearby, at the confluence of the north and south forks of the Umpqua, and the area is also home to many wineries. △ *2 double rooms with baths, 2 doubles with basins share bath, 1 2-bedroom suite. Air-conditioning in rooms. TV/VCR in living room, video library, laundry facilities. $50–$75; full breakfast. MC, V. No smoking.*

MCGILLIVRAY'S LOG HOME BED AND BREAKFAST ☙
88680 Evers Rd., Elmira, OR 97437, tel. 541/935–3564

Utter serenity pervades the forest around the small town of Elmira, just 14 mi west of bustling Eugene. In the midst of it is McGillivray's Log Home, a large and sturdy structure that has all the peace and comfort of its surroundings. Whether it's the cozy feeling of all that wood, or owner Evelyn McGillivray's congeniality, the bed-and-breakfast is welcoming and homey.

The shell of the house was erected by a builder, but the rest—from the split-log staircase to the colorful stained-glass windows on the second-floor landing—is all the McGillivray's work. Rough strips of wood frame old photos of loggers hard at work, appropriate in this structure of pine, fir, oak, chinquapin (an Oregon hardwood), and other woods. Ruffled curtains; quilted pillows and bedspreads; and hand-hewn wood-slab headboards, bedside tables, and dressers add to the rustic atmosphere. Window valances are done in the McGillivray tartan.

Breakfast is an event. Evelyn stands before her antique wood-burning stove preparing fresh coffee, bacon-wrapped eggs, and buttermilk pancakes; other culinary trimmings might include fresh-squeezed juice, baked fruit, hazelnut-honey butter, and maple or chokecherry syrup. Guests can walk off the ample meal on the landscaped grounds, or head to nearby Fern Ridge Reservoir for boating or birding. △ *2 double rooms with baths. Air-conditioning in rooms. $70–$80; full breakfast. MC, V. No smoking.*

OVAL DOOR BED AND BREAKFAST ☙
988 Lawrence St., Eugene, OR 97401, tel. 541/683–3160 or 800/882–3160, fax 541/485–5339; www.ovaldoor.com

This 2½-story, pitch-roof house with a wraparound porch was built in 1990 but matches the surrounding homes from the '20s and '30s in this centrally located, older neighborhood near the University of Oregon and the Hult Center for the Performing Arts in Eugene. A whimsical purple door hints at the unconventional things to come.

Inside is a collection of centuries-old antiques and comfortable, modern American furniture. The dining room has an 1860 Eastlake walnut dining table and floral prints filling one wall; another wall has glass doors that open onto a broad wraparound porch with cushioned chairs and a swing for resting beneath the rustling leaves of the shade trees.

Guest rooms are furnished with a mixture of antique pieces and reproductions; an open steamer trunk that serves as a dresser in one room is especially striking. Extra room touches include sparkling water and glasses on doily-covered trays, fresh and dried flower arrangements, candles and books of poetry, a choice of pillows (down, poly, or orthopedic), robes, and a selection of current paperbacks that you are free to take when you leave. The cozy, two-person whirlpool tub room is adorned with candles, flower arrangements, mirrors, and a selection of scented bath salts and oils. The heated towel rack is a rare joy to find in the United States.

Hostess Judith McLane came to Eugene to run the inn after being downsized out of the California corporate fast lane. She uses a large tile set on the dining room buffet as a blackboard to announce the breakfast menu of the day, which always features fresh-baked bread; her specialties include Popeye's Morning (creamed spinach) and Idaho Sunrise (a twice-baked potato stuffed with a poached egg). ♦ *4 double rooms with baths. Phone, ceiling fan, individual heat control in rooms. $75–$110; full breakfast. AE, D, MC, V. No smoking.*

STEAMBOAT INN ☙

42705 N. Umpqua Hwy., Steamboat, OR 97447, tel. 800/840–8825, fax 541/498–2411; stmbtinn@rosenet.net

Deep in the Umpqua National Forest, 38 winding mi east of Roseburg, this 1955 river-rock and pine lodge sits alongside the luminous blue North Umpqua River. Fisherfolk from around the globe come here to test their skills against the elusive steelhead and trout. Owners Jim and Sharon Van Loan were themselves frequent visitors and worked as members of the inn's summer crew for three years before buying it in 1975.

While its fishing tradition is still much in evidence—rehabilitated fly-tying cabinets serving as the reception desk and fly shop—the Steamboat has seen a shift toward a more refined country inn. The rough edges of this fishing camp have been delicately hewn down with coordinated bedding, draperies, and carpets, as well as thoughtful decorative touches of dried flowers, botanical prints, and hand-quilted comforters in the refurbished riverside cabins. Knotty pine paneling and rustic Americana furnishings in the guest rooms echo the decor of the main lodge.

Recent additions to the property include two detached suites along the river and five roomy, lofted chalets a half-mile up the road, the latter perfect for families or small groups. The riverside suites offer intimate seclusion, with large wood-burning fireplaces, two-person Japanese-style soaking tubs, and large private decks over the river.

The Steamboat's famous candlelit evening dinner might include Northwest wines, salad spiced with roasted local nuts or garden-fresh herbs, fresh bread, a vegetable dish, and roasted lamb or fresh spring salmon. Wine-maker dinners, with guest chefs from the state's best restaurants, are the highlight of winter weekends.

Nonfishing activities in the area include hiking on the trails of the surrounding Umpqua National Forest, soaking in swimming holes, or making a day trip to cross-country ski at Diamond Lake or to admire the breathtaking, crystal-blue waters of Crater Lake. ♦ *8 cabins with baths, 2 suites, 5 2-bedroom housekeeping cottages, 4 3-bedroom houses each share a bath. Fireplace in cabins. Library, conference facilities, bicycles. $125–$235; breakfast extra, dinner available. MC, V. No smoking, closed Jan.–Feb., limited midweek food service Mar.–May.*

WESTFIR LODGE ☙
47365 1st St., Westfir, OR 97492, tel. and fax 541/782–3103

Anchoring the tiny community of Westfir, just west of the crest of the Cascade Mountains, Westfir Lodge was long the hub of activity in the town, which had a population of several thousand in its heyday a half-century ago. You can't tell by looking at the two-story clapboard Arts and Crafts–style building, however, that it was formerly the main office of the Westfir Lumber Company.

Gerry Chamberlain and Ken Symons, who bought the building in 1990, added bathrooms to the building and converted the offices, which ring the first floor, into bedrooms. Over the years, four additional guest rooms were added on the second floor. The large central space became a living area, kitchen, and formal dining room. Antiques—some family heirlooms, others procured in Southeast Asia, and some purchased at local estate auctions—as well as heavy formal drapes on the windows and a wood-burning stove create a mixture of Asian and English-country ambience in the common rooms.

Some rooms face a road traveled by logging trucks that often leave town before daylight, and the many trains that whistle past Westfir can be heard from here, but windows have recently been refitted with thicker glazing to cut down on the noise. The Willamette River is just across the road from the lodge, and if you're a sound sleeper, the river views and larger room size are inducements to opt for the accommodations on the east side of the building.

Ken, who is Australian, makes full English breakfasts featuring eggs, bangers with fried potatoes, and a broiled stuffed half-tomato. Accompaniments include scones and other breakfast breads, as well as fresh fruit. The garden offers a view of the 180-ft-long Office Bridge, the longest covered bridge in Oregon. A nearby kennel happily boards pet traveling companions. △ *7 double rooms with baths. $70–$85; full breakfast. No credit cards. No smoking.*

WINE COUNTRY
Including Salem

Years ago, researchers at Oregon State University concluded that the soils and climate of the Willamette Valley were unsuitable for the cultivation of fine varietal wine grapes. Fortunately for oenophiles everywhere, a few dedicated souls were to prove them wrong; persuaded by the climatic similarity between Western Oregon and Burgundy, they ignored the naysayers, and Oregon's first vineyards took root during the mid-1960s. Caressed by moisture-laden breezes off the Pacific and coddled by Oregon's long, warm summers and crisp autumns, cool-climate varietals such as Pinot Noir, Riesling, and Chardonnay—and increasingly, a good many others besides—thrive in Northwest Oregon's wine country.

The vintages of 1983 and 1985 put the stamp of greatness on Oregon's Pinot Noir, as wines from the Yamhill and Willamette valleys won numerous gold medals in blind tastings against the best from California and France. Perhaps afflicted with Pinot envy, Burgundy's Drouhin family bought 180 acres here in 1987; they released their first bottling in 1991.

If you've been to California's famous Napa and Sonoma wine regions, you'll have an idea of what the Oregon wine country is not. The state's 100-plus bonded wineries have about 7,500 acres under cultivation, compared with California's 800 wineries and 700,000 acres of vineyards. Oregon's wineries tend to be small, personal, and family run. In fact, if you have a question about your Pinot Noir in the tasting room, you may find yourself asking the winemaker-owner, who, it just so happens, is pouring out the samples.

Oregon's wine country lacks the sumptuous splendor, and the pretensions, of California's. Its wineries are scattered from the Columbia River gorge, just across the river from Washington, all the way south to Ashland, near the California border. But the greatest concentration—more than 60 in all—is found within an hour's drive of Portland, dotting the hills as far south as Salem. Geographically, the wine country occupies a wet, temperate trough between the Coast Range to the west and the Cascades to the east. The landscape is a beguiling one—green and rugged, and rich with soothing views that invite picnicking.

The small towns along the way—Forest Grove, McMinnville, Yamhill, Dundee—retain their rural charm. If that means they have yet to succumb to rampant commercialism, it also means you may have to hunt a bit for the best available food, lodging, and other amenities. Oregon's wine country is a quiet region, heavy on bucolic serenity but lightly endowed with sites of noteworthy historical significance, national parks, or other tourist attractions. Napa Valley it's not, but Oregon's wine country makes a fine side trip from Portland—and it's an even better destination for two or three days of quiet R&R.

PLACES TO GO, SIGHTS TO SEE

Bush House (600 Mission St. SE, Salem, tel. 503/363–4174), just south of Salem's downtown district in the 105-acre Bush's Pasture Park, is a creaky, gaslit Italianate mansion from 1878 with 10 marble fireplaces. (Next door is the Bush Barn Art Center, a gallery selling works by Northwest artists.) A few blocks away, the fanciful 1894 *Deepwood Estate* (1116 Mission St. SE, Salem, tel. 503/ 363–1825) is in better taste. Built in the Queen Anne style, the estate is noteworthy for its splendid interior woodwork, original stained glass, and formal English-style garden.

The **Lafayette Schoolhouse Antique Mall** (Hwy. 99W, between Newberg and McMinnville, tel. 503/864–2720), a large, restored 1910 schoolhouse, hosts Oregon's largest permanent antiques show. It's filled with a vast assortment of collectibles and antiquities—from toys to clothing to furniture, china, glass, silver, and Native American artifacts.

McMinnville is the largest (population 22,000) and most sophisticated of Oregon's wine-country towns. Its central location, excellent restaurants and shops, and collection of top-notch B&Bs make it the headquarters of choice for most wine-country tourers. Founded in 1849, *Linfield College* (tel. 503/434–2200), an oasis of brick and ivy in the midst of McMinnville's farmers' market bustle, hosts Oregon's International Pinot Noir Celebration, which attracts a who's who of international wine makers each July. When it opens, McMinnville's *Evergreen Airventure Museum* (Three-Mile La., east of downtown) will be a spectacular new addition to the wine district's roster of attractions. You won't be amazed by its more than 30 rare antique aircraft, many restored to flying condition, including a B-17G, a Ford Trimotor, a P-40, a P-51, a Corsair, and a Spitfire—that is, not after you've caught sight of Howard Hughes' *Spruce Goose*, the largest airplane ever to fly. However, at press time they had only just broken ground on the museum, so call ahead to see if it's open.

Mission Mill Village and Thomas Kay Woolen Mill Museum (1313 Mill St. SE, Salem, tel. 503/585–7012) in Salem offers a vivid glimpse of a late-19th-century woolen mill, complete with waterwheels and mill stream. Teasel gigging and napper flock bins are just two of the processes and machines on display at the museum complex. Everything still works; it looks as if the workers have merely stepped away for a lunch break. The *Marion Museum of History* displays a fine collection of pioneer and Calipooya Indian artifacts. The spare simplicity of the *Jason Lee House, John D. Boone Home,* and the *Methodist Parsonage,* also part of the village, offer a glimpse of domestic life in the wilds of pioneer Oregon.

Newberg is a graceful old pioneer town in a broad bend in the Willamette River, half an hour southwest of Portland. One of the oldest and most significant of the town's original structures is the *Hoover-Minthorn House* (115 S. River St., tel. 503/538–6629), the boyhood home of President Herbert Hoover. Built in 1881, the beautifully preserved frame house includes many original furnishings and features, as well as the woodshed that no doubt played a formative role in shaping young "Bertie" Hoover's character.

The **Oregon Wine and Food Festival** (Oregon State Fair and Exposition Center, 2330 17th St. NE, Salem, OR 97310, tel. 503/378–3247) is held each January at the State Fairgrounds in Salem. Dozens of Oregon's top wineries bring their current releases, and wine lovers can taste to their heart's content for a modest fee. For the resilient of palate, it's an excellent opportunity to compare wines, styles, and vintages.

Salem, Oregon's state capital, is on the 45th parallel about 45 mi south of Portland, precisely halfway between the North Pole and the equator. Even if you have no political ambitions, make time for a visit to the *Capitol* complex (900 Court St., tel. 503/378–4423). The view of the city, the Willamette Valley, and the mountains from its 140-ft-high dome is impressive; there are surprisingly good murals and sculptures inspired by the state's history; and when the legislature is in session, you can observe Oregon's political movers and shakers in action. Tours of the rotunda, the House and Senate chambers, and the governor's office leave from the information counter under the dome. Just across State Street are the tradition-steeped brick buildings and immaculate grounds of *Willamette University* (tel. 503/370–6303), the oldest college in the West. Founded in 1842, Willamette has long been a mecca for aspiring politicians. The tall, prim Waller Hall, built in 1841, is one of the five oldest buildings in the Pacific Northwest. The university hosts theatrical and musical performances, athletic events, guest lectures, and art exhibitions year-round.

Wine Touring, by car or bicycle, is obviously the star attraction here. First pick up a copy of *Discover Oregon Wineries,* a free guide available at visitor information centers and at most places where Oregon wines are sold (it's also available from the Oregon Winegrowers' Association, 1200 Naito Pkwy., Suite 400, Portland, OR 97209, tel. 503/228–8403). The guide is an invaluable companion, with maps to each winery, opening hours, and suggested itineraries.

Day tourers can begin anywhere, but if you're planning a more extended exploration of the wine country, you should choose a base of operations central to the area you intend to explore. McMinnville has the best concentration of restaurants and bed-and-breakfasts. Salem to the south and Forest Grove to the north also make good headquarters.

Opening hours vary widely. The tasting rooms of some wineries are open daily year-round; others are either open only on weekends or closed for lengthy periods during the winter. Some of the state's best wineries, such as Adams, Adelsheim, Cameron, and Eyrie, have no tasting rooms and are open to the public only on special occasions such as Thanksgiving weekend or by appointment (call the individual wineries for details).

The etiquette of Oregon wine tasting is simple. You select a winery and present yourself at its tasting room. The attendant provides glasses and offers samples of the wines available for tasting that day. There is seldom a charge for tasting, though an exception may be made for particularly rare bottlings. Feel free to try any or all of the available wines; swishing and spitting are encouraged, and you're not compelled to buy.

Many of the establishments command hilltop views and maintain picnic areas for visitors' use. McMinnville and Hillsboro offer the greatest variety of delis and specialty food shops. During the summer and fall, the wine country's many roadside produce stands yield luscious strawberries, raspberries, marionberries, pears, nectarines, peaches, plums, apples, kiwis, and other local fruits.

Choosing Oregon's top wineries is as subjective as choosing its top wines. It's fair to say the state's most esteemed operations include *Adelsheim Vineyard* (22150 N.E. Quarter Mile La., tel. 503/538–3652) in Newberg; *Cameron Winery* (8200 Worden Hill Rd., tel. 503/538–0336) in Dundee; *Eyrie Vineyards* (935 E. 10th St., tel. 503/472–6315) and *Panther Creek Cellars* (455 N. Irvine St., tel. 503/472–8080) in McMinnville; *Erath Winery* (Worden Hill Rd., tel. 503/538–3318) in Dundee; *Ponzi Vineyards* (14665 S.W. Winery La., tel. 503/628–1227) near Beaverton; and *Ken Wright Cellars* (Box 190, tel. 800/571–6825) in Carlton. *Chateau Benoit* (6580 N.E. Mineral Springs Rd., off Hwy. 99W, tel. 503/864–2991) in Carlton; *Elk Cove Vineyards* (27751 N.W. Olson Rd., tel. 503/985–7760) in Gaston; *Laurel Ridge Winery* (46350 N.W. David Hill Rd., from Hwy. 8, tel. 503/359–5436) in Forest Grove; *Rex Hill Vineyards* (30835 N. Hwy. 99W, tel. 503/538–0666) in Newberg; and *Yamhill Valley Vineyards* (16250 S.W. Oldsville Rd., off Hwy. 18, tel. 503/843–3100) in McMinnville have some of the most beautiful winery views and picnic grounds in the area.

RESTAURANTS

The wine country's culinary star is undoubtedly **Nick's Italian Cafe** (tel. 503/434–4471) in McMinnville. A favorite of tourists and local wine makers alike, Nick's serves up spirited northern Italian home cooking in modest surroundings. The five-course, fixed-price menu changes nightly to reflect the region's exquisite seasonal produce. Don't overlook the extensive wine list of Oregon's vintages. Just down the street from Nick's, innovative preparations of regional and seasonal ingredients are the focus at the **Third Street Grill** (tel. 503/435–1745). **Lavender's Blue, A Tea Room** (tel. 503/472–4594), in McMinnville, serves an impeccably English high tea, great homemade desserts, light lunches, and dinners. Tiny Dundee, between Newberg and McMinnville on Hwy. 99W, now has not one but two outstanding eateries. **Red Hills Provincial Dining** (tel. 503/538–8224) offers lovely and imaginative dinners featuring local seafood, game, mushrooms and garden-fresh herbs. **Tina's** (tel. 503/538–8880) roams the far corners of the globe for its culinary inspirations, and features impeccably prepared risottos, grilled fish and meat, and dishes from Pacific Rim regions. In Dayton, just off Hwy. 99W between Dundee and Lafayette, the **Joel Palmer House Restaurant** (tel. 503/864–2995) is renowned throughout the Northwest, particularly for the magic they make with mushrooms. **DaVinci's** in Salem (tel. 503/399–1413) serves Italian cuisine, much of it made in a wood-burning oven, and has a terrific wine list besides.

TOURIST INFORMATION

McMinnville Chamber of Commerce (417 N. Adams St., McMinnville, OR 97128, tel. 503/472–6196). **The Oregon Wine Center** (1200 Naito Pkwy., Suite 400, Portland, OR 97209, tel. 503/228–8403 or 800/242–2363). **Portland/Oregon Visitors Association** (3 World Trade Center, 26 S.W. Salmon St., Portland, OR 97204, tel. 503/222–2223 or 800/963–3700). **Salem Convention & Visitor Association** (Mission Mill Village, 1313 Mill St. SE, Salem, OR 97301, tel. 503/581–4325 or 800/874–7012).

RESERVATION SERVICES

Northwest Bed and Breakfast (1067 Hanover Ct. S, Salem, OR 97302, tel. 503/243–7616, fax 503/316–9118).

FLYING M RANCH 🍃

23029 N.W. Flying M Rd., Yamhill, OR 97148, tel. 503/662–3222, fax 503/662–3202

The mysterious red "M" signs begin in downtown Yamhill—a somnolent town of 700 or so in the very press of the wine country—and continue west for 10 mi into the Chehalem Valley, along in the rugged foothills of the Coast Range. Following them alertly will bring you to the 625-acre Flying M Ranch, perched above the Yamhill River.

The centerpiece of this rough-and-ready, Wild West–flavored amalgam of motel, campground, dude ranch, timber camp, and working ranch is the great log lodge, decorated in a style best described as Paul Bunyan Eclectic and featuring a bar carved from a single, 6-ton tree trunk. On weekends, this is *the* happening place; the adjoining restaurant serves thick steaks and prime rib, and there are even a few fish dishes on the menu now. Sensitive souls may notice the accusing eyes of dozens of taxidermic trophies watching while they eat.

You have a choice of eight secluded cabins and 28 motel units. The motel is modern and clean, but lacks personality. The cabins, a better choice, are equipped with kitchens, living rooms, wood-burning stoves, and decks overlooking the river. The cozy Honeymoon Cabin has a huge stone-and-brick fireplace and a double whirlpool tub. The two-story Wortman Cabin sleeps up to 10 and has the newest furnishings.

A longtime Flying M specialty is the Steak Fry Ride. Participants ride a tractor-drawn hay wagon to the ranch's secluded creekside elk camp for a barbecued steak dinner with all the trimmings, including a crooning cowboy. There are also horseshoe pits, a big swimming hole, and good fly-fishing. As if this weren't enough, the wineries are a half-hour drive away over backcountry gravel roads. Be sure to make it back by dusk, because finding the Flying M in the dark can be a real challenge. ⚹ *24 double rooms with baths, 1 suite, 5 housekeeping cabins, 1 2-bedroom housekeeping cabin. TV in 2 cabins. Restaurant, bar, live entertainment, conference and catering facilities, swimming hole, tennis court, fishing, hiking trails, horseback riding, horseshoe pits, campsites, airfield. $75–$200; breakfast extra. AE, D, DC, MC, V. Limited service Nov.–Mar., closed Dec. 24–25.*

HOWELL HOUSE 🍃

212 N. Knox St., Monmouth, OR 97361, tel. 800/368–2085; www.moriah.com/howell

If Clint and Sandra Boylen hadn't happened along at just the right time, the 1891 Victorian known as Howell House would have ended up as a heap of scrap lumber. Built by carpenter and son of Oregon Trail pioneers John Wesley Howell, the house spent most of this century housing students at Western Oregon University (or the Oregon Normal School, as it was called at the turn of the century); it was, in fact, the oldest student rooming house in the state. Like off-campus housing everywhere, it suffered the ravages of a hard life and had been condemned when the Boylens bought it and began a 2½-year restoration. It is now on the National Register of Historic Places.

The period feel here goes beyond the house itself. Clint and Sandra collect vintage clothing and cars, and their antique furnishings have been accumulated over years of local estate-sale shopping. Even the musical entertainment is old; Sandra is a classical pianist who might sit down after breakfast at her antique parlor piano (in period dress, of course) and serve up some Chopin. The one concession to modernity is the backyard hot tub, tastefully housed in a Japanese-style enclosure.

The rooms upstairs—the Seniors Guest Suite, Juniors Guest Room, and Alumni Parlor, which can be made into a guest room in a pinch—are filled with tasteful collegiate memorabilia and historical pieces and have 7-ft Victorian beds with matching marble dressers, lace curtains, and fluffy comforters. The House Mother's suite downstairs has its own entrance, and just outside is a flower-filled gazebo and the hot tub. Bathrooms have large claw-foot tubs and showers.

Breakfast, served on antique china, includes such dishes as blackberry pancakes, hazelnut Belgian waffles, omelets and frittatas, and homemade breads and muffins. In the evening you can sit outside and enjoy the fragrance of the 80 or so varieties of roses, some heirloom. △ *1 suite with private bath, 1 double and 1 suite share bath. Hot tub. $59–$89; full breakfast. MC, V. No smoking.*

KELTY ESTATE ☞
675 Hwy. 99W, Lafayette, OR 97127, tel. 503/864–3740 or 800/867–3740

This simple white-clapboard farmhouse, built in 1872, is on busy Highway 99 between Newberg and McMinnville, directly across the street from the great browsing at the Lafayette Schoolhouse Antique Mall.

Owners Ron Ross, a former facilities manager, and his wife, JoAnn, a nurse, renovated the property themselves, and their hard work is reflected in the house's handsome living areas. Sunlight from tall windows gleams on newly refinished oak floors and tasteful wine-color patterned rugs; an elegant border of green and blue paisley circles the freshly painted walls.

The two upstairs guest rooms have received similar care. Outfitted with antiques, one follows a French theme (with window sheers, 1910 French bedstead, and 1920 Victrola), the other turn-of-the-century American (with oak antiques and white lace curtains). Both rooms have queen-size beds, hardwood floors, and private baths with pedestal sink and tile shower. If possible, reserve the room at the back of the house; the front room, overlooking Highway 99, is a little noisier. You have a choice of Continental or full farmhouse breakfast, typically featuring traditional standbys such as French toast or eggs Benedict.

The Rosses also operate an RV park next door, so there are plenty of comings and goings. △ *2 double rooms with baths. Cable TV in living room, billiards table, coin laundry. $70–$80; full breakfast. No credit cards. No smoking.*

MAIN STREET BED & BREAKFAST ☞
1803 Main St., Forest Grove, OR 97116, tel. 503/357–9812, fax 503/359–0860; aumamarie@aol.com

The first inn in this part of the wine country, Main Street Bed & Breakfast is in a quiet and well-tended neighborhood in Forest Grove, 25 mi west of Portland and near such highly regarded wineries as Tualatin, Shafer, and Elk Cove.

The B&B occupies a 1913 Craftsman bungalow that has a stone foundation, cross-gabled roof, and a wide front porch with glider. The corner lot is filled with flowers and trees. Inside, innkeeper Marie Mather has decorated with a mix of contemporary furnishings and her various collections: owls, kaleidoscopes, and old handmade aprons. Though modern, the carpets, couches, and baths are softened with old-fashioned touches—a lace tablecloth here, a claw-foot tub there.

The three upstairs guest rooms are country quaint, if a little fussy, with florals, ruffles, and dried flowers. The Sweetheart Rose Room is done in shades of pink and powder blue, while the appropriately named Sunshine Room has brightly painted yellow walls. In two rooms, Marie has turned the home's original oversized closets into small sitting rooms, adding a single bed suitable for children. The full breakfasts are hearty: Apple Pan Puffs and Tahitian Butterflies (a split croissant with ham and egg) are some of Marie's specialties. △ *3 double rooms share bath. Phone in rooms. $55–$65; full breakfast, afternoon refreshments. AE, MC, V. No smoking.*

MARQUEE HOUSE 🐦

333 Wyatt Ct. NE, Salem, OR 97301, tel. 503/391–0837 or 800/949–0837,
fax 503/391–1713; www.oregonlink.com/marquee

From the outside, this 1938 Colonial looks like a cross between George Washington's Mt. Vernon and *Gone With the Wind*'s Tara. Inside, amiable innkeeper Rickie Hart, who lived in Hollywood for years and developed a penchant there for collecting costumes and other theatrical memorabilia, has followed through on the movie theme, decorating and naming her five guest rooms after classic comedy films.

An inverted top hat serves as a planter in Topper, appointed with early American barber stands, a straw boater, a bowler, and other vintage hats. More antique hats, hat stands, and a fox hunting outfit are the highlights in Auntie Mame (the master bedroom of the house), while razor straps, an old sitz bathtub, and red long johns accent Blazing Saddles. Christmas in Connecticut, in a Christmas scheme, of course, has French Empire antiques and great views of the lovely creek and lawns behind the house.

Evenings bring movies, complete with popcorn and candy, screened in the living room, which follows the theme from *Harvey* (notice all the rabbits in the decor). Daytime entertainment is provided by live performers: the ducks that swim in Mill Creek, which winds along the back yard. Rickie's hearty breakfasts feature edible flowers, herbs, blackberries, and hazelnuts grown on the grounds. △ *3 doubles with baths, 2 doubles share bath. TV/VCR and video collection in living room. $55–$90; full breakfast. D, MC, V. No smoking, 2-night minimum during holidays and university events.*

MATTEY HOUSE 🐦

10221 N.E. Mattey La., McMinnville, OR 97128, tel. 503/434–5058,
fax 503/434–6667; mattey@pnn.com

Mattey House is a genteel Queen Anne mansion nestled behind its own little vineyard a few miles north of McMinnville. Its tasteful, distinctively western Victorian ambience and its experienced hosts make Mattey House the area's consummate B&B.

The house itself was built in 1892 by Joseph Mattey, a local butcher and cattle rancher. Jack and Denise Seed, originally from England, bought it in 1993 and have lavished great care on the guest rooms, public areas, and grounds. Their affable English sheepdog, Emma, is happy to show you around.

To wine-country visitors tuckered out by a long day's slurping, Mattey House is an oasis of welcoming warmth. Entering the living room, which is framed by Ionic columns and fretwork, you'll find a beckoning fire in the old carved-wood-and-tile hearth, reproduction William Morris wallpaper, and a cheerful mix of period furnishings and more informal modern pieces. There's a porch swing over-looking the vineyard, and 10 acres of grounds for those in a strolling mood.

The four guest rooms are named for locally grown grape varieties. The Chardonnay Room has tall windows and crisp white decor, and the Riesling Room is furnished with an antique pine dresser and a 6-ft-long claw-foot tub. A connecting door joins Chardonnay and Pinot Noir; you can reserve them as a two-couple suite. All bathrooms come with wine-glycerine soaps.

Breakfast features fresh local fruit, followed by fresh-baked scones and the house specialty, an Italian-style frittata, or Dutch apple pancakes. At the end of a day's wine touring, you are rewarded with hors d'oeuvres and one last cheering glass of the Oregonian grape. ⚫ *3 double rooms with bath, 1 double with separate bath. Robes in rooms. $85–$95; full breakfast, afternoon refreshments. MC, V. No smoking, 3-night minimum stay during Pinot Noir Festival (late July) and Linfield graduation, 2-night minimum on holiday weekends.*

ORCHARD VIEW INN 🐦
16540 N.W. Orchard View Rd., McMinnville, OR 97128, tel. 503/472–0165

In 1990, Wayne and Marie Schatter escaped the southern California rat race to run Orchard View Inn. Southern California seems a world away from the long, sunlight-warmed deck of this octagonal redwood house, 1,000 ft up in the Chehalem Mountains about 5 mi west of McMinnville. Birdcalls, the rustle of wind through the evergreen canopy overhead, and the music of water cascading from pool to pool down the hill are the only sounds.

Inside, the inn mixes contemporary vaulted ceilings and velour-upholstered couches with beautiful Chinese antiques. Spacious guest rooms with vaulted ceilings are modern and simply furnished. The Antique Room displays a framed collection of Marie's family heirlooms: 19th-century lace gloves, purses, fans, a silver cane handle that belonged to her mother. The lower-level Studio Room has a private entrance and bath; a mixed-tweed carpet is complemented by a series of gorgeous vintage 1930s Chinese prints on the wall.

Wineries are the most obvious nearby attractions, but there is also good boating, fishing, and swimming. If you kick back on the deck for a while, you may find yourself doing some wildlife watching as well, as the local deer are frequent visitors. In the winter, a spot by the fieldstone hearth of the large wood-burning fireplace is a perfect spot for taking the chill off. ⚫ *2 double rooms with baths, 2 doubles share bath. Laundry facilities. $70–$80; full breakfast. No credit cards. No smoking, 3-night minimum during Pinot Noir Celebration (late July).*

PARTRIDGE FARM 🐦
4300 E. Portland Rd., Newberg, OR 97132, tel. 503/538–2050

This wine country B&B sits on a 5-acre farm just west of the Rex Hill winery, surrounded by raised-bed vegetable gardens, lush orchards, and a finely landscaped perennial border.

Run like a small European guest house by innkeepers Megan and Chris Streight, this yellow, 1920-vintage classic American farmhouse is fittingly decorated with antiques from Germany and France. The three guest rooms are furnished with a simple mix of English and American antiques and contemporary pieces, with a focus on comfort rather than frill. Each has a small private bathroom. The prettiest, with floral papered walls and angled ceilings, also happens to be the least expensive; the other two have small bedrooms but spacious sitting rooms.

The Partridge Farm's chief drawback is not in the inn itself, but rather just outside: Highway 99W, the main artery through the wine country, creates a considerable din, particularly at rush hour. The house muffles the noise well but not entirely, so light sleepers may wish to bring earplugs.

Breakfasts, as might be expected, are farmhouse-hearty and filling, featuring in-season fruits, berries, and vegetables from the grounds. The warm blueberry muffins are an especially appreciated treat, as are the homemade fruit compotes. △ *1 double room with bath, 2 suites. TV/VCR in library, nearby kennel for pets. $80–$110; full breakfast. MC, V. No smoking.*

SPRINGBROOK HAZELNUT FARM 🐚

30295 N. Hwy. 99W, Newberg, OR 97132, tel. 503/538–4606 or 800/793–8528; www.nutfarm.com

Chuck and Ellen McClure have owned this quiet, 60-acre hazelnut farm, with its lovely Craftsman-style farmhouse—listed in the National Register of Historic Places—for almost 30 years. The sense of place is evident, from the bucolic nut-tree stand out front to the fine collection of Northwest contemporary art on view inside.

The entry hall alone is magazine worthy (and, indeed, has been featured in several national publications): An expanse of high-beamed ceilings and hand-screened French wallpaper in shades of yellow leads through the house to the flower-filled rear garden. An enormous fireplace of brick and carved wood welcomes you in winter. Guest-room furnishings are farmhouse comfortable. Water closets were added to the two downstairs rooms, which share a bath across the hall.

If you're craving post-breakfast exercise after the morning meal served on antique Wedgwood china, you can choose between playing tennis on the private court, swimming in the pool, or strolling through the inn's orderly hazelnut orchard. The newest addition to the accommodations is the farm's old cottage, recently beautifully restored. It is very sweet and very private, and features a striking Craftsman-style tile fireplace, bright fir floors, kitchen, bath, and laundry machines. In the carriage house are a large suite and, in a barnlike space on the second floor, Northwest artist Larry Kirkland's *Soul Boat,* a remarkable piece of kinetic sculpture that hung for a time in the Smithsonian. Children are accommodated by arrangement. △ *4 double rooms share 2 baths, carriage-house with bath and kitchen. TV in parlor, library, tennis court, pool, trout pond. $90–$135; full breakfast. No credit cards. No smoking, carriage house and cottage open year-round, main inn closed Nov.–Apr.*

STATE HOUSE 🐚

2146 State St., Salem, OR 97301, tel. 503/588–1340 or 800/800–6712, fax 503/585–8812; www.teleport.com/~mikwin

State House, Salem's oldest bed-and-breakfast, is on busy State Street in one of the city's older residential neighborhoods. A meandering creek, which provides habitat for nutria, beavers, ducks, and geese, runs along the landscaped back yard of this 1920s Craftsman, just past the gazebo and hot tub. The effect isn't exactly bucolic, unfortunately; just across the gravel parking area, heavy traffic makes a continuous din.

Guest rooms on the second floor are furnished with basic mix-and-match contemporary pieces; the largest has a sitting area and a kitchenette, and the smaller two share a bath down the hall. The third-floor penthouse suite is equipped with small kitchenette, TV, and stereo. Friendly proprietors Mike Winsett and Judy Unselman, longtime residents of Salem, are happy to point the way to Bush Park, the capitol building, and other local sites of interest. The inn is conveniently located within a short walk of the Capitol Mall, where the grounds are landscaped with native trees and other plants of Oregon, and Willamette University.

Mike often whips up a mean strawberry crepe or eggs Benedict in the morning, but he's a pretty flexible cook, summing up his approach as "Whatever you want, whatever time you want it." △ *2 double rooms share bath, 2 housekeeping suites. Air-conditioning and phone in rooms. TV in suites. TV in common room. $50–$70; full breakfast. D, MC, V. No smoking, 2-night minimum during university graduation in May.*

STEIGER HAUS ☙

360 Wilson St., McMinnville, OR 97128, tel. 503/472–0821 or 503/472–0238, fax 503/472–0100

"Zsa Zsa Gabor slapped here," proclaims the plaque in Steiger Haus's hallway, covered with hundreds of pictures of guests. Well, actually it says "slept." These little mementos aren't just there for show; they're an illustration of the genuine affection innkeepers Susan and Dale DuRette, who purchased the property in 1996, feel for their guests. After a weekend at Steiger Haus, you feel like family.

On a quiet residential street near downtown McMinnville, the modern, cedar-sided structure was built in 1984 as a B&B. Linfield College, the site of Oregon's annual International Pinot Noir Celebration, is just across the creek at the back of the property.

The inn's public areas have a country-contemporary charm. On the main level are an open kitchen with breakfast bar, a brick fireplace, an antique deacon's bench, and an oak dining suite with Windsor chairs built by an Oregon craftsman. In summer and fall, most of the action shifts outdoors to the inn's four decks and parklike, oak-shaded grounds.

Steiger Haus's five unfussy guest rooms are cool and contemporary, enlivened with dried floral arrangements, fresh paint, and sunlight. (Two of them can be linked to form a suite.) Handmade quilts in many of the rooms provide a warming touch. The downstairs room, which opens onto one of the decks, has a brick fireplace, a small, cozy sitting area, and a large private bath. The Treetop Room upstairs features a mission-style pine slat bed, tall windows, and a huge skylighted bath. An adjacent room is equipped with two single beds and a delicately carved oak armoire.

Breakfast is a hearty affair, when Susan garners rave reviews for her fresh-fruit crepes. △ *4 double rooms with baths, 1 suite. Fireplace in 1 room. Cable TV/VCR, bicycle storage, horseshoe pit. $70–$130; full breakfast. D, MC, V. No smoking, 2-night minimum during college events and holiday weekends.*

YOUNGBERG HILL VINEYARD ☙

10660 Youngberg Hill Rd., McMinnville, OR 97128, tel. 503/472–2727 or 888/657–8668, fax 503/472–1313; www.youngberghill.com

Like ghostly twilight sentinels, the deer come down to greet you at Youngberg Hill Farm. They have free run of this 700-acre estate, high in the hills west of McMinnville. Well, nearly free run—you must remember to close the gate of the deer fence that surrounds the house itself and its 10 acres of young Pinot Noir vines, a favorite midnight snack for these graceful thieves. This rural B&B, recently bought by silicon forest workers Kevin and Tasha Byrd, is a monster-size replica of a classic American farmhouse commanding breathtaking views over mountain and valley from atop a steep hill.

Youngberg Hill is a comfortable place with a proper, lived-in warmth. The common areas are spacious, modern, and high-ceilinged, with Victorian bellyband molding and bull's-eye corners. The furnishings are largely golden oak period reproductions; the sitting room's deep sofa and settee, upholstered in an unusual grapevine-patterned chintz, are a welcoming touch, as are the suede-covered armchairs and wood-burning stove. Big windows make the most of the hilltop estate's romantic views. The five guest rooms are small to medium in size; furnished with golden oak and Victorian Cottage reproductions, they have a cozy modern ambience. Fresh flowers in the room and truffles on the pillow add a touch of romance.

The wine interest carries into the house from the vineyard: Rooms are named after clones of Pinot Noir, and among the inn's special attractions are a nicely stocked, reasonably priced wine cellar, including older vintages and small high-quality producers. Soon to join the cellar will be a winery, plans for which are just getting under way. Each morning, tea and fresh-brewed coffee can be enjoyed in your room or on the porch. Breakfast is served in a room with floor-to-ceiling windows and includes fresh fruit, homemade muffins, and a full country menu. △ *5 double rooms with baths. Air-conditioning in rooms, fireplace in 2 rooms. Conference and wedding facilities. $130–$150; full breakfast, afternoon refreshments. MC, V. No smoking, 2-night minimum over holidays.*

PORTLAND

Portland's easy charm rests on twin foundations: its beguiling urban amenities and its access to a wealth of recreational treasures. About 75 mi east of the Pacific Ocean, near the confluence of the Willamette and Columbia rivers, it is one of the largest inland ports on the West Coast. Within the city limits are more than 9,400 acres of forested parkland—home to deer, hawks, and what are probably the last urban old-growth trees in the world. Portland is known as the City of Roses, but the 10 distinctive bridges spanning the Willamette River and connecting the east and west sides of the city have also earned it the name Bridgetown.

The first settlers didn't arrive in Portland—then the highest easily navigable point on the broad Willamette—until the 1840s. In 1844 pioneers Asa Lovejoy and William Overton used an ax to mark a few boundary trees in the dense riverbank forest (near what are now Bill Naito Parkway and Southwest Washington Street), paid a 25¢ filing fee, and took possession of the 640 acres that are now downtown Portland. A year later Overton sold his share to Francis Pettygrove for $50 worth of trade goods. Pettygrove, a Maine native, and Lovejoy, a Bostonian, tossed a coin to decide who would name the town-to-be; Pettygrove won, and with homesick fondness chose Portland.

With its moist, temperate climate, the city is something of a paradise for gardeners. Portland became the City of Roses thanks to the efforts of Leo Samuel, a turn-of-the-century insurance mogul who planted a jungle of roses in front of his mansion and hung out shears so that passersby could help themselves to choice blooms. One legacy is the city's internationally renowned International Rose Test Garden (in Washington Park), overlooking the downtown skyline and Mt. Hood, whose snowbound 11,235-ft summit towers 50 mi to the east. The Rose Festival, an annual event with two parades and city-wide celebrations, draws thousands of visitors every June.

Downtown Portland, with its award-winning mix of green public spaces, efficient mass transit, modern skyscrapers, and beautifully restored historic buildings, ranks as one of the best-planned urban centers in the United States. Pioneer Courthouse Square, a broad brick piazza with a splashing fountain, is a fine place from which to begin a ramble through the heart of the city and is convenient to many of the city's bed-and-breakfasts. The nearby Portland Center for the Performing Arts is home to the Oregon Symphony, the highly regarded Oregon Ballet Theatre, and Portland Center Stage. The revamped Portland Art Museum, the Oregon History Center, and other theaters and art galleries are also close at hand.

But Portland is equally well-known for its many distinctive residential neighborhoods. On the west side, Victorian mansions line the wide, leafy streets of Nob Hill and Portland Heights, and a trendy new neighborhood called the Pearl District is being created in a former industrial area. Irvington, an east-side neighborhood of fine old homes, is close to the mammoth new Rose Quarter, where the National Basketball Association's Portland Trail Blazers play home games, the Oregon Convention Center, and Memorial Coliseum, a venue for large touring shows.

In the past decade, Portland has become one of the fastest-growing cities in the country. To ward off suburban sprawl, planners are encouraging development within the inner city. The resulting spate of construction and development has given the city a new vitality—but, to the chagrin of many, has also increased traffic congestion. One of the side benefits of the city's expansion and newly acquired urban chic—and one you won't hear anyone complaining about—is the number of new restaurants. In fact, Portland is now said to have more restaurants per capita than any other West Coast city.

PLACES TO GO, SIGHTS TO SEE

Exploring Portland is easy—you don't need a car. The city's popular light-rail system, *MAX* (tel. 503/238–7433 for *Tri-Met* information), makes a loop from downtown Portland to the suburb of Gresham, 13 mi east. Along the way, it forms a handy link between the bed-and-breakfast establishments in northeast Portland's *Irvington* district and many of the city's most important destinations. Using MAX, you can reach the museums, shops, restaurants, and historic districts of the downtown core, including *Pioneer Courthouse Square* (bounded by S.W. Broadway and S.W. 6th Ave. and S.W. Morrison and S.W. Yamhill Sts.), the *Portland Art Museum* (1219 S.W. Park Ave., tel. 503/226–2811), the *Portland Center for the Performing Arts* (S.W. Broadway and S.W. Main St., tel. 503/796–9293), and the *Oregon History Center* (1200 S.W. Park Ave., tel. 503/306–5200). On the west side, MAX provides easy access to the new 21,700-seat *Rose Quarter* stadium (1 Center Ct., tel. 503/797–9617), home of the NBA's Portland Trail Blazers; the *Oregon Convention Center* (777 N.E. Martin Luther King Jr. Blvd., tel.

503/235–7575); the *Memorial Coliseum* (1 Center Ct., Rose Quarter, tel. 503/ 321–3211), a venue for large events of all kinds; and the *Lloyd Center* (N.E. Multnomah St. and N.E. 9th Ave., tel. 503/282–2511), with more than 170 shops. A newly opened MAX extension now runs west to Beaverton as well, making a stop at the *Metro Washington Park Zoo* (*see* Parks and Gardens, *below*). The city's efficient bus system (tel. 503/238–7433 for Tri-Met information), another transportation option, can be used to reach the *International Rose Test Gardens* in *Washington Park.*

Outside the city, the *Columbia River Gorge National Scenic Area*, a remarkably unspoiled expanse of waterfalls, hiking trails, and lush fern-draped grottoes, unfolds along I–84 just 30 minutes east of downtown Portland (the Historic Gorge Highway, which winds along the bluffs parallel to the highway, is slower but far more scenic). Mt. Hood, with its historic *Timberline Lodge* (Timberline Rd., Timberline 97028, tel. 503/272–3311 or 800/547–1406) and year-round skiing, is a half hour farther on. Ninety minutes west of Portland, the tumultuous Pacific Ocean thunders against Oregon's spectacular coastal headlands and white-sand beaches. Award-winning wineries along the way help to enliven the journey.

Parks and Gardens. Portland's *Washington Park* and *Forest Park* occupy more than 5,000 acres in the city's West Hills, forming the largest contiguous municipal park in the United States. At its southeast end, where Washington Park meets the upscale Portland Heights neighborhood, is Portland's famed *International Rose Test Garden* (400 S.W. Kingston Ave., tel. 503/823–3636), which sports more than 10,000 bushes in 400 varieties as well as gorgeous views out over the downtown skyline to Mt. Hood and Mt. St. Helens. On the opposite side of the avenue, the serene expanse of manicured sand, boulders, trees, shrubs, rills, and ponds that form the *Japanese Gardens* (611 S.W. Kingston Ave., tel. 503/223– 4070), the most authentic Japanese garden outside of Japan, are a reminder of Portland's close links with the Pacific Rim. *Hoyt Arboretum* (4000 S.W. Fairview Blvd., tel. 503/228–8733), just up the hill, contains 10 mi of forested hiking trails and more than 700 species of trees and plants. *Metro Washington Park Zoo* (4001 S.W. Canyon Rd., tel. 503/226–7627), founded in 1887, is one of the world's most prolific breeding grounds for Asian elephants, and contains major exhibits on the Alaskan tundra, the Cascade Mountains, and the African plains.

Powell's City of Books (1005 W. Burnside St., tel. 503/228–4651) may also owe a debt of gratitude to Portland's wet climate. With more than a million volumes, it's one of the world's great bookstores—and a browser's haven on a gray afternoon. Patrons can borrow a volume from the shelves and read over cups of caffe latte or espresso in the commodious Ann Hughes Coffee Room.

Shopping. Powell's is midway between Portland's three main west-side shopping districts. In the downtown core are the three flagship department stores, *Meier and Frank* (621 S.W. 5th Ave., tel. 503/223–0512), *Nordstrom* (701 S.W. Broadway, tel. 503/224–6666), and *Saks Fifth Avenue* (850 S.W. 5th Ave., tel. 503/226–3200); as well as *Pioneer Place* (700 S.W. 5th St., tel. 503/228–5800), an upscale mall; the original *NikeTown* (930 S.W. 6th Ave., tel. 503/221–6453); and *The Portland Pendleton Shop* (900 S.W. 5th Ave., tel. 503/242–0037). Northwest Portland's *Nob Hill District*, along Northwest 21st and (more particularly) Northwest 23rd avenues, and the newly fashionable *Pearl District* (north from W. Burnside St. to N.W. Marshall St. between N.W. 8th and 15th Aves.) are home to an eclectic array of clothing, gift, and food shops as well as cafés, art galleries, ethnic eateries, and bookstores. Northeast Portland's revamped *Broadway* district, extending from Martin Luther King Boulevard to about N.E. 42nd Street, is another new and trendy area for shopping and restaurants. A bit more countercultural, but becoming more upscale by the day, is southeast Portland's *Hawthorne District* (along S.E. Hawthorne Blvd. from S.E. 17th Ave. to S.E. 43rd Ave.).

Wineries and brew pubs are another local amenity that have put Portland on the map. The superb Pinot Noir and Chardonnay varietals grown in the nearby Yamhill and Tualatin valleys are consistent international award winners. Close-in wineries include *Ponzi Vineyards* (14665 S.W. Winery La., Beaverton, tel. 503/628–1227), *Shafer Vineyard Cellars* (6200 N.W. Gales Creek Rd., Forest Grove, tel. 503/357–6604), and *Montinore Vineyards* (3663 S.W. Dilley Rd., Forest Grove, tel. 503/359–5012). The City of Roses is also home to more microbreweries and brew pubs—small breweries with attached public houses—than any other city outside Europe. The following are among the most popular of Portland's many highly regarded microbreweries; all of them have attached restaurants where you can get a good meal and ales fresh from the brew house: *Bridgeport Brew Pub* (1313 N.W. Marshall St., tel. 503/241–7179); *Brewhouse Tap Room and Grill* (2730 N.W. 31st Ave., tel. 503/228–5269); *Widmer Brewing and Gasthaus* (955 N. Russell St., tel. 503/281–2437); and McCormick & Schmick's *Pilsner Room* (309 S.W. Montgomery St., tel. 503/220–1865) at RiverPlace, which features rarely encountered microbrewed pilsner. *Portland Brewing Co.* (1339 N.W. Flanders St., tel. 503/222–3414; 2730 N.W. 31st Ave., tel. 503/228–5269) has two pubs. *McMenamin Brewing* has over 30 brew pubs scattered throughout Portland and surrounding areas; some are in renovated historic buildings, including old movie theaters that show nightly double features for a minimal charge. Best-known and most popular are *Bagdad Theatre and Pub* (3702 S.E. Hawthorne Blvd., tel. 503/230–0895), *Mission Theater and Pub* (1624 N.W. Glisan St., tel. 503/223–4031), *Ringlers* (1332 W. Burnside St., tel. 503/225–0543), *Blue Moon Tavern and Grill* (432 N.W. 21st Ave., tel. 503/223–3184), and *Kennedy School* (5736 N.E. 33rd Ave., tel. 503/249–3983).

RESTAURANTS

For a relatively small city, Portland has a surprisingly rich restaurant scene, particularly for lovers of Pacific Northwest produce and seafood. Hip places serving a variety of cuisines are opening in different neighborhoods all the time, but many of them have yet to stand the test of time. The following restaurants are well-established and stand out both for their outstanding quality of food and elegant surroundings: **Atwater's** (111 S.W. 5th Ave., tel. 503/275–3600), with its superb service, inspiring views, and intensely rich Northwest cuisine; the contemporary French artistry of intimate **Couvron** (1126 S.W. 18th Ave., tel. 503/225–1844), the city's best French restaurant; **The Heathman** (1001 S.W. Broadway, tel. 503/241–4100), where a sophisticated, seasonally changing menu features local fish, game, and produce; and the more exotic Southeast Asian and Mediterranean flavors and textures of chic **Zefiro** (500 N.W. 21st Ave., tel. 503/226–3394). At **Jake's Famous Crawfish** (401 S.W. 12th Ave., tel. 503/226–1419), a Portland landmark since 1892, two white-aproned waiters serve up impeccably fresh Northwest seafood from a lengthy sheet of daily specials in a warren of wood-paneled dining rooms. Italian cuisine has been gaining popularity for some years now; the best places to find it are **Assaggio** (7742 S.E. 13th Ave., tel. 503/232–6151) in the Sellwood district, and **Bastas** (410 N.W. 21st Ave., tel. 503/274–1572) in Nob Hill. For intensely flavored Thai, Vietnamese, and Indian food, try **Yen Ha** (6820 N.E. Sandy Blvd., tel. 503/287–3698), **Indigine** (3723 S.E. Division St., tel. 503/238–1470), and **Misohapi** (1123 N.W. 23rd Ave., tel. 503/796–2012). If a juicy steak alongside succulent onion rings suits your palate, **The Ringside** (2165 W. Burnside St., tel. 503/223–1513), a Portland landmark for over 50 years, can't be beat.

TOURIST INFORMATION

Portland/Oregon Visitors Association (3 World Trade Center, 26 S.W. Salmon St., Portland, OR 97204, tel. 503/222–2223 or 800/963–3700).

RESERVATION SERVICES

Northwest Bed and Breakfast (1067 Hanover Ct. S, Salem, OR 97302, tel. 503/243–7616, fax 503/316–9118). **A Travelers Reservation Service** (14716 26th Ave. NE, Seattle, WA 98155, tel. 206/364–5900).

CLINKERBRICK HOUSE 🐦

2311 N.E. Schuyler St., Portland, OR 97212, tel. 503/281–2533, fax 503/281–1281, clinker@teleport.com

A facade bristling with fancifully twisted and fused "clinkers" (a Dutch word for bricks) gives this 1908 Dutch Colonial its name and lends personality to the structure. The gabled house, surrounded by gardens and stately chestnut trees, is conveniently located in northeast Portland's Irvington neighborhood. Innkeepers Peggie and Bob Irvine opened this small, comfortable B&B in 1987.

The house's public spaces have an American country feel without the clutter. Beautiful old quilts spill from pine cabinets; an intriguing V-shape corner bench invites fireside conversation. The interior, with its brickwork, unusual tin wainscoting, and leaded-glass cabinetry, is snug and casually comfortable. Still more brick has been used to create the quiet back patio, where breakfast is served on fine mornings. A typical breakfast is seasonal fruit with waffles (gingerbread in wintertime) or scrambled eggs with smoked salmon, juice, and freshly ground coffee.

The three upstairs guest rooms have their own entrance, accessed from the patio, and share a common area with a TV and full kitchen. In the sunny Strawberry Room, dark-green carpeting, a crewel-embroidered wing chair, and a pine pencil-post bed pull the room together. The Rose Room, decorated with pink roses and white wicker, has a canopied bed, and a daybed covered by crocheted spread. The largest room, dubbed the Garden Room, has windows on three sides and its own private balcony. ⚠ *1 double room with shower, 2 doubles share bath. Kitchen, phone, and TV in common room. $55–$70; full breakfast. MC, V. No smoking.*

GENERAL HOOKER'S B&B 🐦

125 S.W. Hooker St., Portland, OR 97201, tel. 503/222–4435 or 800/745–4135, fax 503/295–6410, lori@generalhookers.com

You might not peg Lori Hall, the fourth-generation Portlander who owns and manages this Victorian B&B five minutes from downtown, as a movie buff. But sitting on the coffee table of her 1888 Queen Anne house is a tantalizing card catalogue filled with the some 3,700 movie titles in her video collection. "After dinner, a lot of our guests like to kick back and relax with a movie," says the former fashion designer and special education teacher. All of her guest rooms have TVs with VCRs so guests can chill out with a flick of their choice.

In Lair Hill, a neighborhood in southwest Portland that still has many of its small, unpretentious Victorian homes, this is a good place for guests who want to be close to downtown but not in it. Hall has unobtrusively modernized and updated the interior, adding skylights in the upstairs rooms, an outdoor second-story deck, and data ports for her many business travelers.

Three of the guest rooms are on the second floor, off a small landing made smaller by a large guest refrigerator (stocked with wine, beer, and juice). The Rose, with a super king-size bed and skylighted bathroom, is the largest. The Iris is a comfortable space with a Civil War–era armoire. Both rooms have doors out to a commonly shared deck. The guest room in the basement has a loft bed (double below, twin above), refrigerator, and its own bathroom down the hall.

A light vegetarian breakfast—usually juice, coffee or tea, fresh fruit, and muffins— is served from 7 to 9. ♠ *2 double rooms with baths, 2 doubles share bath. Airconditioning, robes, cable TV/VCR, and data port in rooms. ½-price YMCA passes. $75–$125; Continental-plus breakfast. AE, MC, V. No smoking, 2-night minimum Apr.–Oct.*

GEORGIAN HOUSE ☜

1828 N.E. Siskiyou St., Portland, OR 97212, tel. 503/281–2250 or 888/282–2250, fax 503/281–3301

White neoclassical columns flank the front door of this striking redbrick Georgian Colonial–style house, and legend has it that in 1922, when the house was built, a dozen $20 gold pieces were buried in its foundation for good luck. Willie Ackley, who bought the house in 1987, has restored it to mint condition, added a wrought-iron fence, and landscaped the grounds with meticulous care. The house sits on a brilliant-green patch of manicured lawn on a quiet, tree-lined street in the historic Irvington neighborhood.

Ackley has kept the interior public spaces open and airy and furnished them with comfortable reproductions of Colonial furniture. Off the living room, with its quiet blue-gray walls and light oak floor, a solarium overlooks the formal gardens in back. The gardens can also be enjoyed from a broad vine-canopied deck and gazebo. A full breakfast, with the summertime addition of fresh fruit from the garden, is served outside or in the dining room at the front of the house.

Each guest room has a personality of its own. The smallish Eastlake Room, with a century-old cherry-wood bed, marble-top dresser, and dark burgundy walls, has a private veranda overlooking the gardens. In the more masculine Pettygrove Room are 150-year-old German-pine twin beds and a striking handmade quilt. Largest and sunniest of the rooms is the Lovejoy Suite, with a tile fireplace, ornate brass canopy bed, private bath with claw-foot tub and shower, and a sitting room. ♠ *1 double room with bath, 2 doubles share 1½ baths, 1 suite. Air-conditioning in 3 rooms, TV in 2 rooms. TV/VCR and phone in common room. $65–$100; full breakfast. MC, V. No smoking.*

HERON HAUS ☜

2545 N.W. Westover Rd., Portland, OR 97210, tel. 503/274–1846, fax 503/248–4055

A sense of luxurious seclusion is what sets Heron Haus apart. It's right in the heart of Nob Hill, northwest Portland's oldest and prettiest neighborhood, but occupies its own hilltop kingdom at the end of a secretive drive. From the driveway, a long flight of wooden stairs leads down not only to the mansion, but to another hidden charm, a secluded orchard of pear, apple, cherry, and filbert trees.

Both urban and urbane, this is one of the most accomplished B&Bs in the Rose City. The house itself is a sturdy Tudor built in 1904 from stucco and Port of Portland ballast stone. It's convenient to the hiking trails and gigantic old-growth trees in Forest Park and the binge of shops, cafés, and restaurants lining Northwest 23rd Avenue. Julie Keppeler, the effervescent owner, worked in investment real estate, publishing, convention planning, and adult education before settling into the B&B business.

Keppeler renovated the 10,000-square-ft house in 1986 with taste, assurance, and charm. The modern touches, such as Southwestern artwork and Scandinavian-flavor furnishings, subtly complement the house's existing features. There's an extra-large breakfast room with herringbone-pattern oak floors and fireplace; a warm, carpeted sunroom overlooking the backyard pool; and, in the mahogany-accented library, leaded-glass cabinets filled with everything from Isak Dinesen to Audubon.

The six guest suites on the second and third floors are extraordinarily large and impeccably furnished with a stylish blend of clean-lined modern pieces offset by one or two fine antiques. Each has a private bath, an enticing sitting area, a working fireplace, a phone, VCR, work desk, and a data port. The most splendid of all is the Kulia Suite, with a roomy, romantic spa tub for bubbly, candlelit baths overlooking the downtown skyline. The Ko Room, just down the hall, is distinguished by its original 1904 seven-head shower and two sitting areas. (These two rooms can be converted into a $400-per-night suite.) At the top of the house, the Manu Room and the Mahina Room sprawl over a space so large that three average-size B&B rooms would easily fit into just one of them.

Breakfast is a Continental affair, with fresh fruits, croissants, pastries, and cereal. △ *6 suites. Air-conditioning, fireplace, phone, data port, and cable TV/VCR in rooms. Pool. $95–$400; Continental-plus breakfast. MC, V. No smoking.*

HOTEL VINTAGE PLAZA ℡
422 S.W. Broadway, Portland, OR 97205, tel. 503/228–1212 or 800/243–0555, fax 503/228–3598; www.vintageplaza.com

When it opened in 1991, this small, "boutique" hotel was the first of its kind in downtown Portland. Its intimate, clublike ambience, central downtown location, and service-oriented staff make it a favorite with corporate business travelers during the week; on weekends, a series of "Romance Packages" draws in another crowd. Dedicated to Oregon's now-famous wine country, the hotel features a complimentary Oregon wine-tasting hour every night, has named its rooms after local wineries, and stocks the minibars with Oregon-made wines and other products.

There are several types of rooms to choose from. The most romantic are the nine Starlight Rooms on the top floor. From bed you can stargaze (or watch the rain) through slanted solarium windows. All suites, including the roomy two-level ones, have two-person whirlpool tubs; standard doubles have spacious baths. Ironing boards and irons, robes, and umbrellas are found in all rooms. By the time this book hits the press, all rooms will be completely refurbished and have a "sexy" new color scheme. Beds will have rich red spreads and carpets will be black and beige.

The Vintage Plaza is within easy walking distance of the Center for the Performing Arts, numerous restaurants, and downtown Portland shopping. The hotel restaurant, Pazzo, serves good Italian food; guests have signing privileges at Red Star, the restaurant of their sister hotel, Fifth Avenue Suites. A Continental breakfast of fresh squeezed juice, coffee, and muffins is included in the tariff. △ *82 double rooms with baths, 19 suites. 2 phone lines, TV, air-conditioning, voice mail, fax, and data port in rooms, whirlpool bath in suites. Restaurant, 24-hour room service, piano lounge, no-smoking rooms, concierge, valet parking. $170–$400; Continental breakfast. AE, D, DC, MC, V.*

LION AND THE ROSE 🦁

1810 N.E. 15th Ave., Portland, OR 97212, tel. 503/287–9245 or 800/955–1647, fax 503/287–9247; www.lionrose.com

When it was built in 1906 for Portland brewing magnate Gustave Freiwald, this startlingly ornate, Queen Anne–style mansion was one of the city's showplaces. Its grounds, occupying nearly a full city block, featured parklike gardens, a stable for Freiwald's matched team of Clydesdale horses, and, later, a garage for one of Portland's first horseless carriages.

By the time the house's current owners, Kay Peffer, Sharon Weil, and Kevin Spanier, took possession, Freiwald's showplace had been turned into a down-at-the-heels boarding house. The hard-working trio has since restored this neighborhood landmark, which now retains the splendor of its pre-Prohibition days.

Since its opening in 1993, The Lion and the Rose has been one of Portland's premier B&Bs. From the gleaming floors of oak inlaid with mahogany to the ornate period light fixtures (many original to the house) and the coffered dining room ceiling, The Lion and the Rose has set a new standard of formal elegance among Portland inns.

The public areas offer an expanse of polished wood, antique silver, and delightful turn-of-the-century touches. The Freiwalds' original carved mahogany sofas share the front parlor with an 18th-century Miller pump organ and a 1909-vintage Bush & Lane walnut piano. The overall feel is substantial and ornate, but just short of florid. The same attention to detail is evident throughout the six guest rooms. Lavonna, the nicest, features a round, sunny sitting area in the mansion's cupola, with an iron canopy bed and cheerful white wicker furniture. This room is also one of the most affordable because it shares a bath (across the hall) with an Eastlake dressing table and a deep claw-foot tub swathed in lace curtain.

A three-course breakfast as opulent as the surroundings is served in the dining room from 8 to 9:30; it starts with a fruit plate and muffins, continues with a pear pancake, crepe, or pumpkin waffle, and ends with a baked egg dish or omelet with bacon. Earlier risers can get a Continental breakfast at 7. Afternoon tea is also available. The inn is just a block from Northeast Broadway in an area filled with fine restaurants and shopping. ☖ *4 double rooms with baths, 2 doubles share bath. Air-conditioning, phone, robes, and TV/VCR (on request) in rooms. $99–$140; full breakfast. AE, MC, V. No smoking.*

MACMASTER HOUSE 🏠

1041 S.W. Vista Ave., Portland, OR 97205, tel. 503/223–7362 or 800/774–9523; www.macmaster.com

Portland Heights, the toniest of southwest Portland's neighborhoods, is noted for its outsized mansions. But for sheer size and historic charm, few of them can match the MacMaster House. Set high on King's Hill, less than 10 minutes by foot from fashionable Northwest 23rd Avenue and only two blocks from Washington Park (home of the city's famous International Rose Test Gardens), this 17-room Colonial Revival mansion was built in 1886 by the same architectural firm that produced Portland's City Hall and Public Library. An enormous relic of bygone splendor, it features a colossal portico, a huge leaded-glass Palladian window, and seven fireplaces.

The interior is both funky and fascinating. Cecilia Murphy, the vivacious innkeeper, has stuffed (some might say overstuffed) the parlor and dining room with a hybrid assortment of Victorian furniture and antiques. The overall decor is comfortable and old-fashioned. This is the sort of place that invites conversation, but there are plenty of nooks and crannies where you can curl up with a good book and not be disturbed.

The seven guest rooms on the second and third floors are charming without being cute. The only drawback is that five of them share a bath. The two suites have outsize bathrooms with large, claw-foot soaking tubs. Especially nice is the spacious Artist's Suite, tucked garretlike up under the dormers, with a high brass bed and fireplace. The McCord Suite, also with a fireplace, has its own small balcony and a second, separate bedroom.

The breakfasts served here are probably the best in Portland. A different gourmet entrée, often with a pan-Asian influence, is cooked up every morning by Patrick Long, who was once Perry Ellis's private chef. According to Murphy, "Good food is conducive to good breakfast-table conversation." She also sees to it that her complimentary wines, a treat at cocktail hour, are good vintages.

The house mascot, Domino, a *very big*, very friendly Dalmation, fits right in and sees to it that you are properly welcomed. He will not, however, carry your bags. △ *5 double rooms share 2½ baths, 2 suites. Air-conditioning and cable TV in rooms. Bicycle storage. $80–$120; full breakfast. AE, D, DC, MC, V. No smoking.*

MCMENAMINS EDGEFIELD ✿

2126 S.W. Halsey, Troutdale, OR 97060, tel. 503/669–8610 or 800/669–8610, fax 503/665–4209; www.mcmenamins.com

It takes a certain amount of chutzpah to turn a former county poor farm into an intriguing inn. But that's what Mike and Brian McMenamin have done with this property 15 minutes east of downtown Portland and five minutes west of the magnificent Columbia River Gorge National Scenic Area. The McMenamins have rescued several historic properties and converted them into brew pubs, but this was their first venture into innkeeping, and it's been a popular success since it opened in 1993.

The original residents of the Multnomah County Poor Farm, which operated from 1911 to 1947 and is now on the Register of National Historic Places, would still recognize the buildings, but little else. Today, this 25-acre estate has its own vineyard, winery and tasting room, brewery, bustling village pub, craft shops, meeting facilities, fine-dining restaurant, movie theater, and beautifully landscaped gardens. The past is not ignored, but it's been transformed into a kind of funky, populist eccentricity.

Most of the guest rooms are in the complex's enormous four-story Colonial Revival centerpiece, Edgefield Manor. Historic photographs and artwork adorn the doors and hallways, softening the sense of institutional anonymity. A major renovation added 91 additional guest rooms to the original 14, as well as dormitory space for 24 guests (two single-sex rooms). The quietest double rooms are in the former administrator's Colonial-style house, set about 100 yards from the main building. The rooms all have scrubbed wood floors and are furnished with a few simple antiques; the ambience throughout is reminiscent of a comfortable, old-fashioned lodge. There are no telephones or TVs.

You are given vouchers for your breakfast of choice, chosen from the menu of the Black Rabbit Restaurant, also open for lunch and dinner. Choices include omelets, crunchy French toast, corned beef hash with poached eggs, fresh local fruit, and eggs Benedict. △ *100 double rooms share 55 baths, 3 suites, 2 hostel rooms. Restaurant, bar, brewery, pub, winery, outdoor beer garden (in summer), cinema, conference facilities. Single $50, double $85–$200; full breakfast. AE, D, MC, V. No smoking.*

PORTLAND GUEST HOUSE ☙

1720 N.E. 15th Ave., Portland, OR 97212, tel. 503/282–1402; www.teleport.com/&pgh

Northeast Portland's Irvington neighborhood used to be full of neatly kept working-class Victorians just like this one, with its flower-filled yard and window boxes. Most of them fell to the wrecking ball when the prosperous 'teens and '20s transformed Irvington into a neighborhood for the nouveau riches.

This house endured decades of neglect until longtime neighborhood residents Susan and Dean Gisvold brought it back to life in 1987. Now, with its exterior painted mocha and its interior rebuilt from the studs outward, the house breathes a quiet, comfortable sense of place and history. It's not as grand as The Lion and the Rose (*see above*), half a block away, or the nearby Portland's White House (*see below*), but it has a fresh, sunny authenticity all its own.

Each of the seven smallish, high-ceiling guest rooms has some special touch: an ornately carved walnut Eastlake bed or armoire, an immaculately enameled claw-foot tub, or a shady deck overlooking the back garden. A large, simply decorated suite in the sunlit basement is configured with families in mind. The tasteful mauve and gray walls of the downstairs living and dining rooms are finished with white bull's-eye molding; an Oriental rug cushions the hardwood floor. The Eastlake living room suite has been reupholstered in pretty rose satin.

Fifteenth Avenue, which runs by the etched-glass front door, can be busy in the mornings and afternoons, but this is barely noticeable in the soundproofed house. The conveniently central northeast Portland neighborhood is close to the MAX light-rail line and served by three major bus routes to downtown. Closer to home, the shops on Broadway offer Oregon wines and produce, imported cheeses, and fresh-baked breads for picnics in the landscaped yard.

The Gisvolds don't live on the premises, but Susan is around every day, and a full-time manager occupies a downstairs apartment. Breakfast—typically juice, coffee, fresh fruit, and a hot entrée such as quiche or homemade pumpkin waffles—is served in front of the cheerful dining room fireplace or alfresco on the back porch when it's nice out. ♦ *5 double rooms with baths, 2 doubles share bath. Air-conditioning and phone in rooms. Bicycle storage. $65–$95; full breakfast. AE, MC, V. No smoking.*

PORTLAND'S WHITE HOUSE ☙

1914 N.E. 22nd Ave., Portland, OR 97212, tel. 503/287–7131 or 800/272–7131, fax 503/249–1641; www.portlandswhitehouse.com

The splash of falling water provides a melodious welcome at this memorable northeast Portland B&B. Listed on the National Register of Historic Places, the house was built in 1912 in Southern Federal style. Except for the tile roof, it bears an uncanny resemblance to its District of Columbia namesake—a resemblance indicative of the chief-executive personality of its builder, timber tycoon Robert Lytle. Its circular driveway, carriage house, and Greek columns all speak of bygone elegance.

Innkeepers Lanning Blanks, a hotel-restaurateur originally from South Carolina, and Steve Holden, a former CPA, bought the Irvington mansion in 1997 and—with the help of Joanne Young, a third innkeeper—have lavished their time and attention on the sumptuous interior. The public areas gleam with hand-rubbed Honduran mahogany and ornately inlaid oak. The dramatic hand-carved stairway is lit by Pulvey stained-glass windows. Hand-painted scenic murals, commissioned in the '20s, line the walls of the foyer. Downstairs is a cavernous ballroom. Outside, Lanning and Steve have added sunny patios and courtyards with more fountains and are in the process of creating a large new garden from an adjoining lot.

The six spacious, high-ceiling guest rooms in the main house are furnished with a tasteful mix of antiques, period pieces, and reproductions. The Canopy and Baron's rooms feature ornate canopy beds and huge claw-foot soaking tubs. In the Garden Room, French doors open onto a private veranda. The Balcony Room has a tile Art Deco bathroom and a small balustrade balcony overlooking the courtyard fountain. In 1997, the former carriage house was converted into three smartly furnished new rooms; the Chauffeur's Quarters, on the first floor, has a four-poster bed and private whirlpool bath.

The breakfasts here, served in the formal dining room on heavy linen, are among the best in Portland. Native American French toast, one of the signature dishes, is black bread soaked in egg and heavy cream, slow-cooked to a custard, and covered with sautéed apples and oranges. The breakfast frittata, made with pears, apples, cheeses, and Portobello mushrooms, is served with pepper bacon. Afternoon tea is available. Groups often rent the entire house, so it's best to reserve as far in advance as you can. ⬧ *9 double rooms with baths. Air-conditioning, phone, and TV (on request) in rooms. $98–$159; full breakfast. AE, D, MC, V. No smoking.*

RIVERPLACE HOTEL ⬧

1510 S.W. Harbor Way, Portland, OR 97201, tel. 503/228–3233 or 800/227–1333, fax 503/295–6161; www.riverplacehotel.com

The popular RiverPlace Hotel is the only downtown hotel sited directly on the banks of the Willamette River, which flows through the heart of Portland. The downtown skyline rears up behind the hotel, but it is the river—with its nearby yacht marina, floating restaurant, and pedestrian and bike trails—that makes RiverPlace special. Part of a 1985 development scheme that infused new life into downtown Portland's Waterfront Park, the hotel complex includes shops, restaurants, condominiums, and offices.

Inside, the RiverPlace has the feel of an intimate European hotel. The subtle luster of teak and green Italian marble is everywhere, and the staff provides a level of service seldom seen in this casual western city. (The 150 employees outnumber the guest rooms nearly two to one.) The lobby, bar, and restaurant are handsome spaces, luxuriously appointed with wood-burning fireplaces, rich fabrics, and Oriental rugs.

The 84 guest rooms overlook river, skyline, or, least desirable, a narrow courtyard. Thickly carpeted and well-soundproofed, they are painted a subtle yellow and furnished with modern, comfortable pieces that add blue to most of the color schemes. Junior suites have huge tile bathrooms and separate sitting areas. Fireplace suites are larger, with marble-top wet bars, king-size beds, small whirlpool baths, two color TVs, and tile, wood-burning fireplaces. You can reserve the hotel's whirlpool bath and sauna room for private use. Another nice feature is that you can get the complimentary Continental breakfast served in your room.

Dinner at the Esplanade Restaurant off the lobby is an experience to savor. The nightly menu varies according to what's in season, but always includes fresh seafood. You might find grilled wild salmon with huckleberry honey, sautéed razor clams on wild greens dressed in lemon and lavender, seared halibut stuffed with Dungeness crab, or grilled steelhead. The Patio is open for outdoor riverside dining from Memorial to Labor days. ⬧ *39 double rooms with baths, 35 suites, 10 apartments. Air-conditioning, phone, cable TV, and voice mail in rooms. Restau-*

rant, 24-hour room service, bar, sauna, valet parking. $210–$800; Continental breakfast. AE, D, DC, MC, V. Pets allowed (prior arrangement).

TUDOR HOUSE 🐚

2321 N.E. 28th Ave., Portland, OR 97212, tel. 503/287–9476, fax 503/288–8363; www.moriah.com/tudor

Dolph Park, a four-block area on the edge of Irvington in northeast Portland, is notable for its gigantic houses set in park-size gardens. Back in the late 1920s, when the area was first being developed, exclusivity was maintained by restricting the number and size of the lots. Tudor House is a perfect example of that oversized planning. The 5,400-square-ft house, set on estate-size grounds rimmed by tall laurel bushes, hawthorn trees, and azaleas, was built to resemble a Tudor manor.

Milan Larsen, the sprightly owner and innkeeper, was an antiques dealer in San Francisco before she moved up to Portland. Not surprisingly, her B&B is loaded with fine pieces of antique furniture and paintings. Luckily, there's enough space—and then some—to accommodate all of it, but the overall effect may strike some as a bit ponderous.

Of the three guests rooms on the second floor, the Antique Suite is largest and best equipped. It has a fireplace, separate seating area, a large bathroom, and an adjacent snack room with refrigerator and microwave. The Blue Room, with windows on two sides, is furnished with a splendid turn-of-the-century French armoire and matching bed. Across from it is the Bordeaux Room, which has an Art Deco armoire and a small reading alcove. Larsen usually rents out only one of these rooms at a time, so guests have a private bathroom; couples or families renting both rooms and sharing the bath receive a discount. A large room on the lower level, suitable for families or friends traveling together, has its own bathroom and two beds.

Breakfast, served in the antiques-laden dining room, is a generous affair, which might include a spinach and bacon omelet, pan-fried potatoes, poached pears, and muffins. ♠ *1 double room with bath, 2 doubles share bath, 1 suite. Phone and cable TV/VCR in rooms. $75–$100; full breakfast. AE, D, MC, V. No smoking.*

NORTH COAST

If the rest of the world had heeded the warnings of early explorers along Oregon's north coast, the area would still be a lonely, windswept wilderness of towering headlands, untracked beaches, and rivers teeming with fish. As it happens, virtually all of these descriptions still apply—except for the "lonely" part.

Four hundred years after Spanish and English adventurers wrote the area off as too stormy to be settled, the 150-mi-long north coast, stretching from Newport in the south to Astoria in the north, is sprinkled with small towns and villages. Fishing fleets leave from Newport, Garibaldi, Depoe Bay, Astoria, and, most quixotically, from tiny Pacific City. Small wineries, galleries, and antiques shops abound. Highway 101 plays tag with the rugged coastland all the way, providing easy access to an otherwise sparsely populated area.

Sir Francis Drake and Bruno Heceta, two 16th-century explorers who found the area uninhabitable, went a little overboard in their pessimism. But this is a stormy place—more than 80 inches of rain a year is the norm. The good news is that all the rain keeps the thick forests a deep, damp green. The bad news is that swimming in the North Pacific is recommended only for seals, salmon, and the odd overly ambitious surfer. Since the temperature rarely climbs above 75°F, beach walking has always been more popular than taking a dip.

Happily, long, uninterrupted public beaches are a staple of the area. In fact, Oregon has virtually no private beaches; an early 20th-century conservation law declared all land seaward from where the beach grass stops to be public. True, access is sometimes blocked, but seldom for long stretches. And more than 70 state parks—about one every other mile—ensure good access.

PLACES TO GO, SIGHTS TO SEE

Antiques. Small antiques shops are as much a part of the north coast as sand and spray. The broadest selection is to be found in the 30-mi stretch between Newport and Lincoln City. A strong association of merchants produces an up-to-date directory available at virtually every antiques shop in the area. Specialties include nautical items, Asian wood carvings, and furniture from the Civil War period.

Beaches. The popular, wide *Cannon Beach* has monoliths and great tide-pooling. Kite flying is the activity of choice at *Lincoln City Beach;* if you didn't bring one along, you can buy one at the many kite stores near the beach. Fossils, clams, mussels, and other aeons-old marine creatures, easily dug from soft sandstone cliffs, make *Beverly Beach State Park* (5 mi north of Newport) a favorite with young beachcombers.

Columbia River Maritime Museum (1792 Marine Dr., tel. 503/325–2323). Astoria's history as a seaport dates back to 1811, when it was the only American settlement west of the Rockies. This informative museum features a retired Columbia River lightship and nautical artifacts. The mainstay of the museum is a collection of U.S. Coast Guard rescue vessels once used over the last century to pluck the unlucky from a part of the ocean shoreline known as the Pacific Graveyard.

Depoe Bay. This is the world's smallest harbor, barely 40 ft across as it meets the pounding Pacific between basalt cliffs. A fishing village lies about 100 ft above the sea, but still in reach of the Spouting Horn, a hole in the cliff that allows the ocean to spray completely over Highway 101 during storms.

Ecola State Park (tel. 503/436–2844) lies between artsy Cannon Beach and touristy Seaside. A trail to the top of 800-ft-high Tillamook Head affords views of Tillamook Light, a 19th-century lighthouse abandoned to the storms in 1957.

Flavel House (441 8th St., tel. 503/325–2563). A tour of this Astoria Queen Anne Victorian built by Captain George Flavel in 1855 will give you a clue as to what life in Astoria was like over 100 years ago.

Fort Clatsop National Memorial (Rte. 3, tel. 503/861–2471). In 1805–06, the Lewis and Clark expedition spent a miserable, stormy winter at this site in Astoria. A reproduction of the fort, with all its discomforts, has center stage. In summer, park rangers don buckskins and demonstrate frontier skills such as making dugout canoes, smoking salmon, and fashioning clothes out of animal skins.

Fort Stevens State Park (tel. 503/861–1671). Originally built to defend the Oregon countryside against Confederate attack during the Civil War, this former military reservation in Hammond is one of the only places in the continental United States attacked during World War II: A Japanese submarine lobbed a shell that landed harmlessly on the beach. A museum lodges a display exploring the fort's history. On the beach lie the remains of the *Peter Iredale*, an Irish bark that ran aground in 1906.

Galleries. Virtually every town in the area has a worthwhile gallery. One of the most interesting is *Artspace* (9120 5th St., tel. 503/377–2782) in Bay City, a restaurant that features works both large and small—mostly modern, all eclectic, and all for sale. *Ricciardi Gallery* (108 10th St., tel. 503/325–5450), a 4,000-square-ft espresso café in Astoria, features an array of regional arts and crafts. More mainstream works by Northwest artists are displayed at *Maveety Gallery* (Market Pl. at Salishan, tel. 541/764–2318) in Gleneden Beach.

Hatfield Marine Science Center (2030 S. Marine Dr., tel. 541/867–0100). Inside the marine science center, an extension of Oregon State University just south of Newport, are displays of birds and other wildlife native to the shoreline; the skeletal remains of a whale; and numerous tanks of local marine life, including a shallow pool where you can touch starfish and anemones. The star of the show is the large octopus in a round low tank near the entrance; he seems as interested in human visitors as they are in him, and he has been known to reach up and gently stroke children's hands with his suction-tipped tentacles. **Oregon Coast Aquarium** (2820 S.E. Ferry Slip Rd., tel. 503/867–3474). Close to the Hatfield Center is this delightful, family-oriented aquarium. Special exhibits allow children and adults to view the teeming life indigenous to shallow tidal pools. Otters, seals, and sea lions flash by in outdoor tanks whose viewing areas, cut out of natural stone, give close-up looks at these playful showmen of the sea. Keiko, the star of the movie *Free Willy,* joined residents of the aquarium in 1996; at press time, plans to return the orca to the wild are proceeding, so you have a limited time to see him without going deep-sea diving in the North Atlantic.

Three Capes Scenic Loop. Running about 30 mi from Cape Meares in the north to Pacific City in the south, this drive embraces some of the state's most impressive coastline. The small community of Oceanside clings to a steep, forested slope overlooking offshore rocks that loom 200 ft high. *Cape Lookout State Park* includes a 1,000-ft headland, miles of trails, and 15 mi of undisturbed beaches. In the lee of *Cape Kiwanda* is a bright orange sandstone headland jutting out into the sea just north of Pacific City; here brave (some say crazy) dory fishermen run their small craft straight into the waves to reach fertile fishing areas offshore.

Tillamook County Creamery (4175 Hwy. 101, tel. 503/842–4481). The world's largest cheese factory, 2 mi north of town, specializes in cheddar, with tours, gift shops, and, of course, dairy delis.

RESTAURANTS

The best dining in Cannon Beach is found at the **Stephanie Inn** (tel. 503/436–2221) where the four-course, prix fixe meal showcases creative Northwest cuisine and wines; reservations are a must. On the more casual end, **McMenamins Lighthouse Brewpub** (tel. 541/994–7238) in Lincoln City serves up excellent veggie-burgers and "french fries for 100" to accompany tasty house-made brews and wines. **Mo's,** a favorite local chain that built its reputation on clam chowder and seafood, also serves chicken, salads, and sandwiches. All six Mo's (Florence, Cannon Beach, Lincoln City, Otter Rock, and two in Newport) are clearly marked on blue state highway signs along Highway 101. **Chez Jeanette** (tel. 541/764–3434) in Gleneden Beach is unpretentious, but its food is the match of any big-city classic French restaurant. **The Dining Room at Salishan** (tel. 541/764–2371) is often rated as the state's finest; it offers a remarkable Continental menu plus a full retinue of Northwest specialties, such as grilled salmon, crab, and oysters. **Roseanna's** (tel. 503/842–7351) in Oceanside may be in an out-of-the-way place, but it's worth finding; try the delicacies proffered on the fresh board and hope they're making mussels in pesto. Tiny Manzanita features two great choices for dining: **Jarboe's** (tel. 503/368–5113), easily one the finest restaurants on the Northwest coast, features innovative preparations focusing on Pacific Northwest fare; and the **Queen Bess Tea Room** (tel. 503/368–4255), which serves artfully presented Continental cuisine prepared by a Cordon Bleu–trained chef.

TOURIST INFORMATION

Astoria Area Chamber of Commerce (111 W. Marine Dr., Box 176, Astoria, OR 97103, tel. 503/325–6311). **Cannon Beach Chamber of Commerce** (207 N. Spruce St., Box 64, Cannon Beach, OR 97110, tel. 503/436–2623). **Lincoln City Visitor Center** (801 S.W. Hwy. 101, Suite 1, Lincoln City, OR 97367, tel. 541/

994–8378). **Newport Chamber of Commerce** (555 S.W. Coast Hwy., Newport, OR 97365, tel. 541/265–8801). **Seaside Chamber of Commerce** (7 N. Roosevelt, Box 7, Seaside, OR 97138, tel. 503/738–6391). **Tillamook Chamber of Commerce** (3705 Hwy. 101 N, Tillamook, OR 97141, tel. 503/842–7525).

RESERVATION SERVICES

Northwest Bed and Breakfast (1067 Hanover Ct. S, Salem, OR 97302, tel. 503/243–7616, fax 503/316–9118).

ANDERSON'S BOARDING HOUSE
208 N. Holladay Dr., Seaside, OR 97138, tel. 503/738–9055 or 800/995–4013

Seaside is a small town with a bad case of schizophrenia. Downtown is dominated by a mile-long loop that turns back at the edge of the sea: Arcades, restaurants, candy stores, and gift shops crowd the narrow street. Yet just a few blocks away from the clamor is Old Seaside, an area of well-preserved Victorian homes in a quiet, orderly neighborhood. Some are now finding second lives as bed-and-breakfasts; one such is Anderson's Boarding House, which dates from 1898, when Seaside was a mere village.

The house's original character has been well preserved. Details include a fir-paneled parlor and dining room, box-beam ceilings, and a Victrola that innkeeper Barb Edwards cranks up for the period finishing touch. You'll pass through a time warp on entering the guest rooms, though; each is outfitted with the trappings of a different decade, with magazines, calendars, and furnishings from the 1890s through the 1940s. The favored colors throughout are blue and white with rose accents. A restored Craftsman cottage that sleeps five and has its own deck is the inn's gem. A sleeping loft allows a good look at the Necanicum River, home to grebes, heron, and other wildlife.

Barb offers daybeds with trundles and an emphasis on holidays, making the Boarding House a good spot for families. With its bustle of beach bicycle carriages and bumper cars, Seaside is better suited to family vacations than romantic getaways. △ *5 double rooms with baths, 1 housekeeping cottage. TVs, bicycle storage. $70–$115; full breakfast (guests in main house only). MC, V. 2-night minimum during July, Aug., and special events.*

ASTORIA INN
3391 Irving Ave., Astoria, OR 97103, tel. 503/325–8153

Mickey Cox fell in love with Astoria after seeing it in the movie *Kindergarten Cop*, and she moved here from Reno in 1994 to take over the Astoria Inn. In the bed-and-breakfast, you will clearly see her other loves as well, namely pigs (echoed throughout the country-fresh decor) and English bulldogs (the house mascot goes by the name Wrinkles).

The inn, a Queen Anne farmhouse with gingerbread ornament, sits atop a hill in a sedate residential area. From its position high above the Columbia River, the views are inspiring. The house is appealingly decorated with antiques, chair rails, and other touches such as an old wedding dress and a feather boa hanging on the wall, and wingback chairs and a trickling fountain in the second-floor library. Of the pastel-hue guest rooms, all named after North Coast landmarks, Cape Lookout has the best views. Cape Virginia has a claw-foot tub in its bathroom.

Mickey's sense of humor shines through in all that she does. Breakfast, she says, is "ready when the smoke detector goes off." All joking aside, she whips up delightful morning entrées such as German puff pancakes, apricot cream French toast, and "Mickey Surprise" (a croissant stuffed with banana and cream cheese, dipped in an egg batter, and fried, then dusted with powdered sugar). ▲ *4 double rooms with baths. Cable TV/VCR and karaoke machine in living room, bicycle storage. $70–$85; full breakfast, afternoon refreshments. D, MC, V. No smoking.*

BENJAMIN YOUNG INN ☞

3652 Duane St., Astoria, OR 97103, tel. 503/325–6172 or 800/201–1286; benyoung@willapabay.org

This handsomely restored Queen Anne overlooking the Columbia River is on the National Register of Historic Places. The 5,500-square-ft inn surrounded by 100-year-old gardens underwent a name change when purchased by Carolyn and Ken Hammer in 1994 (people still come by looking for K. C.'s Mansion by the Sea). Ken works as a pastor across the river in Washington, while Carolyn runs the inn. In addition to seeing to the needs of bed-and-breakfast travelers, she also caters meetings, family reunions, and especially weddings, for which the Benjamin Young is a picture-perfect location.

The home itself, with its ornate period woodwork and fixtures, is the primary draw. Preservationists and old-house aficionados will marvel at the details: faux graining on frames and molding, shutter-blinds in windows, and Povey stained glass, all original. The living room has an imposing brick fireplace, large velvet Victorian couches, and the original, elaborate light fixtures hanging from the 12-ft-high ceiling. The house was in the same family for a century, and the Hammers have tracked down and bought back some of the old furnishings that were sold years ago but still remained in the area.

The four spacious guest rooms are simply furnished, with a mix of contemporary pieces and antiques, and offer views of the river through their tall windows. Roll-out beds and sofas expand the capacity of some rooms to 5 or 6 guests. The most popular is the Fireplace Suite, with a king-size bed, whirlpool bath, and (of course) a fireplace. ▲ *4 double rooms with baths, 1 2-bedroom suite. Fireplace and whirlpool bath in suite. $75–$135; full breakfast. AE, D, MC, V. No smoking, 2-night minimum on holiday weekends.*

CHANNEL HOUSE ☞

35 Ellingson St., Box 56, Depoe Bay, OR 97341, tel. 541/765–2140 or 800/447–2140, fax 541/765–2191; www.channelhouse.com

The town of Depoe Bay is perched above the sea on high black-lava cliffs and surrounded by wooded slopes rising above the tiny harbor. Depoe Bay's fishing fleet shoots through a 40-ft-wide aperture at full speed, heading straight into the turbulent Pacific. Right above this meeting of waves and man is the Channel House, where the setting is everything.

The house has some Cape Cod touches, but this is no ordinary saltbox. Indeed, the desire to have all the rooms face the sea has made for some odd interiors. Baths, often cramped, are manageable only because of the judicious use of sliding doors. Aside from a few brass beds, furnishings are sturdy and comfortable but undistinguished in a cool, contemporary way. Channel House is managed by a vacation rental company rather than by live-in owners, so it's not for you if you're looking for the usual bed-and-breakfast bonhomie.

The views, however, are breathtaking: The sight of the boats braving the neck of the harbor seemingly at arm's reach is a unique experience. They are best taken in from the top-floor rooms, where privacy is optimal. Most of the rooms have hot tubs on decks facing the ocean, and on the lower floors you can't help feeling that the fishing and tour craft coming and going have as good a look at you as you do at them. ♣ *5 double rooms with baths, 4 suites, 3 housekeeping suites. Cable TV and binocular in rooms, kitchen in 3 rooms, whirlpool bath in most rooms. $60–$200; Continental breakfast. D, MC, V. No smoking.*

FRANKLIN ST. STATION ☞
1140 Franklin Ave., Astoria, OR 97103, tel. 503/325–4314 or 800/448–1098, fax 503/325–2275

At the edge of downtown Astoria, this cream-color Victorian with slate blue trim was built in 1900 by shipbuilder Ferdinand Fisher of the Fisher Brothers Chandlery. Not surprisingly, it features remarkable craftsmanship in its moldings and built-ins. The main floor is sumptuous, with a high-back Victorian-style mahogany love seat and matching mother and father chairs covered in turquoise velvet in the living room, delicate spindlework spandrels in the archways, and a fine old greenstone fireplace with oak mantel in the dining area.

Guest rooms are surprisingly spacious. The main-floor Lewis & Clark Room, once part of the dining room, has a large china cupboard as a dresser. Upstairs, the Astor Suite is most impressive, with iron and brass beds, original light fixtures, large arched windows covered by hand-stitched balloon shades, and a deck. In the basement is a separate vacation rental, a modern, functional suite with rattan furniture, and in the attic is a cozy suite with fireplace, sitting area, wet bar, and big bathroom with claw-foot tub.

Innkeeper Renee Caldwell prepares a full breakfast; her French toast stuffed with almonds, cream cheese, and preserves is very popular. The dining area has a parquet table and a small niche displaying family china dating back to the early 1800s, one of four such displays in the house. ♣ *3 double rooms with baths, 2 suites. Fireplace, Cable TV/VCR, and stereo in 1 suite; wet bars in both suites. $68–$120; full breakfast. MC, V. No smoking.*

GILBERT INN ☞
341 Beach Dr., Seaside, OR 97138, tel. 503/738–9770 or 800/410–9770, fax 503/717–1070; www.clatsop.com/gilbertinn

Natural fir tongue-and-groove walls and ceilings dominate the Gilbert Inn, a block from the Seaside's busy downtown and the beach. The 1892 home, built by erstwhile Seaside mayor Alexander Gilbert, reminds you why anyone bothered to settle this area in the first place: lumber.

The Gilbert is a large Queen Anne inn with eight spacious double rooms and two suites. Popularity almost swamped the Gilbert a few years ago, but innkeepers Dick and Carol Rees managed to add five rooms without disturbing the integrity of the existing house. The best part of the inn is still the original core, where the fir detail creates a warm, rough-hewn atmosphere. The decor is country French, with wallpaper, down comforters, and bathrooms in matching prints, and ruffled valances and balloon shades at the windows. Some of the bedrooms have brass and ceramic bedsteads; in the Turret Room, you'll dream away on a four-poster rice bed. The newer guest rooms are attractively furnished with natural wicker, reproduction black iron and brass beds, and old wardrobes of oak and pine.

Gilbert, the feisty apricot-point Siamese watch cat, garners his own fan mail and gifts from adoring guests, all of whom, he seems certain, visit the inn to keep him entertained. Carol has perfected her breakfast specialties: one of the guests' favorites is the cream cheese–and–walnut–stuffed French toast that's grilled and served with apricot sauce and fresh fruit; she also makes a mean English-muffin bake, with maple sausage and Tillamook cheese. ♨ *9 double rooms with baths, 1 suite. Phone and TV in rooms. Conference facilities. $79–$105; full breakfast. AE, D, MC, V. No smoking, 2-night minimum on weekends, closed Jan.*

GRANDVIEW BED & BREAKFAST ☙

1574 Grand Ave., Astoria, OR 97103, tel. 503/325–0000 or 800/488–3250; www.bbonline.com/or/grandview

Seen from a quiet residential street in Astoria, the Grandview Bed & Breakfast doesn't stand out. But once you're inside the nearly 100-year-old shingle-style house, you'll know what's special about it. Because the Grandview rises so precipitously from a hill that falls away steeply, the views from the inn are spectacular and the sensation of floating can be intense. Innkeeper Charlene Maxwell quickly brings you back to earth, however. She has steeped herself in local lore and shares it with you in an easygoing but authoritative manner.

The guest rooms upstairs are eccentrically decorated with a mixture of period furnishings and odd modern touches (for example, plastic patio furniture). A few rooms have canopy beds, and all are outfitted with faux fireplaces that heat the rooms. With unobstructed vistas of the Columbia River and the Coast Range of southern Washington, and of the dozens of church steeples of Old Astoria, you'll feel as if you're in an aerie. If you prefer to be earthbound, there is a very plain two-bedroom suite in the lower level of the house, with a separate entrance that's perfect for families. The arrangement of some of the guest rooms is flexible: Seven double rooms on the second and third floors can be divided into two suites or rented separately. Prices depend on whether you have a private bath. The entrance hall is cluttered with Charlene's work desk, which is only a few feet from the main door.

The dining area, however, is very inviting, positioned in a light-filled turret that offers views of the river and town. For more privacy, you might opt to dine in a smaller bullet turret on the other side of the kitchen, ideal for a twosome. Breakfast consists of five types of coffee, hot chocolate or cider, fresh fruits and juices, homemade muffins, and usually bagels and lox. ♨ *4 double rooms with baths (or 6 doubles share 2 baths, depending on bookings), 1 suite. $59–$159; Continental-plus breakfast buffet. D, MC, V. No smoking, no alcohol on premises.*

HUDSON HOUSE ☙

37700 Hwy. 101 S, Cloverdale, OR 97112, tel. 503/392–3533, fax 503/392–3533

At Hudson House, in Cloverdale, the photo album tells the story. Clyde Hudson, a son of the original builder, was a pioneer photographer on the north Oregon coast. He was among the first to show the world the area's raw beauty through his postcards. The Victorian house in which he lived from the early 1900s has been beautifully restored, although it's more Folk Artsy than frilly.

The Victorian Suite downstairs is the largest guest room; it has an attached parlor and a private porch that looks out over the pastoral Nestucca Valley. The upstairs suite, with its claw-foot tub, hardwood floors, family antiques, hand-stitched quilts, and angled bedroom in the house's turret, is the more popular room. There are also two more antiques-filled rooms tucked under the high gabled roof on the second floor. At press time, new innkeepers Irma and Ron Scroggins were busy sprucing up the place, painting and landscaping. They are also planning to improve handicap access, install a whirlpool bath, and add CD players to the rooms.

The inn is a short drive on scenic roads from great hiking and beachcombing at Cape Kiwanda, Robert W. Straub, and Cape Lookout state parks. Breakfast is a special treat here, a medley of hot and cold cereals, cakes, and American-style dishes and Mexican specialties; on slower days Irma might make *huevos rancheros*, eggs with homemade corn tortillas, fresh salsa, refried beans, and home fries. The innkeepers discourage children under 12. △ *2 double rooms with baths, 2 suites. Coffee and tea in rooms. TV/VCR in library. $75–$85; full breakfast, refreshments throughout the day. MC, V. No smoking.*

INN AT MANZANITA ☞
67 Laneda St., Box 243, Manzanita, OR 97130, tel. 503/368–6754, fax 530/368–7656

Manzanita is a small, quiet town of summer homes clinging to the shoulders of Neah-Kah-Nie Mountain, a 1,700-ft cliff that towers over the Pacific between Tillamook and Cannon Beach. Built in 1987, the Inn at Manzanita makes the most of its location in what amounts to the center of Manzanita. The feel is Scandinavian modern, with high-beamed ceilings and blond wood everywhere.

The property is surrounded by shore pines, so patios on upper floors have a treehouse feel. Favorite rooms are on the top floor of the North Building; these feature gas fireplaces and cozy captain's beds in curtained nooks beneath skylights. Breakfast is not served on the premises—there is a café nearby, open in the morning hours—which may discourage mingling with others, but more than half the guests are either honeymooning or celebrating anniversaries and appreciate the privacy. The owners have recently added a new building with three more rooms; built in a style to match the original structures, it blends seamlessly into the complex.

Manzanita is one of the best-loved spots on the North Coast, and accommodations at the inn are highly sought after in the summer. It makes an ideal winter destination, however, when the hubbub has died down, and you sit by the fire or recline in the tub and watch the storms roll in. △ *13 double rooms with baths. Wet bar, TV, VCR, and whirlpool bath in rooms, kitchen in 2 rooms. Masseuse. $100–$145; no breakfast. MC, V. No smoking, 2-night minimum on weekends and July–Aug.*

NYE BEACH HOTEL ☞
219 N.W. Cliff St., Newport, OR 97365, tel. 541/265–3334, fax 541/265–3622; www.teleport.com/~nyebeach

Every so often, guests will insist that they remember the Nye Beach Hotel from way back when, maybe in the '50s, before it was restored. Innkeeper Crea Williams has to politely disagree, informing them that the building is less than 10 years old. She should know: She opened it with her husband David Baker, the architect who designed the 1992 structure to fit in with the turn-of-the-century style of its neighbors. Not that she can blame them; even a prominent guidebook to the region lists the Nye Beach as "a restored 1910s hotel."

The 18 guest rooms all have ocean views, private baths, fireplaces, and willow love seats; those on upper floors have balconies, and several are equipped with whirlpool tubs. The beds, covered with down comforters, were made in Holland, and they are so comfortable and cleanly designed that many guests inquire about where to buy them (unfortunately, they're not imported anymore). With pastel decor, potted tropical plants, and a macaw in the lobby, the hotel has a funky, distinctive personality that wouldn't be out of place in Key West.

A roomy café and full bar, with a grand piano and fireplace, occupies the beachfront portion of the bottom floor; one of Newport's better restaurants, Nye Beach Cafe serves three meals a day and specializes in spicy seafood dishes. Heaters on the adjoining deck make it an ideal space to take in the surf, sunsets, and nearby Yaquina Head lighthouse, even on chilly evenings. ♠ *18 double rooms with baths. Down comforter, cable TV, fireplace in rooms, whirlpool bath in some rooms. $60–$125; breakfast extra. AE, D, MC, V. No-smoking rooms available.*

ST. BERNARDS 🍍

3 E. Ocean Rd., Box 102, Arch Cape, OR 97102, tel. and fax 503/436–2800 or tel. 800/436–2848

Imagine having an extra million dollars and several years to travel the world collecting antiques and art that would one day fill your fantasy inn. After years spent visiting B&Bs and inns, the dream came true for gregarious innkeepers Don and Deanna Bernard. They built their enormous shingle castle, complete with turret and drive-through tunnel, on the scenic Oregon coast a few miles south of Cannon Beach. Together, the Bernards designed and constructed the châteaulike structure, from the foundation to the scenes ingeniously depicted in the exterior shingles. Now they are content to stay at home, traveling vicariously through their many guests.

As one would expect of a fantasy castle, the guest rooms are quite grand. Decorated by Deanna with an artist's eye, they are appointed with every amenity for comfort and romance—down comforters on firm beds, plush robes, supersoft cotton sheets, large soaking tubs with ocean views, and gas fireplaces. A spacious workout room with sauna rounds out the well-thought-out amenities of this adult-oriented inn.

Ginger, appointed with ornate Austrian bedsteads dating from the 1860s takes its palette from a collection of ginger jars. The walls of Gauguin employ the same muted pastels used by the painter, whose prints are hung on the walls. Tower, with it's incredible Louis XIV Bombay bed, has an attached sitting room in the turret. Provence, on the garden level with a private patio overlooking the ocean, features terra-cotta floors, antique pine furniture, Pierre Deux fabrics in country French yellow and blue, and a two-person whirlpool bath.

Breakfast, served in the rounded dining room beneath the inn's cupola, is also a grand affair, with fresh juice, coffee cakes, seasonal fruits, and a hot entrée served on Deanna's fine collection of china and crystal. ♠ *6 double rooms with baths, 1 suite. Phone, TV/VCR, down comforter, robes, soaking tub, fireplace, and individual heating in rooms, whirlpool bath in 1 room. Sauna, exercise room. $129–$189; full breakfast, evening refreshments. AE, MC, V. No smoking.*

SANDLAKE COUNTRY INN 🍍

8505 Galloway Rd., Cloverdale, OR 97112, tel. 503/965–6745, fax 503/965–7425

On Christmas morning in 1890, the Norwegian schooner *Struan* was wrecked off Cape Lookout, leaving tons of heavy bridge timbers on their way to Australia strewn on the beach. Storm-weary homesteaders with few building materials hauled the timbers off and made sturdy homes. Only a few of these are still standing, the most notable of which is the weathered-shingle Sandlake Country Inn, where innkeepers Femke and Dave Durham preside.

The natural woodwork has been restored and part of the dining room ceiling was removed to reveal the old bridge timbers. The sitting room is a cozy creation, with velvet-covered Victorian settees, a stone fireplace, and views of flowering rosebushes outside. Upstairs is the honeymoon suite, taking up the entire floor and opening onto a deck that surveys the 2½-acre property; keep a look out for deer and elk.

Just off the dining room is The Timbers, a wheelchair-accessible guest room with an outdoorsy feel, complete with a 1920s wicker fishing creel slung over the sturdy timber bedposts, a timber-framed fireplace, a deck in the garden, and a fragrant cedar-lined bathroom. There is also a charming cottage outside, about 100 ft from the main house: The interior is plush, with thick carpeting and huge throw pillows on the floor before a black marble fireplace. A large hot tub is strategically located between the bed and the deck. As in the suites, Arts and Crafts oak period pieces and reproductions predominate.

Homemade baked apple oatmeal is a breakfast staple, as are fruit parfaits and soufflés. The Durhams like to focus on providing a romantic retreat, so they see to it that you are treated to breakfast in bed: Every morning a tray with the multicourse repast elegantly presented on Royal Doulton china is delivered to your room. △ *2 double rooms with baths, 1 suite, 1 housekeeping cottage. Radio/cassette player in rooms, TV/VCR in most rooms, fireplace and whirlpool bath in suite. Hot tub, bicycles. $90–$135; full breakfast. AE, D, MC, V. No smoking, 2-night minimum on weekends May–Oct., closed Christmas week.*

STEPHANIE INN ℘

2740 S. Pacific Rd., Cannon Beach, OR 97110, tel. 503/436–2221 or 800/633–3466, fax 503/436–9711; stephinn@transport.com

This casually elegant oceanfront country inn overlooks Haystack Rock at Cannon Beach. Despite its size—with over 40 rooms, it is considerably larger than its peers—and the cool gloss of its marketing, it is *the* intimate inn on the Oregon coast.

The inn itself is named for the daughter of owner Jan Martin, and guest rooms are named for other members of the family. Plaids, florals, and contemporary cushioned and wicker furnishings figure in the comfortable room decor. Each room features a fireplace, TV, and VCR tucked away in an armoire; whirlpool bath for two; thick terry robes; and an adoptable teddy bear on the firm bed. Most also have an ocean view balcony or patio. A new building, under construction at press time, will provide an additional four suites.

Every evening, guests gather for wine and hors d'oeuvres in the chart room and every morning for a hearty breakfast served in the dining room; both are included in the tariff, as is the morning paper and 24-hour coffee service in the lobby. A four-course, prix-fixe dinner showcasing the fine wines and cuisine of the Pacific Northwest is also available; reserve a spot early. △ *42 double rooms with baths, 4 suites. Wet bar, phone, TV/VCR, fireplace, and whirlpool bath in rooms. Library, video library, masseuse, free shuttle into town. $149–$399; full breakfast buffet, evening refreshments, dinners available. AE, D, DC, MC, V. No smoking, 2-night minimum in Aug., weekends, and holidays.*

SYLVIA BEACH HOTEL ℘

267 N.W. Cliff St., Newport, OR 97365, tel. 541/265–5428

Built in 1911, the Sylvia Beach Hotel was long known as a flophouse with a view until Portland restaurateur Goody Cable and Roseburg partner Sally Ford decided to make it a kind of literary lodging—or a library that sleeps 40. The Sylvia Beach in the name is not the sandy strip just outside (that would be Nye Beach) but rather the renowned patron of literary arts who in the 1920s and '30s ran the Shakespeare & Co. bookstore in Paris. Each room is dedicated to an author, with appropriate books and decorating scheme. The Hemingway Room, for example, is all the manly Papa could have hoped for: a bed made out of tree limbs under a mounted antelope head, and an old Royal typewriter in the corner.

Down the hall is the Oscar Wilde Room, a smallish place resembling a Victorian gentleman's lodgings. The view, which faces a roof from the other side of the hotel, is far from awe-inspiring. But the managers are way ahead of you. Right next to the window is a framed Wilde quote: "It's altogether immaterial, a view, except to the innkeeper who, of course, charges it in the bill. A gentleman never looks out the window."

The most popular rooms are the Poe Room, an eerie chamber in black and red, complete with raven and pendulum suspended over the bed, and the Colette Room, a sexy French suite with lace canopies, velvet window seat, and peach-color headboard. The upper reaches of the hotel are turned over to a large library (some 1,000 books), with plenty of nooks and crannies and comfortable armchairs for book lovers.

The food at the hotel's restaurant—Tables of Content—is excellent, an exception to the unwritten traveler's rule that one should sup and sleep in different places. That's not to say you should skip breakfast here, which starts with a buffet of juices, pastries, and fruits and moves on to a hot entrée such as quiche, French toast, or omelets. ♙ *20 double rooms with baths, 1 separate dormitory room with 8 bunks for women and 4 bunks for men. Fireplace in 3 rooms. Restaurant, library. $69– $152, dormitory bed $22; full breakfast, evening refreshments. AE, MC, V. No smoking, 2-night minimum on weekends, closed 1st wk in Dec.*

TYEE LODGE ☙

4925 N.W. Woody Way, Newport, OR 97365, tel. 541/265–8953 or 888/553–8933; www.newportnet.com/tyee/home.htm

The home of local teachers Mark and Cindy McConnell was built in the 1940s on a portion of what was once the Bush family estate. The old manor house, once home to composer Ernest Bloch, is next door. In 1995, they and their house were ready for a change; they expanded the oceanfront structure and added five second-floor guest rooms and a new living and dining area to accommodate bed-and-breakfast guests. They did their homework, and decided to name their inn after the salmon that once drew Coast Salish Yaquina natives to the premises as summer fishing grounds.

Guest rooms, in muted shades of pine green, mauve, and pale yellow taken from the inn's natural environment, are outfitted with pine furniture and afford ocean views through towering Sitka Spruce trees. Each follows a theme, from fish and birds to native peoples and coastal lighthouses.

The property is tucked up against Yaquina Head, providing both guests and gardens refuge from the summer winds. A private trail leads to numerous tide pools along the beach, and an outdoor fire pit makes for a warm place to while away the evening. Yaquina Head Lighthouse, the Hatfield Marine Science Center, the Oregon Coast Aquarium, and other Newport attractions are all nearby.

In the bay-windowed breakfast room overlooking the ocean, breakfast is served family style and is so good that guests usually end up skipping lunch. Mark and

Cindy take full advantage of ingredients available in the Pacific Northwest. A typical day will feature baked grapefruit or poached pears, Mark's excellent cinnamon rolls or scones, and a hot dish such as "Tyee" quiche, with smoked salmon, or layered whole-wheat-and-orange pancakes with ricotta-and-orange sauce. A complimentary beverage bar, refrigerator, and microwave are available all day. ⚐ *5 double rooms with baths. Fireplace in 1 room. Bicycles, beach trail. $95–$120; full breakfast. AE, D, MC, V. No smoking.*

WHISKEY CREEK BED & BREAKFAST ❦

7500 Whiskey Creek Rd., Tillamook, OR 97141, tel. 503/842–2408; whiskeycreekb&b@oregoncoast.com

Built in 1900 by the operator of a custom sawmill, the cedar-shingle Whiskey Creek Bed & Breakfast is paneled inside with rough-hewn spruce. Originally, the mill operator made spruce oars and used the odd pieces of leftover wood for the main floor. For years, the home and the mill were powered by a small hydroelectric turbine on Whiskey Creek, about 100 ft away at the southern boundary of the property.

The house is split into two guest rooms and an apartment with a private entrance; these can be rented nightly or by the week. Upstairs, the guest rooms are paneled with the original rough-hewn spruce and have terraces overlooking Netarts Bay; the cathedral-ceiling dining area is decorated with owner Allison Asbjornsen's rabbit objet d'art collection. A wood-burning stove keeps the smallish rooms warm and cozy when it's cold. Adorning the white walls of the one-bedroom downstairs apartment, which also offers a view of the bay and the lawn, are Allison's oil paintings, watercolors, collages, and sculptures. Both units have queen-size futon beds and overstuffed chairs, a living room, a bathroom, and a kitchen for cooking your own meals.

Allison will happily answer questions about the area and serve a full breakfast, perhaps involving omelets or oysters. Otherwise she leaves you alone to enjoy the beautiful natural surroundings, where bear, elk, and deer still roam. Blue herons are a common sight. Tillamook means "land of many waters," and there are streams everywhere for exploring. The inn is a retreat in winter, with yoga and shiatsu massage on site. ⚐ *1 apartment, 2 double rooms with shared bath. $65–$90, additional cost for more than 2 people, weekly rates available; full breakfast. MC, V. No smoking.*

COLUMBIA RIVER GORGE
AND MT. HOOD

The gorge, the mountain—to Portlanders, no other names are necessary. The Columbia River gorge, stretching some 70 mi east from the city, supplies the good and the bad: Dozens of waterfalls, high cliffs, mountain trails, and sweeping vistas provide an array of recreational activities.

The bad comes largely in the form of weather. The Columbia River gorge is one of the few places in the world where a river cuts through a major mountain range. That provides unique scenery, but since the 4,000-ft-deep gash in the Cascade Range connects the high, arid Columbia Plateau with the low, moist western valleys, the collision of weather systems can spell trouble. Most frequently, the product created by this accident of nature is wind, which, in the finest Oregon tradition, the locals have latched onto. These days Hood River, a small town wedged in between Mt. Hood and the Columbia, bills itself as the windsurfing capital of the world.

Overlooking the gorge is snowcapped Mt. Hood, which at 11,235 ft above sea level is the highest point in Oregon. Its five ski areas and hundreds of miles of hiking trails are all within a 90-minute drive of downtown Portland. Sprinkled around the mountain are dozens of clear blue lakes—among them Lost Lake, Timothy Lake, and Badger Lake—each with its particular angle on the ever-changing profile of Mt. Hood. And the rivers spiral out from the glaciers of the mountain: Hood River, White River, Warm Springs River, Salmon River, Zig Zag River, Sandy River, and Bull Run River.

Despite the area's wild appeal, it is easily reached by good roads. Interstate 84 zips through the gorge to Hood River. Highway 35 climbs through the colorful orchard country of the Hood River valley to the icy slopes of Mt. Hood, and Highway 26 swoops down the south side of Mt. Hood back to Portland.

Each season has its pleasures. Fall brings the apple trees to full color in the Hood River valley, and the reds and golds of the deciduous trees blend into the deep green of the fir and pine forests. Winters can be a skier's par-

adise, with most ski areas receiving at least 8 ft of snow. But ice storms and blizzards fueled by 100 mph winds sometimes close the gorge freeway for a few days each winter, leaving motorists stranded. The spring thaw brings snow-melt to the rivers and, once the streams clear, runs of salmon. Summer is the time for hiking, camping, and exploring the alpine country before the fall snows return—sometimes as early as September.

PLACES TO GO, SIGHTS TO SEE

Bonneville Dam (Cascade Locks, tel. 541/374–8820). This mammoth structure, the first dam ever to span the river, stalls the Columbia long enough to generate a million kilowatts of electricity (enough to supply 700,000 single-family homes). Although the dam, opened in 1937, wiped out the most spectacular rapids on the river, it has many wonders of its own. You can view its great turbines from special walkways during self-guided powerhouse tours, and, at the visitor center on Bradford Island, watch migrating salmon and steelhead as they struggle up the fish ladders. The adjoining *Bonneville Fish Hatchery* (tel. 541/374–8393) has ponds teeming with large salmon, rainbow trout, and sturgeon that are used to repopulate the river.

Cascade Locks. During pioneer days boats needing to pass the rapids had to portage around them. In 1896, the locks that gave the town its name were completed, allowing waterborne passage for the first time. Today the locks are used by Native Americans for their traditional dip-net fishing, and Cascade Locks is notable mainly as the home port of the 600-passenger stern-wheeler *Columbia Gorge* (Marine Park, tel. 541/374–8427). From June through September, the ship churns its way upriver, then back again, on daily two-hour excursions through some of the gorge's most awesome scenery.

Columbia River Gorge Scenic Highway (Hwy. 30). Built in the early 1900s by lumber magnate Simon Benson expressly for sightseeing, this narrow, curving 22-mi road strings along the upper reaches of the gorge from Troutdale to The Dalles. While the journey affords some awe-inspiring views—there are a dozen waterfalls in a single 10-mi stretch—the road itself is quite an attraction: Graceful arched bridges span moss-covered gorges, and hand-cut stone walls act as guardrails. The route is especially lovely during the fall, but it is often impassable during the winter.

Crown Point/Vista House (tel. 503/695–2240). Here, atop a 733-ft-high bluff, visitors get their first full glimpse of the grandeur of the gorge. Built a few years after the scenic Crown Point Highway on which it is located, Vista House provides a 30-mi view of the gorge and of the lights of Portland.

The Dalles. This historic town at the eastern end of the Columbia River gorge has a fine Old Town district of brick storefronts that date from the 1840s. It was here that Oregon Trail pioneers took a breather to decide whether the final leg of their 2,000-mi journey would be down the wild Columbia River or over the treacherous passes of Mt. Hood. The 130-year-old *Wasco County Courthouse* (404 W. 2nd St., tel. 541/296–4798) and the 1857 *Ft. Dalles Surgeon's Quarters* (15th and Garrison Sts., tel. 541/296–4547) have been converted into museums; both contain outstanding displays and collections illustrating the incredible ordeal of the pioneers' journey. Today The Dalles has windsurfing second only to that found in Hood River.

Hood River Valley. Orchards abound in this hanging valley draped down the eastern shoulder of Mt. Hood. At its foot is the town of Hood River, which features some of the best windsurfing in the world, and its own small brewery tasting room and pub, *Full Sail Brewing* (506 Columbia St., tel. 541/386–2281). There are even two wineries: *Hood River Vineyards* (4693 Westwood Dr., tel. 541/386–3772) and *Three Rivers Winery* (275 Country Club Rd., tel. 541/386–5453).

Mt. Hood National Forest (tel. 503/666–0771). Mt. Hood, reached by Highway 35 south from Hood River, is believed to be an active volcano, quiet now but capable of the same violence that decapitated nearby Mount St. Helens in 1980. The mountain is just one feature of the 1.1 million-acre forest. You'll find 95 campgrounds and 150 lakes stocked with brown, rainbow, cutthroat, kokanee, brook, and steelhead trout. The Sandy, Salmon, and other rivers are known for their fishing, rafting, canoeing, and swimming. Both forest and mountain are crossed by an extensive trail system for hikers, cyclists, and horseback riders. The Pacific Crest Trail, which begins in British Columbia and ends in Mexico, crosses here at the 4,157-ft-high Barlow Pass.

Multnomah Falls (tel. 503/695–2376). At 620 ft, Multnomah Falls is the highest in the gorge, a breathtaking plunge over the lip of a high basalt cliff. A steep paved trail switchbacks to the top, but the less hearty can retire to the comfort of Multnomah Falls Lodge, an old stone structure at the foot of the falls that houses a restaurant, bar, and an inn.

Oneonta Gorge. This narrow cleft hundreds of feet deep is right off the scenic highway a few miles east of Multnomah Falls. The walls drip moisture year-round; hundreds of plant species—some of which are found nowhere else—flourish under these conditions. In late summer the intrepid can walk up the shallow creek; the gorge is so narrow that you can touch both sides.

Timberline Lodge (tel. 503/231–7979). At the 6,000-ft level of Mt. Hood's southern slope, Timberline is the mountain's oldest ski area. The lodge (*see* Restaurants, *below*), 6 mi from the intersection of Highway 26 and Timberline Road, was handmade out of mammoth timbers and stone by local craftsmen as part of a 1930s Works Progress Administration project; it's been used as a setting in many films, including *The Shining*, with Jack Nicholson. The Palmer Chair Lift takes skiers to the 8,400-ft-level for year-round skiing.

Wasson Winery (41901 Hwy. 26, Sandy, tel. 503/668–3124). Best known for its fruit-and-berry wine, this small winery in the rolling hills outside Sandy is gaining a growing reputation for its grapes.

RESTAURANTS

The **Cascade Dining Room** at the Timberline Lodge (tel. 503/272–3311) in Timberline features Continental cuisine with a Northwest alpine twist. **Stonehedge Inn** (tel. 541/386–3940) in Hood River offers excellent European fare in a restored country house. Also in Hood River, The **Mesquitery** (tel. 541/386–2002) grills lean beef, chicken, and pork over aromatic mesquite, with the emphasis on fresh herbs and tangy marinades. **Rendezvous Grill & Tap Room** (tel. 503/622–6837) in Welches has innovative food at reasonable prices, a tasty dinner menu, and an award-winning wine rotating wine selection.

TOURIST INFORMATION

The Dalles Area Chamber of Commerce (404 W. 2nd St., The Dalles, OR 97058, tel. 541/296–2231). **Hood River County Chamber of Commerce** (405 Portway Ave., Hood River, OR 97031, tel. 541/386–2000). **Mt. Hood Area Chamber of Commerce** (Box 819, Welches, OR 97067, tel. 503/622–3017). **Port of Cascade Locks Visitors Information** (Box 307, Cascade Locks, OR 97014, tel. 541/374–8619).

RESERVATION SERVICES

Northwest Bed and Breakfast (1067 Hanover Ct. S, Salem, OR 97302, tel. 503/243–7616, fax 503/316–9118).

BERYL HOUSE 🌿

4079 Barrett Dr., Hood River, OR 97031, tel. 541/386–5567; www.moriah.com/beryl

Before it became a popular spot for windsurfing, Hood River was best known for its fruit orchards. Even though Beryl House is run by a one-time windsurfer, its location amid apple and pear trees keep you in touch with the town's roots.

John Lovell and Kim Pfautz found this 1910 house, a few miles out of Hood River, in 1994 and left their California occupations behind to renovate it. One of their favorite discoveries was a large pocket door entombed behind some molding. They now use it to block off the guest living room so that the wood stove doesn't have to work as hard in winter.

John and Kim have created a remarkable place that feels like the well-kept old home of friends. Upstairs, the original old fir floors, accented by old-style braided rugs, lend the house a warm feeling. The decor is whimsical—a framed turn-of-the-century marriage license hung on the wall of the bridal suite, for example, and lodge-style furnishings in most of the rooms.

Breakfast may be served on the sundeck overlooking Asian pear trees, when weather permits. But even inside, blackberry cornmeal pancakes with local sausage—a cuisine John calls "Paul Bunyan meets Alice Waters"—always pleases. △ *4 double rooms share 2 baths. Robes and slippers in rooms. TV/VCR, CD player, and video and CD library in common room. Equipment storage. $60–$70; full breakfast. MC, V. No smoking.*

BRIDAL VEIL LODGE 🌿

Box 87, Bridal Veil, OR 97010, tel. 503/695–2333

In 1921, Virgil Amend hauled timbers from the mill down the hill to an empty spot beside the Historic Columbia River Highway, in the tiny gorge community of Bridal Veil. There, within the sound of delicate Bridal Veil Falls, he built a lodge.

After years of functioning as a lodge, years of being a family residence, and years of being not much of anything, the old rustic Bridal Veil Lodge has reverted to its original purpose. Amend's great-granddaughter Laurel Slater and her husband have created a country-style bed-and-breakfast within 20 minutes of Portland's bustling waterfront.

But if Portland's lights are visible just to the west, it's what lies to the east that makes Bridal Veil's location special. The log structure is on the edge of the Columbia River Gorge National Scenic Area, a 90-mi-long preserve of trails, dizzying waterfalls, rock formations, high cliffs, and wilderness. Trails going through this region can be found within a mile of the lodge.

Inside, the inn is warm and the sense of family is unmistakable. Old photos adorn the shelves in the dining area, which is dominated by a large, 1920s-vintage harvest table and a huge wrought-iron cook stove. In the main common area, a player piano holds sway beneath high, exposed fir beams. Quilts adorn the walls of the two upstairs rooms. Grandpa's Room, with knotty pine walls and a hand-carved oak headboard and matching dresser, evokes the rough days when the lodge was built. Grandma's Room, slightly bigger, has a feminine feel, with table skirts, curtains, and plenty of light.

Perhaps the inn's greatest asset is Laurel Slater, who grew up in the house and can answer questions about local history. Laurel's breakfasts tend to be healthy and hearty, and often include German-style pancakes, fresh fruit, and plenty of sausage and bacon as regular fare. △ *2 double rooms share 1½ baths. TV in common area. $62–$70; full breakfast. No credit cards. No smoking.*

BRIGHTWOOD GUEST HOUSE ℘

64725 E. Barlow Trail Rd., Box 189, Brightwood, OR, 97011, tel. 503/622–5783 or 800/503–5783

Innkeeper Jan Colgan has created a romantic Japanese-style guest house nestled in a garden of Oriental plantings, situated on 2 acres of the historic Barlow Trail. The house is surrounded by a clear mountain stream, tall firs, and has its own water garden. A footbridge and miniature koi pond complete the landscape.

The house is always filled with fresh flowers from the garden. The main level offers a cozy sitting area, and a small eating area with kitchenette. Herbs, spices, and an exotic variety of teas—even microwave popcorn—fill the cupboards. There's also a handy supply of bird seed and fish food for a little serene outdoor entertainment by the koi pond. In the spacious bathroom, Jan provides an enticing assortment of bath oils and salts, and many personal items often forgotten from home. In the guest house, steps lead up to the sleeping loft and a heavenly featherbed with views of the water garden. There are also several futons on the main level that can be used as additional beds.

Jan, who once owned a bakery and managed a restaurant, has a particular appreciation for preparation and presentation. Breakfast can be vegetarian on request and may include a Hawaiian Treasure Fruit Plate. Otherwise, expect dishes such as waffles with freshly sliced berries or a roasted potato-and-onion omelet. △ *1 guest house with sleeping loft. TV/VCR, videos, kimonos, and slippers in guest house. Bikes. $125; full breakfast. No credit cards. No smoking.*

BROOKSIDE BED AND BREAKFAST ℘

45232 S.E. Paha Loop, Box 1112, Sandy, OR, 97055, tel. 503/668–4766

Innkeepers Jack and Barbara Brooks have made certain that Brookside is the perfect home-style B&B for families. This hillside country home has plenty to keep children fascinated—chickens, ducks, and geese wander about the property, and there are friendly goats, shaggy llamas, and colorful peacocks as well. Add Barbara's lush perennial beds and borders, and the setting is a pretty, homey sight.

Both Jack and Barbara are friendly and easy to engage in conversation. They've been to many exotic places, most recently to Mali, West Africa; treasures from their travels are found throughout the house. Jack is also a talented amateur photographer, and his landscapes of the local area decorate the walls.

The cozy sitting-kitchen area is the center of the action in this household and features many antiques and collectibles. Guest rooms on two levels are comfortable; the Brooks' sense of humor is apparent in naming The Room Next to Ours. One of the upstairs bedrooms looks out over the koi pond and has a king-size bed and a trundle bed. The Teddy Bear room has a private bath and looks out over the deck. A hearty breakfast is served family-style in the dining area. △ *1 double room with bath, 2 double rooms with shared bath. $35–$65; full breakfast. No credit cards. No smoking.*

CHAMBERLAIN HOUSE 🐚

36817 E. Crown Point Hwy., Corbett, OR 97019, tel. 503/695–2200; naw1150@aol.com

Although it's only 30 minutes from downtown Portland, Corbett is country through and through. The old town clings to the western edge of the Columbia River gorge about 1,000 ft up the steep slopes. In the middle of Corbett is Chamberlin House, a plain blue Craftsman farmhouse that has been weathering gorge winds since 1912 and has always been in owner Nancy Wilson's family.

The house retains its hardwood interior. The rooms are small, and you are always very much aware that you're in a family home; the only public area is essentially the family living room. But those creaking stairs and upright iron beds have an undeniable appeal that harks back to the early part of the century. History is Nancy's hobby, and she serves on the board of the Corbett Historical Society.

Breakfast is filling and seemingly endless. Orange-baked French toast and chocolate waffles complement baked-egg dishes and plates of muffins and homemade preserves. ⚱ *2 double rooms with shared bath. $50–$70; full or Continental breakfast, champagne splits in evening. No credit cards. No smoking.*

COLUMBIA GORGE HOTEL 🐚

4000 Westcliff Dr., Hood River, OR 97031, tel. 541/386–5566 or 800/345–1921, fax 541/387–5414; www.columbiagorgehotel.com

Staying at the Columbia Gorge Hotel is one of those irresistible, classic experiences. Just west of Hood River, the stucco hotel sits above a 200-ft waterfall that drops into the Columbia River.

Built in 1921 by Oregon lumber magnate and philanthropist Simon Benson, the property has been the Phelps' Mill and the Wah Gwin Gwin Hotel (a Native American name for the waterfall nearby) and a retirement home for the Neighbors of the Woodcraft. Today, although the grounds surrounding the hotel are beautiful, a pleasant stroll through the gardens is tempered by the modern-day distraction of I–84, which runs directly in front of the property.

Despite the hotel's size—the public rooms are huge, with plaster beams to match—the feeling is intimate. Louis XV–style armchairs surround a huge fireplace in the lounge, while such Victorian touches as round tufted velvet seats and dome lamps with hanging crystals enliven other rooms. Guest accommodations range from grand top-floor rooms that feature fireplaces and spectacular views over the falls to more pedestrian offerings on the lower floors.

As good as the dinners are, breakfast is the big production here: baked apples, apple fritters, smoked pork chops, pancakes—it goes on. And when honey is ceremoniously poured over the biscuits from on high, it's pure theater. ⚱ *40 double rooms with baths. TV and phone in rooms, fireplace in 2 rooms. Restaurant, bar, lobby lounge, bikes, conference facilities, turn-down service. $150–$375; full breakfast, dinner and catering available. AE, D, MC, V. No smoking in restaurant.*

DOUBLEGATE INN 🐚

26711 E. Welches Rd., Welches, OR, tel. 503/622–4859; www.mthoodlodging.com

Tucked beneath towering cedars, the Doublegate Inn is a welcoming sight. Gaining its name from the double-gated, gray, hand-chiseled wall in front, this big blue house is actually one of the area's most comfortable inns—especially if you like soaking in a tub.

Two of the four rooms have spa tubs, while a third has a luxurious soaking tub. Old-fashioned wainscoting surrounding the modern tubs add to the get-away-from-it-all ambiance. Each of the rooms has its own flair, from the warm cedar walls of the Bit O'Country to the happy bursts of color in the English Cottage room. The second-story deck, where breakfast is sometimes served in summer months, overlooks the calming Salmon River.

Innkeepers Gary and Charlene Poston maintain a friendly place where you can spend your evenings working on a giant jigsaw puzzle in front of a brick fireplace and munch on fresh-baked chocolate-chip cookies, a specialty of the inn. Both the Great Room and the Oregon Lodge Lounge are fitted with TVs, VCRs, games, puzzles, books, and magazines.

The Postons serve a hearty, filling breakfast usually including fruit, fresh fruit juice, and a hot entrées such as stuffed French toast or baked oatmeal. The innkeepers prefer not to house kids under 14. △ *2 double rooms with baths, 2 suites. Whirlpool bath in some rooms. TV/VCR in common rooms, video library, gift shop. $80–$115; full breakfast. AE, D, MC, V. No smoking.*

FALCON'S CREST INN 🐦

87287 Government Camp Loop Hwy., Box 185, Government Camp, OR, 97028, tel. 503/272–3403 or 800/624–7384, fax 503/272–3454; www.virtualcities.com/or/falconscrestinn.html

Perched at the 4,000-ft level on the south flank of Mt. Hood, the chalet-style Falcon's Crest Inn, trimmed with warm woods and a mix of contemporary and traditional furniture, is just 44 mi from Portland. From its two-story glass-front living room and dining area, this intimate inn enjoys an expansive view of the Mt. Hood Skibowl recreational area. In the winter months, guests sitting in the upstairs common areas can watch night skiers make their way down the mountain while enjoying a jigsaw puzzle, card game, or simply relaxing.

Each of the rooms and suites are decorated and furnished individually. Family heirlooms and keepsakes of innkeepers Bob and Melody Johnson are found throughout the house. Most of the rooms have mountain views, and all have in-room phones and private baths.

The Mexicali Suite on the first level of the inn, with a whirlpool tub for two, is decorated in the muted desert tones and vibrant colors of the Southwest. The trunk used as a coffee table in the spacious sitting room was used by Melody's grandfather to bring all his earthly possessions to America from Sweden. The Safari Suite on the main level is a guest favorite. Glass sliding doors open onto a deck overlooking the ski area below, which you can observe at night from the bamboo-cage bed beneath the room's own glowing star-studded ceiling. Rattan furniture and playful stuffed exotic animals complete the well-done theme.

Bob and Melody also operate an acclaimed fine-dining establishment at the inn, and have a strong following. You enjoy multiple-course gourmet dinners at individual tables throughout the main common area (reservations required). In addition to containing a full breakfast for overnight guests, in-room morning trays are delivered with treats such as Falcon's Crest Magic Muffins with cranberry butter. △ *4 suites with private baths. Soak tub on deck in 1 room, whirlpool bath in 1 room. TV/VCR, videos, games, restaurant. $100–$179; full breakfast, wine and beer available. AE, MC, V. No smoking.*

FERNWOOD AT ALDER CREEK ❦

54850 Highway 26 E, Sandy, OR 97055, tel. 503/622–3570

Nestled in the trees and ferns just off busy Highway 26, this vintage log home feels miles away from anything noisy or modern. A huge, multipaned window set into one log wall seems vaguely Bavarian, but the atmosphere is purely Northwest. The highway's hum is washed away by Alder Creek, about 100 ft below the inn and in a major hurry to meet up with the Sandy River just beyond the highway bridge.

Inside, a warm and rustic feeling pervades with a collection of local handmade furniture and some antiques from the families of innkeeper Darrell Dempster and his wife Margo. Part of the house is a bit dark, but the spacious dining room—library, with an immense supporting pole running vertically through it, is filled with natural light from a large window. Books and a collection of *Life* magazines dating back to the 1930s are displayed on the walls of this grand room, which has a loft that's perfect for reading or sleeping.

Both of the inn's two suites have decks and creek views. The Red Huckleberry Suite, downstairs, also features a private entrance and a small kitchen. It's easy to relax in the suite's knotty pine bath, with its bucolic view of the creek and canyon. The Hallberg House, with its full kitchen, fireplace, and large living room overlooking the creek, is a good place for groups.

The Curly Willow Suite upstairs has a whirpool tub. Its furnishings are more distinctive, especially the wrought-iron bed and the oak, American Empire rocking chair. The view from the window seat is peaceful; it's not hard to imagine curling up with a good book here.

The hearty and creative family-style breakfasts served in the dining room on the main floor might include fresh fruit juice, a meat dish, and raspberry puffed pastries or blueberry waffles with homemade syrup. △ *2 suites, 1 cabin. Kitchenette in 1 suite, whirlpool bath in suites. $75–$125; full breakfast. MC, V. No smoking.*

HOOD RIVER HOTEL ❦

102 Oak St., Hood River, OR 97031, tel. 541/386–1900, fax 541/386–6090;
www.hoodriverhotel.com

Although Hood River now bills itself as a kind of rustic Riviera for windsurfers, the Hood River Hotel is a reminder of the town's older character. True, Hood River's fresh identity as a recreational center is the reason the hotel was worth fixing up, but the hotel existed as a simple railroad stopover as early as 1910.

The 41-room brick-faced structure sits just off Main Street. At the front desk is innkeeper Pasquale Barone, a veteran of the European hospitality industry, who brings his Continental flair to Hood River. The rooms are furnished with Victorian reproductions; the beds add a much-needed touch of individuality, be they brass, four-poster, or canopy. In the hotel's two-story-high lobby—which flows into the restaurant and bar—there is a corner where children can find toys to pass the time.

The imposing wooden bar serves local beers and wines in a classy yet laid-back atmosphere. (Windsurfers are often big spenders, but they hang around in wet suits or Lycra shorts.) The bar and the dining room, which extends up to the mezzanine over the lobby, are immense, featuring the building's original pine woodwork.

The food continues the hotel's theme of being at once traditional and trendy. Dinners can get pricey, but the perfectly done seafood is worth it. Continental breakfasts are included as part of the room rate; full breakfasts are extra, but they are worth the money with specials such as chiles rellenos with home fries.

The hotel is close to Hood River's antiques shops and also near the town's liveliest nightspots. A few blocks away is the White Cap Brew Pub (tel. 541/386–2247), home of the Hood River Brewery, which serves its Full Sail Ale, one of the Northwest's most popular local ales. Closer to the hotel is the Brass Rail, a hopping dance club that features bands from the Portland and Seattle club scene. **△** *41 double rooms with baths, 9 suites. Air-conditioning, TV, and phone in rooms; kitchens in suites. Exercise room, sauna, hot tub, room service, full banquet room. $69–$145. AE, MC, V. No smoking.*

LAKECLIFF ESTATE BED & BREAKFAST 🐦
3820 Westcliff Dr., Box 1220, Hood River, OR 97031, tel. 541/386–7000

From the front room of the stately Lakecliff Estate Bed & Breakfast, the Columbia River gorge is like a three-dimensional postcard. Framed by a window that stretches the width of the large, oak-beamed room, the river view is nothing short of transfixing. When the wind cooperates, legions of little specks with colorful sails—the gorge's latest fun seekers, windsurfers—dot the water.

The estate, now on the National Register of Historic Places, was designed by A.E. Doyle, a turn-of-the-century Portland architect who also designed the Multnomah Falls Lodge and several public buildings in Portland, as well as Portland's charming downtown drinking fountains. Originally built for a Portland merchant family as a country getaway, the large home is something of a grand bed-and-breakfast by Northwest standards. Three of the four guest rooms feature rugged fireplaces made with rocks found on the property when it was built in 1908. Three also have views of the gorge, while the fourth looks back on the woods between the estate and the highway. All are done in country French style, with oak beams and down comforters on the beds.

Innkeepers Bruce and Judy Thesenga have created an impressive place to relax while taking in the sights of the gorge. In the dining area, Judy's collection of antique milk bottles rings an upper shelf. Bruce, who runs a horse ranch in the hills across the river from the Lakecliff, often takes a turn in the kitchen, where he produces Lakecliff bacon, a sweet, crunchy bacon served cold. Other breakfast mainstays are huckleberry pancakes, frittatas, Dutch babies, and oven-baked French toast. **△** *2 double rooms with baths, 2 double rooms share bath. Fireplace in 3 rooms. Shuffleboard court. $90–$110; full breakfast. No credit cards. No smoking, closed Oct.–Apr.*

MAPLE RIVER 🐦
20525 E. Mt. Country La., Box 339, Brightwood, OR, 97011, tel. 503/622–6273

Maple River innkeepers Jim and Barbara Dybvig found the perfect location and, after much work, have remodeled an unassuming contemporary home into an attractive, spacious, and elegant bed-and-breakfast.

The property sits high above the rushing Salmon River, with decks overlooking the river offering peaceful refuge from the everyday world. In the front of the house, gardens, a pond, and a large lawn are surrounded by tall trees, giving the place a completely secluded feel. Inside, a large common room with a massive stone fireplace and vaulted ceilings invites guests to curl up on the deep, soft sofas and relax.

The inn has two suites, the St. Andrews and the Northwoods Room. At this writing, a small outbuilding is steadily being converted into a Honeymoon Suite. Both suites have private entrances, fireplaces, river views, and pleasant environments. The St. Andrews Suite is tastefully golf themed, with plaid fabrics and memorabilia, while the Northwoods Room offers a more lodgelike feel. The private entrances open onto to a shared patio, and an outdoor hot tub is steps away.

Breakfast at Maple River is served family-style in the warm atmosphere of the country kitchen dining area. Breakfast includes fruit, muffins, and a hot entrée such as Swedish pancakes, a pear soufflé, Dutch babies, or an egg dish. △ *2 suites with baths. Fireplace, robes, and sandals in rooms; TV/VCR, videos in 1 room. Hot tub. $90–$120; full breakfast, refreshments. MC, V. No smoking.*

OLD WELCHES INN ❦

26401 E. Welches Rd., Welches, OR 97067, tel. 503/622–3754;
www.innsandouts.com/property/old_welches_inn.html

During the days of the Oregon Trail, wagons frequently stopped in Welches on the Salmon River, well below the glaciers of Mt. Hood and its steep passes. Below spread the fertile Willamette Valley, the goal of the weary pioneers. By 1890 the valley had become civilized, and Welches Hotel lured the carriage trade from Portland with the promise of hiking, fishing, and relaxation.

A simple, white clapboard house is all that remains of the hotel. The inn combines the atmosphere of a laid-back ski lodge and an old country estate. Bleached woodwork accentuates the sunny, airy feel of the place. Much of that feeling comes from Judi Mondun, who operates the inn with her husband, Ted.

The covered patio, with a floor of hand-fitted river stones and lattice walls, features an 8-ft-high stone fireplace that was originally part of the old hotel. Three upstairs rooms share two baths, and the newly added Forget-Me-Not room has a private bath. The largest, which overlooks Resort at the Mountain's 27-hole golf course and has views of Hunchback Mountain, has a sleigh bed, Georgian hunting scenes on the raw silk-covered walls, and a floral upholstered rocking chair. A second room lacks a dramatic view, but the rich cedar paneling and ornate iron bedstead more than compensate. The remaining room on that level has a cannonball-style headboard and is festooned with duck decoys.

An outlying cabin is even closer to the river and the golf course—it overlooks the first hole. The 1890 structure has its own kitchen, two bedrooms, and a river-rock fireplace. A full breakfast is served bright and early—from 7:30 to 9—in the dining room or on the patio; the favorite among guests is Grandma's Special Casserole, an herbed egg dish with sausage and cheese. △ *1 double room with bath, 3 double rooms share 2 baths, 1 2-bedroom housekeeping cabin. TV in 1 room, kitchen and fireplace in cabin. $75–$175; full breakfast (except for cabin). AE, MC, V. No smoking, 2-night minimum on holiday weekends.*

SUITE RIVER BED AND BREAKFAST ❦

69437 E. Vine Maple Dr., Box 530, Welches, OR, 97067, tel. 503/622–3547

Fifty miles from downtown Portland on a quiet gravel road, Suite River Bed and Breakfast is surrounded by tall firs and cedars. Overlooking the Sandy River and mountains, this small inn has a lot to offer a city-weary traveler. The area is close to skiing, and also offers canoeing, rafting, fishing, and general peace and quiet.

Innkeepers Pat Dutmers and Steve Rickeard chose this private location for its natural beauty. Guests at Suite River can have as much or as little privacy as they choose, as the inn's only guest room—the Marie Francis Suite—was created with that in mind.

The suite was named for Pat's Aunt Marie, whose skillful hands made the dining room tablecloth and the suite's lace bedspread. The bedspread was a wedding gift to Pat's parents; other such family heirlooms and keepsakes are found in the house. Decorated in mauves, greens, and beiges, the room has an uncluttered and cozy feel. Double French doors lead outside to a private deck and into Pat's gardens. The riverbank is a short walk away. Resident squirrels, chipmunks, and birds chitter about the Adirondack chairs outside. The large bathroom comes with all the trimmings, including a double spa tub.

You can opt for a Continental breakfast or a full breakfast offering choice of beverage, pastry, entrée, meat, and fruit salad. It is served to candle light, with fine china, silver, crystal, and fresh flowers, all resting on Aunt Marie's lace tablecloth. △ *1 suite. TV, VCR, videos. $95; choice of full or Continental breakfast. No credit cards. No smoking.*

CENTRAL AND EASTERN OREGON
Including Bend

Drop unsuspecting travelers into the part of Oregon that's east of the snow-capped Cascade Mountain range and they'll swear they're someplace else—Utah, Arizona, Texas, Switzerland.

While the western third of the state is lush and green, the eastern two-thirds is high, dry, and wild—sparsely populated, too. The 17 counties of eastern Oregon make up an area of pine forests, rangeland, and mountains the size of Missouri, but the population is less than 350,000. There is only one town with more than 20,000 people, just two commercial TV stations, and one congressional representative, whom the vast area shares with southern Oregon.

Central and eastern Oregon begin very visibly in the west as soon as you reach the summit of the Cascade Mountains. There the forests turn from fir to pine and the ground underfoot from soggy to crunchy. The difference rests simply in the presence of the Cascades, which drain most of the precipitation out of the Pacific storms, dumping it on the western slopes of the mountains. Whereas western Oregon averages 45 inches of rain a year, the mean to the east is less than 15 inches.

Once you're out of the mountains, the land settles down to a broad plateau that gradually slopes toward the Columbia River to the north. On this high plain, much of it more than 3,500 ft in elevation, are large mountain ranges: the lumpy Ochocos; the stately Strawberry Range; the majestic Wallowas; and the immense, complex Blue Mountains. And in the southern deserts, gargantuan fault-block mountains—Steens Mountain, Hart Mountain, Abert Rim—thrust straight out of the sagebrush.

Deer, elk, antelope, cougars, and even wild horses roam these plains. Ranches, some running more than 10,000 head of cattle, are sprinkled throughout the big country. Although there are few developed tourist areas outside the Bend area, the adventuresome are seldom idle in central and eastern Oregon.

The Deschutes River, a cold green stream that heads near Mt. Bachelor, shoots along the eastern edge of the Cascades, providing better than 100 mi of fishing and rafting opportunities. The John Day River winds through thousands of square miles of fossil beds in north central Oregon. Farther east, the Snake River, bordering Oregon and Idaho, dominates the terrain with Hells Canyon—apologies to the Grand Canyon—the deepest gash on the continent.

Northeastern Oregon's Wallowa Mountains, often called the American Alps because of their combination of granite peaks and hanging glacier valleys, lie just to the west of Hells Canyon, with hundreds of miles of hiking and pack trails.

Only in the southeastern corner of the state, an area about the size of South Carolina, does Oregon have a true desert environment—the Great Basin. Here, in an area of more than 30,000 square mi, rivers from the mountains flow into the plain and evaporate in marshes and alkali flats, and birds gather from all along the western flyway.

This is lonely, self-sufficient country, and people are friendly and likely to wave at you as you drive down the long, lonesome highways. But passersby are few and far between. Sudden snowstorms or flash floods can come out of nowhere virtually anytime of the year. It is advisable to be prepared to fend for yourself at all times.

PLACES TO GO, SIGHTS TO SEE

Baker City. On the old Oregon Trail, this former mining town quickly takes you back to the Gold Rush days of northeastern Oregon. Just east of town is the *Oregon Trail Interpretive Center* (tel. 800/523–1235), an excellent museum depicting pioneer life in the 1840s.

Bend. The largest town east of the Cascades and sitting very nearly in the center of Oregon, Bend is a good fueling-up spot for the recreational activities nearby: A half hour to the east, skiers whiz down the slopes of Mt. Bachelor, and the fishing and rafting of the wild Deschutes River are within easy reach. Bend is filled with decent restaurants, nightclubs, wilderness outfitters and equipment-rental places, as well as a surprising number of good hostelries. At the *High Desert Museum* (59800 S. Hwy. 97, 4 mi south of Bend, tel. 541/382–4754), you can walk through a Paiute Indian encampment, a pioneer wagon camp, an old mine, an Old West boardwalk, and other detailed dioramas, with authentic relics, sounds, even odors. A 150-acre outdoor section features porcupines, birds of prey, and river otters at play. At press time a new Native American wing focusing on the Indian cultures of the Columbia River Plateau was scheduled to open in fall 1999.

Century Drive. For 100 mi, this forest-highway loop beginning and ending in Bend meanders among dozens of high mountain lakes offering fishing, hiking, waterskiing, and camping. Take Highway 46 for the first two-thirds of the trip and switch to Highway 97 at LePine to return to Bend.

John Day Fossil Beds National Monument (2 mi north of the junction of Hwys. 26 and 19, tel. 541/987–2333). Millions of years ago, the arid canyons of east central Oregon were tropical forests inhabited by sloths and the prehistoric ancestors of horses. Their remains in the form of well-preserved fossils, many in lake beds of volcanic ash, are found in the valley of the John Day River.

Kah-Nee-Ta (11 mi from Warm Springs on Hwy. 3, tel. 800/831– 0100). In the heart of the 600,000-acre Warm Springs Indian Reservation sits this posh resort. The hot mineral springs feeding the Warm Springs River form the focal point of Kah-Nee-Ta, which is operated by the Confederated Tribes of Warm Springs. A double Olympic-size mineral-water pool is open to nonguests for a nominal fee; golf, tennis, hiking, and fishing are also available. At the *Museum at Warm Springs* (10 mi north of Kah-Nee-Ta on Hwy. 26, tel. 541/553–3331) you can see traditional dwellings and maybe have the chance to attend a real Wasco wedding. Established in 1993, the museum chronicles the history of the Wasco, Paiute, and Warm Springs tribes.

Ontario. A stone's throw from the Idaho state line, this town of 10,000 features the new *Four Rivers Cultural Center* (676 S.W. 5th Ave., tel. 541/889–8191), devoted to the area's fivefold heritage: Basques and others of European descent, Northern Paiutes, Japanese, and Hispanics together created a unique cultural mix.

Owyhee River Country. The far southeastern corner of Oregon is named for the wild, thrashing river that shoots through the canyons. White-water rafting is popular here, as are fishing, hiking, and studying Native American petroglyphs. The town of Vale, at the junction of Highways 20 and 26, is the best base for exploring the area.

Pendleton. Famous for its annual mid-September rodeo, this cattle town, reached by I–84, is situated on a plain between the scenic Blue Mountains and the brown Columbia Plateau. An important staging area for shipping cattle, Pendleton seems almost Texan in atmosphere.

Smith Rocks State Park (tel. 541/548–7501). The muddy Crooked River winds through these high precipices north of Redmond. A favorite with rock climbers, 300- to 500-ft-deep canyons form high spires, the most famous of which is called Monkey Face. The park, which also encompasses dense pine forest, offers excellent hiking.

Steens Mountain is one of the most unusual desert environments in the West. The 60-mi-long ridge has 5,000-ft glacial gorges carved into its sides. The summit, 9,700 ft above sea level, is reached by a passable but rugged road, and overlooks the sandy Alvord Desert. To the north, 6 mi off Highway 205, lies the mammoth *Malheur National Wildlife Refuge* (tel. 541/493–2612), home to hundreds of species of migratory birds, among them sandhill cranes, snowy white egrets, and white-faced ibis.

Wallowa Mountains. Oregon's northeastern corner is a surprise to most visitors. The mountains form a giant U-shape fortress between Hells Canyon to the east and the Blue Mountains to the west. Hundreds of alpine lakes, many more than 7,000 ft high, dot the remote hanging valleys that fall between ridges of 9,000-ft-plus peaks. The most scenic route through the area is Highway 82; take it for 80 mi, starting and finishing at either LaGrande or Joseph.

RESTAURANTS

Pine Tavern (tel. 541/382–5581) in Bend takes its name from the two pine trees growing through the roof. But the place's reputation comes from its flaw-

lessly prepared seafood and fresh trout served up in typically hearty Western help-
ings. The **Halfway Supper Club** (tel. 541/742–2027), presided over by Babette Beatty, gives visitors to the tiny town of Halfway an unexpected chance
to sample top-flight gourmet cooking in an area where you'd least expect it.
Ask any cowpoke in the Baker Valley who serves the best steak and potatoes,
and there's only one answer—**Haines Steak House** (tel. 541/856–3639). One
caveat: If you order it rare, that's how you'll get it. In Baker City, the **Geiser Grand
Hotel**'s Swans dining room and Palm Court (tel. 541/523–1889), the latter underneath a stunning stained-glass skylight, offer upscale fare and an impressive wine list. The **Buckaroo Room** (tel. 541/493–2738), in Steens Mountain
Inn (*see below*) in tiny Frenchglen, serves a simple menu of high-quality fare such
as filet mignon and Basque roast chicken, with fresh produce brought in regularly from Portland. Travelers in the Sisters area will find excellent dining at
the **Kokanee Cafe** (tel. 541/595–6420) in Camp Sherman. A hot spot for guests
at Black Butte Ranch, the restaurant is open between mid-April and the end
of October; reservations are essential.

TOURIST INFORMATION

Baker County Chamber of Commerce (490 Campbell St., Baker City, OR
97814, tel. 541/523–5855). **Bend Chamber of Commerce** (63085 N. Hwy.
97, Bend, OR 97701, tel. 541/382–3221). **Grant County Chamber of Commerce** (281 W. Main St., John Day, OR 97485, tel. 541/575–0547). **Harney
County Chamber of Commerce** (18 W. D St., Burns, OR 97720, tel. 541/573–
2636). **Ontario Chamber of Commerce** (676 S.W. 5th Ave., Ontario, OR 97914,
tel. 541/889–8012). **Pendleton Chamber of Commerce** (501 S. Main St.,
Pendleton, OR 97801, tel. 800/547–8911).

RESERVATION SERVICES

Northwest Bed and Breakfast (1067 Hanover Ct. S, Salem, OR 97302, tel. 503/
243–7616, fax 503/316–9118).

BED-AND-BREAKFAST BY THE RIVER ☙
HCR 77, Box 790, Prairie City, OR 97869, tel. 541/820–4470

The Emmel Brothers Ranch sits at the foot of the stunning Strawberry Mountains near Prairie City on more than 3,000 acres of rangeland and forest, with
the John Day River winding through it. Within a few miles are hot springs and
abundant opportunities for hiking, bird-watching, fishing, and hunting.

The bed-and-breakfast operated by Helen Emmel is a modern ranch–country-
style home, comfortable and simple. The guest rooms, once the children's bedrooms, are decorated with a mix of Georgia antiques from the 1813 plantation
house where the family lived until they came out west in 1969. There are some
interesting touches: The family room has a hand-carved walnut and pecan mantel and a pie safe from the plantation's slave quarters. Guests may also avail
themselves of a games room, piano, and private entrance.

Bed-and-Breakfast by the River is a working cattle ranch where the morning
begins with biscuits, waffles, homemade bread and preserves, and meat—beef,
pork, venison, or elk—all from the ranch or the family's hunting trips. The house
is right by the riverbank, and the Emmels have done a lot of work on maintaining the ranch's riparian areas; there is a great view from the breakfast table of
the salmon spawning. ♣ *1 double room with bath, 2 doubles share bath. TV/VCR,*

pool table in games room. $40–$60; full breakfast. No credit cards. No smoking, no alcohol.

CHANDLERS BED, BREAD & TRAIL INN 🕊

700 S. Main St., Box 639, Joseph, OR 97846, tel. 541/432–9765 or 800/452–3781; www.eoni.com/~chanbbti

From the small cattle town of Joseph, the pine-covered, snow-capped Wallowa Mountains rise some 5,000 ft. Nestled at the foot of these dominating peaks, just south of town, is Wallowa Lake, a popular spot for swimming, fishing, and hiking. As you make the turn between Joseph and the lake, you'll find Chandlers Bed, Bread & Trail Inn.

This modern, lodgelike house is surrounded by an extensive deck. The rustic, sparely furnished rooms have high, beamed ceilings, and much of their paneling is made of old barn wood; although the deep brown carpets are a bit dark, skylights provide plenty of eastern Oregon light. One room has a loft furnished with twin beds. The best view of the mountains is from the sunroom on the second floor.

The inn's unusual name is a clue to its attractions: Innkeeper Ethel Chandler makes her own bread—a staple in the hearty breakfast she fixes (as are sausage casseroles and tasty hazelnut pancakes). And the wild Wallowas include a wilderness area the size of Rhode Island, where trail hiking and backpacking either by horse or llama are popular. Both Ethel and her husband, Jim, can advise you on the best places to go in the area. ⚲ *3 double rooms with baths, 2 doubles share 1½ baths. TV/VCR in common area, computer available. Free shuttle to nearby trailheads. $50–$80; full breakfast. MC, V. No smoking.*

CLEAR CREEK FARM BED-AND-BREAKFAST 🕊

Rte. 1, Box 138, Halfway, OR 97834, tel. 541/742–2238 or 800/742–4992, fax 541/742–5175; www.neoregon.com/ccgg

Coming out of the sagebrush country at the southern edge of the Wallowa Mountains into the woods and streams of the Pine Valley is like entering another world—you might feel as though you'd suddenly stepped into a verdant valley in Colorado or Vermont. This is the setting of Clear Creek Farm, 160 acres of forest, fields, orchards, and gardens; it's often used as the starting point for excursions to Hells Canyon, but it's worth a visit in itself. Hosts Mike and Rose Curless, former Coloradans, offer simple but comfortable accommodations in a cozy 1880s Craftsman farmhouse that looks out onto nearby orchards. When it's warm, two artist-built bunkhouses are also available.

The main house—with its large, airy kitchen, broad porch, and wood-walled living area—invites lounging, and a substantial renovation underway at press time will allow even more room to do so. Accommodations remain rustic in the distinctive bunkhouses. With ceilings to keep out the occasional summer showers but no windows, they're perfect for families and those seeking an unadulterated hit of the great outdoors. Of the two, Lakeview, with a balcony overlooking a small pond, is the best.

Rose's breakfast specialties, served in an outdoor kitchen in warm weather, include buffalo sausage, Dutch babies, home-grown raspberries and peaches in season, and egg dishes. Optional dinners are heavy on steak, featuring bison meat raised on the neighboring 70-head bison ranch, which Mike manages. ⚲ *4 double rooms share 3 baths, 3 cabin rooms with three detached baths. Hot tub, library, bicycles, conference facilities, horse lodging. $60–$66, $30 per* *person for parties of 2 or more; full breakfast. MC, V. No smoking, bunkhouses closed Nov.–Apr.*

ELLIOTT HOUSE 🐚
305 W. 1st St., Prineville, OR 97754, tel. 541/416–0423, fax 541/416–9368; www.empnet.com/elliotthouse

Despite a rough-hewn reputation, Prineville has always been the most genteel town in central Oregon. Elliott House, a 1908 Queen Anne Victorian on the National Register of Historic Places, keeps that tradition of class in the outback alive. With its thick green lawns, wraparound porch, Tuscan columns, and bay windows, the house stands out like a well-groomed dowager in a quiet but otherwise undistinguished neighborhood. Re-creating the past has become a full-time occupation for the innkeepers, Andrew and Betty Wiechert. Once they found their "dream house," they moved up from the Bay Area and began carefully restoring it.

Fueled by their life-long passion for antiques, the Wiecherts have filled Elliott House with a marvelous collection of turn-of-the-century furnishings, most of it oak. There is an interesting piece wherever you look, including a working 1916 Wurlitzer nickelodeon in the parlor.

The two guest rooms on the second floor are also filled with vintage pieces and accessories. A 100-year-old mahogany side table and English oak commode with black marble graces one of them. In the second room, which has cabbage-rose wallpaper, there's a double cast-iron bed with a high mattress and an embroidered quilt that came by wagon train, as well as an 1890 oak "potty chair" (decorative, of course). The rooms share a large sumptuous bathroom with floral-print wallpaper, original brass fixtures, and a marble-top sink.

Betty custom designs breakfasts. Served by candlelight on antique china, the morning's repast might include a bowl of fresh fruit or homemade applesauce, Swedish waffles or crepes with raspberries, or eggs with sausage rolls. To accompany it all, she cranks up the Edison cylinder phonograph and fills the dining room with period music. The innkeepers ask that guests refrain from bringing children under 12. ⚠ *2 double rooms share bath. Cable TV/VCR in attic lounge, golf and fishing gear, bicycles. $70; full breakfast, afternoon refreshments. No credit cards. No smoking.*

FRENCHGLEN HOTEL 🐚
Frenchglen, OR 97736, tel. 541/493–2825, fax 541/493–2828; fghotel@ptinet.net

It's impossible to miss the Frenchglen Hotel—that is, once you *find* Frenchglen, a tiny spot on the map deep in the eastern Oregon desert. Built in 1920, still pioneer days in this remote region, the state-owned hotel resembles a simple prairie church, with a gabled roof visible from miles away as you approach from the north. Manager John Ross spent years as a cook on Alaskan fishing boats, so remoteness is nothing new to him. At least here, at the foot of Steens Mountain, he gets a fresh supply of faces every few days.

The hotel's interior is simple and rustic. A huge camp-type coffeepot is always on the hob in the combination lobby–dining room, where you can absorb local history and whet your appetite for touring with a collection of picture books. The two long pine dining tables serve as a gathering place for ranchers and visitors.

The food here has long been a standout. Every evening a large, hearty family-style dinner is served for overnight guests and the general public. A typical group might include a ranching couple who have driven 60 mi to celebrate their anniversary, a pair of bird-watchers, and a local mechanic. John whips up huge salads, rich casseroles, home-baked rolls, and a main meat dish for à la carte dining. Breakfast is also bountiful, although it's served individually from a menu and isn't included in the room rate.

Most of the people who stay at the hotel, which is on the National Register of Historic Places, are devoted bird-watchers who are drawn by the nearby Malheur National Wildlife Refuge. In the fall, however, Steens teems with hunters. The mix of hunters, ranchers, and conservationists can make for some lively conversations over breakfast. ⌂ *8 double rooms share 2 baths. Restaurant. $53–$56; full breakfast (not included). D, MC, V. No smoking, closed mid-Nov.–mid-Mar.*

GEISER GRAND HOTEL ☜

1996 Main St., Baker City, OR 97814, tel. 541/523–1889 or 888/434–7374, fax 541/523–1800

You needn't ask for directions to the Geiser Grand; as you approach Baker City on the interstate, the brown highway signs that designate national parks and monuments lead the way. Few hotels get this kind of roadside publicity, but few hotels have undergone the kind of painstaking restoration that has made this remarkable Italian Renaissance Revival structure once again the jewel of eastern Oregon.

The wealth of the Geiser family's Bonanza gold mine, and the sophistication of Czechoslovakia-born, Chicago-trained architect John Benes, went into building the 1889 hotel. Its opulence, from the rich architectural detail and fine materials to the expansive scale of the rooms (10-ft windows and 18-ft ceilings), gave it a reputation as the finest hotel between Salt Lake City and Portland, and even now there are few that equal it in either city. It closed in 1968, however, and nearly fell to the wrecking ball after decades of disuse and decrepitude; it is thanks to the commitment and expertise of Barbara and Dwight Sidway that it stands today.

The Sidways have extensive experience in historic preservation, and their renovation of the Geiser Grand adhered to the strict guidelines of the National Park Service, down to laboratory analysis of paint flecks to determine and reproduce the original color scheme. The three-year, $6 million restoration earned the hotel National Historic site status—hence the road signs.

Not only is the building itself a marvel, but the way the Sidways manage it is also highly professional and accommodating. Its ground-floor restaurant is Baker City's finest, with an accomplished menu and a respectable wine list, and tables arrayed underneath the largest stained glass ceiling in the Northwest. ⌂ *30 double rooms with baths. Room service, restaurant, bar, exercise room, concierge, meeting rooms, library. $79–$199; breakfast not included. AE, D, DC, MC, V. No-smoking floors.*

HOTEL DIAMOND ☜

HC 72, Box 10, Diamond, OR 97722, tel. 541/493–1898, fax 541/493–2084; www.central-oregon.com/hoteldiamond

On the eastern boundary of the famed Malheur National Wildlife Refuge, about 54 mi south of Burns, Hotel Diamond with its adjacent general store and post office comprise most of the town of Diamond. The people who stay in this remote spot are usually bird-watchers, rock hounds, writers, and nature photographers.

The plain redwood exterior of the square, two-story hotel, built in 1898, looks perfectly at home in this Western landscape of juniper-covered hills. Jerry and

Judy Santillie, who formerly managed the Frenchglen Hotel (*see above*), bought the place in 1986 and restored it and the grounds over the winter months when the Frenchglen was closed. Entirely refurbished, the hotel opened in 1990—50 years after it last offered lodgings.

The interior, though it verges on the utilitarian, still manages to preserve something of an Old West feel. Just off the wide, screened porch there's a combined sitting and dining area with wooden tables and two large sofas. Mounted deer and elk heads preside over the upstairs lounge. The guest rooms, with brass bedsteads and quilts, are plain and comfortable. Full breakfasts and ranch-style dinners are served for an additional charge.

The Santillies also sell gas to guests at cost, which is a nice, hospitable touch; you use a lot covering the great distances, and it tends to be expensive. Even if you have children equipped for road trips, the owners ask that you keep the young ones at home. ♨ *3 double rooms with baths, 3 doubles share 2½ baths. TV, radio/CD player, and air-conditioning in rooms. Mountain bikes. $55–$90; Continental breakfast, dinner by reservation. MC, V.*

LARA HOUSE ℞
640 N.W. Congress St., Bend, OR 97701, tel. and fax 541/388–4064 or 800/766–4064

Staying at Lara House, a cross-gabled Craftsman house built in 1910, gives you a glimpse of what life was like in Bend when it was a four-day trip to Portland instead of the present-day three-hour drive. Beside peaceful Drake Park on the Deschutes River near downtown, Lara House stands out; it's on a huge lot with a sloping lawn atop a retaining wall of native lava rocks.

The house's original woodwork can be seen in the trim and door frames and in the alderwood-coffered ceiling of the living room. There a massive, lodge-size fireplace dominates, to be enjoyed from two cream-and-blue patterned camelback love seats or from the ladder-back chairs about the gaming table. The walls here are heavily stuccoed. Walk through the double French doors and the atmosphere changes radically. Restored to its original style, the huge sunroom, with a glass table, overlooking the 11-acre riverside park is an airy, light-filled haven.

The large, carpeted guest rooms, all on the second floor, have seating areas and private bathrooms. The L-shape Drake Room, furnished in dark oak, has a duck theme: wallpaper borders swimming with them, framed prints of them, and a wall unit displaying knickknacks of these fine-feathered friends. The black claw-foot tub in the bathroom is the original. Softer and more romantic is the Shevlin Room with its alcoved, lace-covered bed, Queen Anne–style couch and chair, and Cupid prints. A masculine tone predominates in the Cascade Room, which has handsome black-striped wallpaper.

There is a choice of venues for the full, home-style breakfast: the formal dining room, sunroom, or terraced redwood deck that surrounds the house. ♨ *6 double rooms with baths. Hot tub. $55–$110; full breakfast, afternoon and evening refreshments. D, MC, V. No smoking.*

PARKER HOUSE BED AND BREAKFAST ℞

311 N. Main St., Pendleton, OR 97801, tel. 800/700–8581

The eastern Oregon town of Pendleton is perhaps best known for its Round-Up, four days of rodeos, races, and related events that annually bring the area's raw and untamed (and recent) past to the fore. In the context of this Wild West atmosphere, the Parker House, on Main Street just across the Umatilla River from downtown, seems more than a little incongruous. The tile-roof, pink stucco Italianate structure bespeaks a grace and sophistication one doesn't expect from a place once known for its proliferation of saloons and bordellos.

The family who sold it in 1989 was the same family for whom it was built in 1917; in their seven decades there, the Rodgers apparently maintained everything and changed little. Owner Sandy Parker, who grew up in Pendleton and found the house for sale when she returned for her 20-year class reunion, has followed suit. The original exquisite millwork still adorns windows, doors, and walls, and the original custom fixtures are everywhere. The five guest rooms range from the Gwendolyn Room (after matriarch Gwendolyn Rodgers), with French doors, a fireplace, and semiprivate balcony, to the Maid's Room, a snug accommodation with an heirloom silk Oriental rug.

Preserving the house without changes has meant that the rooms share the one original bath. Many bed-and-breakfast travelers steer clear of inns without private baths, but if they stick to their guns in Pendleton, they'll be missing a gem. △ *5 rooms share 1 bath. Phone and TV in rooms. Fax and secretarial service on request, meeting room. $75–$85; full breakfast, afternoon refreshments. AE, MC, V. No smoking.*

PINE VALLEY LODGE AND HALFWAY SUPPER CLUB ℡
163 N. Main St., Halfway, OR 97834, tel. 541/742–2027;
www.neoregon.net/pinevalleylodge

Pine Valley Lodge, on Main Street in "downtown" Halfway, is really just another art project for owners Dale and Babette Beatty. Both have had their share of fame: Dale is a nationally recognized home and furniture builder, and Babette is *the* Babette, who graced the cover of *Sports Illustrated*'s first swimsuit issue, January 20, 1964. Both say they've had their time in the limelight and now it's time to settle down and make an honest living.

From the outside, the large house is styled like many others that were built in eastern Oregon during the timber boom of the late 1920s. Inside, the common area is artfully cluttered with a mixture of antique Florida fishing gear, Native American artifacts, and Babette's paintings. Like most of the property, the two rooms upstairs reveal the funky hand of an artist, with eiderdown comforters on sleigh beds, bold patterns and linens, and walls painted in bright colors with colorful stencils. A common room has board games galore.

The Beattys continue to play a major role in preserving, in their own idiosyncratic way, the old houses of Halfway, acquiring and artistically transforming structures that otherwise would have been demolished. Both the rustic Love Shack, the oldest building in town, and the little house called the Blue Dog, have been outfitted to provide guest accommodations. Renowned for her superb cooking, Babette also runs the Halfway Supper Club and bakery, in the 1891 church across the street from the lodge. The menu includes everything from Thai peanut noodles and green-chili burritos to Cuban roast pork sandwiches. △ *7 double rooms share baths, 2 suites share connecting bath, dormitory-style accommodation sleeps up to 10. Restaurant, bicycles. $65–$140; full breakfast. No credit cards. No smoking.*

SATHER HOUSE BED-AND-BREAKFAST ℡
7 N.W. Tumalo Ave., Bend, OR 97701, tel. 541/388–1065 or 888/388–1065,
fax 541/330–0591; www.moriah.com/sather

Bend is booming, and its recent "discovery" has inevitably led to a great deal of undistinguished, fast-track development along its peripheries. Luckily, the charm and dignity of Bend's older neighborhoods can still be savored at the Sather House, a spacious historic home on the northwest side of town, three blocks from the riverside Drake Park and walking distance from downtown.

Built in 1911 for the Sather family, who occupied it for 75 years, the house reveals characteristics of both Colonial Revival and Craftsman styles, and is on the National Register. Owner Robbie Giamboi extensively renovated the house, and her meticulous taste is evident the moment you step inside. Period furnishings are used throughout, and the original Douglas fir woodwork has been beautifully restored. Robbie sponged and rag-rolled the walls herself. The light-filled living room, with lace-curtained windows, has wingback chairs and a comfortable sofa gathered near a fireplace. Built-in benches in the parlor are used for a games area. There is also a big, airy kitchen and a butler's pantry, where you can get an early morning coffee.

Of the four guest rooms, all on the second floor, the largest and lightest is the Garden Room. It has a sofa and a rocking chair; Battenburg and lace are used for curtains and the comforter. The English Room is darker and more traditionally masculine. The Victorian Room, decorated in blues and pinks, has a 1910 claw-foot tub in the bath. Robbie says her goal is to "pamper the women and feed the men." Breakfast, served in the formal dining room, typically consists of French toast with raspberries and almonds, or banana pancakes with lemon sauce. She serves fireside tea in winter and lemonade, iced tea, and cookies on the veranda in summer. ⚘ *2 double rooms with baths, 2 doubles share bath. Cable TV in 1 room. TV, fireplace in common room. $75–$85; full breakfast, afternoon tea or refreshments. D, MC, V. No smoking.*

SHANIKO HOTEL ☙
4th and E Sts., Shaniko, OR 97057, tel. 541/489–3441 or 800/483–3441, fax 541/489–3441

Bed-and-breakfasting in a ghost town may not strike everyone as a good bet. But here on the high dusty plains south of The Dalles, the Old West feel of the restored Shaniko Hotel is palpable. Guest rooms at the hotel, which first opened in 1901, are spare and a bit antiseptic. (The mock old-fashioned wooden iceboxes acting as night tables *are* clever, however.) Still, there's plenty of atmosphere just outside; you need only peek out of the window to see a town falling down as the wind wails through the old buildings and shutters flap eerily.

Shaniko has been a ghost town since the 1940s, when the last rail line leading to town washed out. Yet in 1900, the town's population numbered in the thousands and it was the world's biggest shipper of wool. Stagecoach lines spoked into the frontier of eastern Oregon, and Shaniko was the rail head for the only line that then penetrated the high plains.

Despite the slightly sterile feel of the place, owners Jean and Dorothy Farrell give a personal warmth to the hotel and to their guests. Jean, a retired plumbing contractor, is also the mayor of Shaniko, a delicate job that involves keeping the town looking run-down without allowing it to collapse completely.

Shaniko's old firehouse has been kept up to house ancient horse-drawn fire rigs. The blacksmith shop is run by a small company that makes reproduction carriages. For real culture shock, you can tour the tiny, false-front Shaniko Post Office. Across the lonesome highway is the old, creaking water tower, the tallest building in town. The first new structure to be built in Shaniko in decades—a combination ice-cream parlor and photo studio—is right next to the hotel, which also has a highly browseable antiques store. Breakfast presents the standard choices of all-you-can-eat pancakes; eggs with bacon or sausage and hash browns; or French toast. ⚑ *17 double rooms with baths, 1 suite. Whirlpool bath in suite. Restaurant. $56–$96; Continental or full breakfast. AE, D, MC, V. No smoking.*

STANG MANOR 🍃

1612 Walnut St., La Grande, OR 97850, tel. 541/963–2400 or 888/286–9463; www.eoni.com/stang

When Marjorie McClure was growing up during the late 1940s in La Grande, the Stang mansion, just a few blocks away, seemed a place of unattainable glamour. Owned by lumber baron August Stang, the richest man in the county, the 1926 Georgian Revival house on the western edge of this small college and ranching town was an obligatory stop for any political figure and celebrity passing through. It wasn't until 1992, when Marjorie and her husband Pat returned from California for her father's 100th birthday, that she finally got her chance to stay at the elegant manor. Three months later, the McClures had closed the deal to buy the place that Bing Crosby and Guy Kibbe had visited during Marjorie's childhood.

Stang Manor's interior is full of stylish details from the 1920s. You can enjoy the large Italian stone fireplace in the living room from a semicircular sectional couch upholstered in a rose-print tapestry fabric. Throw open the French doors of the Sun Room, complete with a working wall fountain of teal-color Italian tiles, and the years quickly melt away. Built-in benches line the perimeter of the window-filled room, affording views of the property. White rattan furniture adds to the Jay Gatsby aura of the room.

Extraordinary features are found in every room of this historic house, which has remained unmodified except for its wall coverings. The master suite boasts a turn-of-the-century mahogany four-poster bed and matching dresser with tilting mirror. The bathroom has its original "foot washer," fed with running water.

Breakfast is a lavish affair of fruit, homemade breads and muffins, and a hot dish served in the dining room under a pewter and crystal chandelier. Usually Pat and Marjorie will join you for breakfast, which might be considered an intrusion if they weren't so cordial, informative, and easygoing. ⚑ *2 double rooms with baths, 2 2-bedroom suites. Cable TV and fireplace in 1 suite. $75–$90; full breakfast, afternoon tea. MC, V. No smoking.*

STEENS MOUNTAIN INN 🍃

Hwy. 205, Frenchglen, OR 97736, tel. 541/493–2738, fax 541/493–2835

In the 1920's, the home of the first schoolteacher in the tiny town of Frenchglen underwent an expansion, with the addition of a two-story dance hall hauled in from a ghost town not far away. The town hasn't grown much since then, but the recent conversion of the house into a quietly elegant inn by Lance and Missy Litchy has considerably increased its allure.

The Litchys are a young couple who traded in careers in Bend—hers as an art director, his working at the Mt. Bachelor ski area—to buy the 1876 Frenchglen Mercantile and the adjacent house. Careful craftsmanship, well-chosen art and antiques, and unsparing attention to detail have all gone into making the inn a standout destination in Oregon's desert country. The two upstairs guest rooms share a deck with an alder grove to one side and views of Steens Mountain to the other; white-tile private baths are just down the stairs. The Litchys' spare aesthetic is a sure antidote for bed-and-breakfast travelers who have overdosed on frills and Laura Ashley–style prints.

Next door, the Mercantile has also undergone a transformation, from a basic country store to a not-so-basic country store: Travelers essentials such as maps, guidebooks, sunscreen, film, and cold drinks are available, as are Navajo rugs, Native American jewelry, and assorted antique accessories. The Litchys also run the adjacent Buckaroo Room, one of eastern Oregon's best restaurants, with a simple but sophisticated menu of filet mignon, pasta, roast chicken, and salads made from high-quality fresh produce. Breakfast choices vary daily; specialties include Black Forest ham and Tillamook cheddar scrambled eggs with home-style red potatoes, and *huevos rancheros.* 🔔 *2 rooms with detached private baths. Guide service, room service, laundry. $75; full breakfast. AE, D, MC, V. No smoking.*

Washington

Vancouver Island

Strait of Georgia

CANADA BR

542 **U.S.A.** *Mt. Baker Nat'l. Forest*

North Cascades National Park

Ferndale

5

Eastsound *Lummi Island*

Bellingham

9

Deer Harbor **Olga**

Orcas

Friday Harbor

Victoria

SAN JUAN ISLANDS

Lopez Island

Anacortes Burlington

20

Mt. Vernon

Stehek

Neah Bay

Strait *of Juan de Fuca*

Cape Flattery 112

Olympic Peninsula

Clallam Bay

Lake Ozette

113

Port Angeles

Dungeness National Wildlife Refuge Dungeness

Whidbey Island

La Conner

Coupeville

405

Sequim

Forks

Quilcene

101

Port Townsend

104

Greenbank

Langley

Freeland

Clinton

Mountains

Snoqualmie National Forest

Cascade

2

110

La Push

101

OLYMPIC MOUNTAINS

Olympic National Park

Port Gamble

Poulsbo

Bainbridge Island

Kirkland

203

Kalaloch

Queets

101

Quinault

Olympic National Forest

Bremerton

Port Orchard

Bremerton

Seattle Bellevue

Puget Sound

Renton Issaquah

Snoqualmie

Snoqualmie Falls

90

Quinault Indian Reservation

16

Maple Valley

Roslyn 970

Moclips

109

101

Shelton

Tacoma

Buckley

South Cle Elum

Ocean Shores

Aberdeen

12

8

⭐ **Olympia**

410

410

Montesano

105

Westport

12

5

7

Mt. Rainier National Park

North Cove

Leadbetter State Park

Oysterville

Nahcotta

Ocean Park

Chehalis

Elbe 706

Ashford

12

103

Long Beach

101

Naselle

6

Morton

12

Seaview

Ilwaco

Chinook

4

Cathlamet

Gifford Pinchot National Forest

▲ *Mt. Adams*

Yakima Indian Res.

Cape Disappointment

Astoria

Columbia River

Kelso

Glenwood

Seaside

OREGON

503

Trout Lake

PACIFIC OCEAN

N

Vancouver

14

White Salmon

Bingen

8

Portland

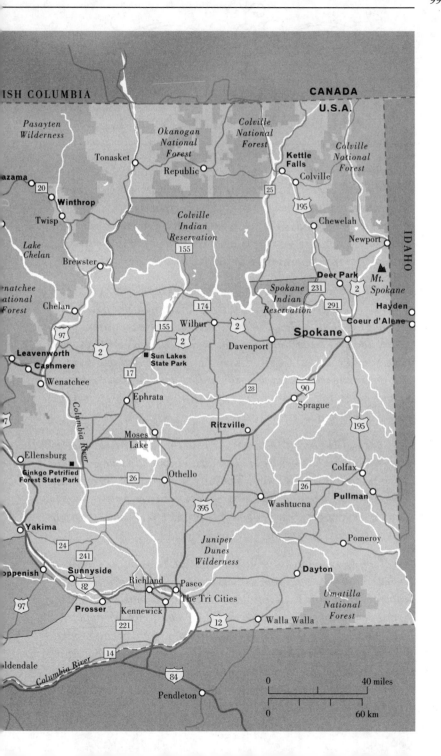

COLUMBIA RIVER AND
LONG BEACH PENINSULA

The Columbia River Valley and Long Beach Peninsula offer a variety of outdoor experiences. Scenery in the valley is striking, with a deep gorge cutting through forested hills and rugged cliffs. Farther west, visitors flock to the peninsula for its sandy beaches, ocean swells, and migrating birds. The peninsula's reputation for fine cuisine is another big drawing card. Both areas offer many opportunities for hiking and nature walks.

The mighty Columbia River, which forms much of the Washington–Oregon border, has a rich geological, cultural, and natural history. Its bounty of salmon once fed many native tribes and later supported a thriving fishing industry. Today, in addition to providing electrical power to much of the Northwest and the West Coast, the river provides water-sports enthusiasts with one of the world's prime sailboarding sites—with winds often at 30 mph or more, the 70 mi of river from Bingen to Roosevelt draws more than 200,000 windsurfers annually.

An 80-mi stretch of Highway 14 traces the wild and scenic river where it slices through a canyon between walls of basalt, designated as the Columbia River Gorge National Scenic Area. The only sea-level cut through the Cascade Mountains, the gorge divides areas of very diverse climates: The wetter western portions get up to 80 inches of rain each year, while the high-desert area on the east may get as little as 10 inches.

Northeast of the Gorge, across the Yakima Indian Reservation, is Washington's wine country. Bitterly cold winters make the Yakima Valley nearly inhospitable to grapevine cultivation, but long, hot summer days bring the fruit to super-ripeness, while cool nights help to retain the acids that give wines structure. The result is that Washington vintners can produce warm-climate varietals, such as Merlot and Cabernet Sauvignon, which in balance and depth of flavor rival those of California. The Valley's wineries stretch from Yakima in the north downriver nearly to the Columbia; most are within easy reach of I–82.

Just north of the mouth of the Columbia, in the southwest corner of the state, is the Long Beach Peninsula, with a chain of small fishing villages and the longest uninterrupted stretch (28 mi) of sandy ocean beach in North America. The area offers good hiking and beachcombing, but because of tremendous undertows and shifting sands, this is not a very safe place for swimming—there are several drownings each year. Driving on the beach is still a hotly disputed issue among residents, but in 1990 the state legislature closed about 40% of it to motor vehicles from April through Labor Day. A half-mi-long wooden boardwalk in Long Beach features disabled-access ramps, benches, telescopes, and great views, but no vendors. The entire peninsula is a perfect place to enjoy a winter storm, with howling winds and huge breakers crashing on the beach.

A favorite pastime in the area is bird-watching. Migrating white trumpeter swans frequent marshes a mile or two inland, and on Long Island— an islet on the bay side of the peninsula that is home to an old-growth red cedar grove—are found the highly controversial spotted owl and the marbled murrelet.

PLACES TO GO, SIGHTS TO SEE

Bingen. The area's first white settler, Erastus Joslyn, arrived in 1852 and built his home and farm close to the Columbia River, just west of the present town of Bingen. The home was destroyed in a conflict with Native Americans, but Joslyn eventually built another one in town on Steuben Street; it came to be called the *Grand Old House* for its ornate Victorian architecture. On Jefferson Street, the *Theodore Suksdorf House* was the home of Bingen's founder, who originally hailed from Bingen-on-the-Rhine in Germany—thus the town's name. The *Wilhelm Suksdorf House,* built in 1905 by Theodore's son, a renowned botanist who named many native plant species, stands on Lincoln Street. Tours are offered at the *Mont Elise Winery* (315 W. Steuben St., tel. 509/493–3001), one of the oldest family-owned wineries in Washington. The 1911 Methodist Church, at the corner of Steuben and Maple streets, is now the *Gorge Heritage Museum* (tel. 509/493–3228).

Cape Disappointment. This cape at the start of the peninsula got its name from English fur trader Captain John Meares because of his unsuccessful attempt in 1788 to find the Northwest Passage here. On the bluff is one of the oldest lighthouses on the West Coast, first used in 1856. Below the bluff is the *U.S. Coast Guard Station Cape Disappointment* (tel. 360/642–2384), the largest search-and-rescue station on the Northwest coast. The rough conditions of the Columbia River Bar provide intensive training for its *National Motor Lifeboat School,* the only school of its kind. Here, rescue crews from all over the world learn advanced skills in navigation, mechanics, fire fighting, and lifesaving. The observation platform on the north jetty at *Ft. Canby State Park* (tel. 360/642–3078)—site of an active military post until 1957—is a good viewing spot for watching the motor lifeboats during regular surf drills.

Cascade Locks. Before the dams were built on the Columbia River, locks were needed to allow river traffic to bypass the Columbia's dangerous rapids. At Cascade Locks, you can board the stern-wheeler *Columbia Gorge* (tel. 503/223–3928 or 503/374–8427), where a spirited narrator relates tales of the past to the rhythm of the giant paddle wheel. Day trips, dining cruises, and special excursions are offered. The *Cascade Locks Historical Museum* (tel. 503/374–8535) offers a look at the now obsolete locks, a steam locomotive, and other historical artifacts.

Cathlamet. The name of this river town—about an hour west of I–5, and the seat of Wahkiakum ("wa-*ki*-a-kum") County—comes from a Chinook word meaning "stone," so named because the tribe lived here along a stretch of rocky river bed. Today you will find a pleasant marina, some 19th-century houses perched on the hill overlooking the river, and the *Wahkiakum County Historical Museum* (65 River St., no phone). From Cathlamet, you can take a bridge or a ferry—*The Wahkiakum* is the only ferry remaining on the lower Columbia—to *Puget Island.* Settled in 1884 by Scandinavians who brought herds of dairy cattle and built large barns and dikes on the low-lying island, it is popular with bicyclists for its pleasant views of boat moorages, gill-netting boats, dairy farms, and historic churches. About a mile and a half west of Cathlamet on Route 1 is the *Julia Butler Hansen National Wildlife Refuge* (tel. 360/795–3915), named for a woman who served in the U.S. House of Representatives from 1960 to 1975. In addition to protecting the endangered Columbian white-tailed deer, a small deer of the Northwest, the refuge is a wintering area for waterfowl on the Pacific flyway, and home to bald eagles, great blue herons, swans, and herds of elk.

Ft. Columbia State Park and Interpretive Center (Hwy. 101, tel. 360/777–8221). Built in 1903, this fort was one of 27 coastal defense units of the U.S. Army. Many of its 30 structures have been restored to show military life. The park is just 2 mi east of Chinook, a town named for the Native Americans who assisted Lewis and Clark—credited with "discovering" the peninsula—during their stay here in the early 1800s.

Goldendale. The *Presby Mansion* (127 W. Broadway, tel. 509/773–4303 or 509/773–5443) was built in 1902 for Winthrop Bartlett Presby, a lawyer who migrated from New Hampshire in 1888 and eventually served four years as a Washington state senator. His 20-room mansion is now a museum that illustrates pioneer life in Klickitat County and displays Native American artifacts and a collection of coffee grinders. On the northern edge of the town, the *Goldendale Observatory* (1602 Observatory Dr., tel. 509/773–3141) offers interpretive presentations concerning stars and telescopes, as well as tours and other programs; you are welcome to use its 24½-inch Cassergrain reflecting telescope.

Ilwaco. This community of about 600 has a colorful past linked to the fishing industry: From 1884 to 1910, gill-net and trap fishermen were so competitive about rights to the fishing grounds that they fought each other with knives, rifles, and threats of lynchings. Since then fishermen have developed more amicable relationships, and today charters are available for salmon, crab, tuna, and sturgeon fishing. The *Ilwaco Heritage Museum* (115 S.E. Lake St., tel. 360/642–3446) presents the history of southwestern Washington through such exhibits as dioramas on Native Americans, traders, missionaries, and pioneers. It also contains a model of the "clamshell railroad," a narrow-gauge train that ran on a bed of ground clam and oyster shells to transport passengers and mail up and down the peninsula.

Leadbetter State Park (call Ft. Canby State Park for information; *see* Cape Disappointment, *above*). At the northern end of the peninsula, this wildlife refuge is a good spot for bird-watching. The dune area at the point is closed from April through August to protect nesting snowy plovers. Biologists have identified some 100 species here, including black brants, yellowlegs, turnstones, and sanderlings.

Long Beach. Go-cart and bumper-car concessions, an amusement park, and beach activities attract tourists to this town of 1,200, which each year hosts the Washington State International Kite Festival during the third weekend in August. Other peninsula festivals include the Garlic Festival, a tasty tribute to that pungent bulb, held in mid-June, and the Water Music Festival, featuring chamber music at various locations on the third weekend in October.

Maryhill Museum of Art (35 Maryhill Museum Dr., Goldendale, tel. 509/773–3733). Built as a "ranch house" in 1914 and resembling a European château, the museum—opened in 1940—is the result of the efforts and resources of three people: Sam Hill, transportation mogul and heir to the fortune of the Great Northern Railway; his friend Loie Fuller, a pioneer of modern dance who found fame in Paris during the 1890s; and Queen Marie of Romania (Sam did war relief work in Romania after World War I; indebted, the queen came to Washington for the dedication). It includes one of the country's largest collections of Rodin sculpture; an impressive array of Native American baskets, clothing, and photographs; and royal costumes and furniture from the late queen. Nearby is a replica of Britain's Stonehenge, Sam Hill's memorial to soldiers who died in World War I.

Mt. Adams (Ranger Station, Trout Lake, tel. 509/395–2501). At 12,276 ft, Mt. Adams is the second-highest mountain in Washington, but in sheer bulk it is larger than Mt. Rainier. In the vicinity are ice caves, a self-guided-tour area formed by molten lava, and *Big Lava Bed*—12,500 acres of sculptural shapes and caves to be viewed from its edge.

Mt. Hood Scenic Railroad (110 Railroad Ave., Hood River, tel. 503/386–3556). Built in 1906, the train links the Columbia River gorge with the foothills of snowcapped Mt. Hood, at 11,235 ft the highest peak in Oregon. The route offers views of the Cascades, including Mt. Hood and Mt. Adams. Along the way, the train may pick up a carload of lumber or pears—it's still a working freight train.

Mt. St. Helens National Volcanic Monument (Rte. 1, Amboy, tel. 360/247–5473). Devastated by a great volcanic eruption in 1980, Mt. St. Helens is today a national monument. Hiking trails lead up through a regenerated evergreen forest to the mile-high crater, its lava dome, and Ape Cave, an extremely long lava tube (12,810 ft). Sporadic eruptions continue to spew steam and gases, giving lucky hikers a free show. There's a visitor center in *Castle Rock* (3029 Spirit Lake Hwy., tel. 360/274–6644).

Oysterville. This tiny community once thrived on the oyster industry but nearly turned into a ghost town when the native shellfish were harvested to extinction. Tides have washed away homes and businesses, but a handful of late-19th-century structures still exist. Free maps inside the restored Oysterville Church direct you through the one-street village, now on the National Register of Historic Places.

Yakima Valley Wineries. The more than two dozen wineries between Yakima and Richland range in size from tiny *Thurston Wolfe* (Prosser, tel. 509/786–3313) to the 500,000-case *Columbia Crest* (Paterson, tel. 509/875–2061), whose winery building alone covers 9 acres; most have tasting rooms open to the public. *Staton Hills* (tel. 509/877–2112) in Wapato and *Horizon's Edge* (tel. 509/829–6401), in Zillah, boast panoramic views of the valley and parts of the Cascades. The gift shop at *The Hogue Cellars* (tel. 509/786–4557) offers award-winning wines as well as products from the Hogue family farm. Opening hours and facilities vary widely; they're listed in a brochure published by the *Yakima Valley Wine Growers Association* (tel. 800/258–7270).

RESTAURANTS

The Ark Restaurant & Bakery (on Willapa Bay, Nahcotta, tel. 360/665–4133) was praised by the late James Beard for its fresh local seafood. The **Shoalwater Restaurant** at the Shelburne Inn (Seaview, tel. 360/642–4142, *see below*) serves nationally acclaimed Northwest cuisine—lots of seafood and local produce such as edible ferns—offering vegetarian options and a children's menu. Also in Seaview, **Cheri Walker's 42nd St. Cafe** (tel. 360/642–2323) is a neighborhood restaurant with intriguing gourmet preparations of seafood, steaks, and pasta at reasonable prices. The **Sanctuary** (Chinook, tel. 360/777–8380), in a former church, serves a varied menu, including decadent desserts.

TOURIST INFORMATION

Goldendale Chamber of Commerce (Box 524, 903 E. Broadway, Goldendale, WA 98620, tel. 509/773–3400). **Long Beach Peninsula Visitors Bureau** (Box 562, Long Beach, WA 98631, tel. 360/642–2400 or 800/451–2542). **Tri-Cities Visitor & Convention Bureau** (Box 2241, Tri-Cities, WA 99302-2241, tel. 509/735–8486 or 800/254–5824). **Washington State Tourism** (Box 42500, Olympia, WA 98504-2500, tel. 800/544–1800).

RESERVATION SERVICES

Pacific Reservation Service (Box 46894, Seattle, WA 98146, tel. 206/439–7677 or 800/684–2932). **Washington State Bed & Breakfast Guild** (Box 355-FD, 2442 N.W. Market St., Seattle, WA 98107, tel. 800/647–2918).

BINGEN HAUS 🐚
Box 818, Bingen, WA 98605, tel. 509/493–4888, fax 509/493–2771

After pioneers Erastus and Mary Joslyn's first home was burned to the ground in a Native American uprising, they built the house that is now Bingen Haus in 1860. Besides holding church services here, they also offered travelers passing through town by boat or horse free lodging for the night. The tradition endures now, although the B&B is no longer free. Still it's well-worth a visit to this sturdy old Victorian in the Columbia River Gorge. Innkeepers Tom Leiner and Sheila Brown have made it into a solid B&B with an offbeat feel.

Before opening in 1994, Leiner had the house blessed by a Native American shaman to rid the place of any bad vibes hanging over from pioneer days. Each room is eclectically decorated. One has a king-size, vintage 1970s waterbed and ceiling mirrors; another has a 48-star flag and Old Glory pillow cases; and a third has a delicate brass bed.

Breakfasts can be a bit rich, with French oven pancakes, Haus Kuchen, and German bread pudding all competing for attention. Guests can work off the calories with a walk around the town's historic sites, including the homes of Theodore Suksdorf and his son Wilhelm, the important botanical explorer. △ *6 double rooms share 2 baths. Hot tub. $65–$85; full breakfast. MC, V. No smoking.*

BIRCHFIELD MANOR 🐚
2018 Birchfield Rd., Yakima, WA 98901, tel. 509/452–1960 or 800/375–3420, fax 509/452–2334

What is now Birchfield Manor, 2 mi outside Yakima, was once the headquarters of a sprawling, 15,000-acre sheep ranch. The scale of the property is considerably diminished these days, but the elegance of the 1910 manor house remains. If anything, things have improved at Birchfield with the arrival of chef and owner Wil Masset.

Masset, who apprenticed in Switzerland, came with his wife, Sandy, and family to the Yakima Valley from Issaquah, where he taught classic cuisine. In addition to turning the ground floor into an award-winning restaurant, the owners have greatly expanded the accommodations with a large guest cottage. Rooms in the new building have TVs and private-line telephones, and most have whirlpool tubs and private decks with panoramic views of the valley. There are fewer modern amenities in the original structure, but there's more old-house charm, with a sunporch in one room and corner bays in two others.

The Birchfield's dinner menu changes seasonally, and may include king salmon in puff pastry, filet mignon, and rack of lamb; guests in the cottage can arrange to have dinner delivered to their room. The extensive wine list is particularly strong in wines of the Northwest. Breakfast involves a large country spread of quiche and other egg dishes, breakfast meats, and fresh local fruits. The Massets have also turned the 1893 carriage house into a cigar lounge; with a refined interior and an array of wing chairs, it looks as though it were taken straight out of an exclusive private club. △ *11 double rooms with baths. TV and whirlpool bath in some rooms. Restaurant. $80–$175; full breakfast. AE, DC, MC, V. No smoking.*

BOREA'S BED & BREAKFAST INN ▧
607 North Blvd., Long Beach, WA 98631, tel. 360/642–8069 or 888/642–8069;
www.boreasinn.com

The North Wind blows over the Long Beach Peninsula in the summer and sweeps away the fog, creating the clear warm weather that prevails over the Pacific beaches. In appreciation of this natural benevolence, Boreas Bed & Breakfast is named after the Greek god of that wind.

The 1920's beach home is close enough to the center of Long Beach for convenience, but far enough away from town for peace and quiet. Two large living rooms look out onto the ocean, and a path winds through beach grasses down the long city lot that stretches all the way to the sand. Just outside the back door is a hot tub in a newly constructed cedar and glass enclosure; there is just one key for it, hanging in the kitchen, so guests can use it in total privacy.

Rooms are furnished with a mixture of antiques and contemporary furniture; all have ample natural light, some have ocean views, and one has its own whirlpool tub. Owners Susie Goldsmith and Bill Verner usually serve their expertly prepared breakfasts, which feature homemade breads, fresh fruit, and hot entrées, in the dining room—but in keeping with the romantic character of the place, they'll be happy to bring it to your room instead. △ *5 double rooms with baths. Whirlpool bath in 1 room. Hot tub. $105–$135; full breakfast. AE, D, DC, MC, V. No smoking.*

BRADLEY HOUSE BED & BREAKFAST ▧
61 Main St., Cathlamet, WA 98612, tel. 360/795–3030 or 800/551–1691;
bradleyhouse@transport.com

Perched on a hill in Cathlamet overlooking the Columbia River is this Eastlake-style house built in 1907. Real estate appraiser Tony West and his wife, Barbara, a teacher, bought the place in 1991 after seeking a change from their San Francisco Bay area jobs.

The house has never been remodeled; except for wallpaper, curtains, and paint, it's all original, including oak floors inlaid with mahogany, the Douglas fir staircase off the foyer, and striking Povey stained glass from Portland. The living room features built-in bookcases, an overstuffed pink velvet sofa and chair, a pink Oriental rug from the 1930s, and the same Morris chair shown in a 1910 photo of the room when the house was still owned by the Bradleys, a prominent Cathlamet family at the turn of the century.

Each guest room is filled with comfortable, grandma's-attic-type furniture. The Monet Room is decorated in pink and white, with white-painted furniture. The Rose Room has a king-size bed with floral canopy and spread, an Oriental rug, and a large bay window. These two front guest rooms overlook the river and the marina; the back rooms overlook the gardens. Breakfast includes muffins and a hot dish such as apple pancakes, cheese and herb soufflés, veggie frittatas, or, in winter, poached fruit. △ *2 double rooms with baths, 2 doubles share bath. $75–$95; full breakfast, afternoon refreshments. MC, V. No smoking.*

CASWELL'S ON THE BAY 🐚
25204 Sandridge Rd., Ocean Park, WA 98640, tel. 360/665–6535;
www.site-works.com/caswells

Bob Caswell's grandmother built a cabin on the Long Beach peninsula nearly a century ago, and the family has been coming to visit ever since. Now Bob and his wife Marilyn have built their own place here as a working retirement, and a modest family cabin it's not: the 6,500-square-ft Victorian-style home treats its guests to luxurious accommodations in a spectacular setting on the shore of Willapa Bay. The interior of the house is designed to showcase the location to maximum effect. From enormous windows under 22-ft ceilings in the common room, the panorama includes the Coast Range, Long Island (part of the Willapa National Wildlife Refuge), and the pristine waters of the bay itself—which during high tides seems quite close indeed. You can also enjoy the view from the huge covered veranda.

Even among antiques-filled inns, Caswell's is a standout. The rooms are furnished with entire bedroom sets, including an Eastlake ensemble in walnut and a 1793 French oak set in superb condition; not only are they remarkable pieces, but they also help to tone down the newness of the house. Modern amenities include monogrammed robes, freshly pressed 250-thread-count cotton sheets, and individual temperature control in each guest room.

The Caswells prepare their ample breakfasts with an emphasis on presentation and quality of ingredients. Fresh fruit, a warm dish, and a breakfast dessert, such as marionberry cobbler or lemon soufflée, are always on the menu. △ *5 double rooms with baths. $95–$150; full breakfast, afternoon refreshments. D, DC, MC, V. No smoking.*

CHICK-A-DEE INN AT ILWACO 🐚
120 Williams St., Ilwaco, WA 98624, tel. 360/642–8686 or 888/244–2523, fax 360/642–8642

Perched on a knoll in the fishing village of Ilwaco, at the mouth of the Columbia River, is this inn, built in 1879 and then later moved and rebuilt, in 1928, as a Presbyterian church. The Georgian-style building has recently undergone extensive sprucing up inside, and innkeepers Chick and Delaine Hinkle keep the parking area in style as well, with a restored 1940 Cadillac limo.

The salmon-and-white common area is spacious, with 13-ft ceilings, large windows, Oriental rugs, a fireplace, and eclectic furnishings, including a French Provincial sofa and chair upholstered in soft green. The most outstanding accommodation is a two-bedroom suite just off the common room, dubbed the Captain's Quarters. The suite features deep navy blue carpeting and quilts, nautical charts on the walls, a wet bar, and waste baskets from the Hotel Queen Mary. The second room is more befitting an ensign, but still as crisp in blue and white as an Annapolis morning. Upper floor guest rooms, occupying the former Sunday school, are cozy, with country furnishings and fir floors with throw rugs. Several feature dormer windows with window seats, and some have the original board-and-bead wood paneling.

The sanctuary is sometimes used as a wedding chapel or meeting place, but on a day-to-day basis it serves as a backdrop to breakfast, which is served on the altar stage. Breakfast features such entrées as quiche or French toast with cream cheese and nuts, topped with a sauce of walnuts, bananas, and cranberries. △ *8 double rooms with baths, 1 suite. $76–$180; full breakfast. MC, V. No smoking, 2-night minimum for summer weekends and holidays.*

COAST WATCH BED & BREAKFAST ☙

Box 841, Ocean Park, WA 98640, tel. 360/665–6774; www.willapabay.org/~kmj/cw

When Karen Johnston came to the peninsula for a weekend one spring, she saw this contemporary ocean-front house, overlooking an expanse of grass-covered dunes, for sale. Partway home to Bellingham, she turned around, returned to the peninsula, signed an agreement to buy it, then rushed back home just in time for work.

Each of the two airy guest suites has a private entry and living room, and either a telescope or binoculars for watching shorebirds, stars, or passing ships on the horizon. Both are decorated with contemporary furnishings in earth tones and have views of the Pacific Ocean, the dunes, and the beach. One suite includes prints by local artist Eric Wiegardt and Norma Walker; a fishing net hangs on the wall over the bed.

Karen provides a mini-refrigerator in each suite to chill guests' wine bottles. Breakfast includes caffe latte, deadly-to-your-waistline cinnamon rolls served under glass domes, and individual platters of up to eight kinds of fresh fruit, which Karen sometimes drives as far as 40 miles to get. △ *2 suites. Mini-refrigerator in suites. $95; Continental-plus breakfast. MC, V. No smoking.*

FARM BED AND BREAKFAST ☙

490 Sunnyside Rd., Trout Lake, WA 98650, tel. 509/395–2488; www.gorge.net/business/farmbnb

Dean and Rosie Hostetter had passed through the Trout Lake Valley for almost 30 years on the way to their cabin in the hills. When retirement time came, the Portland couple, who both worked in insurance, decided to come down to the valley and run a bed-and-breakfast.

The 1890 farmhouse on 6 acres leapt out at them. Since opening the B&B in the spring of 1995, the Hostetters have fashioned a fun, relaxing getaway for world travelers and weekenders from Portland and Seattle. The inn is close to Trout Lake Farm, the nation's largest certified organic grower of botanicals and herbs.

The Hostetters have decorated the place with their collection of antiques, including a Queen Anne buffet and Dean's authentic turn-of-the-century pharmacy dispenser complete with original ointments. Also on display is the couple's collection of old pattern glass, Beam figures, and Steuben glasswork.

Both guest rooms are upstairs. The quilt room features early 1900s quilts on the bed, heirlooms from Rosie's family. Across the hall is the 1890 room, which includes local, turn-of-the-century Native American baskets, a Victorian love seat, and primitive paintings of the Cascade range. The two rooms share a modern bath with a double shower, glass bricks, and sponge-painted walls.

Breakfast is served near the woodstove; favorites are huckleberry pancakes, scones, fresh fruit, local sausage, Dutch babies, and the special "400 mile" oatmeal. △ *2 double rooms share bath. Robes in rooms. Bicycles, area tours. $70–$80; full breakfast, box lunches available. No credit cards. No smoking.*

FLYING L RANCH 𝕎
25 Flying L La., Glenwood, WA 98619, tel. 509/364–3488 or 888/682–3267, fax 509/364–3634; www.gorge.net/lodging/flyingl

About 30 mi north of the Columbia River, nestled in the ponderosa pines and meadows of the Glenwood Valley, is the Flying L Ranch, with spectacular views of Mt. Adams—at nearly 13,000 ft, the second-highest peak in the state—only 15 mi away. Jaquie Perry and Jeff Berend have recently bought the ranch, but they still run it in the style of the former owners, who grew up there.

The look of the interior is rustic Western ranch–style, with well-worn and mismatched but comfortable furniture. The large common area has wood paneling, a beamed ceiling, Navajo rugs, a stone fireplace whose log mantel is emblazoned with the Flying L brand, and Western art. The simply furnished, almost austere guest rooms feature firm beds with comforters.

You can rent bicycles to explore the area, or stroll the ranch's more than 2 mi of marked trails, pond, and picnic areas where lupine, Indian paintbrush, and other wildflowers grow. Mt. Adams is a popular and relatively easy ascent for novice climbers, and the trailhead at Cold Creek campground is not far away. Three-night summer packages include escorted day hikes on the mountain, naturalist programs, and dinners at local restaurants. Breakfasts are hearty, with baked egg dishes, huckleberry pancakes—often on the hob—and plenty of fresh fruit. △ *8 double rooms with baths, 2 doubles share 2 baths, 3 cabins. 2 common kitchens, bicycles, hot tub. $70–$110; full breakfast. AE, MC, V. No smoking.*

INN AT WHITE SALMON 𝕎
172 W. Jewett St., White Salmon, WA 98672, tel. 509/493–2335 or 800/972–5226; www.gorge.net/lodging/iws

After 30 years, Roger Holen had had enough of the computer business, so in 1990 he and his wife, Janet, a nurse, became innkeepers. From the outside, their place is short on appeal: a plain brick hotel built in 1937 and set on the main street of the small river town of White Salmon. But don't let appearances deceive you: The interior has a lot of charm.

Highlights of the lobby include beveled glass and a large brass cash register on a marble-top mahogany desk. The parlor features an 8-ft-tall oak sideboard from the 1890s and hand-painted lithographs. Each guest room features a few antiques, such as brass or ornate wood headboards. The bridal suite has a sitting area with a mahogany Eastlake settee upholstered in rose. Breakfast is an extravaganza: some 20 pastries and breads, including a chocolate raspberry cheesecake, and a choice of entrées such as artichoke frittata, broccoli quiche, and other egg dishes.

The easterly wind blows incessantly here, and the stretch of the Columbia just below town is a boardsailing mecca; Hood River, the capital of the windsurfing world, is just across the water. Whether or not you're here to ride the whitecaps, White Salmon is a more sedate alternative to Hood River, which gets crowded with "boardheads" in the summer. ⚿ *16 double rooms with baths. Air-conditioning, TV, phone in rooms. Hot tub. $99–$129; full breakfast. AE, D, DC, MC, V. No smoking in common rooms.*

KOLA HOUSE BED & BREAKFAST ☞
211 Pearl Ave., Ilwaco, WA 98624, tel. 360/642–2819; ljl@willapabay.org

During the 1930s, Oscar Luokkala used to stay at Kola House when it was in its first incarnation—a boardinghouse in the windswept fishing community of Ilwaco. In 1980, Luokkala bought the old place just off the harbor, on the edge of a quiet residential neighborhood, and set about redoing it in his spare time when he wasn't working on his busy construction business in the Portland area. Now the Kola House, bearing the name of the boat-building family that constructed it in 1919, is a sturdy bed-and-breakfast in the little town best known as a jumping-off place for deep-sea fishing off the mouth of the Columbia River. In recognition of the builder's heritage (and Oscar's, too), the doormat reads "Tervetuloa"—Finnish for "Welcome."

The decor is very basic, but two of the upstairs rooms offer harbor views. Three rooms have skylights in the bath, and the suite hosts a fireplace and a cozy Finnish sauna. Just seaward of the house is a small cabin that is often booked by fishermen heading out early in the morning.

The dining area is dominated by a large built-in oak cupboard featuring family china. Breakfasts also tend toward the basics, with ham, eggs, pancakes, and muffins being common fare. ⚿ *4 double rooms with baths, 1 suite, 1 cabin. Fireplace and Finnish sauna in suite. $60–$75; full breakfast. MC, V. No smoking.*

LAND'S END ☞
Box 1199, Long Beach, WA 98361, tel. 360/642–8268

Isolated amid the sand dunes of the peninsula and facing the Pacific Ocean, Land's End is the large, contemporary, Northwest-style home of former teacher Jackie Faas. Aptly named after the windswept westernmost point in England, the house offers a private path to the beach and equally private accommodations.

The living room is spacious and remarkably bright, with a marble fireplace, grand piano, Eastlake furnishings, Oriental rugs, and 6-ft-high windows framing panoramic ocean views. So distinctive is the interior, it was once selected for an Eddie Bauer catalogue photo shoot. On the ground floor are the two guest rooms, done up in country style. The larger room has an ornamental Dutch enamel cookstove; its bath features a large soaking tub with a dark wood surround. A framed antique quilt that may have been made in the 1850s in an Oregon Trail wagon train is the focal point of the smaller bedroom.

Jackie prides herself on pampering her guests, stocking each room with fresh fruit, flowers, and candy. Breakfast—typically featuring apples baked in sherry and poached eggs over smoked salmon with a white wine sauce—is presented on silver and china in the formal dining room, in view of the ocean. ⚿ *2 double rooms with baths. Cable TV in rooms. $95–$120; full breakfast. MC, V. No smoking.*

MOBY DICK HOTEL AND OYSTER FARM 🦪

Sandridge Rd., Box 82, Nahcotta, WA 98637, tel. 360/665–4543, fax 360/665–6887;
www.nwplace.com/mobydick.html

Built in 1929 by a railroad conductor who had struck it rich mining gold in Alaska, the Moby Dick has seen many years of service both as a hotel and, during World War II, barracks for the U.S. Coast Guard Horse Patrol. A rather utilitarian piece of architecture on 7 acres of forest, it has a boxy simplicity softened by kitchen gardens and landscaping. Inside, a Southwestern color scheme and funky, artsy decor capitalizes on abundant natural light. The inn's owners, Fritzi and Edward Cohen, also own the Hotel Tabard Inn, a well-known "literary" hotel in Washington, D.C.

Guest rooms are simply furnished; each is provided with a copy of *Moby Dick* or another Herman Melville classic, along with an artwork or a bedspread that reflects the room's theme, such as a mended heart, birds, or the sea. Bathrooms have become miniature art galleries for the hotel's eclectic collection. A new addition to the hotel is a stately cedar sauna pavilion about 50 yards from the main building, with a porch overlooking the bay. Also on the grounds is the "Spartina Institute," a paper-making workshop devoted to turning the peninsula's curse of spartina, an invasive species also known as cordgrass, into a blessing.

The hotel has its own oyster bed, and breakfasts regularly feature oysters done many ways, as well as organic produce from the garden. ♦ *1 double room with bath, 9 doubles share 5 baths. TV in common area. $75–$95; full breakfast. AE, MC, V. No smoking, 2-night minimum on summer weekends.*

SCANDINAVIAN GARDENS INN 🦪

1610 California St., Long Beach, WA 98631, tel. 360/642–8877 or 800/988–9277;
www.aone.com/~rdakan

When you enter the Scandinavian Gardens, innkeepers Rod and Marilyn Dakan will ask you to take off your shoes. It may have nothing to do with Scandinavian custom, but you can immediately see a practical reason—the white wool carpeting that covers the ground floor. The house is immaculate; there doesn't seem to be a single corner where even the most fastidious person wouldn't feel comfortable eating lutefisk off the floor.

The main common area, with its white carpet and blond-wood furnishings, is somewhat intimidating, but the colorful guest rooms easily compensate for it. On the main floor is the Icelandic Room, done in plums and greens, with an antique armoire and love seat and rosemaling on wall cabinet doors. The Danish Room, all blue and cinnamon tones, is decorated with hearts and nautical knickknacks. The Norwegian Room features greens and golds and a simple pine bed.

Upstairs, the teal and red Finnish Room offers such special touches as a skylight in the bath and an antique vanity. The main attraction here, however, is the Swedish Suite, done in soft pinks and light blues. The view is pedestrian— guests look out on the surrounding residential area— but inside there's a hot tub for two with an overhead skylight. The bedroom features a teak bed set, antique vanity, and a half-bath of its own.

Even if you haven't booked the honeymoon suite, you need not go without a hot soak: The recreation room offers a hot tub, sauna, and exercise equipment. You can also enjoy the games in the social room, which doubles as the dining area. Breakfast is a feast, including traditional creamed rice and fruit soup, granola, sorbet, pastries, and a hot entrée. ♦ *4 double rooms with baths, 1 suite. Hot tub and mini-refrigerator in suite. Exercise room, hot tub, sauna, games room. $85–*

$140; full breakfast. D, MC, V. No smoking, 2-night minimum on holiday and local festival weekends.

SHELBURNE INN 🍍

4415 Pacific Way, Box 250, Seaview, WA 98644, tel. 360/642–2442 or 800/466–1896, fax 360/642–8904; www.theshelburneinn.com

The Shelburne Inn, a green wood-frame building on the peninsula's main thoroughfare, is the oldest continuously-run hotel in the state. Opened in 1896, the Craftsman-style inn joined to a late Victorian building is owned by Laurie Anderson and David Campiche. David met Laurie—who had worked for a cruise line and traveled widely before settling here—when he helped pull her vehicle out of the sand.

The inn has a homey, country atmosphere. The lobby is somewhat cramped, with a seating area around a fireplace, a church altar as a check-in desk, a large oak breakfast table, and more. The original beaded-fir paneling, as well as large panels of Art Nouveau stained glass rescued from an old church in England, are found throughout the inn. A new section, built in 1983, is quieter than the older sections, though the latter have been soundproofed and carpeted.

Fresh flowers, original artwork, and fine art prints adorn the guest rooms, most of which have decks or balconies. Some rooms feature country pine furnishings, others mahogany or oak. Beds have either handmade quilts or hand-crocheted spreads. Some rooms are rather small, but the suites are spacious.

The Shelburne's breakfast is one of the top three, if not *the* best, in the state. David makes use of regional produce from wild mushrooms to local seafood, and Laurie does all the baking. You can choose from among five or six entrées, which may include an asparagus omelet or grilled oysters with salsa. The highly regarded Shoalwater Restaurant, housed in the enclosed front porch, offers such elegant entrées as duck with dried cherry sauce. The wine list has more than 400 titles. The Heron and Beaver Pub serves light meals, along with the best concoctions from the Northwest's microbreweries. △ *13 double rooms with baths, 2 suites. Restaurant, pub. $109–$179; full breakfast. AE, MC, V. No smoking, 2-night minimum on weekends and holidays.*

SOU'WESTER LODGE 🍍

Beach Access Rd., Box 102, Seaview, WA 98644, tel. 360/642–2542

Just behind the sand dunes on the peninsula is this red-shingle, three-story inn. Make no mistake about it: The Sou'wester is not for everyone. Perhaps more than any other B&B in the state, it is an experience weighted as much by the unique character of the innkeepers as it is by the setting, a big old lodge built in 1892 as the country estate of Senator Henry Winslow Corbett of Oregon.

Len and Miriam Atkins left their native South Africa in the early 1950s to work in Israel, then moved to Chicago to work with the late child psychologist Bruno Bettelheim. With the idea of establishing a treatment program on the West Coast for emotionally disturbed children, they spent six months in 1981 in a camper, scouting potential sites. Instead, they opted to help adults unwind from the stresses of daily life.

An unusual aspect of the Sou'wester is that it bills itself not as a B&B but as a B&MYODB (make your own darn breakfast), with kitchen access provided (but not food). Second- and third-story accommodations are suites with full kitchens and views of the Pacific. Guest rooms are furnished with the occasional antique but more often Salvation Army furniture, with marbleized linoleum floors; nicer touches are the handmade quilts or chenille bedspreads and artwork done by various artists while staying in that room.

Another slightly offbeat note that adds to the Sou'wester's charm is the collection of guest cabins and trailers scattered among the firs. The cabins are a bit more rustic than the guest rooms. Trailers feature handsome blond-wood interiors with lots of 1950s rounded corners. The Disoriented Express features an exterior mural of a train full of animal passengers. Tent and RV spots are also available. ♨ *3 double rooms share bath, 6 suites, 4 cabins, 15 trailers. Kitchen in suites, cabins, and trailers; cable TV on request in some units. $39–$119; no breakfast. D, MC, V. No smoking, pets allowed in outdoor units only.*

SUNNYSIDE INN ♥

800 E. Edison Ave., Sunnyside, WA 98944, tel. 509/839–5557 or 800/221–4195, fax 509/839–5350; www.bbhost.com/sunnysideinn

If you spend much time in the Yakima Valley, you'll understand how Sunnyside got its name; with 300 sunny days a year, the valley might make you forget that you're in the Pacific Northwest. All that sun makes for abundant natural light in the Sunnyside Inn, a large 1919 Craftsman-style home close to the center of town.

The 10 rooms are uncommonly spacious—even the bathrooms are larger than some guest rooms you may have stayed in. All are equipped with cable television and phones, and all bathrooms but one have "double occupancy" whirlpool tubs. The other bathroom stills boasts its 1919 fixtures, including a remarkable original bathtub. Four of the rooms have their own entrances, and three have extra twin beds, one in an enclosed sunporch.

Owners Karen and Don Vlieger, who moved here from Southern California in 1989, make ample breakfasts of hot muffins and pastries and main dishes featuring Yakima valley produce, and there's plenty to do to work them off, with golf, tennis, and fishing nearby. Sunnyside is also about as close to the center of the Yakima Valley wine country as you can get. The town itself is pretty sedate, though it may not seem that way amid heavy daytime traffic; once evening rolls around, however, the cars vanish, and the neighborhood around the inn is a great place for a long after-dinner walk. ♨ *9 double rooms with baths, 1 suite. Whirlpool baths in most rooms. $59–$89; full breakfast. AE, D, MC, V. No smoking.*

TOUCH OF EUROPE BED AND BREAKFAST INN ♥

220 N. 16th Ave., Yakima, WA 98902, tel. 509/454–9775 or 888/438–7073; www.winesnw.com/toucheuropeb&b.htm

At the foot of the stairs of A Touch of Europe, the "History Wall," a collection of framed photographs, tells much of the story of this gracious 1889 Queen Anne Victorian on the National Register of Historic Places. The house was built by Yakima pioneer and lumber baron Charles Pollock Wilcox, and was later home to Ina Phillips Williams, one of Washington's first women legislators. It was while she lived here that President Teddy Roosevelt came to stay, which explains why his picture hangs among those of the former residents.

The house is now owned by Jim and Erika Cenci, former Tacoma restaurateurs who bought it in 1995 and turned it into one of the Yakima Valley's finest bed-and-breakfasts. They have taken care to preserve the house—with its box-beam ceiling, extensive millwork, and stained glass—as well as its history; the library includes an archive of documents, letters, and clippings dating back a century. Guest rooms are furnished with antiques, including a superb mid-1800's fainting couch.

Erika, whose mother was a chef at Berlin's Rathskeller, is a superb cook, with three cookbooks to her credit. Her breakfasts include omelettes from farm-fresh eggs, assorted cheeses and meats, and freshly-baked crumpets or popovers. ♠ *1 double room with bath, 2 doubles share bath. Library. $65–$110; full breakfast, lunch and dinner by arrangement. AE, MC, V. No smoking.*

TROUT LAKE COUNTRY INN ☙
15 Guler Rd., Trout Lake, WA 98650, tel. 509/395–2898

In 1904, pioneers in the upper Trout Lake Valley built a large hall for community meetings. Since then the rustic western-style building, with its distinctive false front, has been everything from a post office to a bowling alley to a public bath house.

Whatever the incarnation, the building has always been the center of the small community of ranchers and farmers wedged up against the bulk of Mt. Adams about 25 mi north of the Columbia River. Since 1988, it has been a charming bed-and-breakfast run by Gil and Milly Martin. Besides catering to guests who may be on their way to a rigorous hike in the wilderness or a breezy drive around the northeast side of Mt. St. Helens, the Trout Lake Country Inn offers a restaurant, country store, soda fountain, dinner theater, and small video store for locals.

Straight past the soda fountain–cum–cash register–cum–registration desk, lies the main hall. Across the stage up front is a hand-painted drop curtain emblazoned with "Trout Lake Art Players" in the style of old vaudeville acts. Gil writes his own plays, usually comedy revues or melodramas starring Milly.

Accommodations—two rooms upstairs and one in a nearby cabin—are simple and rustic. The pine walls are original, cut by a local mill at the turn of the century. The creekside cabin is a treat, built on top of the icehouse that once served the whole settlement. The cabin's deck provides perhaps the best view of Mt. Adams in the valley and is just above a swimming hole in the creek.

Served in the main hall, breakfast is a tasty collection of fresh fruit, huckleberry pancakes, and baked egg dishes. Besides the dinner theater, meals and snacks are also available to you from a small, but diverse menu. ♠ *1 double room with bath, 1 suite, 1 cabin. Restaurant, soda fountain, dinner theater, gift shop. $55–$90; full breakfast. MC, V. No smoking.*

WINE COUNTRY INN ☙
1106 Wine Country Rd., Prosser, WA 99350, tel. 509/786–2855, fax 509/786–7414

The small, dusty town of Prosser lies on the Yakima River, near the area's abundant cherry orchards and within close reach of some of the state's best wineries. Right on the riverbank is the Wine Country Inn, a simple turn-of-the-century house featuring comfortably modest lodging and sophisticated dining.

Built in 1898, the house was transformed into apartments in the 1950's, which explains the kitchenette in one of the upstairs rooms. Ten years ago, Chris Flodin and Audrey Zuniga, friends from the area, bought it and converted it to a bed-and-breakfast. The four quiet guest rooms are decorated in a spare and unpretentious way, like an old country farmhouse. One upstairs room has wood floors and a skylit bath with shower, and a room on the main floor overlooks the river.

The restaurant, just off the lobby, is one of the wine country's finest, with entrées including duck with spicy Madeira sauce, New York steak with wild mushrooms, and ravioli Florentine. The wine list, naturally, features the products of top local vintners. In good weather, which is pretty common in Prosser, you can dine on the deck while you watch the river flow lazily by. ☺ *2 double rooms with bath, 2 doubles share bath. Restaurant. $65–75; full breakfast. AE, MC, V. No smoking.*

OLYMPIC PENINSULA

Rugged and remote, the Olympic Peninsula lies at the northwest corner of the contiguous United States and is dominated by jagged mountains and (within Olympic National Park, at least) dense, almost impenetrable forests. To the west, the Pacific Ocean rages wild. The Strait of Juan de Fuca is to the north, and the Hood Canal, an 80-mi-long natural inlet to Puget Sound, borders the peninsula on the east. Just a bit inland, and visible from more than a hundred miles away, are the snowcapped Olympic Mountains.

These peaks trap incoming clouds, creating the rain forests of the Olympic National Park to the west and a dry "rain shadow" to the north and east. As a result, the peninsula has both the wettest and the driest climates on the Pacific Northwest coast.

The interior of the peninsula is accessible only to backpackers, but Highway 101, in a 300-mi loop, offers glimpses of some of its spectacular wilderness. Along the ocean side of the peninsula, you can hike, clam, beachcomb, collect driftwood, explore tide pools, and fly kites. Olympic National Park preserves nearly a million acres of mountains, old-growth forest, and wilderness coast in their natural states. Mountain hikes are popular, especially around Hurricane Ridge, just south of Port Angeles. Fishing is a major activity throughout the peninsula. Anglers pull in trout and salmon from the rivers; charter boats out of Neah Bay take halibut and salmon, while others ply the Westport area for bottomfish and salmon.

A good perch for launching Olympic Peninsula excursions is Port Townsend, on Puget Sound. Here, in this picturesque little town of 6,800, a number of exquisite Victorian homes built by sea captains, bankers, and business-people have been turned into inviting bed-and-breakfasts.

 PLACES TO GO, SIGHTS TO SEE

Hurricane Ridge. Drive 30 minutes—17 mi—south from briny Port Angeles and you're a mile high in the craggy Olympics at Hurricane Ridge, with its spectacular views of the Olympic Mountains, the Strait of Juan de Fuca, and Vancouver Island. Despite the steep grade, the road is easily traveled. A small visitor center offers interpretive talks, ranger-led walks, and a museum. Leading off from the center are nature paths and miles of hiking and cross-country skiing trails. Herds of deer, unconcerned with human onlookers, and chubby-cheeked Olympic marmots are frequent visitors.

Neah Bay. The water of Neah Bay offers an abundance of king and silver salmon, while its beaches yield treasures of driftwood, fossils, and agate rocks. Trails lead along the shore and through surrounding deep forests to Cape Alava, an important archaeological discovery. More than 55,000 artifacts were taken from this ancient Makah village before it was covered back up, leaving nothing to see. Many are on display at the *Makah Museum* (Hwy. 112, Neah Bay, tel. 360/645–2711), where the life of the tribe is documented through relics, dioramas, and reproductions.

Olympia. At the southern tip of Puget Sound, Olympia was founded in 1850 and is the capital of the Evergreen State. It retains a relaxed feel and is home to many artists and musicians. For travelers, one of the biggest draws is the *Capitol Campus,* which has monuments, lovely flowers, and gardens. The Japanese cherry trees come into a glorious bloom at the end of April. The handsome, neo-Roman style *Legislative Building,* (Capitol Way between 10th and 14th Aves., tel. 360/586–8687), was erected in 1928; its 287-ft dome closely resembles that of the Capitol Building in Washington, D.C. Free tours are offered from 10 to 3 on the hour. Also worth a visit is Olympia's *Percival Landing Park,* a wooden pier that runs more than a half mile from Fourth Avenue along the western arm of Budd Inlet. Paralleling it are lawns and—at the northern end—shops and restaurants. It also offers good views of pleasure boats both large and small, as well as the Capitol dome.

Olympic National Park. An information center operated by the U.S. Forest Service is along Quinault Lake on the South Shore Road. At the road's end is the trailhead to the Enchanted Valley, whose many waterfalls make it one of the peninsula's most popular hiking areas. The Hoh Rain Forest, with an average annual rainfall of 145 inches and a salmon-rich river, is one of the few old-growth ecosystems remaining in the lower 48 states, an incredibly complex web of flora and fauna sheltering such wildlife as elk, otter, beaver, and flying squirrels. Nature trails lead off from the Hoh Visitor Center, at the campground and ranger station–information center, which also contains a small museum. There are eight other ranger stations, each with its own visitor center, scattered throughout the park; check at the stations about periodic road washouts. *Port Angeles Visitors Center* (600 E. Park Ave., tel. 360/452–0330), just outside the park, is the most comprehensive.

Port Gamble. This New England–style waterfront town, dating from about 1853, has been designated a National Historic Site as one of the few company-owned towns left in the United States. Along with the oldest continuously operating lumber mill in North America, visitors to this town south of Port Townsend will find an 1870 church; the *Of Sea and Shore Museum* (Rainier Ave., tel. 360/297–2426), with fishing and natural history artifacts; and a town historical museum in the General Store.

Port Townsend. This waterfront town, with its carefully restored Victorian brick buildings, was first settled in 1851, becoming a major lumber port in the late 19th century. Several of the grand Victorian homes built on the bluff during these prosperous years overlook downtown and Puget Sound. Today Port Townsend is home to a flourishing community of artists, writers, and musicians; the late Frank Herbert, author of *Dune,* lived here. The restored buildings of *Fort Worden* (tel. 360/385–2021), a former Navy base that is a National Historic Landmark, include officers' homes, barracks, a theater, and parade grounds, and was used as the location for the film *An Officer and a Gentleman.* The *Centrum Foundation* (tel.

360/385–3102), an arts organization based at the fort, presents workshops and performances throughout the summer. A jazz festival is held each July.

Poulsbo. Technically on Puget Sound's Kitsap Peninsula, but considered part of the larger Olympic Peninsula, Poulsbo was once a small Nordic fishing village. Although tourists now outnumber fisherfolk, there are many reminders of its heritage, including murals on sides of buildings depicting Scandinavian life; flower-filled window boxes; rosemaling on shutters and signs; and the *Sluys Bakery* (18924 Front St., tel. 360/779–2798), known for its Scandinavian delicacies and nationally distributed whole-grain Poulsbo Bread.

Quilcene. Famous for its Canterbury oysters and the largest oyster hatchery in the world, Quilcene is about 15 mi south of Port Townsend on Highway 101. It's also the site of a fish hatchery and a ranger station for the Olympic National Park.

Sequim and Dungeness. A wide variety of animal life can be found in Sequim (pronounced "skwim") and the fertile plain at the mouth of the Dungeness (pronounced "dun-ja-*ness*") River. *Dungeness Spit,* part of the *Dungeness National Wildlife Refuge* (tel. 360/457–8451) and one of the longest natural sand spits in the world, is home to abundant migratory waterfowl as well as to clams, oysters, eagles, and seals. Hikers sometimes see killer whales—also known as orcas—cruising nearby and playing in the strait, or looking for a tasty meal of salmon or seal. The small *Sequim-Dungeness Museum* (175 W. Cedar St., tel. 360/683–8110) displays mastodon remains discovered nearby in 1977 as well as exhibits on Captain George Vancouver (a late-18th-century English explorer of the Pacific coast), and the early Klallam Indians. *Sequim Natural History Museum* (503 N. Sequim Ave., tel. 360/683–8364) features exhibits on more than 80 varieties of birds and wildlife on the Olympic Peninsula. Dioramas show preserved creatures in their natural habitats—saltwater beaches, marshes, and forest.

RESTAURANTS

Port Townsend provides a number of good dining options. The **Fountain Cafe** (tel. 360/385–1364) specializes in seafood and pasta. The **Restaurant at Manresa Castle** (tel. 360/385–5750) offers elegant regional cuisine and fabulous Sunday brunches. **Khu Larb Thai** (tel. 360/385–5023), with its explosive Thai noodles and curries, and **Cafe Piccolo** (tel. 360/385–1403), with its home-style Italian cuisine, are esteemed by locals.

Olympia has several good restaurants. **La Petite Maison** (tel. 360/943–8812) serves imaginative French cuisine in a converted 1890s farmhouse. **Capitale Espresso-Grill** (tel. 360/352–8007) has a Pacific Rim menu with salmon, inventive pizzas and salads. The **Spar Cafe-Bar and Tobacco Merchant** (tel. 360/357–6444) has been an Olympia tradition since 1935. The fare for breakfast, lunch and dinner is dinerlike, but tasty.

TOURIST INFORMATION

North Olympic Peninsula Visitor & Convention Bureau (Box 670, Port Angeles, WA 98362, tel. 800/942–4042). **Port Townsend Visitors Center** (2437 E. Sims Way, Port Townsend, WA 98368, tel. 360/385–2722 or 888/365–6978). **Sequim-Dungeness Valley Chamber of Commerce** (Box 907, Sequim, WA 98382, tel. 360/683–6197 or 800/737–8462). **Washington State Tourism Hotline** (Box 42500, Olympia, WA 98504-2500, tel. 800/544–1800).

RESERVATION SERVICES

Pacific Reservation Service (Box 46894, Seattle, WA 98146, tel. 206/439–7677 or 800/684–2932). **A Travelers Reservation Service** (14716 26th Ave. NE, Seattle, WA 98155, tel. 206/364–5900).

ANN STARRETT MANSION ❧

744 Clay St., Port Townsend, WA 98368, tel. 360/385–3205 or 800/321–0644, fax 360/385–2976; www.olympus.net/starrett

This improbably ornate Queen Anne in Port Townsend, painted in cream, teal, and rose, was built by George Starrett, a contractor, mortician, and sawmill owner, in 1889 at a cost of $6,000 as a wedding present for his wife, Ann. In 1996, it was awarded fourth place in the Great American Home Search sponsored by the National Trust for Historic Preservation. You may find the almost museum quality of the mansion off-putting, but hosts Bob and Edel Sokol are low-key and friendly. Bob is a retired Air Force pilot and was navigator on *Air Force One* for President Jimmy Carter. Edel, a native of Germany, is an avid collector and baker.

The foyer—with a front desk handcrafted in Port Townsend when Washington was a territory—opens to a dramatic free-hung, three-tier spiral staircase of Honduran and African mahogany, English walnut, oak, and cherry. At the top is the eight-side tower dome, frescoed by George Chapman with allegorical figures of the four seasons and the four virtues. The dome was designed as a solar calendar: Sunlight coming through small dormer windows on the first days of each new season shines onto a ruby glass, causing a red beam to point toward the appropriate seasonal panel.

The Master Suite looks like a museum period room. Once the Starretts' master bedroom, it features Persian rugs, a Brussels tapestry tablecloth, an 1880 mahogany Eastlake bedroom suite, and a floral tapestry canopy that extends from the floor to the 12-ft ceiling. The Drawing Room has a little antique tin tub painted with cherubs, and an 1860 Renaissance Revival mahogany bed. The contemporary Gable Suite offers a view of Puget Sound and the Cascades, as well as a two-person hot tub.

Breakfast, served in the elegant dining room, includes champagne, juice, New Orleans French toast stuffed with chocolate cream and berries, and topped with a spirited berry sauce; homemade muffins, German griddle cakes stuffed with apples and cinnamon. ♨ *8 double rooms with baths, 2 doubles share bath, 2 suites, 2 cottages. Hot soaking tub in 1 suite, whirlpool bath in 1 suite. $80–$185; full breakfast. AE, D, MC, V. No smoking, 2-night minimum on holiday and festival weekends.*

ANNAPURNA INN MASSAGE AND RETREAT CENTER ❧

538 Adams St., Port Townsend, WA 98368, tel. 360/385–2909 or 800/868–2662

With its porch garlanded with clematis and its gardens lush with flowers, fruit trees, and vegetables, the Annapurna Inn fits right into its Port Townsend neighborhood. The inn also lives up to its Sanskrit name, which means "Goddess of Plenitude". Inside this late-19th-century bungalow-style house you'll find more than just the typical B&B. Owner Robin Sharan, a licensed massage therapist, has created a retreat where you can take advantage of a steam room, sauna, yoga classes, massage facilities, reflexology, and craniosacral therapy, or choose to simply relax in the serene atmosphere.

A graceful structure with fir floors, cedar trim, and a spattering of murals, the house was built in 1881 by Captain Benjamin Sewell. While his neighbors were building three-story "Grand Dames," Captain Sewell constructed a home to remind him of his boat and his life on the sea. He built it low and wide with elliptical portholes in the porch, which now are softly framed with clematis vines that bloom in early May.

The inn was beautifully restored by Robin herself. The airy and comfortable guest rooms are filled with plants and a hodgepodge of antiques. Delicious vegan breakfasts (without meat or dairy products) are prepared daily and often include fruit salad, waffles, tofu scramble, and fresh-baked muffins. There are also many restaurants only a short stroll down the bluff. ⚠ *6 double rooms with baths. Sauna, steam room, massage and reflexology services, yoga instruction, accommodations for groups up to 18, conference facilities. $70–$110; full vegan breakfast. MC, V.*

DOMAINE MADELEINE 🍍

146 Wildflower La. (8 mi east of town), Port Angeles, WA 98362, tel. 360/457–4174, fax 360/457–3037; www.domainemadeleine.com

Bed-and-breakfast connoisseurs have been known to travel the breadth of the continent for a stay at Domaine Madeleine, one of the Olympic Peninsula's most remarkable inns. Blessed with incomparable views of the Strait of Juan de Fuca, romantic gardens patterned after Monet's Petites Allées at Giverny, and the culinary artistry of French-born chef/owner Madeleine Chambers, the B&B has cultivated a fervently devoted clientele.

The atmosphere at this very French inn is a mixture of Continental sophistication and quiet, natural charm. Madame Chambers, who speaks five languages—including Farsi, the Persian tongue—has decorated the house with Asian art, as well as the works of Olympic Peninsula artists. The rooms, public and private, are filled with European antiques and Persian carpets from Iran. In the dining area, a gigantic basalt fireplace presides over high-windowed views of the Strait, where sailboats, sea kayaks, and huge tankers drift by.

Fruit, wine, and cheese await your arrival, to say nothing of designer robes and French perfume. This B&B has a total of five units: the expansive home has three rooms with private baths and fireplaces. Two of them have hot tubs and one—the Ming Room—has a huge private balcony that runs along the entire north face of the house. In a nearby building the Rendezvous Room has a two-person hot tub and a northerly view of the Strait of Juan de Fuca. For very private stays, the honeymoon cottage has a queen-size bed, fireplace, and a comfortable kitchen/sitting area. Windows cover the south side, which looks out onto a flower garden and the Olympic mountains beyond. The bathroom, which has a two-person whirlpool bath, shares the view.

The comfortable dining room is doubly memorable because it is here that you will encounter Madeleine's plentiful five-course breakfasts (brunches really) that are designed to fuel hikers on treks into the Olympics. These delicious meals often include a fresh fruit platter, poached pear, French bread, banana nut bread, chocolate or almond croissant, a meat entrée, tiny chocolate cups with fruit, chocolate hazelnut torte, and baked apple with flan. Madeleine and her husband, John, guarantee that if you eat lunch before 2 PM, they'll pay for it. The innkeepers prefer not to host children under 12. ⚠ *3 double rooms with baths, 2 suites, 1 cottage. Fireplace, TV/VCR, CD player, and phone in rooms. Kitchen in cottage. Video library. $125–$175; full breakfast. AE, MC, V. No smoking.*

HARBINGER INN 🍍

1136 E. Bay Dr., Olympia, WA 98507, tel. 360/754–0389

The Harbinger Inn has the quintessential Northwest view. It sits on a street above Budd Bay, looks out over a marina with sailboats and motor launches, and has a stunning view of the Olympics to the north and the state Capitol to the south. Built in 1910 in the American Four Square style, the interior of the house is filled with a warm, oak trim typical of that period.

The three-story mansion is made of finely detailed, gray, concrete block. Its white pillars with wide balconies give it somewhat of a Southern plantation look. The distinctive grounds feature a street-to-house tunnel and hillside waterfall fed by an artesian well. The rooms, which have original wall stencils, are decorated with turn-of-the-century antiques. Guests are encouraged to borrow books from the library, snack on late afternoon tea and cookies, and watch the sun set over the Olympics from a balcony.

Owned and operated since 1990 by Marisa and Terrel Williams—she's an Alaska Airlines flight attendant and he's retired—this inn has a classy feel to it that makes it the Olympia area's most popular B&B. Breakfasts include fresh fruits, homemade granola, oatmeal, scones, omelets and other egg dishes, coffee, and juices. The Williams also rent a four-bedroom waterfront bungalow across the street for $350 a day. This B&B is not recommended for those traveling with children under 12. ♨ *5 double rooms with baths, $60–$125; full breakfast. AE, MC, V. No smoking.*

JAMES HOUSE ☙

1238 Washington St., Port Townsend, WA 98368, tel. 360/385–1238 or 800/385–1238, fax 360/379–5551; www.jameshouse.com

The picture-perfect location—high atop a bluff, with sweeping views of Port Townsend's waterfront, the Cascade and Olympic mountains, and Puget Sound—is only one of the many striking features of the 1889 James House. The gray wood-frame Queen Anne house, with gables, dormers, porches, and five red-brick chimneys, is one of Port Townsend's grandest Victorian accommodations. In an era when a large house could be built for $4,000, this one, with 8,000 square ft of living space, cost $10,000.

The entrance hallway, dominated by a hand-carved cherry staircase made from logs that came around Cape Horn, is a monument to fine woodworking. Like the two front parlors, the hall features original parquet floors in elaborate patterns of oak, walnut, and cherry. Breakfast is served in the large dining room or in the homey kitchen by the Great Majestic cookstove.

Years of restoration work preceded the house's 1973 opening as one of the first Northwest bed-and-breakfasts. It is furnished with period antiques (some original to the house), Oriental rugs, an antique player piano, and many beveled- and stained-glass windows. Four of the house's nine original fireplaces remain, with carved mantels and Minton tile framing.

Guest rooms are on three floors of the house and in the cottage out back. The house's master or bridal suite offers unsurpassed views, its own balcony, a sitting parlor, a fireplace, a private bath, and the original late Victorian bed, armoire, and fainting couch. The cottage, which sleeps four, has lots of windows and a more contemporary feel.

Innkeeper Carol McGough, a health care professional, moved here from Boston in 1990. She enjoys tending the roses, daisies, geraniums, herbs, and other plants that spill out of the inn's gardens, as well as making potpourris for her guests. Breakfast includes fruit, scones or muffins, and soufflés or quiches, all made from fresh ingredients. ♨ *7 double rooms with baths, 2 doubles with detached baths, 3 suites, 1 cottage, 1 bungalow. $75–$165; full breakfast. AE, MC, V. No smoking.*

LAKE CRESCENT LODGE

416 Lake Crescent Rd., Port Angeles, WA 98362, tel. 360/928–3211

When he inspected the Olympic Peninsula in 1937, then a candidate for a national park, President Franklin Delano Roosevelt stayed at this 1920 lodge on the shores of Lake Crescent, 20 mi west of Port Angeles. Today it's one of two places that offer lodging inside Olympic National Park.

In the antique-furnished lobby you can relax in the Arts and Crafts–style chairs and sofa before a huge stone fireplace, above which hangs a stuffed elk head. Accommodations include five guest rooms in the lodge with a shared hall bath, private-bath motel units, and 17 individual cottages (best bets are the four cottages with fireplaces, overlooking the lake). Not much attention has been paid to room decoration, which has a rather spartan feel, with red cedar paneling and utilitarian pine and maple furniture. Guest rooms are paneled in red cedar and filled with nondescript contemporary pine and maple furniture. Most, however, have fine mountain vistas and water views, and that makes up for the simple decor. With rowboats for rent, you may want to take a short tour of this breathtakingly beautiful—and chilly—Northwest lake.

The lakeside dining room features a selection of Northwest seafood and wines, and the gift shop offers Native American crafts and hiking supplies. The kitchen can supply you with boxed lunches for outings. Pets are allowed but must be on a leash. *47 double rooms with baths, 5 doubles in lodge share bath. Restaurant, lounge, gift shop, rowboats. $67–$170; breakfast and box lunches extra. AE, D, DC, MC, V. Closed late Oct.–late Apr.*

LAKE QUINAULT LODGE

S. Shore Rd., Box 7, Quinault, WA 98575, tel. 360/288–2900 or 800/562–6672, fax 360/288–2901

If you're discouraged by the clearcut at the junction of Highway 101 and South Shore Road, Lake Quinault Lodge will hopefully lift your spirits. When this fine, old-fashioned country resort in Olympic National Park was being built, more than 70 years ago, men had to haul the lumber, brick, glass, and plumbing fixtures over 50 mi of dirt road. The large cedar-shake structure above Lake Quinault was completed at a cost of $90,000—a hefty sum in 1926.

The heart of the shingle-covered lodge is the large lobby, with Douglas fir beams, a massive brick fireplace, original wicker settees and chairs, large-burl coffee tables, Northwest art, Native American crafts and stencils, and cozy corners. President Roosevelt also visited this lodge on his 1937 tour of the Peninsula. Chances are good he may have tried the fresh salmon and oysters that still highlight the restaurant's menu. Try the oyster appetizer, the baked salmon in capers and onions, or the seafood fettuccine with Dungeness crab, lobster, salmon, scallops, and shrimp. The old-fashioned bar off the lobby is also lively and pleasant.

Guest rooms in the lodge are small, simple, and rustic, with country furnishings, some antique. The 36 spacious rooms in the Lakeside Wing—completed in 1990—are decorated with contemporary white wicker, a sofa, and a private balcony. The Fireplace Wing features large rooms with gas fireplaces. The eight-unit annex is quite rustic, used most often by fishermen and guests traveling with pets. *89 double rooms with baths, 3 suites. Restaurant, no-smoking rooms, indoor pool and hot tub, sauna, pool tables, gift shop, fishing, hiking, boat rentals. $62–$250; breakfast extra. AE, MC, V. No smoking in dining rooms.*

LIZZIE'S VICTORIAN BED & BREAKFAST ❦

731 Pierce St., Port Townsend, WA 98368, tel. 360/385–4168 or 800/700–4168;
www.kolke.com/lizzies

This Italianate Victorian in Port Townsend, built in 1887 by a tugboat captain and his wife, Lizzie, is owned by Bill Wickline, an optometrist, and his wife, Patti, a former interior designer. A woodworking hobbyist, Bill has built a replica of the inn in the backyard for their dog.

Lizzie's is furnished in Victorian style, with antiques in exotic woods and light Victorian-pattern wallpapers. Three cast-iron fireplaces hand-painted to look like marble, wood graining on door panels, and the Parisian wallpaper in the front parlor are all original to the house. You are encouraged to use the two 19th-century grand pianos in the parlors. Just off the foyer, Lizzie's Room has a half-canopied queen mahogany bed, a bay window with sitting area, a fireplace, and a clawfoot tub.

Breakfast is served in the country kitchen, paneled in oak and knotty pine. Offerings are all made from natural ingredients and often include fruit, a baked egg dish, ginger bread scones, almond pastries, or an oatmeal souffle. A back porch with Adirondack chairs affords views of the pear, apple, cherry, and plum trees in the orchard. △ *7 double rooms with baths. $70–$135; full breakfast. D, MC, V. No smoking; 2-night minimum on holiday and festival weekends.*

MANOR FARM INN ❦

26069 Big Valley Rd. NE, Poulsbo, WA 98370, tel. 360/779–4628,
fax 360/779–4876; www.manorfarminn.com

The Manor Farm Inn is an oasis of elegance and country charm just across Puget Sound from Seattle. Here, a classic 1886-vintage white clapboard farmhouse is the centerpiece of a 25-acre "gentleman's farm," complete with sheep, horses, donkeys, and other animals. Innkeeper Jill Hughes-Day, a former teacher, provides rods, flies, even floppy fishing hats for those who want to try their luck in the well-stocked trout pond. Bicycles, the best way to explore the inn's extensive grounds, are also available. (Jill prefers not to house families with children under 17.)

The interior of the Manor Farm Inn is filled with special touches. White walls, oatmeal-color carpets, rough-hewn beams, and wide, sunny windows give the spacious guest rooms a clean and soothing simplicity. French and English pine armoires, writing desks, and tables are arranged around the king-size beds, warmed by stylish comforters.

The large kitchen is another special feature at Manor Farm. A sonorous old brass bell summons you to the comfortable drawing room. The farm-style breakfast, which begins with warm scones and coffee delivered to each room, includes oatmeal, fresh eggs from the farm chickens, oven-roasted potatoes, bacon, and sausage. Be sure to save a slice or two of home-baked bread for the inn's friendly goats, Cinammon and Nutmeg, who occupy a fenced pasture down by the trout pond. △ *7 double rooms with baths. Bicycles, croquet, fly-fishing, horseshoes. $100–$170; full breakfast. MC, V.*

OLD CONSULATE INN ❦

313 Walker St., Port Townsend, WA 98368, tel. 360/385–6753 or 800/300–6753,
fax 360/385–2097; www.oldconsulateinn.com

Another Port Townsend Queen Anne Victorian on the bluff overlooking the water—similar to the James House (*see above*)—this redbrick beauty comes complete with conical turret, dormers, an unusual sloping "wedding cake" porch with a bay-view swing, well-tended gardens, and lots of white Adirondack chairs for lounging. Also known as the F.W. Hastings House, the inn was built as a private home in 1889 by the son of the town's founder and served as the German consulate from 1908 to 1911. The inn is owned by Rob and Joanna Jackson. Transplanted Californians, they fell in love with Port Townsend on their 25th anniversary, chucked their old jobs and became innkeepers.

The oak-paneled front parlor features its original chandelier, with large bunches of green glass grapes, and a fireplace framed in Italian tile. A large sitting room is comfortable for reading and conversation, with a fireplace, Queen Anne sofas and chairs, a baby grand piano, a pump organ once owned by England's royal family, and a chinoiserie chest original to the house and inlaid with mother-of-pearl. In the evening, the Jacksons serve complimentary port and sherry by the fire, as well as tasty desserts, including Joanna's infamous hot bourbon bread pudding. A smaller anteroom off the dining room offers cable TV, a VCR, and lots of books. The doll, beer stein, and other collections displayed throughout the house can get a bit overwhelming.

Guest rooms on the second and third floors have a Victorian ambience, with floral wallpapers, custom-made comforters, dolls placed on bureaus, and a picture hat here and there on the walls. From the Tower Room there is a sweeping view of the bay. All suites have claw-foot tubs.

Joanna is a cookbook author and her breakfasts show it. They are are leisurely seven-course affairs and usually include brandy baked apples topped with fresh brandied applesauce and cream; a Greek puffed-egg dish stuffed with goat cheese, sautéed bell peppers, and onions and topped with a lemon-cheese sauce; fresh biscuits; and a small fruit quick-bread laced with a matching cordial. ♠ *5 double rooms with baths, 3 suites. Air-conditioning in rooms. Billiards, hot tub. $96–$195; full breakfast, afternoon refreshments. AE, MC, V. No smoking.*

QUIMPER INN ☙
1306 Franklin St., Port Townsend, WA 98368, tel. 360/385–1060 or 800/557–1060, fax 360/385–2688; www.olympus.net/biz/quimper/quimper.html

With its flared, shingled second story and broad walking porch overlooking Admiralty Inlet, the square Georgian-style Quimper Inn is a nice change from most of Port Townsend's bed-and-breakfasts, which tend to be relentlessly Victorian. Also known as the Harry G. Barthrop House, it was built by Henry Morgan in 1888 and purchased by Harry and Gertrude Barthrop in 1904. The Barthrops wanted a bigger, more ornate house, so they added the third floor with the gables and dormers typical of the Chicago School of Modern Architecture.

During its 110 years, the Quimper Inn has also served as a boarding house; living quarters for nurses; and, sadly, a warehouse for furniture. One of the Northwest's first B&Bs, it was originally renovated in 1972, but had reverted to a private residence when new owners Ron and Sue Ramage bought it in 1991. Now spiffed up and filled with a tasteful mix of antiques and modern reproductions, the home lives again.

Two of the inn's five guest rooms are especially memorable. The ground-floor Library Room, just off the front entrance, is a light, charming chamber with floor-to-ceiling bookshelves, walls painted an unusual "elephant gray," and a thick down comforter on the queen bed. Upstairs, the more spacious Harry's Room (actually a two-room suite separated by sliding pocket doors) is decorated in white, teal, navy, and charcoal; triple-wide windows look out over the inlet and the Olympic Mountains beyond.

Breakfasts are delicious and often feature fruit, muffins, scones, crepes, quiche, or a layered puffed egg dish called a "strata" with cheese and mushrooms, croissants stuffed with Hollandaise sauce, eggs and cheese, and French toast stuffed with cheese and covered with sautéed apples and nuts. Sue also is happy to prepare meals for guests' special diets. ▲ *3 double rooms with baths, 2 doubles share bath. $75–$140; full breakfast. MC, V. No smoking.*

RAVENSCROFT INN ☞

533 Quincy St., Port Townsend, WA 98368, tel. 360/385–2784 or 800/782–2691, fax 360/385–6724; www.ravenscroftinn.net

A relatively new addition to the Port Townsend B&B scene, this mahogany-hued, clapboard inn is not Victorian. Built in 1987, it was modeled after a Charleston-style shingle house, with porches across its first and second floors, as well as dormers on the third.

Teal, brick red, and ivory are the predominant colors at Ravenscroft Inn. The foyer leads to a comfortable library on one side and, on the other, to a "great room" with a fireplace, a grand piano, and small tables that face the open kitchen. Guest rooms feature a mix of country antiques and contemporary furnishings, including wicker, French doors that open onto balconies, fluffy comforters, and the occasional teddy bear. The gardens have been freshly landscaped, with a winding brick path leading to an outdoor seating area.

The inn is owned by Leah Hammer, who for years was a manufacturer's representative for fine crystal and china. Breakfast includes homemade breads and jams, French toast or crepes, fresh fruit, and juice, served on Leah's collection of china and crystal. A vegan, Leah is more than happy to accommodate particular dietary needs. She would rather not accommodate children under 12. ▲ *8 double rooms with baths, 2 suites. Fireplaces in 3 rooms. $67–$175; full breakfast. AE, D, MC, V. No smoking, 2-night minimum on holiday and festival weekends.*

SIMONE'S GROVELAND COTTAGE ☞

4861 Sequim Dungeness Way, Dungeness, WA 98382, tel. 360/683–3565 or 800/879–8859; www.northolympic.com/groveland

Groveland Cottage—just a half mile from the Strait of Juan de Fuca and the Dungeness National Wildlife Refuge—was built at the turn of the century by Charles F. Seal, a merchant and trader who, along with his wife, raised three daughters in the home. The sturdy Victorian farmhouse, with a lazy front porch and green and maroon trim, indeed looks well cared for and lived in. A profusion of flowers—tulips, daffodils, peonies, lilacs, day lilies, roses, and irises—blooms in the garden in season. You can stroll the garden paths, listen to the nearby gurgling brook, and watch hummingbirds and gold finches in the apple, cherry, and walnut orchard. There are also a few willow and holly trees on the property.

The Great Room, occasionally used for weddings and special dinners, has a massive brick fireplace hewn of river rock. Here you can play cards, read a book, listen to music, or play the 1930s upright M. Schultz piano. The best room in the house is Mr. Seals, with a private bathroom, two-person jetted tub, king-size bed, and antique oak dresser. The Waterfall Room has a fainting couch dating from 1910, an overstuffed chair, and French lithographs from the early 1900s. The room

In case you want to be welcomed there.

We're here to see that you're always welcomed at establishments everywhere. That's why millions of people carry the American Express® Card – for peace of mind, confidence, and security, around the world or just around the corner.

AMERICAN EXPRESS

do more®

Cards

In case you're running low.

We're here to help with more than 118,000 Express Cash locations around the world. In order to enroll, just call American Express before you start your vacation.

do more

Express Cash

And just in case,

We're here with American Express® Travelers Cheques and Cheques *for Two.*® They're the safest way to carry money on your vacation and the surest way to get a refund, practically anywhere, anytime.
Another way we help you...

do more ®

AMERICAN
EXPRESS

**Travelers
Cheques**

is named for its furniture, made in Portland in the 1930s; the grain of the wood forms a "V" and resembles a tumbling cascade. The Happy Room has the same style furniture, as well as an antique armoire and an old rocking chair that once belonged to a Sequim pioneer. It has a large deck that looks to the south and a bathroom with a whirlpool tub, a skylight, and water views.

The French Room is decorated with French plates on the walls and handsome furniture dating from the 1930s. Off the orchard is a small cottage, where visitors with children and pets often stay. It has a wrought-iron, queen-size bed and country antiques, including several painted cupboards. The cottage is set up for longer stays, its kitchen stocked with dishes, a microwave, small refrigerator, sink, and hot plate.

Owner Simone Nichols starts the day by bringing coffee, tea, and juice to your room. Breakfast can include a homemade hot five-grain cereal with raisins, currants, cinnamon, fresh berries, or sautéed apples; scones or popovers; eggs Benedict with spinach; puffy pancakes with fruit; shirred eggs with smoked salmon; or a Dungeness crab quiche. Pets are welcome in the cottage. ♨ *4 rooms with private baths. TV/VCRs in rooms. $80–$110; full breakfast. AE, D, DC, MC, V. No smoking.*

SWANTOWN INN ☙

1431 11th Ave. SE, Olympia, WA 98501, tel. 360/753–9123; www.olywa.net/swantown

The Swantown Inn is Olympia's newest B&B. The 1893 Victorian was built in the Queen Anne, Eastlake style and is on city and state historical registers. The inn once overlooked the Swantown Slough, hence its name. The slough, a southern arm of Budd Bay, was filled in years ago. The original owner, businessman William White, lost the house to foreclosure a year after building it and sold it for a mere $2,000. Since then the 17-room house has gone through many transformations.

For years the place was a boarding house, and at one point it had a store on its ground floor. According to co-owner Stephanie Johnson, the stately home was even a bordello for a time. She said the house's red and black wallpaper—now gone—contributed to the feel. Johnson, who was in charge of the interior design for the house's renovation, disliked the dark shades associated with the Victorian era: after steaming off five layers of wallpaper, she and her family painted the walls in pastels.

Stephanie's parents, Ed and Lillian Peeples, bought the house with their daughter and son-in-law, T.J. Johnson, in 1997. The Peeples are old B&B pros: in their former hometown of Greeley, Colorado, they ran the Sterling House Inn B&B. The Peeples now live at the Swantown Inn and run the place.

The Astoria Room has a queen-size four-poster bed, a sitting area, and a private bath with a two-person whirlpool tub. The Columbia Room, which has a queen brass bed and a view of the capitol dome, includes an adjacent bath with a clawfoot tub and Victorian footbath. The Deschutes Room has an antique Jenny Lind–style bed. Like the others, it offers vistas of the capitol grounds plus views of the B&B's gardens.

Breakfasts include fruit, juices, freshly baked scones and muffins, New Orleans–style French toast, German pancakes, and eggs Benedict. Special diets can be accommodated, and there is complimentary afternoon tea. (The innkeepers prefer not to host families with children under 12.) ♨ *3 double rooms with baths. $85–$115; full breakfast. V, MC. No smoking.*

TUDOR INN 𝍫

1108 S. Oak St., Port Angeles, WA 98362, tel. 360/452–3138, fax 360/457–9360; www.tudorinn.com

On a knoll on a quiet residential street of Port Angeles—roughly 17 mi or 30 minutes from Hurricane Ridge in the Olympic National Park —the Tudor Inn is a half-timbered home surrounded by gardens of lilies, irises, lupines, columbines, and fuschias. Built in 1910 by an English dentist, it is 12 blocks from the center of downtown and the ferry to Victoria, British Columbia. The proprietor is Jane Glass, whose roots are in Texas but who lived for a decade in Norway and England before settling in Port Angeles in 1983 with her late husband Jerry.

Guests can nestle in the sitting room on an antique Victorian Chesterfield sofa. Stained-glass windows from England, fireplaces, and hardwood floors with Oriental rugs adorn the common rooms. The inn underwent a major renovation in 1995 and all guest rooms have been soundproofed. Several have views of the Strait of Juan de Fuca or the Olympic Mountains. The most romantic spot in the house is the Country Room with its cathedral ceiling, pastoral scenes painted on two walls, small balcony, gas fireplace, and antique claw-foot tub and shower. The Tudor room occupies a corner of the house and overlooks the terraced garden. It has a king-size, four-poster bed and an antique Beaconsfield dresser and antique dressing table.

Breakfast specialties include caramel apple French toast, buttermilk blueberry pancakes with homemade blackberry syrup, smoked salmon egg souffles, other egg dishes, bacon, biscuits or muffins, and fruit compote. ♨ *5 double rooms with baths. $75–$120; full breakfast. MC, V. No smoking, 2-night minimum on summer weekends and holidays.*

SEATTLE AND ENVIRONS

Wedged between Lake Washington on the east and Elliott Bay on the west, Seattle is a city of water, parks, and heady views of the Cascade and Olympic mountains. The city's damp reputation is well deserved. The winter drizzle (which also appears during the spring, summer, and fall) keeps the city's extensive park system—designed by Frederick Law Olmsted, creator of New York City's Central Park—lush and green. The rain doesn't hamper people's enjoyment of the city's walking and bicycling paths, especially those at waterfront locations such as Lincoln Park in West Seattle; Seward Park in Southeast Seattle; Myrtle Edwards Park downtown; Greenlake, north of downtown; Discovery Park in Magnolia; and the Burke-Gilman Trail, along the shores of Lake Washington. Clouds, fog, and long winter nights have also helped to make the city a haven for moviegoers and readers.

Ever since a number of national publications "discovered" Seattle's sophisticated but comfortable lifestyle, housing prices have climbed, the population has grown (some half million within the city proper, another 2 million in the surrounding Puget Sound region), and jammed freeways are no longer strictly a rush-hour phenomenon. Suburban growth is rampant. But Seattleites—a diverse bunch, including Asians, Asian Americans, Scandinavians, African-Americans, Native Americans, Hispanics, and other ethnic groups—are a strong political force with a great love for their city and a commitment to maintaining its reputation as one of the most livable cities in the country.

With the success of certain high-profile businesses in the region (e.g., Boeing, Microsoft, Starbucks) has also come a great deal of wealth. The downtown retail core is a showcase of new construction and renovation, including a world-class symphony hall and a new Nordstrom flagship store. These developments follow on the heels of the recently rebuilt Key Arena at the Seattle Center, which serves primarily as a basketball venue, and the renovation of several theaters. A new baseball park is also under construction south of the Kingdome, a venue that is slated for demoli-

tion to make room for a new football stadium. With a new regional transit authority that will construct light-rail lines from the city to the suburbs, and a likely third runway at Seattle–Tacoma International Airport, it is plain to see that the area's growth shows no sign of relenting anytime soon.

PLACES TO GO, SIGHTS TO SEE

Brew Pubs. Seattle has become a hotbed of microbrews—distinctive, flavorful ales made in tiny (by national brewers' standards) batches for local consumption. Brew pubs are drinking establishments that are attached to actual breweries and serve a variety of food and nonalcoholic beverages as well. Some notable establishments include the *Big Time Brewery* (4133 University Way NE, tel. 206/545–4509), *Pyramid Alehouse* (91 S. Royal Brougham Way, at 1st Ave. S, tel. 206/682–3377), *Elysian Brewing Co.* (1221 E. Pike St., tel. 206/860–1920), *Six Arms Brew Pub* (300 E. Pike St., tel. 206/223–1698), *Pike Pub and Brewery* (1415 1st Ave., tel. 206/622–6044), and the *Trolleyman* (3400 Phinney Ave. N, tel. 206/548–8000).

Festivals. The *Folklife Festival* is an annual Memorial Day weekend event, showcasing some of the region's best folk singers, bands, jugglers, and other entertainers at the Seattle Center. In late July and early August, there's *Seafair,* saluting Seattle's marine heritage with a parade in downtown and hydroplane races on Lake Washington near Seward Park. Labor Day weekend means *Bumbershoot,* four days of music that includes classical, blues, reggae, zydeco, and pop, at Seattle Center.

International District. Originally a haven for Chinese workers after they finished the Transcontinental Railroad, the "ID" is a 40-block area inhabited by Chinese, Filipinos, and other Asians. The district, which includes many Chinese, Japanese, and Korean restaurants, also houses herbalists, massage parlors, acupuncturists, and social clubs. *Uwajimaya* (519 6th Ave. S, tel. 206/624–6248), one of the largest Japanese stores on the West Coast, stocks china, gifts, fabrics, housewares, and a complete supermarket with an array of Asian foods. Also in this area is the *Nippon Kan Theater* (628 S. Washington St., tel. 206/467–6807), the site of many Asian and Asian-American performances. The *Wing Luke Museum* (4076 7th Ave. S, tel. 206/623–5124) emphasizes Oriental history and culture.

Museum of Flight (9404 E. Marginal Way S, tel. 206/764–5720). The Red Barn, the original Boeing airplane factory, houses an exhibit on the history of aviation, while the Great Gallery, a dramatic structure designed by Seattle architect Ibsen Nelson, contains 38 airplanes—suspended from the ceiling and on the ground—dating from 1916 to the present.

Pike Place Market (1st Ave. at Pike St., tel. 206/682–7453). Considered by many to be the finest public market in the United States, this Seattle institution began in 1907 when the city issued permits to farmers allowing them to sell produce from their wagons parked at Pike Place. Today the sprawling, rickety old market is a vibrant and highly enjoyable place to browse an afternoon away amid the shouts of fishmongers and produce sellers, the music of buskers, and a wild profusion of foods and craft items from every corner of the world.

Pioneer Square. This old section of the city boasts cobblestone streets and restored brick buildings dating from the late 19th century. Start at *Pioneer Park* (Yesler Way and 1st Ave. S), the site of Seattle's original business district, where an ornate iron-and-glass pergola now stands. In 1889, a fire destroyed many of the wood-frame buildings in the area, but residents reclaimed them with fire-resistant brick and mortar. With the Klondike Gold Rush, this area became populated with saloons and brothels; businesses gradually moved north, and the old pioneering area deteriorated. Today Pioneer Square encompasses 18 blocks, the city's largest concentration of art galleries, restaurants, bars, and shops. *The Elliott Bay Book Company* (101 S. Main St., tel. 206/624–6600) hosts lectures and readings by authors of local and international acclaim. The *Klondike Gold Rush National Historical Park* (117 S. Main St., tel. 206/442–7220) and interpretive center explores Seattle's role in the 1897–98 Gold Rush through film presentations, exhibits, and gold-panning demonstrations.

Seattle Art Museum (100 University St., tel. 206/654–3100). The museum, which specializes in Native American, African, Oceanic, and pre-Columbian art, has a new five-story building designed by Robert Venturi. A work of art itself, the building features a limestone exterior with large-scale vertical fluting, accented by terra-cotta, cut granite, and marble. In August 1994, the museum's exquisite collection of Asian art from Japan, China, Korea, and the Himalayas moved to the *Seattle Asian Art Museum* (1400 E. Prospect St., tel. 206/654–3100), the original Seattle Art Museum Building, in Volunteer Park, just east of downtown.

Seattle Center (305 Harrison St., tel. 206/684–7200). This 74-acre complex built for the 1961 Seattle World's Fair includes an amusement park; the futuristic-looking *Space Needle,* with observation deck, lounge, and restaurant (tel. 206/443–2100); theaters; the *Key Arena* (1st Ave. N and Mercer St., tel. 206/684–7200), where the NBA's Seattle SuperSonics play; exhibition halls; the *Pacific Science Center* (200 2nd Ave. N, tel. 206/443–2001); and shops.

University of Washington. Some 33,500 students attend the U-Dub, as locals call the university, which was founded in 1861. On the northwestern corner of the beautifully landscaped campus is the *Burke Museum of Natural History* (17th Ave. NE and N.E. 45th St., tel. 206/543–5590). Washington's natural history and anthropological museum, it features exhibits on cultures of the Pacific region and the state's 35 Native American tribes. Nearby, the *Henry Art Gallery* (15th Ave. NE and N.E. 41st St., tel. 206/543–2280) displays paintings from the 19th and 20th centuries, textiles, and traveling exhibitions. At the museum, pick up a brochure of self-guided walking tours of the *Washington Park Arboretum* (2300 Arboretum Dr. E, tel. 206/325–4510), adjacent to the museum. Rhododendron Glen and Azalea Way are in bloom from March through June; during the rest of the year, other plants and wildlife flourish. A visitor center at the north end of the park will brief you on the species of flora and fauna you'll see here.

Waterfront. Once the center of activity in Seattle, this area stretches some 19 blocks, from Pier 70 and Myrtle Edwards Park in the north down to Pier 51 in Pioneer Square. At the base of the Pike Street Hillclimb is the *Seattle Aquarium* (Pier 59 off Alaskan Way, tel. 206/386–4320), where visitors can see otters and seals swim and dive in their pools. The "State of the Sound" exhibit explores the aquatic life and ecology of Puget Sound. Just next door is the *Omnidome Film Experience* (Pier 59, tel. 206/622–1868), where 70mm films on such subjects as the eruption of Mt. St. Helens and a study of sharks and whales are projected on a huge, curved screen.

Several guided tours of Seattle's waterfront and nearby areas are available. From Pier 55, *Argosy Sea Cruises* (Pier 55, tel. 206/623–1445) offers one-hour tours exploring Elliott Bay and the Port of Seattle. *Gray Line* (buses to the ships depart from the downtown Sheraton Hotel and Towers, 1400 6th Ave., tel. 206/621–9000) runs similar cruises. *Tillicum Village Tours* (Pier 56, tel. 206/443–1244) sails visitors from Pier 56 across Puget Sound to Blake Island for a four-hour experience of traditional Northwest Native American life, including dinner and a traditional dance performance.

Westlake Center (1601 5th Ave., tel. 206/467–1600). Controversial from the time of its inception—some residents wanted the land to be used for a park—this 27-story office tower and three-story shopping structure with enclosed walkways is the major terminus for buses and the Monorail, which goes north to Seattle Center.

Woodland Park Zoo (5500 Phinney Ave. N, tel. 206/684–4800). Many of the animals are free to roam their section of the 92-acre zoo. The African savanna and elephant house are popular features.

RESTAURANTS

Chef Thierry Rautereau of the nationally acclaimed **Rover's** (2808 E. Madison St., tel. 206/325–7442) presents five- and eight-course prix fixe menus that change daily but always include the freshest, and sometimes most exotic, ingredients available. **The Kingfish Café** (602 19th Ave. E, tel. 206/320–8757) serves contemporary soul food in a Capitol Hill storefront. The Kingfish is closed on Tuesday and doesn't take reservations; come prepared to wait in line with the loyal regulars. Downtown, Tom Douglas's **Palace Kitchen** (2030 5th Ave., tel. 206/448–2001) features a large open apple-wood grill and serves a full dinner menu until 1 AM. The menu at **Lush Life** (2331 2nd Ave., tel. 206/441–9842), a cozy bistro hideaway in Belltown, is inspired by the foods of the Mediterranean. For a view to dine by—and die for—**Ray's Boathouse** (6049 Seaview Ave. NW, tel. 206/789–3770) features Puget Sound outside its windows, plus impeccably fresh seafood at both its elegant restaurant and lower-priced café. **Wild Ginger** (1400 Western Ave., tel. 206/623–4450), below the Pike Place Market is Seattle's premier Asian restaurant and satay bar. Monday night live jazz, professional staff, and consistently exquisite food are what make this restaurant extremely popular. Make your reservations in advance! This place is always busy but worth the wait.

TOURIST INFORMATION

Seattle–King County Convention & Visitors Bureau (800 Convention Pl.; mailing address, 520 Pike St. Suite 1325, Seattle, WA 98101; tel. 206/461–5840).

RESERVATION SERVICES

Pacific Reservation Service (Box 46894, Seattle, WA 98146, tel. 206/439–7677 or 800/684–2932). **Seattle B&B Association Hotline** (Box 31772, Seattle, WA 98103, tel. 206/547–1020). **A Travelers Reservation Service** (14716 26th Ave. NE, Seattle, WA 98155, tel. 206/364–5900). **Washington State Bed & Breakfast Guild** (2442 N.W. Market St., Box 355-FD, Seattle, WA 98107, tel. 800/647–2918).

BACON MANSION/BROADWAY GUEST HOUSE ☞

959 Broadway E, at E. Prospect St., Seattle, WA 98102, tel. 206/329–1864
or 800/240–1864, fax 206/860–9025; www.site/works.com/bacon

On a quiet tree-lined street in the Harvard-Belmont Historical District, only five minutes from downtown, the zestfully run Bacon Mansion/Broadway Guest House was a welcome addition to the Seattle bed-and-breakfast scene. Owners Daryl King and Tim Avenmarg-Stiles opened the doors of this huge, imposing 1909 Edwardian-style Tudor in February, 1993.

The house had been operated as an inn for several years when King and Aven-marg-Stiles bought it; they added seven guest rooms to the original three, installed new bathrooms and furnishings, and in the process created an ambience of comfortable luxury. The inn's public areas are tasteful, with wool carpets in shades of rose, cream, and indigo laid over glossy hardwood floors. Headlining the decor of the main sitting room is a black concert grand piano adorned with a Liberace-style candelabra. French doors overlook the garden courtyard, complete with fountain, out back. Flowers in every room make it feel like June all year around.

Guest rooms at the Bacon Mansion run the gamut from the floral motifs of the Garden Suite and the Iris Room to the more masculine confines of the Clipper Room and the Capitol Suite. The latter is the largest and most impressive of the in-house accommodations, with a pine four-poster bed, carved oak fireplace, wet bar, original tile bath (with two-person soaking tub), and a fine view of the Space Needle. There's also a nice view of Mt. Rainier from the Iris Room, on the top floor at the opposite end of the house.

Out back, past the fountain, is the two-story Carriage House. On the main floor is the spacious Carriage Suite with white plaster walls, forest-green carpeting, and a queen-size brass bed; on the second floor is the Carriage Loft, another, smaller suite. The full-size living-room hide-a-bed on the first floor makes this the best choice for families or other large groups. ♠ *6 double rooms with baths, 2 doubles share bath, 2 suites. Phone and TV in rooms. $74–$139; Continental breakfast. AE, D, MC, V. No smoking.*

BOMBAY HOUSE ☞

8490 Beck Rd. NE, Bainbridge Island, WA 98110, tel. 206/842–3926 or 800/598–3926; www.travelassist.com/reg/wa/085.html

In a quiet, rural setting just a 30-minute ferry ride from Seattle, Bombay House is a three-story Victorian mansion owned by Bunny Cameron, a former caterer, and her husband, Roger Kanchuk, who ran a business that served legal papers. The couple pulled up stakes in Anchorage, Alaska, looking for a better climate. One might question whether Puget Sound is an improvement, but in 1986, after scouring various western locations, Bunny and Roger landed on Bainbridge Island and bought the Bombay House.

The house, which has a widow's walk and wraparound porch, was built in 1907 by a master shipbuilder from Port Blakely (famous for its four-masted schooners built in the heyday of the tall ships). The entrance opens to a spacious, sunny living room with 10-ft-high ceilings and stained-glass windows. A century-old rock maple loom from Maine stands against one wall; a 1912 upright piano stands against another. One of the guest rooms on the main floor has a functioning old tin bathtub, and an open staircase leads up to the other guest rooms. The Captain State Room is a large, airy room decorated in forest green and white, with a wood-burning parlor stove, large bird's-eye maple bed, and clawfoot soaking tub with shower.

In the glass-enclosed breakfast area you can munch on Bunny's special fruit-bran muffins, quick breads, cakes, pastries, and homemade granola while you watch the large white ferries plying the waters of Rich Passage between Bainbridge Island and the Kitsap Peninsula.

The half-acre yard contains a rough cedar gazebo and informal gardens of roses, daisies, peonies, and lilies exploding with color. A favorite activity on the 15-mi-long island is berry picking. If you haven't immediately consumed everything you've picked, you'll have an appetite for the fresh pasta dishes at Ruby's

(4569 Lynnwood Center Rd., tel. 206/780–9303). ♨ *2 double rooms with baths, 2 doubles share 1 bath, 1 suite. $59–$149; Continental-plus breakfast, complimentary beverages. AE, MC, V. No smoking.*

CHAMBERED NAUTILUS ☙

5005 22nd Ave. NE, Seattle, WA 98105, tel. 206/522–2536 or 800/545–8459 or 800/545–8459, fax 206/545–8459; www.chamberednautilus.com

You can't miss the bright red door of this three-story Georgian Colonial Revival home near the University of Washington's campus. Called the Chambered Nautilus after an ornate seashell found in the Pacific Northwest, the house was built in 1915. The owners, Joyce Schulte and Steve Poole and their two cats, happily welcome you to their home.

The spacious living room features Oriental rugs, large windows, and a fireplace. In one corner is a Hardman-Peck baby grand piano. Other interesting pieces in the room include an early English oak fire bench and a collection of rare Peruvian grave artifacts, some 2,000 years old. A 6-ft-tall carved oak headboard from the 1890s is the focal point of the Rose Room, dressed with a rose-and-ivory striped down comforter and floral pillowcases. The Scallop Room takes advantage of the hilltop setting, with windows on three sides. Furnishings include a white iron daybed, carved chestnut armoire, and an early 19th-century commode. The Crow's Nest has a gas fireplace and an art deco–style bathroom with a claw-foot tub and shower.

Steve is a talented chef who loves to go all out with the full breakfasts served in the formal dining room. His recipe for stuffed French toast with orange syrup has appeared in *Bon Appétit* magazine. Other offerings might include rosemary buttermilk biscuits, homemade granola, or a breakfast pie made with salmon, dill, and Swiss cheese. ♨ *6 double rooms with baths. TV (on request) in rooms. $89–$119; full breakfast. AE, MC, V. No smoking, 2-night minimum on weekends mid-Apr.–mid-Oct., 3-night minimum on holiday weekends.*

GASLIGHT INN ☙

1727 15th Ave., Seattle, WA 98122, tel. 206/325–3654, fax 206/328–4803; www.gaslight-inn.com

The three-story, teal-color Gaslight Inn atop historic Capitol Hill was always a showplace. A developer built the Arts and Crafts four-square–style home in 1906 to show prospective customers the kind of home they could build after they had bought their lot from him.

Owners Stephen Bennett and Trevor Logan bought the dilapidated building in 1980, and after four years of painstaking restoration, opened it as a bed-and-breakfast. If you reject the excesses of Victorians, you will love this more austere aesthetic.

The inn, named for its original gaslight fixtures, also retains the original beveled-and stained-glass windows on all three floors, oak millwork, graceful fluted columns, and oak-paneled wainscoting with egg and dart detailing. All the oak and the muted color schemes lend a warm feel to the inn, and large windows and unfussy furnishings—authentic Arts and Crafts, Mission, and Eastlake—give it a bright, clean look.

Each of the guest rooms is unique, with its own distinctive and well-executed decor; every one is equipped with remote-control TV and a small refrigerator. Some rooms have views of downtown, only a short bus ride away. Room 1 has a crisp, hardy appeal, with its ivory-and-blue mattress-ticking wallpaper and lots of wood. It features two Eastlake walnut chests and table, a walnut headboard, a hand-pieced quilt, and a bathroom with dark-stained wainscoting and a small Eastlake mirror. Despite dark taupe walls, Room 2 is warm and sunny, with white millwork, an elaborately carved golden oak bed and dresser, and an Arts and Crafts armoire. Another room is rustic, with a log bed made in the San Juan Islands and pine furniture. The five suites in the house next door, including a very spacious third-floor suite with kitchen, desk, fireplace, and expansive view of the Puget Sound, are elegant, comfortable, and particularly ideal if you're planning an extended stay.

Breakfast at the Gaslight is not a celebrated event, as is the case at other B&Bs. It's a strictly Continental affair of store-bought pastries, fresh fruit, coffee, and juice. △ *6 double rooms with baths, 3 doubles with shared baths, 7 suites. Fireplaces in 1 room and 3 suites, cable TV and refrigerators in rooms. Pool. $68–$158; Continental-plus breakfast. AE, MC, V. 2-night minimum Memorial Day–Labor Day and on weekends.*

HILL HOUSE 🐚

1113 E. John St., Seattle, WA 98102, tel. 206/720–7161 or 800/720–7161, fax 206/323–0772; www.foxinternet.net/business/hillhouse

If you want the bustle of the city right outside your door, this is a fine choice. Two blocks off Broadway on a busy arterial street in the Capitol Hill neighborhood, Hill House occupies two identical single-family homes built side-by-side in 1903. Both houses retain much of their original charm, with lead-glass windows and hardwood floors.

Innkeepers Alea and Herman Foster—originally from Detroit and Houston, respectively—have lived in Seattle long enough to know it is where they want to stay, so they bought the place in 1997. Herman owned a restaurant in Houston and is the primary breakfast chef, except on Sunday, when a student from a local culinary school steps in. Both chefs turn out elaborate made-to-order meals: spinach-and-mushroom omelets with fresh marinara sauce, smoked-salmon eggs Benedict, blintzes, and French toast made from homemade walnut bread. Breakfast is served in the formal dining room, where a Duncan Phyfe table covered in lace, which matches the room's curtains, comfortably seats eight. Framed botanical prints and paintings by local artists adorn the walls. You are welcome to enjoy coffee and the morning paper in the adjoining living room before or after your meal.

Each of the guest rooms is held to impeccable standards, with crisp cotton coverlets on down comforters and gorgeous antiques, including several ornate four-poster beds. Each room is thoughtfully stocked with fresh flowers, homemade soaps, ice water, mints, and plush robes. The Rose Room is the smallest guest room and shares a bathroom with the slightly larger Celadon Room. Both quarters have period queen-size beds and full-length mirrors. The spacious Madras and Bordeaux suites have their own bathrooms, sitting rooms, refrigerators, TVs, phones with data ports and answering machines, and private entrances. △ *1 double with bath, 2 doubles share bath, 2 suites. TV, phone, and refrigerator in suites. Free parking. $90–$145; full breakfast. AE, D, MC, V. No smoking.*

INN AT HARBOR STEPS
1221 1st Ave., Seattle, WA 98101, tel. 206/748–0973 or 888/728–8910,
fax 206/682–6045; www.foursisters.com

This B&B is located conveniently on the Harbor Steps, across the street from the Seattle Art Museum and the Benaroya Symphony Hall and two blocks south of Pike Place Market. It is housed on the lower floors of an elegant high-rise residential building built in 1997. The inn is a departure for Four Sisters's Inns, whose collection of bed-and-breakfasts focuses on plush getaways in painstakingly restored Victorians and cozily appointed country homes. But you can still expect the warm hospitality for which this group has become known, in this sleek, modern setting. The staff at the front desk provides friendly yet unobtrusive assistance somewhere between the service at a small boutique hotel and a B&B in a home.

Although the entrance and corridors have a sort of "yuppie dormitory" feel to them, the double rooms are spacious, with high ceilings, gas fireplaces, tidy kitchenettes, and comfortable king-size beds. An eclectic mix of traditional and contemporary furnishings and fabrics, the decor is in sync with the building's modern architectural style but is softened with warm, homey overstuffed chairs and pillows and lighting choices that range from bright to warm and glowing. On the walls are framed botanical prints. The bathrooms are particularly luxurious—all have tubs and oversized glass-enclosed shower stalls, and in five doubles are whirlpool tubs large enough for two people. There are double sinks and plenty of thick white towels. You have access to the same amenities as condo owners from the upper floors, making this inn particularly pleasant for an extended stay. There is a well-equipped exercise room, sauna, basketball court, swimming pool, and hot tub, as well as a coin-operated laundry room.

A generous breakfast buffet is laid out in the sage green breakfast room; small tables with floral tablecloths dot one end of this pleasant (though windowless) room, while brocade-upholstered sofas occupy the other. Breakfast includes seasonal fruits and juices, a selection of cold and hot cereals, pastries, and one or two entrées, such as vegetable quiche, huckleberry pancakes, or *huevos rancheros*. Every afternoon a substantial tea is served in the library. ⚐ *20 double rooms with baths. Kitchenette, phone, cable TV, and fireplace in rooms. Pool, hot tub, sauna, basketball, exercise room, coin laundry. $150–$200; full breakfast. AE, D, MC, V. No smoking.*

INN AT THE MARKET
86 Pine St., Seattle, WA 98101, tel. 206/443–3600 or 800/446–4484,
fax 206/448–0631; www.innatthemarket.com

Ever see a 20-pound chinook salmon fly? Take a stroll through Seattle's renowned Pike Place Market, and you might—thanks to the ebullient resident fishmongers. It's all part of the show at the Inn at the Market, in the heart of Pike Place, a warren of intriguing shops, galleries, pubs, and restaurants.

Another of Seattle's ubiquitous small downtown luxury hotels, the inn is entered through a neo-Venetian courtyard; the quiet lobby is sunny and cheerful, with a cozy wood-burning fireplace and the comfortable, lived-in luxury of an old English country manor house.

The 70 rooms are large and bright, with big windows that maximize views of Elliott Bay or the city; the king-size beds are seductively comfortable. The Laura Ashley Suite is adorned with yellow and cornflower-blue fabrics from the namesake designer's collection and has a large private deck with white Adirondack chairs overlooking the stalls of the public market and Elliott Bay.

The inn shares its courtyard with three restaurants. Formal and elegant, Campagne (tel. 206/728–2800) specializes in the flavors of Provence; its less formal yet equally romantic café spin-off is open for breakfast, lunch, and dinner, with such menu offerings as a *croque monsieur* (ham and cheese sandwich dipped in egg and grilled) and lamb burgers served with shoestring *pommes frites*. Campagne provides dinner room service for the hotel, while Bacco (tel. 206/443–5443), the third and smallest of the restaurants sharing the courtyard, turns out tasty variations on breakfast classics to the hotel guests ordering room service. (Breakfast is not included with the rates, but morning coffee is on offer.) ⚊ *60 double rooms with baths, 10 suites. Cable TV, refrigerator, robes in rooms. Restaurants, room service, rooftop deck, access to athletic club, conference facilities. $150–$335; breakfast extra, complimentary morning coffee. AE, D, DC, MC, V.*

M.V. *CHALLENGER* 🖋

1001 Fairview Ave. N (park at Yale St. Landing shopping center and marina), Seattle, WA 98109, tel. 206/340–1201, fax 206/621–9208

In a city that's defined by water, what could be more appropriate than a stay on a tugboat? Doing the improbable, owner Jerry Brown, a real-estate appraiser from the Midwest, bought the 96-ft working tug, built in 1944 for the U.S. Army, renovated it, and opened the *M.V. Challenger* as a bed-and-breakfast. It's definitely not hyperbole to call it unique.

Moored on the south end of Lake Union, a small lake 10 blocks from the heart of Seattle and filled with sailboats, cruisers, and charter boats, the *Challenger* is not for the claustrophobic. Common areas inside the vessel are open and fairly spacious, but some cabins are very snug.

You are asked to remove your shoes as you enter the main salon, built over the former cargo hatch, now decorated in ivory, blue, and beige with wood trim, brass candlesticks, and nautical gauges. The aft-deck solarium, which affords panoramic views of the waterfront, can be opened to the sky on sunny days and, more typically, enclosed with canvas and vinyl for Seattle's fog and drizzle.

Staterooms, some no bigger than a walk-in closet, are papered with nautical maps. Two cabins have bunks, the others double or queen-size beds. All come equipped with radios and phones. The red-striped comforter and matching pillowcases and curtains, towels, and a small painted radiator, also in red, make the Captain's Cabin cozy and bright. If you've been assigned to the Master's Cabin, you might be tempted to take to your bed, from which you can observe the busy comings and goings on the lake. Two new boats have been added to the "Challenger fleet": A modern trawler with wooden boat charm and a newer power boat, which is more spacious but lacks the personality of the tug and trawler.

An extensive Continental breakfast, complete with cereals, pastries, fruits, juices, hot chocolate, coffee, and tea, is served in the main salon. ⚊ *9 double rooms with baths, 3 doubles share bath, 1 suite. Phone and TV/VCR in rooms. $55–$275; Continental-plus breakfast. AE, MC, V. No smoking, no shoes indoors.*

ROBERTA'S BED & BREAKFAST 🖋

1147 16th Ave. E, Seattle, WA 98112, tel. 206/329–3326, fax 206/324–2149; www.robertasbb.com

For 30 years Roberta Barry has ruled the roost at her eponymous bed-and-breakfast in Seattle's elegant, tree-shaded Capitol Hill neighborhood, luring repeat customers with a mix of humor, energy, and genuine warmth. "People come here to have a good time," she says, explaining her innkeeping philosophy. "I just want them to be comfortable."

Roberta's freshly painted, flower-trimmed, square-frame house, built in 1903, sits in the quiet residential Capitol Hill neighborhood across 15th Avenue from green Volunteer Park and its sumptuously restored conservatory. One small drawback is that Capitol Hill, which contains several of the city's most enjoyable B&Bs, can be a little hard for first-time Seattle visitors to find. Calling for directions will save headaches later. Note, too, that because of local zoning laws, there's no sign out front. Arriving at Roberta's, you'll make your way past a covered sitting porch. Inside, the common areas are bright and sunny, personalized with a piano of antique oak, a beautifully tiled gas fireplace, and an ornate cast-iron–and–nickel wood-burning stove. The gregariously natured Roberta loves to read, and there are books everywhere.

The five guest rooms are on the small side, with bright sunlight filtering through white lace curtains. The rugs on the hardwood floors and the comforters on the queen-size beds are modern and unpretentious. The third-floor Hideaway Suite, decorated in pale green and ivory, is the most spacious. Tongue-and-groove walls and a crazily angled ceiling enliven the space, which also includes a big claw-foot bathtub, oak chairs and tables, and a queen-size bed. Window seats in one alcove offer a view of the Cascade Mountains. Phones with data port and voice mail are in all rooms.

The breakfasts served in the dining room are vegetarian, featuring such dishes as baked eggs, fluffy omelets, and Dutch babies (oversized popovers drizzled with lemon juice and powdered sugar). △ *3 double rooms with baths, 1 double with hall bath, 1 suite. Phone in rooms. $90–$135; full breakfast. MC, V. No smoking.*

SALISBURY HOUSE ❦

750 16th Ave. E, Seattle, WA 98112, tel. 206/328–8682, fax 206/720–1019; www.salisburyhouse.com

On a wide, tree-lined avenue in an old residential neighborhood on Seattle's Capitol Hill sits Salisbury House. The Craftsman-style house, built in 1904, is owned by Mary Wiese, a former real-estate broker in California, and her daughter Cathryn.

The house is spacious and elegant, with maple floors, high coffered ceilings, and large leaded-glass windows. The furniture is eclectic, with few noteworthy antiques but lots of comfort. You might prefer to take a volume from the library up to the second-floor sunporch. There you can settle into the wicker chairs and make use of a refrigerator and hot pot.

Guest rooms are individually decorated in a warm, contemporary style. The Rose Room, a large corner room with a canopy bed in rose chintz, is especially pretty. The Blue Room gets the morning sun and has a private deck overlooking the garden. In 1998 the basement was transformed into the luxurious Lower Level Suite, with its own entrance, a sitting room with a fireplace, a private phone line, cable TV, and a 6-ft whirlpool tub. Mary's favorite room is the Lavender Room, where a country French suite painted pale yellow combines with white wicker chairs and headboard, the lavender walls and purple floral duvet providing the chief color notes.

A full breakfast of seasonal fruits and fresh baked goods is served in the sunny dining room overlooking the side garden. You are welcome to take your coffee in the library while reading from a selection of morning newspapers. △ *4 dou-*

ble rooms with baths, 1 suite. Phone and TV in suite. $89–$140; full breakfast. AE, DC, MC, V. No smoking, 2-night minimum holiday and summer weekends.

SORRENTO HOTEL ☞

900 Madison St., Seattle, WA 98104, tel. 206/622–6400 or 800/426–1265, fax 206/343–6159; www.hotelsorrento.com

The wings of this venerable hotel enfold its fountain courtyard like the covers of an open book. Arriving, you will run a gauntlet of palm trees, valet parking, and doormen, finally winning access to the hushed interior of the ornate Sorrento Hotel, an Italianate throwback to a more gracious time, perched high on Seattle's Pill Hill.

Since 1909, visiting dignitaries ranging from President Harding and the Vanderbilt family to David Bowie have made the Sorrento their lair while in the Emerald City. With good reason: The Sorrento provides a level of European luxury small-hotel service rarely encountered in the laid-back Northwest. Crackling fireplaces, hand-burnished Honduran mahogany, and elaborate flower arrangements make a memorable first impression.

In the guest rooms, the amenities and service successfully walk the line between gracious attentiveness and overkill. The home-baked butter cookies and miniatures of Dow's Port on the book-lined entertainment complex are warming touches; the Sorrento Hotel matchboxes, gold-embossed with the guest's name, are a flicker of Trumpian excess. There's plenty of space; no two rooms are exactly alike, although rose-colored carpets, cream walls, down pillows, and tasteful antique furnishings are consistent features. The vast, $1,200-per-night Penthouse Suite, popular with reclusive rock and movie stars, has a deck with an outdoor soaking tub and a view of the Seattle skyline, as well as a wood-burning fireplace, four-poster bed, and its own library.

Downstairs, in the octagonal, mahogany-paneled Fireside Room, cocktails are served beside a huge green-tile fireplace. In the Hunt Club, chef Brian Scheehser presents his interpretation of Pacific Northwest cuisine. Breakfast is on your own (but the room service is excellent). ♨ *34 double rooms with baths, 42 suites. Air-conditioning, cable TV, and phone in rooms, fireplace in suite. Restaurant, bar, on-premises shiatsu masseur, concierge, access to health club, complimentary downtown limousine service. $210–$270 (Penthouse Suite $1,200); no breakfast. AE, D, DC, MC, V.*

VILLA HEIDELBERG ☞

4845 45th Ave. SW, Seattle, WA 98116, tel. 206/938–3658 or 800/671–2942, fax 206/935–7077; www.villaheidelberg.com

Villa Heidelberg owner Barb Thompson remembers her husband's reaction the first time they walked into the graceful, 1909 Craftsman, which had been neglected for more than 30 years. "I said, 'Wouldn't this make a great B&B?' John visibly paled." Today, several years later, Barb's dream has become a freshly painted, neatly landscaped reality.

Outside are manicured lawns and flower-filled gardens, a broad porch with views over Puget Sound, and a facade of irregular clinker brick and straight-grained fir. Inside, hardwood floors, heavily embossed wallpaper, lace tablecloths, a silver tea service, and a bowl of pink roses from the garden create a spare Edwardian feel, reinforced by sturdy but comfortable Arts and Crafts furniture.

The deluxe suite on the main floor has the original beadboard and box-beam ceilings and a view of the gardens and Puget Sound. The five guest rooms upstairs are named for the Thompsons' favorite German towns. The Garmish Room is bright, sunny, and floral, with a private deck. The larger Heidelberg Room, done in hardwoods and floral prints, has its own fireplace, phone, and TV. Oberammergau, on the third floor, is the most recent addition. Though not the best choice for people who might have difficulty climbing up two flights of stairs, it has a spectacular view of Puget Sound and the Olympic Mountains. This spacious room has a king-size bed and a private bath.

A full breakfast is served in the formal dining room, which has its original wainscoting and box-beam ceiling. Barb likes to change the menu and the look of the table daily. One morning you may be served croissant French toast with raspberry syrup on pink Depression glass plates, and the next day a parfait of seasonal fruit, homemade granola, and vanilla yogurt await at a table adorned with lace tablecloths and fresh-cut flowers. △ *4 double rooms share 2 baths, 2 suites. Cable TV in rooms, fireplace and phone in suite. $80–$120; full breakfast. AE, MC, V. No smoking.*

WALL STREET INN 🐚

2507 1st Ave., Seattle, WA 98121, tel. 206/448–0125, fax 206/448–2406; www.travel-in-wa.com/ads/wallstreet

The Wall Street Inn was originally built as a land base for the Sailors of the Pacific Union. Between voyages spanning 1952 to 1996, merchant marines lodged in the 500-square-ft studio apartments in Seattle's Belltown. This former rough-and-tumble waterfront neighborhood has been invigorated over the past 10 years and is now home to a thriving collection of nightclubs, boutiques, art studios, and some of the city's best restaurants.

While living in a Seattle suburb raising their three children, innkeepers Greg and Kirsten Waham always knew they wanted to own a B&B. And when they found this two-story 1950s apartment building on the market in 1996, they knew it was the place to start. They sold their home, converted two of the apartments into living quarters for their family, then got started renovating the rest of the building. Greg has owned and managed several restaurants and now spends his days running the inn, while Kirsten works at a local department store.

No two of the 20 guest rooms are alike. Seven of the rooms have glorious views of Elliott Bay and the Olympic Mountains, four have kitchenettes, and half of the rooms still have the original Murphy beds from the old sailor days (the other half have queen-size beds). The corner rooms are a bit larger, but all rooms have sitting areas, refrigerators, and an infectiously comfortable mix-and-match approach to furnishing. Each room has its own bathroom with either a tub or a shower, plus hair dryers, terry-cloth robes, and slippers.

A breakfast of fruit, quiche, and fresh pastries from neighborhood bakeries is laid out in the reception area each morning. Guests are free to enjoy their coffee and morning paper in the leather chairs in front of the fireplace. When the weather permits, breakfast can be taken on the interior courtyard patio, where on some evenings Greg, Kirsten, and their children invite you to join them for barbecues. △ *20 double rooms with baths. Cable TV, phone, terry-cloth robes, and slippers in rooms. $100–$135; Continental-plus breakfast, AE, MC, V. No smoking.*

WHIDBEY ISLAND

Over the years Whidbey Island has been settled by farmers, retirees, executives who don't mind the commute, and families who want to get away from the hubbub of city life. They all grow attached to the rolling terrain of forests and meadows, to the high cliffs and sandy beaches, and to the dramatic views. Come here to tread the bluffs of Fort Ebey, marvel at the sunsets at Fort Casey or Deception Pass, feast on famous Penn Cove mussels, pick summer flowers or berries, bike along the many miles of wooded country roads and shoreline, or boat and fish off the same long shore.

The first white settlers included Colonel Walter Crockett and Colonel Isaac Ebey, who arrived during the early 1850s and gave their names to Crockett Lake and Ebey's Landing National Historic Reserve. Wildlife is plentiful: eagles, great blue herons, oystercatchers in the air; orcas, gray whales, dolphins, and otters in the water.

Lying 30 mi northwest of Seattle, the island ranks as the second-longest (60 mi; its width is only 8 mi) in the contiguous United States. It's easily accessible from Seattle via a ferry from Mukilteo ("muck-il-tee-oh") or a drive across Deception Pass on Highway 20.

PLACES TO GO, SIGHTS TO SEE

Coupeville. Founded in 1852 by Captain Thomas Coupe, this seaport village (population 1,300) on the island's east coast passed its early years trading in timber, farm produce, and animal pelts. Much of the original town has been restored—it has some 54 historic landmarks. The *Island County Historical Museum* (Alexander and Front Sts., tel. 360/678–3310) displays artifacts of pioneer families and the town's sea captains. Coupeville hosts an Arts and Crafts Festival in August; a Harvest Festival, with fall foods and a flea market, in October; and the "Greening of Coupeville" when it decorates for the holidays in mid-December. A farmers market is open Saturday from 10 to 2, early April to early October.

Deception Pass State Park (5175 N. State Hwy. 20, Oak Harbor, tel. 360/675–2417). You can take in the spectacular vista and stroll among the peeling, reddish-brown madrona trees. While walking across the Deception Pass Bridge, you'll have a view of the dramatic gorge below, well known for its tidal currents. The bridge links Whidbey Island to Fidalgo Island and the mainland; from here, it's just a short distance to Anacortes and ferries to the San Juan Islands.

Ebey's Landing National Historic Reserve (902 N.W. Alexander Rd., tel. 360/ 678–6084), west of Coupeville off Highway 20, encompasses more than 1,000 acres—including the areas of Keystone, Coupeville, and Penn Cove. Established by Congress in 1978, the reserve is the first and largest of its kind. It's dotted with some 91 nationally registered historical structures (mainly private homes), as well as farmland, parks, and trails with fine views.

Fort Casey State Park (1280 S. Fort Casey Rd., tel. 360/678–5632) lies just north of Keystone off Highway 20. The fort, built in 1890, was one of three coastal forts constructed at the entrance of Admiralty Inlet to protect Puget Sound. The park includes the fort, bunkers, and 10-inch disappearing guns, as well as a small interpretive center, campgrounds, picnic sites, fishing areas, and a boat launch.

Fort Ebey State Park (395 N. Fort Ebey Rd., Coupeville, WA 98239, tel. 360/ 678-4636). Part of the original "Triangle of Death," Fort Ebey protected Puget Sound from invasion. Now part of a state park, the World War II fort still stands guard over the sea with bunkers and gun batteries. The park offers nearly 700 acres of hiking trails, picnic areas, trailer and tent sites, rest rooms and parking, as well as breathtaking views of Port Townsend and the Olympic Peninsula. A trail runs from the day use area to Lake Pondilla, known for good bass fishing and freshwater swimming.

Greenbank. The tart-sweet loganberry is grown on farms all over the island; now the 125-acre *Whidbey Greenbank Berry Farm* (76 S.E. Wonn Rd., tel. 360/ 678–7700) also produces Whidbeys Loganberry Liqueur. Self-guided tours are offered daily 10–5 from Memorial Day through Labor Day and 11–5 the rest of the year. Greenbank is also the site of the 53-acre *Meerkerk Rhododendron Gardens* (3531 S. Meerkerk La., off Resort Rd., tel. 360/678–1912), with 1,500 native and hybrid species of the flowering shrub along numerous trails and ponds. The prime time for viewing blossoms is April and May. Adults are admitted for $3 9–4 daily.

Langley. This quaint town on the island's southeastern shore sits atop a 50-ft-high bluff overlooking Saratoga Passage. A bluff-top sidewalk park offers spectacular views over the passage to Camano Island and the mainland beyond. Sculptor Georgia Gerber's bronze *Boy and Dog* stands sentinel over First Street, which is lined with quaint restaurants and boutiques. The town's small-boat harbor, a 35-slip facility, is protected by a 400-ft timber-pile breakwater and has a 160-ft-long fishing pier–cum–walkway. The adjacent commercial marina offers fuel and supplies.

Winery and Brewery. In addition to the delicately sweet liqueur produced in Greenbank (*see above*), the island has its own winery, the *Whidbey Island Winery* (5237 S. Langley Rd., tel. 360/221–2040), and brewery, the *Whidbey Island Brewing Company* (630 2nd St. B, tel. 360/221–8373). Both are in Langley and are open Thursday through Sunday from noon to 5 for tastings.

RESTAURANTS

The Garibyan brothers serve up Continental and Greek dishes, including lamb and fresh seafood, in a Mediterranean atmosphere at **Café Langley** (tel. 360/221– 3090). At the edge of Langley on a deck looking out at Saratoga Passage and the Cascade Mountains, **Star Bistro** (tel. 360/221–2627) presents contemporary Northwest cuisine (which focuses on its indigenous seafoods), accompanied on Friday and Saturday evenings by live jazz. Weather permitting, you can dine on the deck; outdoor heaters chase the chill. **Christopher's** (tel. 360/678– 5480), in Coupeville, features views of the harbor as well as great stuffed island mussels and other seafood. Also in Coupeville, **Rosi's Garden Restau-**

rant (tel. 360/678–3989), grandly housed in a restored Victorian, offers a large menu featuring seafood and prime rib. Romantic European decor and fine Continental cuisine draw locals to **Kasteel Franssen** (tel. 360/675–0724) in Oak Harbor for special-occasion dinners.

TOURIST INFORMATION

Central Whidbey Chamber of Commerce (5 S. Main St., Box 152, Coupeville, WA 98239, tel. 360/678–5434). **Island County Visitor Information** (Box 1641, Coupeville, WA 98239, tel. 888/747–7777). **Langley Chamber of Commerce** (Box 403–B88, Langley, WA 98260, tel. 360/221–6765). **Washington State Tourism** (Box 42500, Olympia, WA 98504-2500, tel. 800/544–1800).

RESERVATION SERVICES

Pacific Reservation Service (Box 46894, Seattle, WA 98146, tel. 206/439–7677 or 800/684–2932). **Washington State Bed & Breakfast Guild** (2442 N.W. Market St., Box 355–FD, Seattle, WA 98107, tel. 800/647–2918).

ANCHORAGE INN ☞

807 N. Main St., Coupeville, WA 98239, tel. 360/678–5581; www.whidbey.net/anchorag

The Anchorage Inn, a reproduction Victorian home just up the hill from the shops and restaurants of Main Street in Coupeville, opened in 1991. The white-walled, red-roof house rises three stories with such fanciful touches as gables, dormer windows, and a tower. From the hardwood floors to the reproduction furniture, most of the Anchorage Inn is less than 10 years old, although antiques are interspersed among the inn's newer furnishings.

The foyer has a fireplace and a large, open staircase. In Room 2 you'll find a cherry-wood four-poster bed with a fluffy white comforter, a dresser, and a view of the harbor. Splendid harbor views through broad windows draw attention to the outside, competing with the queen-size brass beds and Victoriana decor dominating the remaining guest rooms. The owners' concern for guests' comfort and solitude is evident in each room's own hot water heater, and the ¾-inch concrete floors providing peace and quiet between rooms.

In "a working retirement," owners Don and Joanne Storer moved from Boston to run the inn. They are often found chatting with guests in the crow's nest on the third floor, which the Storers stock with cookies and drinks, reading matter, games, and an extensive video collection. △ *6 double rooms with baths. Air-conditioning, cable TV in rooms. $75–$90; full breakfast. D, MC, V. No smoking.*

CAPTAIN WHIDBEY INN ☞

2072 W. Captain Whidbey Inn Rd., Coupeville, WA 98239, tel. 360/678–4097 or 800/366–4097, fax 360/678–4110; www.captainwhidbey.com

The Captain Whidbey nestles along the shore of Penn Cove near Coupeville. Built in 1907 from local madrona logs, the lodgelike inn is rustic, warm, and inviting. The sitting room has smooth log walls and a double-sided beach rock and brick fireplace whose other side faces the dining room.

Guest rooms in the main building open off the upstairs hallway. All have cozy feather beds, down comforters, and sinks. (The sinks help alleviate waits as these guest rooms share two bathrooms: one for men, and one for women). The rooms on one side have a water view, while those on the other side have a garden view. One of the suites has a four-poster bed, blue woven curtains, and a reading chair with matching upholstery. Three cottages have fireplaces and, in some cases, kitchens, while four cabins offer simple, private lodging with views of Penn Cove. Another building contains the spacious Lagoon Rooms, all with verandas and private baths.

Guests may find relaxing pursuits by land or by sea. Pathways extend around the entire property, which includes herb, vegetable, and flower gardens. In the summer, boats are for rent.

A full breakfast is served in the lodge building's dining room. Additionally, multicourse, gourmet candlelight dinners and an ample wine selection are available in the dining room, which looks onto Penn Cove. After dinner, you can relax in the Chart Room, a rustic bar. Sailing charter captain John Colby Stone owns The Captain Whidbey; Dennis Argent, who grew up in the area, manages it. ⌂ *12 double rooms with baths, 10 doubles and 2 suites share 2 baths, 3 cottages and 4 cabins with baths. Phone in some rooms, kitchen in cottages. Restaurant, bar, conference facilities. $95–$225; full breakfast. AE, D, DC, MC, V. 2-night minimum on weekends, 3-night minimum on holiday weekends.*

CLIFF HOUSE AND SEA CLIFF COTTAGE 🐚

*727 Windmill Rd., Freeland, WA 98249, tel. 360/331–1566;
www.whidbey.com/cliffhouse*

High on a cliff above Admiralty Strait, on 400 ft of secluded waterfront, stand the Cliff House and Sea Cliff Cottage. Natural beauty and tranquility led owner Peggy Moore to build her incredible home on Whidbey Island. The 1981 Cliff House—a contemporary statement in glass, wood, and stone—has brought awards to its architect, Arne Bystrom, and is elegantly appointed in art and artifacts.

A large open kitchen and dining area stands on one side of a 30-ft glass atrium; a study and seating area is on the other side. The sunken living room has a fireplace and a sectional with a perimeter of tiny lights that make it appear to float at night. Floor-to-ceiling windows allow glorious views of Admiralty Strait, Puget Sound, and the Olympic Mountains.

Because guests share living and dining facilities, Peggy will only rent the two spacious loft bedrooms to acquainted parties. The larger room opens out over the living area. Amenities include a king-size feather bed, whirlpool bath, and two upholstered swivel chairs so guests can fully appreciate the sun setting over the mountains. The second bedroom overlooks the kitchen and dining area to the forest beyond. A skylight brightens the dark-blue tile bathroom. Comprehensive music and video libraries can keep you entertained on chilly evenings.

Sea Cliff Cottage is as romantic and cozy as Cliff House is airy and elegant. The porch has a bit of gingerbread among the driftwood railing, and Adirondack chairs. There's a country feel to the living room: whitewashed pine walls, pine armoire, wicker chairs and love seat, and a brick fireplace. Ralph Lauren linens on the bed and a cushioned window seat overlooking the trees and the water add to the comfort. There is also a fully equipped kitchenette and a dining area, as well as a bathroom. ⌂ *2 double rooms with baths in house, 1 cottage. Kitchen and fireplace in cottage, hot tub with house. $165–$385; Continental breakfast. No credit cards. No smoking, 2-night minimum.*

COLONEL CROCKETT FARM ☙

1012 S. Fort Casey Rd., Coupeville, WA 98239, tel. 360/678–3711;
members.aol.com/crocketbnb

Colonel Walter Crockett, a relative of Davy Crockett, built this house in 1855. It was derelict in 1984 when Robert and Beulah Whitlow found it; today the house is listed in the National Register of Historic Places. They spent 18 months and $235,000 transforming the old farmhouse into an inn, which stands amid 3 acres of lawn and flower gardens.

The Victorian cross-gabled structure has Doric pilasters on pedestals, lending an incongruous grandeur to the otherwise modest house. The entry hall and small solarium have stained- and leaded-glass windows and wicker furniture. The main public room is a well-stocked library with red oak paneling, a slate fireplace, an English brass rubbing, and a collection of bulldogs in an antique case. Furnishings include a mirror-back English settee and matching chairs, an upholstered Eastlake chair and matching rocker, and another hand-carved rocker.

The five guest rooms are individually decorated. The Crockett Room, the inn's bridal suite, is furnished with a four-poster canopy bed, a marble-top washstand, and a Belgian field desk; its extra-long tub has lion's-head feet. The Edwardian fainting couch in the sitting area is a particularly rare piece. The Alexander Room, with a tiger maple bed and dresser, overlooks meadows, Crockett Lake, and Admiralty Bay.

The dining room has a fireplace, a view out to the iris gardens and Crockett Lake, and a telescope for guests' use. Small tables are surrounded by collections of antique porcelain plates; Royal Copenhagen, Wedgwood, and Belleek pieces; and gleaming English silver. Breakfast specialties include eggs California, fruit platters, and homemade muffins with seasonal ingredients. (Beulah may share some of her original recipes).

The farm is on a major flyway, so many migrating birds stop over on Crockett Lake. It's also close to 9 mi of beach with public access and the Port Townsend ferry terminal. △ *5 double rooms with baths. $75–$105; full breakfast. MC, V. No smoking, 2-night minimum on holiday weekends.*

COMPASS ROSE BED AND BREAKFAST ☙

508 S. Main St., Coupeville, WA 98239, tel. 360/678–5318 or 800/237–3881,
fax 360/678–5318; www.whidbey.net/compassrose

The Compass Rose Bed and Breakfast, south of the main part of Coupeville, is in the Will Jenne House, an 1890 Queen Anne Victorian home on the National Register of Historic Places. But the real attraction to the Compass Rose stems not from the 100-plus-year-old house, but from its inhabitants—Captain and Mrs. Marshall Bronson.

For 31 years, Marshall served in the upper echelons of the U.S. Navy and he and Jan lived in the far reaches of diverse continents and nations, from Finland to Uruguay to Indonesia. They've entertained dignitaries in foreign capitals and perused cultures and corners not even imagined by most travelers. Now, they've retired to Coupeville, and have brought with them treasures from around the globe to share with the guests who are becoming their newest friends. Art, artifacts, and antiques carry visitors on a magical journey as the Bronsons warmly share the fascinating tales that accompany each prize.

The Compass Rose is a veritable museum, brimming with unique pieces in every room and hall. Entering the front door, one is met with a collection of globes and, of course, compasses of all sizes and descriptions. Botanical prints and engravings line the walls of the parlor and a massive formal dining room table foretells the Epicurean delights that await guests. (He cooks; she serves— on one of the eight complete sets of china, crystal, and silver she has collected.)

Guest rooms are upstairs. The king-size Scales is true to its name and is appointed with items from four continents, among them a spinning wheel and trunk from Finland. Dragon's Louis XVI queen-size reproduction furnishings hail mostly from South America. The exotic even spills into the rose and herb gardens, which are decorated with sculptures from Zimbabwe. △ *2 double rooms share bath and parlor. Phone, cable TV/VCR. $85; full breakfast, complimentary beverages. No credit cards. No smoking.*

COUNTRY COTTAGE OF LANGLEY ☞
215 6th St., Langley, WA 98260, tel. 360/221–8709 or 800/713–3860; www.virtualcities.com/ons/wa/w/wawc602.htm

The Country Cottage, operated by Bob and Kathy Annecone, stands two blocks from downtown Langley on 2 landscaped acres that were part of a farm until 1980. The two-story farmhouse, with dormer windows and a gabled entrance, went up in 1927. Burgundy, in various shades, is the predominant color, and white-washed wainscoting is used throughout. The walls of the dining room feature murals depicting the four seasons; you can choose to dine there or have a full breakfast delivered to your room.

The large living room has a stone fireplace, and outside, a large deck with umbrella tables and a boardwalk lead to a gazebo, and beyond, a newer building with two large guest rooms. The small structure that once served as the farmhouse creamery has evolved into a quaint cottage with a Dutch door and window boxes. Rooms follow a theme, from Captain's Cove and its nautical decor, water view from the bed and table, and leather couch, to Sand 'n' Sea and its casual beach motif, with shells from Fiji and Bora and views of mountains to the east. Others, including Lynn's Sunrise and the Whidbey Rose, feature floral schemes, fairies and whimsy, and watercolor impressions. All rooms have a featherbed and a down comforter for a good night's sleep. △ *5 double rooms with baths. TV/VCR, CD player, coffeemaker, and refrigerator in rooms, fireplace in 2 rooms. Hot tub, video library. $105–$169; full breakfast. AE, MC, V. No smoking, 2-night minimum on summer weekends and holidays.*

EAGLES NEST INN ☞
4680 Saratoga Rd., Langley, WA 98260, tel. and fax 360/221–5331; www.eaglesnestinn.com

·The ambience of Eagles Nest Inn, just a few minutes' drive from Langley, is one of comfortable elegance. This contemporary octagonal house, with views of the water and the mountains, is serenely rural. The 360-degree perspective from the rooftop deck is breathtaking.

The two-story living room has a 17-ft brick fireplace flanked by elongated octagonal windows in clear and peach-color glass. An adjacent wall sports a 20-ft, free-hand mural by Everett artist Joseph Root. It's a continuation of what you'd see if the wall were a window, depicting Saratoga Passage, eagles and trees.

Every guest room is distinctively decorated and has a private bath and a view of either the woods or Saratoga Passage and the Cascade Mountains. Honeymooners love the fourth-floor peach-and-white penthouse room, which has windows on all eight walls, brass and wicker furnishings, and a deck. New to the accommodations is an English country cottage on a high bluff above the water on the other side of Langley. Its highlights are a stairway to a private beach, hot tub for two both on the covered porch and inside, a fireplace, and an English garden.

Jerry and Joanne Lechner took over the inn in 1994 and added the cottage. Joanne used to teach gourmet cooking, and now puts her culinary talents to good use in preparing bountiful breakfasts. Fresh berry coffeecake and alder-smoked salmon soufflé are among her specialties. To make room for more home-cooking, guests can take advantage of the 400-acre trail system adjacent to the Eagles Nest property. △ *4 double rooms with baths, cottage. Cable TV/VCR and stereos in rooms. Hot tub. $95–$235; full breakfast, complimentary beverages. D, MC, V. No smoking; 2-night minimum on weekends.*

FORT CASEY INN 🐦

1124 S. Engle Rd., Coupeville, WA 98239, tel. 360/678–8792

The Fort Casey Inn is the former officers' quarters of the old coastal defense fort, built in 1909. Gordon and Victoria Hoenig have been the owners since 1956, but turn daily operation of the inn over to an on-site manager.

Victoria renovated, one at a time, the four two-story Georgian Revival duplexes herself. Each one has a kitchen and a living room on the lower floor and two bedrooms and a bath upstairs. The houses are individually decorated, with painted floors and braided rag rugs; the high ceilings in the living rooms retain their original tin, and rooms are accented with tin chandeliers, lace curtains, folk art, hand-painted furniture, and claw-foot bathtubs.

The Doctor's House has two bedrooms and a bath, and Garrison Hall, which is used for weddings and seminars, also has a small suite, dubbed the Eagle's Nest because of the abundance of the regal bird in it's decor (the handmade eagle quilt is quite fetching). There's a wild bird sanctuary just across the street, but you'll need to bring your own identification guide and binoculars.

The Hoenigs leave fixings for a Continental breakfast in each kitchen (and in the suite that has no kitchen, under glass on its dining table). △ *1 suite, 1 2-bedroom cottage, 8 2-bedroom units. Wood-burning stoves and kitchens in most units. Bicycles. $75–$125; Continental breakfast. AE, MC, V. No smoking.*

GUEST HOUSE LOG COTTAGES 🐦

24371 State Hwy. 525, Greenbank, WA 98253, tel. 360/678–3115,
fax 360/678–3115; www.whidbey.net/logcottages

The Guest House Log Cottages sit at the edge of a pond in a rural area between Langley and Coupeville. Mary Jane and Don Creger first started renting their log-cabin guest house as a couple's private retreat. Over the years, the Cregers added more accommodations on their 25 acres and now have six separate and secluded cottages and cabins. They seldom interact with guests, preferring instead to assure guests' privacy.

Five cottages are nestled in woodsy settings in the midst of abundant wildlife, from deer and frogs to bald eagles and owls. The custom-built lodge cabin combines luxury and the rustic, perfect for star-gazing through a glass ceiling from one of two large whirlpool tubs or relaxing in front of the big stone fireplace.

The country ambience of the Emma Jane cottage is similar to the others, with old scythes, a runner sled, and a lantern on the front porch. The living room has pine floors spread with braided rugs, knotty pine walls, a stone fireplace, a blue mohair overstuffed sofa, rocking chairs, and Pilgrim-style trunks.

An outdoor swimming pool, hot tub, and exercise room are the shared facilities. Potpourri and white chocolate candies are among the thoughtful touches in the cottages. Dining tables come set for breakfast, and the refrigerators are stocked with breakfast fixings, including fresh, free-range Aracuana eggs. △ *5 cottages and 1 cabin. Fireplace, kitchen, stereo, TV/VCR, video library, whirlpool bath in units. Pool, exercise room, video library, hot tub. $160–$295; full breakfast. AE, D, MC, V. No smoking, 2-night minimum on weekends, 3-night minimum on holiday weekends.*

HOME BY THE SEA COTTAGES ✿

2388 E. Sunlight Beach Rd., Clinton, WA 98236, tel. 360/321–2964, fax 360/321–4378; www.frenchroadfarm.com

Just 15 minutes from the Mukilteo/Clinton ferry and 10 minutes from the seaside town of Langley, Home By The Sea actually includes three nearby properties: Sandpiper Suite, Cape Cod Cottage, and French Road Farm Cottage. All are furnished for comfort, complete with whirlpool tubs, wood-burning stoves, phones, televisions, and fully stocked kitchens. Fresh, hot croissants are delivered on the first morning.

The Sandpiper Suite, attached to the proprietors' beach house and overlooking the Olympic Mountains, is on Useless Bay's waterfront. It's private and ideal for stepping directly off the deck and onto a quiet beach. Down the road is the cute Cape Cod Cottage, circa 1930, that's been lovingly cared for by three generations of the Fritts-Drew family. It, too, has access to the beach and peekaboo views of the bay. The Sandpiper and Cape Cod both are appropriate for families.

Set on 10 acres of perennial gardens, tall timber, and a 3-acre vineyard, French Road Farm Cottage is a short drive away. A links-style, nine-hole golf course across the road is private, but permits public play. Innkeeper Linda Drew-Walsh is lending her own touches to the hospitality family members before her have offered. Among them is her passion for gardening, evidenced by the extensive gardens and rare and unusual plants she cultivates at French Road.

Connected to her love of gardening is Linda's association with a new nearby accommodation, Froggwell House. The custom-built, handcrafted home is surrounded by expansive gardens, including rhododendron varieties from all over the world. The secluded oasis attracts land- and air-born wildlife as well as avid gardeners and romantics seeking retreat. Inquiries about the two-bedroom Froggwell House can be addressed to Linda. △ *1 suite, 2 cottages. Kitchen, phone, TV/VCR, sound system, whirlpool bath in units. $155–$175; Continental breakfast. MC, V. No smoking, small pets welcome, 2-night minimum on weekends.*

INN AT LANGLEY ✿

400 1st St., Box 835, Langley, WA 98260, tel. and fax 360/221–3033

This contemporary structure at the edge of the Langley business district is a contemplative melding of earth, sky, water, wood, and concrete. The two cedar-shake, Mission-style buildings—inspired by Frank Lloyd Wright—are surrounded by quiet gardens of herbs, berries, flowers, and fruit trees.

An archway leads to a long, rectangular reflecting pond, which connects with the Country Kitchen, a restaurant that serves Continental breakfast to guests and opens to the public for dinner on Friday and Saturday. A longer building with similar lines includes the office, 22 guest rooms, and two suites trailing down the bluff to the beach.

An Asian sense of space and understatement shapes the interior in neutral earth tones. The waterside wall in the common area is nearly all glass, affording a staggeringly beautiful view past the deck to Saratoga Passage, Camano Island, and the Cascade Mountains. The fireplace and maple, fir, cherry, and pine appointments meld with the outdoors.

The Country Kitchen might be a wealthy friend's dining room. You'll find no maître d' standing at an official podium, no coat check, and no cash register. A huge river-rock fireplace rises before you; tables for two line the walls unobtrusively. The restaurant, a veritable gallery of local crafts, has a locally made, Wright-inspired "great table" for 10 on the far side of the fireplace.

Steve and Sandy Nogal, the inn's managers, see stressed and exhausted guests arrive and watch with pleasure as they "unwind and blossom". Steve is the creative force behind the incredible dinners served each weekend. He builds menus around Whidbey Island foods, and has a ready group of suppliers that bring in salad greens, eggs, baby vegetables, jams and jellies, and freshly harvested mussels for his artful culinary presentations. ♠ *22 double rooms with baths, 2 suites. Phone with voice mail, TV, VCR, mini-refrigerator, whirlpool bath, and fireplace in rooms. Restaurant, conference facilities. $189–$279; Continental breakfast, dinner Fri. and Sat. AE, MC, V. No smoking, 2-night minimum on weekends.*

INN AT PENN COVE ☞

702 N. Main St., Box 85, Coupeville, WA 98239, tel. 360/678–8000 or 800/688–2683; www.whidbey.net/~penncove/pencv.htm

Two side-by-side stately homes in the middle of historic Coupeville are run as an inn by innkeepers Gladys and Mitchell Howard. Kineth House—a large, peach-color Italianate Victorian—was built in 1887. Next door stands the 1891 Coupe-Gillespie House, which was built for the daughter of the town's sea-captain founder.

Kineth House's parlor has fir floors, dusty pink–and–cream reproduction Victorian wallpaper, wingback chairs facing a faux-marble fireplace, and a pink frosted-glass chandelier overhead. The room also contains an antique pump organ, a Victorian music box, and two 1890s armchairs by the bay window.

Guest rooms are elegant without being stuffy. Elizabeth's Room has pale-pink walls, lavender carpet, a turn-of-the-century bed, and an 8-ft double-mirror armoire. Desiree's is the largest room, with a king bed, whirlpool tub big enough for two, and a gas stove. A dress model clad in a wedding dress lends an air of nostalgia. A large claw-foot tub is among the distinctive features of Amanda's Room.

The Coupe-Gillespie House's three guest rooms are slightly smaller than those of its neighbor, but just as quaint, with stenciled wall trim and Victorian bedsteads. With a games room and reading room, the Coupe-Gillespie House is suitable for families. ♠ *3 double rooms with baths, 2 doubles share bath, 1 suite. Fireplace in 3 rooms, whirlpool bath in suite. Cable TV/VCR in video library in Kineth House. $60–$125; full breakfast, complimentary beverages. AE, D, MC, V. No smoking.*

LOG CASTLE BED & BREAKFAST ☞

4693 Saratoga Rd., Langley, WA 98260, tel. 360/221–5483, fax 360/221–6249; www.whidbey.com/logcastle

The rustic, Northwest-style Log Castle Bed & Breakfast, owned by Congressman Jack Metcalf and his wife Norma, sits on a secluded beach outside Langley. Norma designed the house and Jack started building it in 1974 from local stone, driftwood (used for accent pieces such as door handles), and timber from thinning trees on family lands. The place has a homey, nostalgic feel: stained-glass lamps, tree-root door handles and drawer pulls, plants hanging in macramé holders, and wormwood for the stairway, doors, and kitchen cupboards. The large living-dining room has the aura of a grand old lodge: massive timbers, cathedral ceiling, large leaded-glass windows, red and tan carpets, and a table made from an ancient log slab.

The four guest rooms are named for the couple's four daughters. Anne's room, in the third-story tower, is decorated in white and mauve and features a 1912 wood stove, white furniture (including a metal-frame bed), and a flowered quilt made by Norma's grandmother; it has a peaked roof and a widow's walk around the outside. Also decorated with quilts, Marta's overlooks the water with its own private balcony and swing. Crocheted spreads bedeck the beds in Gayle's and Leah's rooms, both of which also have a private deck or balcony.

Innkeepers Karen and Philip Holdsworth manage the Log Castle for the Metcalfs. Karen has continued with many of Norma's popular recipes and has added her own to the three-course breakfast, trimmed with delicious homemade quick breads and muffins. △ *4 double rooms with baths. Woodstove in 2 rooms. Nature trail. $95–$120; full breakfast, afternoon refreshments. D, MC, V. No smoking, 2-night minimum on holiday weekends.*

LONE LAKE COTTAGE AND BREAKFAST 🐚
5206 S. Bayview Rd., Langley, WA 98260, tel. 360/321–5325; www.whidbey.com/lonelake

Dolores Meeks, who owns and runs the Lone Lake Cottage and Breakfast, was a restaurant manager who wanted an active retirement. Her hobby is raising birds and she keeps an aviary of over 200 rare native and exotic varieties.

At Lone Lake you can stay in a cottage, a lakeside suite attached to the main house, or a houseboat. Dolores's late husband built the small stern-wheeler houseboat, which is moored on its own private dock and restored its antique engine (at one time it toured the lake). The interior is decorated in shades of blue, with a queen-size loft bed and a tiny galley. The two cottages have rattan and soapstone-inlaid furniture, Oriental screens, and extra-firm queen-size beds; both have covered decks with gas barbecues and views of the lake. Color themes vary from one accommodation to another, from black and rose to peach and other muted tones, but all have whirlpool tubs, microwaves, TV/VCRs, and stereos.

You also have use of a mini–tennis court, bikes, boats, a canoe, paddleboat, and fishing gear to angle for the plentiful trout and bass that populate the lake. Dolores delivers breakfast for the first two days of your stay, but after that you're on your own. △ *1 houseboat with detached bath, 1 suite, 2 cottages. Kitchen, TV/VCR, CD player, whirlpool bath in units. Video library, bicycles, canoes, paddleboat, rowboat, fishing gear. $140; Continental breakfast for 1st 2 days. No credit cards. No smoking, 2-night minimum on weekends.*

SARATOGA INN 🐚

201 Cascade Ave., Langley, WA 98260, tel. 360/221–5801 or 800/698–2910, fax 360/221–5804; www.foursisters.com

Formerly known as Harrison House, the Saratoga Inn rests at the edge of downtown Langley, within easy walking distance of the town's shops, restaurants, and arts center. Most rooms offer a view of Saratoga Passage or the Cascade Mountains and the inn's bicycles afford easy exploration of the town or nearby countryside.

The inn was built in 1994 and is owned by a group of architects from Seattle. In 1997, it became the ninth in the collection of Four Sisters Inns, a family-owned group of country inns. Natural wood shingle siding, white trim, gabled rooftops, and wraparound porches lend a Pacific Northwest authenticity to the Saratoga. The feeling extends inside, where wood floors, fireplaces in every room, and private baths with oversize showers enhance the warmth and comfort of this intimate island retreat.

A separate, spacious carriage house suite offers total privacy for guests seeking solitude. With its own entrance, sun deck, kitchen, entertainment center, sleigh bed, Oriental rugs, telescope, desk, and an oversize bathroom with an antique double cast-iron tub, the carriage house is an elegant, understated choice for romantics or urban refugees.

The Library Board Room is a venue for meetings and other gatherings and provides a full range of audiovisual equipment. Additionally, the Saratoga's staff can provide refreshments for meetings. (A full gourmet breakfast and afternoon hors d'oeuvres are served daily.) ♙ *15 double rooms with baths, carriage house. Phone, cable TV, fireplace in units. $110–$225; full breakfast, complimentary snacks and beverages. AE, D, MC, V. No smoking.*

SAN JUAN ISLANDS

The San Juan Islands offer the traveler a relaxed pace in a setting that ranges from tranquil to wildly rain- and windswept. There are no thoroughfares, just meandering roads; fierce storms bring power outages; fresh water is a precious commodity.

The San Juan archipelago contains 743 islands at low tide, a number that drops to 428 at high tide. Of this total, 172 are named, 60 are populated, and 10 are state marine parks. The islands are home to seals, porpoises, otters, some 80 orca whales, and more than 60 actively breeding pairs of bald eagles. The islands offer an unbeatable array of outdoor activities: bicycling, sailing, kayaking, canoeing, golfing, horseback riding, boating, fishing, and on and on.

Non-native residents have moved here to escape the breakneck pace of life elsewhere, and they become as fierce as the natives about protecting what they find: the natural beauty, the wildlife, the privacy. Visitors who respect the island's values are welcome. Ferries stop at Lopez, Shaw, Orcas, and San Juan islands (schedules can vary and you often have to wait in line hours before departure); you'll need a private plane or boat to get to the others.

Lopez Island abounds with orchards, weathered barns, and pastures of grazing sheep and cows. The relatively flat terrain makes it a favorite spot for bicyclists. The Franciscan nuns who run the ferry dock at Shaw Island wear their traditional habits; few tourists disembark here, though, because the island is mostly residential. Orcas, the next in line, is a mountainous, horseshoe-shape island of 56 square mi, with 125 mi of coastline. The last stop, on San Juan Island, is Friday Harbor, with its colorful and active waterfront. The San Juan islands also lie in the so-called Banana Belt, with an annual average of 247 sunny days; compare that with Seattle's gray weather and you'll begin to understand Friday Harbor's holiday atmosphere.

PLACES TO GO, SIGHTS TO SEE

Moran State Park (Star Rte., tel. 360/376–2326) lies just 10 mi from the Orcas Island Ferry landing. It offers 4,600 acres of forest and hiking trails, as well as panoramic views from a lookout tower (at the end of a 6-mi drive on paved roadway) on top of 2,400-ft Mt. Constitution. The park also has 148 campsites.

Roche Harbor (tel. 360/378–2155), at the northern end of San Juan Island, is an elegant resort complex with rose gardens, manicured lawns, a cobblestone waterfront, and hanging flower baskets on the docks. It was constructed during the 1880s as a limestone mining village. A white clapboard restaurant and lounge, the Roche Harbor Restaurant, offers great views of Roche Harbor, though the food is just average. The romantic-looking old Hotel de Haro has seen better days— the guest rooms are very down at the heel. In addition to the harbor, the resort has a private airport. Ask for directions to Afterglow Vista, a fascinating Grecian-columned mausoleum tucked away in the woods on the property.

Rosario Spa & Resort (1 Rosario Way, tel. 360/376–2222 or 800/562–8820), on Orcas Island, was built in 1905 by shipbuilding magnate Robert Moran, who had been told that he had only six months to live and wanted to do it lavishly. Moran put $1.5 million into this Mediterranean-style mansion (there are 6 tons of copper in the roof); the investment turned out to be a good one, since he lasted another 30 years. In 1960 Rosario became a resort; villas and hotel units were added (since fire codes prohibited rental of the mansion's rooms), but they're a far cry from the exquisite teaks and mahoganies of the original structure. The mansion itself, now listed on the National Register of Historic Places, contains the music room (where a free organ concert and slide presentation on the history of the place are given several times each week), the dining room, and the spa with the original pool.

San Juan Goodtime Jazz Festival (Box 1666, Friday Harbor, WA 98250, tel. 360/378–5509) attracts musicians from across the country who perform at four sites in Friday Harbor for three days at the end of July.

San Juan Island National Historic Park (tel. 360/468–3663). For a number of years, both the Americans and the British occupied San Juan Island. In 1859 a Yank killed a Brit's pig, igniting long-smoldering tempers. Both nations sent armed forces to the island, but no further gunfire was exchanged in the "Pig War" of 1859–72. The remains of this scuffle are the English Camp near the north end of the island, with a blockhouse, commissary, and barracks; and the armaments from the American Camp on the southeastern tip of the island. The visitor center is on Spring Street one block up from the ferry terminal.

Whale Museum (62 1st St. N, tel. 360/378–4710). This modest museum in Friday Harbor focuses on the great cetaceans; displays include whale models, whale skeletons, whalebone, whale recordings, and whale videos. Standing on the ferry dock, you can see it at the top of the hill—it has a whale mural painted on the wall. The museum also operates a whale sighting hot line at 800/562–8832 as part of ongoing research; they'll want to know the time of your sighting and any distinctive markings you saw.

Whale-watching. For a chance to see whales cavorting, try the first official whale-watching park in the United States, *Lime Kiln Point State Park* (6158 Lighthouse Rd., tel. 360/378–2044), 9 mi west of Friday Harbor on San Juan Island's west side. Whale-spotting season is mid-May through mid-August. For an even better chance, consider a half-day *Western Prince Cruise* (tel. 360/378–5315 or 800/757–6722), which offers whale-watching during the summer and bird-watching and wildlife tours during the spring and fall. Cruises depart from the Main Dock at the Friday Harbor Marina.

RESTAURANTS

Lopez Island: The **Bay Café** (Lopez Village, tel. 360/468–3700) features innovative dishes, especially fish, in a casual, cottage-style atmosphere. **Gail's** (tel. 360/468–2150) has a natural-wood Cape Cod look and specializes in fresh seafood and local lamb; Gail grows her own herbs and vegetables. For lunch, try the old-fashioned soda fountain at the **Lopez Island Pharmacy** (tel. 360/468–3711), offering soups and sandwiches as well as phosphates, malts, floats, and other fountain treats. Orcas Island: **Christina's** (N. Beach Rd. and Horseshoe Hwy., Eastsound, tel. 360/376–4904) provides fresh local seafood in an elegant atmosphere both inside and on the rooftop terrace. **Bilbo's Festivo** (N. Beach Rd. and A St., Eastsound, tel. 360/376–4728), in a stucco house with a courtyard decorated with Mexican tiles, features creative renditions of burritos and enchiladas as well as mesquite-grilled specialties. Two of Orcas Island's inns, the **Orcas Hotel** (Horseshoe Hwy., tel. 360/376–4300, closed fall–spring; *see below*) and the **Deer Harbor Inn** (tel. 360/376–4110; *see below*), serve casual Pacific Northwest fare utilizing the fresh produce of the islands. San Juan Island's **Duck Soup Inn** (3090 Roche Harbor Rd., tel. 360/378–4878) features the island's Wescott Bay oysters and other fresh seafood prepared in its Mediterranean-inspired kitchen. The **Springtree Café** (310 Spring St., tel. 360/378–4848), in the middle of Friday Harbor, boasts its own organically grown produce as well as fresh fish and pasta dishes. For seasonal Northwest cuisine with an international flare, visit the dining room at **The Friday Harbor House** (130 West St., tel. 360/378–8455), on a hill above the ferry loading area. A rising star on the San Juan culinary scene is **The Place Next to the San Juan Ferry** (tel. 360/378–8707), featuring creatively prepared seafood and pasta dishes, and the best view in town if you're waiting for the ferry.

TOURIST INFORMATION

San Juan Island Chamber of Commerce (Box 98, Friday Harbor, WA 98250, tel. 360/378–5240). **San Juan Islands Visitor Information Service** (Box 65, Lopez, WA 98261, tel. 360/468–3663 or 888/468–3701). **Washington State Tourism** (Box 42500, Olympia, WA 98504-2500, tel. 800/544–1800).

RESERVATION SERVICES

Orcas Island Chamber of Commerce Innkeeper Hotline (tel. 360/376–8888). **Pacific Reservation Service** (Box 46894, Seattle, WA 98146, tel. 206/439–7677 or 800/684–2932). **Washington State Bed & Breakfast Guild** (2442 N.W. Market St., Box 355-FD, Seattle, WA 98107, tel. 800/647–2918).

CHESTNUT HILL INN ☞

Box 213, Orcas, WA 98280, tel. 360/376–5157, fax 360/376–5283;
www.chestnuthillinn.com

High atop a grassy knoll on Orcas Island, overlooking rustic fields and an evergreen forest, sits a proud yellow Victorian farmhouse, the Chestnut Hill Inn. Opened on Mother's Day, 1995 by Marilyn and Dan Loewke, this restored turn-of-the century farmhouse is the quintessential country inn, with a lazy wraparound porch and vistas of tranquil farmland from almost every room. Marilyn and Dan left their suburban life (she managed a pediatrics clinic, he is a marine engineer) for 16 acres of rolling green hills on Orcas Island, home also to deer, rabbits, and soaring hawks.

French country furnishings, polished hardwood floors, and a marble gas fireplace in the parlor set the casually refined tone you can expect throughout your stay. Each of the five guest rooms is named for its view. In the Pond Room, 75 ft of lace scarf is gently wrapped on top of the pencil-post featherbed. There is a fireplace, claw-foot tub, and yes, a view of the pond. The Chestnut Suite is the ultimate retreat, with a cozy sitting area, fireplace, full entertainment center, wet bar, whirlpool tub, and its own private entrance. In the afternoon you can stroll through the century-old pear orchard or enjoy a glass of cool lemonade on the veranda. Marilyn specializes in putting romantic getaway packages together. She'll arrange for a massage or a gourmet picnic for two. Robes, slippers, soaps, lotions, candies, and aperitifs in your room are just some of the extra-special trappings.

Breakfast is also sumptuous: Marilyn prepares a multicourse affair each morning in the main-floor dining room, with offerings that might include pecan butter pancakes, artichoke frittata, and homemade chicken sausage. Dinner is available by reservation during the fall and winter seasons. △ *4 double rooms with baths, 1 suite. Fireplace, robes, and slippers in rooms, TV/VCR in suite. Airport and ferry pickup. $145–$195; full breakfast. MC, V. No smoking.*

DEER HARBOR INN ☞
Deer Harbor Rd., Box 142, Deer Harbor, WA 98243, tel. 360/376–4110, fax 360/376–2237

The Deer Harbor Inn, 15 minutes west of the Orcas Island ferry landing, has two parts. The Old Norton Inn—now the restaurant—overlooks Deer Harbor; this was the original hotel. Up a hill is a two-story log cabin built in 1988, and this is the inn proper. Three small log cabins are lined up next to the inn, providing more private accommodations. Hosts Craig and Pam Carpenter live on the property, but their interaction with guests is usually limited to encounters in the restaurant.

The log cabin has high ceilings and light, simple country-style furnishings. Both levels have decks with views of the water off the common sitting rooms, which feature peeled-log sofas, chairs, and tables, and windows swathed in white muslin tieback curtains. The eight guest rooms are furnished with peeled-log beds with hand-stitched quilts and peeled-log chairs and tables; four have views of the water.

Ideal for romantic getaways, each cottage has its own outdoor hot tub on a private deck, and inside, locally made fir furniture with simple floral country quilts, fireplaces, and TVs. The honeymoon cottage sits on a bluff with a spectacular view of the harbor. Homemade muffins, fresh fruit, and juice are delivered to your door each morning in picnic baskets. The restaurant, open throughout the year, specializes in fresh seafood and pasta dishes; in summer, deck dining, with splendid views of the harbor, is offered. △ *8 double rooms with baths, 3 cottages. TV, fireplace, and whirlpool bath in cottages. Restaurant. $99–$189; Continental-plus breakfast. AE, MC, V. No smoking.*

DUFFY HOUSE ☞
760 Pear Point Rd., Friday Harbor, WA 98250, tel. 360/378–5604 or 800/972–2089, fax 360/378–6535; www.san-juan.net/duffyhouse

The Duffy House sits above Griffin Bay on the southeast side of San Juan Island, 2 mi south of Friday Harbor. Surrounded by 5 acres of orchards, flowering gardens, groomed lawn, and secluded beach, the inn has unobstructed views of the Olympic Mountains. Owners Mary and Arthur Miller fell in love with San Juan Island when traveling through the region on their boat, and ended up buying the B&B in 1992 so that they could stay.

The Tudor-style house has a solid, old-world feel; it has the original leaded-glass windows, cove ceilings, hardwood floors, and mahogany woodwork. Native American artwork covers the white stucco walls. Cream-color leather couches set in front of a wood-burning stove in the common room offer a relaxing setting for afternoon refreshments. The Panorama Room upstairs is romantic, with crisp, white curtains, a garden-print quilt (made by Mary) on the cherry-wood bed, and an exceptional view of Griffin Bay and the mountains beyond. A resident eagle has made its nest near the inn, and viewing the majestic birds is a popular pastime for many guests.

Favorites among the Millers' three-course breakfast offerings include egg and cheese strata; crepes with fresh strawberries; hot, sticky cinnamon rolls; and raspberry cream cheese coffee cake. △ *5 double rooms with baths. Private beach. $90–$110; full breakfast. MC, V. No smoking, 2-night minimum on weekends July–Sept. and holidays.*

EDENWILD INN 🐚
Box 271, Lopez Island, WA 98261, tel. 360/468–3238, fax 360/468–4080; www.edenwildinn.com

The imposing gray Victorian-style farmhouse surrounded by rose gardens in tiny Lopez Village is the Edenwild Inn. Although it looks restored, the inn was built in 1990. After reading about it in the *Wall Street Journal* in 1996, Lauren and Jamie Stephens traveled to Lopez to get a better look. It was love at first sight. They bought the inn within two months, left their suburban life in Bellevue, Washington, and have enjoyed the easy pace of island life ever since.

The entrance opens onto a long hallway with oak floors, handwoven rugs, and framed oils and watercolors by Northwest artists. The muted palette—whitewashed floors, walls of grayed rose and lilac, white woodwork—lends the common areas sophistication. Each of the guest rooms has a different color scheme and individualized furnishings, with custom-made bed frames and wainscoting, botanical prints, large sprays of dried flowers and grapes (and, in season, fresh flowers), Scottish lace curtains, and leaded-glass windows. Four rooms have views of Fisherman's Bay and the San Juan Channel. The blue-gray Honeymoon Suite, overlooking the water, has a fireplace flanked by antique fireplace chairs.

Jamie is the cook in the house and makes everything from scratch, from maple-almond granola to his award-winning breakfast raspberry cake. On summer afternoons, you can linger on the sunny patio with a glass of wine or light alfresco meal. △ *8 double rooms with baths. Fireplace in suite. Conference facilities; ferry, seaplane, and airport pickup. $100–$155; full breakfast. AE, MC, V. No smoking.*

FRIDAY HARBOR HOUSE 🐚
130 West St. (Box 1385, Friday Harbor, WA 98250), tel. 360/378–8455, fax 360/378–8453; www.friday-harbor.net/fhhouse

On a prominent bluff overlooking the marina in San Juan Channel stands the Friday Harbor House. The natural colors of the scenic setting are echoed in the guest rooms and an array of textures give them an outside-in feeling, as do the walls of glass opening on to decks and narrow step-out balconies. Local artwork is showcased throughout the inn, including handmade driftwood benches made by innkeeper Jim Skoog.

Double-size whirlpool tubs and fireplaces set the stage for romantic interludes. Rooms are very spacious, averaging 550 square ft, and appointed with coffeemakers, mini-refrigerators, plush robes, and televisions. In all rooms you can enjoy the radiance of the fireplace while relaxing in the whirlpool tub. The inn is also very family friendly; kids under 17 stay free in their parents' room, and futons and cribs are readily available.

A generous breakfast buffet is offered downstairs in the dining room, with freshly baked pastries, granola, yogurt, bagels, seasonal fruit, and juice. Local produce and herbs, lamb, and seafood play a major role in the critically acclaimed culinary productions created each evening by local chef Laurie Paul. Outdoor dining is available in the summer. Reserve a spot for dinner well in advance. ♨ *19 double rooms with baths, 1 suite. Fireplace, whirlpool bath, mini-refrigerator, phone, data port, and TV/VCR in rooms. Restaurant, conference facilities. $150–$275; Continental-plus breakfast. No smoking, 2-night minimum July–Sept. and holidays.*

HILLSIDE HOUSE 🦜
365 Carter Ave., Friday Harbor, WA 98250, tel. 360/378–4730 or 800/232–4730, fax 360/378–4715; www.rockisland.com/~hillside/house.html

After Dick and Cathy Robinson left San Luis Obispo, California, they spent three years traveling in their 46-ft boat before purchasing Hillside House, a three-story contemporary cedar home that stands—yes—on a hillside a half mile from downtown Friday Harbor. Dick's creative talents are most easily appreciated in his famous, always available, banana–chocolate chip cookies; Cathy's talents shine most in the house's decor.

The open living and dining room areas give onto a spacious and scenic deck above the garden; on clear days, there are spectacular views of Mt. Baker. The living room has a large brick fireplace, an Arts and Crafts coffee table, and overstuffed chairs. Water trickles from Dick's hand-crafted fountains on display throughout the house. The seven sophisticated, comfortable guest rooms are furnished with king- and queen-size beds, oak chests, and window seats. Cathy has created a distinct theme for each room. In the Charlotte's Web Room there's a quilted chintz bedspread with pink cabbage roses on an ivory background, sea-green carpet, and views of hummingbirds and butterflies that visit the two-story atrium just outside. The Eagle's Nest Suite is the most romantic and extravagant of the rooms, replete with king-size bed, whirlpool tub, wet bar, television, and a small private deck.

Dick prides himself on the hearty country-style breakfast that he serves each morning. Along with fresh fruit, juice, granola, and muffins, you can fill up for the day on one of his tasty hot casseroles. ♨ *7 double rooms with baths. Robes in rooms. TV and whirlpool bath in suite. $85–$165; full breakfast. AE, D, MC, V. No smoking.*

INN AT SWIFTS BAY 🦜

Port Stanley Rd., Rte. 2, Box 3402, Lopez Island, WA 98261, tel. 360/468–3636, fax 360/468–3637; www.swiftsbay.com

Rob Aney and Mark Adcock first discovered the Inn at Swifts Bay in 1993 through a gift certificate that they received for being "best men" in their friend's wedding. They loved the place so much that they returned year after year until they found out the inn was for sale. They had always dreamed of owning a B&B, but didn't know where or how, until this enchanting property presented itself to them.

A 1975 mock-Tudor building, 2 mi from the Lopez Island ferry landing, the inn is surrounded by rhododendrons, madronas, and firs amid 3 acres of woods, with another acre of beach a four-minute walk away. The inn's decor is sophisticated, but the rooms feel lived-in and loved. The sunny living room has large bay windows, a fireplace, a chintz sofa and chairs on an Oriental rug, and shelves of books. The den/music room behind the living room features a large brick fireplace, two Queen Anne upholstered wing chairs, a TV/VCR with more than 300 videotapes, and French doors that open onto the deck and the woods.

The individually decorated guest rooms are spacious and airy. Room 2 has hunter green walls with cream accents, window swags of patterned fabric, an Arts and Crafts headboard on the queen-size bed, a gateleg desk, and a large dark-cherry mirror and chest. An attic suite has pale peach walls, a queen-size sleigh bed, and an English armoire and chest; three long, narrow skylights have been cut into the sloping ceiling, and there's a private entrance and small deck.

The raised dining room, pale yellow with hand-stenciled ivy around the ceiling, is the setting for breakfast, which might include hazelnut waffles with fresh island berries and crème fraîche or salmon dill blintzes. ▲ *2 double rooms with baths, 2 doubles share bath, 1 suite. Fireplaces and mini-refrigerators in suite and 2 rooms; TV/VCR in den and suite. Video library, exercise room, hot tub. $95–$175; full breakfast. AE, D, MC, V. No smoking.*

KANGAROO HOUSE ☞

N. Beach Rd., Box 334, Eastsound, WA 98245, tel. 360/376–2175 or 888/371–2175, fax 360/376–3604; www.pacificws.com/kangaroo

Nestled on 2 acres of lawn and gardens less than a mile from the Orcas Island village of Eastsound is the 1907 Craftsman-style home known as Kangaroo House. The innkeepers are Peter and Helen Allen, both retired from careers in the National Park Service. Peter was born in Australia, and so when they spotted an inn for sale with the name "Kangaroo House," they just couldn't pass it up.

There's a solid, old feel to the dark hardwood floors and the Oriental rugs, but there's no need to be anxious about knocking over precious antiques. The living room is spacious, with a sitting area in front of a large stone fireplace, beamed ceilings, lace curtains, settees, and wing chairs. The Louisa Room—forest green and tan—has an old brass bed and a small twin bed with a painted iron headboard, handmade quilts, and angled ceilings. Kathleen's Suite is the most private of the rooms, with its own bathroom and garden view.

The Allens serve a full breakfast with gourmet offerings, including challah French toast with crushed cornflake crust (the batter spiked with rum), poached pears, and sourdough pancakes. They'll also pack a "ferry breakfast" if you're off early to meet a boat. A seat at their Christmas and Thanksgiving dinners are available by reservation. ▲ *1 double room with bath, 3 doubles share 1½ baths, 1 suite. Robes in rooms. Games room, hot tub. $75–$125; full breakfast. AE, D, MC, V. No smoking.*

LOPEZ FARM COTTAGES ☞

Fisherman Bay Rd., Lopez, WA 98261, tel. 360/468–3555, fax 360/468–3966; www.lopezfarmcottages.com

John Warsen had Irish grandparents who owned a farm in upstate New York when he was a child, a place he remembers spending endless summer days with

Earn Miles With Your MCI Card.

Take the MCI Card along on this trip and start earning miles for the next one. You'll earn frequent flyer miles on all your calls and save with the low rates you've come to expect from MCI. Before you know it, you'll be on your way to some other international destination.

Sign up for MCI by calling
1-800-FLY-FREE

All airline program rules and conditions apply. Other terms and conditions apply to ongoing mileage offer and bonus mile offer. MCI, its logo and the names of the products and services referred to herein are proprietary marks of MCI Communications Corporation. American Airlines reserves the right to change the AAdvantage program at any time without notice. American Airlines is not responsible for products and services offered by other participating companies. American Airlines and AAdvantage are registered trademarks of American Airlines, Inc.

Is this a great time, or what? :-)

Earn Frequent Flyer Miles.

Continental Airlines
OnePass.

▲ Delta Air Lines
SkyMiles®

HAWAIIAN AIRLINES.

MIDWEST EXPRESS AIRLINES

NORTHWEST AIRLINES
WORLDPERKS®

Rapid Rewards™
SOUTHWEST AIRLINES®

MILEAGE PLUS.
United Airlines

US AIRWAYS
DIVIDEND MILES

With guidebooks for every kind of travel—from weekend getaways to island hopping to adventures abroad—it's easy to understand why smart travelers go with **Fodor's**.

At bookstores everywhere.
www.fodors.com

scores of relatives. His dream of re-creating a family farm reminiscent of Grandpa's has come true on Lopez Island. He and his partner, Ann Warsen, bought 20 acres of land in 1995 with the intention of being closer to their grandchildren, and fulfilling Ann's dream of owning a B&B. They built four cottages (with four more in the works) in the middle of their century-old orchard with resident sheep, deer, rabbits, and songbirds.

Three miles from the Lopez ferry dock, the farm is tucked away from the road by a thick wild rose hedge and cedar grove. The cottages have raw cedar siding and white-painted trim. There are windows throughout, letting in light and views of the trees and meadow. Each is equipped with a double shower, gas fireplace, kitchenette with microwave, and thick comforters on queen-size beds. The decor is country simple—walls painted cream, sunflower yellow, and purple. The back decks are set in the trees, a secluded place for morning coffee and listening to the chatter of wild birds in the orchard. Guests have access to an outdoor hot tub for private evening spas. A Continental breakfast basket is delivered to your cottage each evening (so as not to disturb your morning sleep). Ann bakes deliciously enormous muffins fresh each day. ♨ *4 cottages. Kitchenettes and fireplaces in cottages. Hot tub, ferry and airport pickup. $125; Continental breakfast. MC, V. No smoking.*

MACKAYE HARBOR INN ☞
Rte. 1, Box 1940, Lopez Island, WA 98261, tel. 360/468–2253, fax 360/468–2393; www.san-juan.net/mackayeharbor

In 1978 Mike Bergstrom retired from professional golfing so that he could be with his wife, Robin, and their young children. In 1985, inspired by family and friends who enjoyed visiting them, the Bergstroms bought a 1920s wood-frame Victorian-style sea captain's house along a quarter mile of beach at the south end of Lopez Island, across the road from MacKaye Harbor.

The sitting room has white wicker furnishings as well as a light blue sofa and love seat in front of a brass-and-glass-doored fireplace, and a stained-glass window with roses designed by Robin. This room looks west out to the harbor, as do three of the guest rooms. The romantic Harbor Suite is appointed with a golden oak bedroom set from Italy, fireplace, and private deck through French doors. The spacious Carriage House Studio sits behind the main farmhouse, with wicker furnishings, a blue-and-white-tile floor, and stocked kitchenette.

The Bergstroms serve fresh-baked pastries in the afternoon, chocolate truffles in the evening, and a gourmet breakfast each morning. For the adventurous, they maintain a fleet of rental mountain bikes and kayaks; a quiet glide on MacKaye Harbor at sunset is the perfect end to the day on Lopez. ♨ *2 double rooms with baths, 2 doubles share 2½ baths, 2 suites, 1 carriage house. Kitchenette in suite. Kayak instruction and rental, mountain bikes, boat buoy, airport and ferry pickup. $99–$175; full breakfast. MC, V. No smoking, 2-night minimum July–Sept.*

MARIELLA INN & COTTAGES ☞
630 Turn Point Rd., Friday Harbor, WA 98250, tel. 360/378–6868 or 800/700–7668, fax 360/378–6822; www.mariella.com

Mariella is the only inn right on the waterfront on San Juan Island. This stately 1902 Victorian has cabins in varying styles and sizes along the waterline, and equipment for outdoor activities. It was a resort from 1926 through World War II, after which it became a private residence; it reverted to seaside retreat status in 1992 and has been growing continually ever since. It should be noted that the inn was on the market at press time, but the current owner is committed to handing the property over to capable hands.

Of the 11 rooms in the main house, Sweet Briar, in the southeast corner, is a favorite: lace-covered windows look out on the garden and harbor, allowing sunshine to stream in on forest-green carpet, wicker and dark-wood trimmed furniture, rose-print wallpapered walls, and the coordinating down-filled duvet on the tall oak bed. The room, as well as others on the main floor, has a fireplace, a whirlpool bathtub, and a glass-walled solarium overlooking the water. A lavish Continental breakfast buffet is served each morning in the dining room.

Several of the waterfront cottages dotting the property have kitchenettes, TV/VCRs, hot tubs, fireplaces, and private decks that jut out over the water. A Continental breakfast basket and newspaper are delivered to you each morning. ♦ *8 double rooms with baths, 3 suites, 12 cottages. Kitchenette, fireplace, and whirlpool bath in some cottages. Hot tub, volleyball court, tennis court, boat dock, private beach, bicycle rentals, sailing and cruise charters. $125–$375; Continental breakfast. AE, MC, V. No smoking, 2-night minimum June–Sept. and 3-night minimum on holidays.*

OLD TROUT INN ☞

Horseshoe Hwy., Rte. 1, Box 45A, Eastsound, WA 98245, tel. 360/376–8282, fax 360/376–3626; www.pacificws.com/oldtroutinn

When owners Sandy and Dick Bronson bought this place in 1995, they were looking to retire to warmer climes after spending two decades in Alaska, where Dick had been stationed as an Air Force pilot. The inn now serves as the Bronson's "working retirement," and they've spent a great deal of time and money spiffing it up; they've even added a waterside annex called The Anchorage Inn, with three private, spacious suites overlooking Eastsound.

The burgundy, gray, and white walls in The Old Trout Inn serve as a palate for subtle artwork hung throughout this large, three-story contemporary. The most stunning features of this inn, less than 3 mi inland from the Orcas Island ferry, are the soaring windows and broad decks that look out over an idyllic 2½-acre pond surrounded by trees and cattails. You may not end up spending much time in your pretty guest room, choosing instead to sit outside on the decks listening to the soothing trickle of a stone waterfall; watching the ducks, hummingbirds, cranes, and woodpeckers; paddling the little canoe on the pond; or soaking in the waterside hot tub on the lower deck. The Waters Edge cottage is ideal for romantic getaways, with a private hot tub, queen-size feather bed, and fireplace. The three waterfront suites at The Anchorage Inn all have a fireplace, kitchenette, and private deck with dramatic views of the water.

A Continental breakfast basket is delivered to your room each morning. A full breakfast is served at the Old Trout Inn during the summer season. ♦ *6 suites, 1 cottage. Robes in rooms; kitchenettes and fireplaces in suites; kitchenette, hot tub, and fireplace in cottage. Hot tub, canoe, ferry pickup. $125–$185; Continental-plus breakfast. D, MC, V. No smoking.*

OLYMPIC LIGHTS ☞

4531-A Cattle Point Rd., Friday Harbor, WA 98250, tel. 360/378–3186, fax 360/378–2097; www.san-juan.net/olympiclights

In 1985 Lea and Christian Andrade took a vacation from the San Francisco Bay area and fell in love with San Juan Island—so much so that they returned a month later and bought this 1895 farmhouse, 5½ mi south of the Friday Harbor ferry landing. Throughout the summer, wildflowers cultivated by the Andrades frame the house in a riot of color.

Many inns are hideaways, but Olympic Lights stands out in a windblown field with few trees to block the view of Puget Sound and the Olympic Mountains. You have the run of the entire house—the hosts live in a small building behind the main house. Decorated almost exclusively in white (save for a few pale pastels), with no curtains except for white valances, the house feels expansive and open to both sunlight and starlight. Guest rooms feature brass reading lamps, wicker chairs and tables, and fluffy duvets and pillows. The parlor has white wicker furniture with pale peach cushions.

A farm-fresh breakfast is served on Lea's aunt's ivory, green, and pink rose-pattern china, either in the parlor or in the kitchen. The Andrades' breakfast includes a hot egg dish, scones, fresh fruit, and coffee. The spacious lawn is an ideal spot for an afternoon game of croquet or horseshoes, or at night for gazing at the stars. △ *1 double room with bath, 4 doubles share 2 baths. Croquet, boccie, horseshoes. $75–$110; full breakfast. No credit cards. No smoking, 2-night minimum June–Sept. and on holiday weekends.*

ORCAS HOTEL 🐚

Box 155, Orcas, WA 98280, tel. 360/376–4300 or 888/672–2792, fax 360/376–4399; orcashotel@thesanjuans.com

On the hill overlooking the Orcas Island ferry landing sits a three-story red-roof Victorian with a wraparound porch and a white picket fence. The Orcas Hotel, a bustling seaside inn, was built between 1900 and 1904 by Canadian landowner William Sutherland. Today the hotel is listed on the National Register of Historic Places; even the flower gardens—drifts of daffodils, wisteria vines, irises, and roses—have been restored. The hostelry is managed by Craig and Linda Sanders and Brad Harlow—three active young people who, when they aren't bicycling, hiking, or playing volleyball or softball, are likely to be in the kitchen cooking gourmet meals.

The hotel has a colorful past. A bullet hole through a veranda post recalls the Prohibition-era escape of a bootlegger who foiled his pursuers by leaping to freedom over the porch railing. Some islanders claim that liquor was smuggled in by small boats and stored in the woodpile and the attic. During the hotel's restoration in 1985, loose planks were discovered in the attic, with enough space underneath to store dozens of bottles of booze.

The main floor features a bakery-espresso café, dining room, and parlor furnished with Queen Anne settees, marble-top tables, and Oriental rugs. The dining room (open to the public) overlooks the ferry landing as well as part of the garden. All public rooms have splendid harbor views, and showcase works by Orcas artists.

Two romantic guest rooms at the front of the inn have French doors opening onto a wrought-iron-furnished sundeck with views of the waterfront. Both rooms feature fluffy feather beds and duvets and marble-top tables. Each has a large bathroom with a double whirlpool bath. △ *2 double rooms with baths, 2 doubles and 1 triple with ½ baths share 2 full baths, 5 doubles and 1 triple share 4 baths. Whirlpool bath in two rooms. Restaurant (June–Sept.), bakery, cocktail lounge, conference facilities, bicycle rentals. $69–$170; full breakfast. AE, D, MC, V. No smoking, 2-night minimum on holiday weekends.*

SAN JUAN INN 🦐

50 Spring St., Box 776, Friday Harbor, WA 98250, tel. 360/378–2070 or 800/742–8210, fax 360/378–6437; www.san-juan.net/sjinn

Annette and Skip Metzger began looking for an inn of their own in 1989; after a nationwide search for the right place at the right price, they settled on the San Juan Inn. Facing Friday Harbor's main street, the 1873 Victorian that once housed the town's wireless station stands a block uphill from the ferry landing.

A rose garden behind the building offers a secluded spot for a picnic or a glass of wine and the chance to relax in the hot tub. The inn is clean and comfortable but not luxurious. The tiny lobby and stairway have stained-wood paneling. An upstairs sitting room features a rose Queen Anne parlor group, a wood-burning stove, a Mission oak rocker, and a peekaboo harbor view.

The nine guest rooms, all upstairs, are fitted with brass, wicker, or painted-iron bedsteads. The San Juan Room has wicker chairs, flowered comforter, iron bedstead, washstand, and soft pink walls hung with framed needlework samplers. The suites, just off the garden, have their own private entrance, kitchen, TV/VCR, and two-person whirlpool bathtub.

The Metzgers serve fresh pastries, bagels, fruit, and coffee on bone china in the second-floor parlor each morning. ⚱ *4 double rooms with baths, 5 doubles share 3 baths, 2 suites. Kitchen, TV/VCR, and whirlpool bath in suites. $78–$220; Continental-plus breakfast. AE, D, MC, V. No smoking.*

SAND DOLLAR INN 🦐

Horseshoe Hwy., Box 152, Olga, WA 98279, tel. and fax 360/376–5696; www.virtualcities.com/ons/wa/j/waj8801.htm

Follow Horseshoe Highway through Eastsound to the quiet side of Orcas Island, and you'll come to the tranquil Sand Dollar Inn. On an incline across the road from Buck Bay, this white-trimmed, gray farmhouse built in 1926 offers fine views of the San Juan Channel, Lopez Island, and the Olympic Mountains in the distance.

Opened in 1989 by Ric and Ann Sanchez, formerly of Carmel, California, the inn is striking but homey; the many Asian antiques reflect the time Ann spent teaching English in Japan. All the guest rooms feature woodblock prints, Japanese tansu chests, queen-size beds, and claw-foot tubs; the three second-floor rooms have terrific ocean views. There are also great vistas from the sunny enclosed porch, which also serves as the dining area where such morning specialties as baked salmon on a croissant topped with a cream sauce, or plum cake and hot coffee help you greet the day.

A rowboat is available to guests for an afternoon adventure on the channel. Hiking trails and the lake in nearby Moran State Park also provide a plethora of activities to occupy you. Olga Art Works and Café (tel. 360/376–5098), within walking distance, is a great option for lunch or an early dinner. ⚱ *4 double rooms with baths. Guest refrigerator, rowboat. $90–$125; full breakfast. AE, MC, V. No smoking.*

SPRING BAY INN 🦐

Obstruction Pass Park Rd., Box 97, Olga, WA 98279, tel. 360/376–5531, fax 360/376–2193; www.springbayinn.com

At the end of the trek to Spring Bay Inn, 20 mi (the last mile on a potholed dirt road) from the Orcas ferry landing, you will be rewarded by seclusion in an incredible waterfront setting. The contemporary cedar inn, nestled on 57 acres of largely undisturbed forestland, is lovely in and of itself, but its innkeepers, Carl Burger and Sandy Playa, make this place special. These retired park rangers have managed to keep their fingers in the environmental pie by purchasing the land bordering Obstruction Pass Park to protect it from subdivision and development. They offer nature tours, either by kayak or on foot, as part of your stay, to impart a better understanding of the uniqueness of the San Juans' flora and fauna.

Airy, sunny guest rooms have wood-burning fireplaces, claw-foot tubs, fresh flowers, and windows overlooking Spring Bay; two larger corner rooms also have private balconies and cozy feather mattresses. The most extraordinary room in the inn is the Ranger Suite, with a 15-ft ceiling, private hot tub, queen-size bed with a puffy down comforter, and 28 windows that face the water. You'll want to call well in advance to reserve this room.

Each morning begins with a Continental breakfast to nibble on while reading the *Spring Bay Today*, a one-page newsletter printed by the innkeepers every morning, reporting local weather, news about guests, and a schedule of activities. And then you're off for a morning nature outing with your hosts, followed by a hearty brunch served in a room that is flanked by twin stone fireplaces and has a fir floor and 15-ft ceiling with exposed beams. △ *5 double rooms with baths. Fireplace in rooms. Guest refrigerator, hot tub, barbecue, nature trails, kayak and hiking tours, binoculars. $175–$225; Continental breakfast and full brunch, dinner available. AE, D, MC, V. No smoking, 2-night minimum Apr.–Oct.*

STATES INN ☙

2039 W. Valley Rd., Friday Harbor, WA 98250, tel. 360/378–6240, fax 360/378–6241; www.karuna.com/statesinn

It was a schoolhouse in the early 1900s and for a time it served as a dance hall, but now the States Inn is a working equestrian center, with boarding for horses and a horsemanship school for children, and a bed-and-breakfast. Horseback tours are generally available to guests, but inquire when you make your reservations, just in case.

Nestled in a tranquil valley not far from British Camp and Roche Harbor, the house retains its original maple floor in the living room and a tall, stone fireplace; otherwise it's thoroughly modern, with casual, ranch-style decor and contemporary American furnishings. Each of the 10 guest rooms feature decorative touches reminiscent of the state for which it's named—white wicker and eyelet in the Louisiana Room, for example, and seashells on the fireplace mantel in the Rhode Island Room. The Arizona–New Mexico suite—awash in subdued Southwestern blues, tans, and rust hues—has two bedrooms, a sitting room, and a shared bath and is ideal for families or couples. The spacious California Room has cathedral ceilings and expansive windows with a spectacular view of the valley and nearby hills.

A hearty two-course breakfast is served in the sunny sitting room by innkeepers Julia and Alan Paschal. Farm-fresh offerings might include seasonal fruit, juice, and muffins, along with a hot entrée such as chili-cheese eggs or baked French toast. △ *8 double rooms with baths, 2 doubles share bath. Fireplace in 1 room. Bicycle storage, horseback riding, ferry and airport pickup/drop off. $85–$125; full breakfast. MC, V. No smoking.*

TRUMPETER INN ☞

420 Trumpeter Way, Friday Harbor, WA 98250, tel. 360/378–3884 or 800/826–7926,
fax 360/378–8235; www.friday-harbor.net/trumpeter

In a peaceful rural valley just 2 mi from the Friday Harbor ferry landing on San Juan Island, this charming 1980 farmhouse is named for the Trumpeter swans that occupy a wetland area on the property in winter. Rolling lawns call for picnics and hammocks strung between fir trees encourage naps in the shade; a pond stocked with fish and the opportunity to pick blackberries for a morning cobbler round out the country retreat appeal.

Don and Bobby Wiesner have done a fine job with their five guest rooms: Each is country comfortable and tastefully appointed with a mix of contemporary and antique furnishings, down comforters, and graceful window treatments framing sunny pastoral views. Local art is proudly featured throughout the inn. The Lavender Room, with Battenburg lace, and a wedding ring quilt wall hanging, is a charmer. The Rosemary Room on the first floor has an elegant country charm, with a fireplace, ivory walls and linens, fresh flowers, and views of the surrounding valley. There's also a wheelchair-accessible room (the only one on the island to date) on the home's lower level next to the lounge.

Views from the dining room of the Olympic Mountains and False Bay are often the main topic of conversation over breakfast. Bobby serves a variety of homemade specialties, paying close attention to seasonally fresh ingredients. In the summer she might make strawberry pancake baskets, in the fall, French toast with apples. Afternoon refreshments are offered. △ *5 double rooms with baths. TV in den, games, hot tub, bicycle storage, ferry and airport pickup. $80–$125; full breakfast. AE, D, MC, V. No smoking.*

TURTLEBACK FARM INN ☞

Crow Valley Rd., Rte. 1, Box 650, Eastsound, WA 98245, tel. 360/376–4914
or 800/376–4914, fax 360/376–5329; www.turtlebackinn.com

Bill and Susan Fletcher abandoned suburban life in the San Francisco Bay area (he was a real-estate broker, she a homemaker) for 80 acres of meadow, forest, and farmland on Orcas Island. Forest green with white trim, the renovated, Folk National–style farmhouse, a 10-minute drive from the Orcas Island ferry landing, stands in the shadow of Turtleback Mountain, with Mt. Constitution to the east.

The cream-color sitting room, with a beamed ceiling and peach-and-green accents, includes a Rumford fireplace, pilgrim-style trunk, cabbage-rose upholstered sofa, and a corner game table. The salmon-color dining room has fir wainscoting and five small oak tables.

The guest rooms are decorated with Cape May Collection wallpaper. All have reading lamps, comfortable seating, cream-colored muslin curtains, and meadow and forest views. The Meadow Room has a private deck overlooking the pasture. The light fixtures and crystal doorknobs in most rooms and the claw-foot tubs and bathroom mirrors were rescued from Seattle's old Savoy Hotel before it was razed, and the sinks and beveled-glass bathroom shelves above them come from Victoria's grand old Empress Hotel. The comforters on the beds are stuffed with wool batting from the Fletchers' own sheep. The Orchard House, a new cedar building appropriately set in the apple orchard, offers four luxurious rooms with king beds, fireplaces, claw-foot tubs, and private decks overlooking the valley.

If you are staying in the main house, breakfast is served in the dining room or, in nice weather, on the deck on tables set with bone china, silver, and linen. Guests staying in the Orchard House enjoy breakfast in the privacy of their room or deck. Breakfast brings fresh fruit and juice, homemade granola, and specialty hot dishes including an egg fritatta and breakfast pizza. If you want the recipes, you can buy Susan's cookbook. Full meal service is available by reservation for groups. △ *11 double rooms with baths. Fireplace in 4 doubles. Walking paths. $80–$210; full breakfast, complimentary beverages. D, MC, V. No smoking, 2-night minimum on holidays and weekends Apr.–Oct.*

WHARFSIDE BED & BREAKFAST ☞
K-Dock, Slip 13, Port of Friday Harbor Marina, Box 1212, Friday Harbor, WA 98250, tel. 360/378–5661; www.san-juan-island.net/wharfside

Board the *Jacquelyn*, a 60-ft motor-sailer anchored near the Friday Harbor ferry landing, and you'll find yourself on the Wharfside, the town's only floating bed-and-breakfast. Clyde Rice and his wife, Bette, decided to combine their love of boating and their flair for hospitality in 1984, when they opened the *Jacquelyn* as a B&B.

The main salon, decorated with art and artifacts from Clyde's earlier days at sea, has two sofas and a skylight, a fireplace, and lots of polished wood and brass. The head has a Japanese-style tile soaking tub as well as a shower. The two guest rooms stand at opposite ends of the boat: the aft stateroom, a romantic low-beamed captain's cabin with a queen-size bed, a small settee, and a half-bath; and the forward stateroom, furnished with a double bed and two child-size bunks. As Bette tells everyone who calls to inquire about a room, this B&B is not for tall people.

Bette serves a four-course, all-you-can-eat breakfast in the salon or on the aft deck if it's sunny. Breakfast aboard on a typical day might include blueberries and peaches with ginger; apple crunch cake with a rum-nut topping; sausage rolls; and a special frittata or a breakfast quiche with San Juan salsa. She provides children with nets and cans for gathering shrimp (and jellyfish and other treasures) from the harbor. △ *2 double rooms share bath. Robes in rooms. Fishing gear, rowboat. $95; full breakfast. AE, MC, V. No smoking, pets allowed, 2-night minimum June–Sept. and holidays.*

WINDSONG ☞
2 Deer Harbor Rd., Box 32, Orcas, WA 98280, tel. 360/376–2500 or 800/669–3948, fax 360/376–4453; www.pacificws.com/windsong; windsong@pacificrim.net

This 1917 schoolhouse, home to grades one–six until 1942, was extensively renovated and reopened to the public as a bed-and-breakfast in 1992. Hand-painted murals brighten the interior walls of the house; Madrona Point, a scenic rocky point on the island, is depicted in the entryway. The 12-ft ceiling in the main 20- by 30-ft school room is awash in fluffy clouds bordered on the walls below by vining ivy. Tall, broad windows pull the rural scenery in; innkeepers Kim and Sam Haines have also tucked hammocks and a hot tub in a stand of fir trees so that you can spend time outdoors soaking in the peaceful setting.

Following the theme set by the inn's name, rooms feature musical monikers. Nocturne, on the main floor, is Southwestern style; antlers hang on the wall above the fireplace flanked by cushioned chairs and twig side tables, and an intriguing pine bedstead. An alder-twig headboard and floral-print pillows and tablecloths lend country charm to the Rhapsody room, which has a peekaboo view of the West Sound. Down comforters, gas fireplaces, comfortable sitting areas, warm robes, and chocolates delivered when the beds are turned down are some of the thoughtful touches.

Sam, who has been cooking since age five, marshals an impressive morning feast, beginning with a fresh fruit sorbet and his homemade apple oat cereal. He also serves dinner in the off-season, featuring local lamb and seafood. ♨ *4 double rooms with baths. Robes, fireplace, and chocolates in rooms. Library, hot tub, barbecue, kayak storage, ferry and airport pickup. $115–$140; full breakfast. MC, V. No smoking.*

WHATCOM AND
SKAGIT COUNTIES
Including Anacortes, Bellingham, and La Conner

*About 90 minutes north of Seattle on the way to Vancouver, British Co-
lumbia, I–5 passes through Skagit and Whatcom counties, where gently
rolling dairy farmland is juxtaposed with flat rectangles of brilliant color—
fields of commercially grown daffodils and tulips that are a major attraction
for gardeners, photographers, and city dwellers in search of a pleasant weekend drive. To the east in these two northernmost counties in coastal Washington, low foothills often wrapped in mist nestle against the snowcapped
mountains of the Cascade range.*

*Far from being exclusively agrarian, however, the three major commu-
nities in Whatcom and Skagit counties are very much associated with
the sea. La Conner, at the mouth of the Skagit River, is a fishing village with
a decidedly artsy accent, a legacy of the 1940s, when modernist painters
Morris Graves and Mark Tobey settled there. Ferries ply the waters of
Anacortes, a fishing and logging town on Fidalgo Island that serves as
the gateway to the San Juan Islands. Bellingham, a center of fishing
and lumber activity and the southern terminus of the Alaska Marine
Highway System, is the site of Western Washington University, a campus
with splendid views of Puget Sound. Nowhere are the ocean views more dramatic than from Chuckanut Drive (Highway 11), a dramatic 23-mi stretch
between Bellingham and Bow along Chuckanut Bay.*

*Today artists and college professors coexist with farmers and fishermen
in this pastoral area. A number of the residents are descendants of the
native tribes that have lived here for the past 12,000 years, or offspring
of relative newcomers: the Spanish, who arrived in 1774, and the English, who followed four years later.*

PLACES TO GO, SIGHTS TO SEE

Bellingham Waterfront. Several spots provide good dock walking, fishing, lounging, and picnicking. *Squalicum Harbor Marina* (Roeder Ave. and Coho Way,

tel. 360/676–2542), the second-largest marina on Puget Sound, is home to more than 1,700 commercial and pleasure boats. An aquarium in the adjacent Harbor Center shopping mall contains examples of many of the local sea creatures; children will especially enjoy the "touch tank." *Boulevard Park* (S. State St. and Bayview Dr.), midway between downtown and Old Fairhaven, is a 14-acre waterfront park with a half mile of shoreline. With views of both the San Juan Islands and the Cascades, it's a perfect choice for picnicking. *Marine Park* (at the foot of Harris St. in Old Fairhaven) is small, but popular for crabbing and watching sunsets.

Birch Bay State Park (5105 Helwig Rd., Blaine, tel. 360/371–2800). Most of this 200-acre park, 10 mi from the Canadian border, is heavily wooded, but the shore and a few of the 167 available campsites offer impressive views of the San Juan Islands. The clamming and crabbing here are excellent, and opportunities for fishing, swimming, and hiking along interpretive trails are plentiful. Campsites are open year-round but can be reserved only from Memorial Day to Labor Day.

Chuckanut Drive (Hwy. 11). It's best to take this 23-mi drive along Chuckanut Bay heading south out of Bellingham; that way you'll have the steep and densely wooded Chuckanut Mountain on your left, with stunning views of Puget Sound and the San Juan Islands relatively unobstructed. The drive begins along Fairhaven Park in Old Fairhaven and joins I–5 in the flat farmlands near Bow in Skagit County. The full loop can be made within a few hours. Several good restaurants are on the southern end of the drive, so you may want to plan your jaunt around lunch or dinner (*see* Restaurants, *below*). In addition to a number of lookout points, there are several other worthwhile stops along the way: *Larrabee State Park* (245 Chuckanut Dr., Bellingham, tel. 360/676–2093), with nearly 1,900 acres of forest and park and 3,600 ft of shoreline; the 6-mi-long *Interurban Trail*, a former train track along the water used for cycling, walking, jogging, and horseback riding (the trailhead begins in the north near 24th Street and Old Fairhaven Parkway and in the south near Larrabee State Park); and the *Taylor United/Samish Shellfish Farm* (188 Chuckanut Dr., Bow, tel. 360/766–6002), where, by appointment, you can watch oysters being harvested, sorted, shucked, and packed. A store on the premises sells oysters, scallops, crabs, and mussels in season.

Ferndale Parks. *Hovander Homestead Park* (5299 Nielsen Rd., Ferndale, tel. 360/384–3444) is a "farm park" complete with a Victorian-era farmhouse, farm animals, vegetable gardens, old farm equipment, a blacksmith's shop, and walking trails. *Pioneer Park* (1st and Cherry Sts., Ferndale, tel. 360/384–6461) features a handful of restored log buildings from the 1870s, including a granary, Whatcom County's first church, a hotel, and several houses. *Lake Terrell Wildlife Preserve* (5975 Lake Terrell Rd., Ferndale, tel. 360/384–4723) is an 11,000-acre spread that allows you to observe a wide variety of waterfowl. Hunting is permitted in season (ducks and pheasants are most prevalent), and fishing on the lake, year-round, yields trout, catfish, bass, and perch. Nearby is *Tennant Lake Natural History Interpretive Center* (5236 Nielsen Rd., Ferndale, tel. 360/384–3444), featuring an early homestead, nature walks around the lake, and an observation tower from which the 200 acres of marshy habitat, bald eagles, muskrats, otters, and other wildlife can be seen. The rich perfumes emanating from the fragrance garden there are intended for the seeing-impaired, but, naturally, sighted visitors enjoy them as well. Special events include crafts fairs and evening walks with a modern-day Henry David Thoreau in 19th-century costume.

Gaches Mansion (703 S. 2nd St., La Conner, tel. 360/466–4288). Ever since Morris Graves, Mark Tobey, Kenneth Callahan, and other pioneering American modernist painters settled in La Conner during the 1940s, the town has been an artists' haven. Aside from sampling the local talent at one of the village's many galleries, you can see the works of area artists at the Valley Museum of Northwest Art, on the first floor of this restored 1891 Victorian Tudor mansion. The first floor is especially popular because you are encouraged to touch and sit on the period furniture that is on display. The second and third floors house a quilt museum. The turret of the house offers an excellent view of La Conner.

Maritime Heritage Center (1600 C St., Bellingham, tel. 360/676–6806). This urban park is a tribute to Bellingham's fishing industry and heritage. On self-guided tours, you can learn about hatcheries and the life cycles of salmon, watch salmon spawn, see how rearing tanks work, watch mature salmon swim up the fish ladders, and actually fish for salmon and trout.

Padilla Bay (10441 Bay View–Edison Rd., Mt. Vernon, tel. 360/428–1558). This estuary features an interpretive center that focuses on the area's natural history, with exhibits and saltwater aquariums, a mile-long nature trail, beach walk, a pair of resident bald eagles, and a variety of waterfowl and sea life.

Skagit Valley Tulip Festival (Box 1784, Mt. Vernon, WA 98273, tel. 360/428–5959). Held during the last two weekends in March or the first three weekends of April in Mt. Vernon, Burlington, Anacortes, and La Conner, the festival centers around more than 1,500 acres of spring flowers—daffodils, irises, and, of course, tulips—with tours of the blossoming fields and bulb sales. Festivities include foot races, an art show featuring local talent, a community fair, horse-drawn wagon rides, a salmon barbecue, sailboat regatta, concerts, dance performances, an antiques show, a food fair, petting zoo, and sky-diving and kite-flying demonstrations.

Western Washington University (516 High St., Bellingham, tel. 360/650–3000) overlooks downtown Bellingham and Bellingham Bay. As you drive through the campus to take in the panorama, you'll be treated to a fine collection of outdoor sculpture, including works by Mark DiSuvero, Isamu Noguchi, Richard Serra, and George Rickey.

Whatcom County Museum of History and Art (121 Prospect St., Bellingham, tel. 360/676–6981). In a large redbrick Victorian building in downtown Bellingham, the museum concentrates on the early coal and lumber industries, the history and culture of Native American tribes that lived in the area, and the habitat and characteristics of local waterfowl. The museum also hosts traveling exhibitions.

RESTAURANTS

At **Randy's Pier 61** (tel. 360/293–5108) in Anacortes, you can dine on some of the town's best seafood while watching the sun set over Guemes Channel. Well-regarded French cuisine is served at the romantic **La Petite** (tel. 360/293–4644). Among Bellingham's dining spots, try **Pacific Café** (tel. 360/647–0800) for an eclectic, beautifully presented blend of Pacific-Asian dishes; the **Orchard Street Brewery** (tel. 360/647–1614) for excellent microbrews and Northwest fare; and the **Wild Garlic** (114 Prospect St., tel. 360/671–1955) for creative Pacific Northwest cuisine. Other good bets in Bellingham include **Il Fiasco** (tel. 360/676–9136), which, despite its name, serves good Italian fare, and **La Belle Rose** (tel. 360/714–0195), a country French restaurant that specializes in seafood. The **Oyster Creek Inn** (tel. 360/766–6179), in Bow, overlooks a rushing creek on Chuckanut Drive and specializes in—what else?—oysters. Also in La Conner, **Palmer's** (tel. 360/466–4261), in the La Conner Country Inn, prepares pasta and seafood in Pacific Northwest style. At **Calico Cupboard** (tel. 360/293–7315), also in La Conner and Mount Vernon, fresh, low-fat, and decadent fill the menu side-by-side for an eclectic blend of comfort food, vegetarian, and Northwest specialties.

TOURIST INFORMATION

Anacortes Chamber of Commerce (819 Commercial Ave., Suite G, Anacortes, WA 98221, tel. 360/293–3832). **La Conner Chamber of Commerce** (413 A Morris St., Box 1610, La Conner, WA 98257, tel. 360/466–4778). **Mount Vernon Chamber of Commerce** (117 N. 1st, Suite 4, Box 1007, Mt. Vernon, WA 98273, tel. 360/428–8547). **Washington State Tourism** (Box 42500, Olympia, WA 98504-2500, tel. 800/544–1800). **Whatcom County Convention & Visitor Bureau** (904 Potter St., Bellingham, WA 98826, tel. 360/671–3990).

RESERVATION SERVICES

Bed & Breakfast Service (445 W. Lake Samish Dr., Bellingham, WA 98226, tel. 360/733–8642). **Pacific Reservation Service** (Box 46894, Seattle, WA 98146, tel. 206/439–7677 or 800/684–2932). **Washington State Bed & Breakfast Guild** (2442 N.W. Market St., Box 355-FD, Seattle, WA 98107, tel. 800/647–2918).

ALBATROSS 🐚

5708 Kingsway W, Anacortes, WA 98221, tel. 360/293–0677 or 800/662–8864; www.cnw.com/~albatros

You'll enjoy the warm hospitality and homey comforts of this 1927 Cape Cod–style inn. It has a wide deck overlooking the harbor at Flounder Bay and is painted—what else?—Cape Cod blue with white trim. Beaches, camping and picnic areas, and trails are just two blocks away at Washington Park, where the opening scenes of *Free Willy* were shot. Additionally, guests enjoy recreational privileges at Flounder Bay's nearby beach club. The Albatross is less than a mile from the ferry terminal for the San Juans and Vancouver Island.

The Scarlett O'Hara Room, with a view of the marina through lace curtains, is named for its authentic plantation furnishings (including an 1860s Victorian half-tester bed covered with a pink silk-moiré comforter, Lincoln rocker, and cranberry glass lamp), while another favorite room, Monet's Garden, is named for its view of the colorful backyard garden.

Linda and Lorrie Flowers, a mother-daughter team, fled the corporate world and moved to Anacortes from Colorado and Texas (via Alaska) in 1997. They purchased the one-level Albatross and set out to establish a new lifestyle as hospitality providers. They take pleasure in discovering how many ways they can make their guests comfortable. At the top of the list is breakfast, which may vary from their choice Baja brunch with Southwestern favorites, to frittatas, fresh fruit pancakes, or stuffed French toast. △ *4 double rooms with baths. Guest phone, cable TV/VCR, library, ferry pickups on request. $85–$95; full breakfast. D, MC, V. No smoking.*

BIG TREES BED & BREAKFAST 🐚

4840 Fremont St., Bellingham, WA 98226, tel. 360/647–2850 or 800/647–2850, fax 360/647–2850; www.nas.com/~bigtrees

Appropriately named, Big Trees Bed & Breakfast is a 1907 Craftsman home nestled among old growth cedars and firs near Lake Whatcom. Naturalized garden areas, rolling lawns and a path to the creek invite exploration.

A corbeled ceiling and massive stone fireplace in the living room, and the dining room's fir woodwork and French doors leading to a covered porch maintain the home's original character. Innkeeper Jan Simmons, who moved to

Bellingham from Santa Monica in the late 1980s, is an avid collector whose passions—quilts, costumed dolls, folk art, and cookbooks—are an asset in her period home.

Each of the guest rooms carries the name of the most prominent subject viewed from that room. The Cedar Room's primary attraction is its lush, king-size feather bed, while the Rhodie Room's decoupage floor invites guests to exercise their creativity. Each has its own bathroom, while the bathless Maple Room is most often occupied by friends or family members who can share with either the Cedar or Rhodie guests.

Breakfast takes the lead at Big Trees. Jan's fondness for cooking prompts her to experiment frequently, take requests, and extend a breakfast invitation to friends and family of her guests. When she presents a savory meal one day, such as Northwest eggs Benedict with salmon, artichokes, and roasted red peppers, she'll follow with a sweet alternative like oatmeal pancakes with orange ricotta and fruit the next day. One guest even persuaded her to concoct a breakfast pizza with sauerkraut and onions. ♙ *3 double rooms share 2 baths. TV/VCR, phone in rooms. Stereo in living room. $95–$115; full breakfast. MC, V. No smoking.*

CHANNEL HOUSE ☙

2902 Oakes Ave., Anacortes, WA 98221, tel. 360/293–9382 or 800/238–4353, fax 360/299–9208; www.channel-house.com

Midway between downtown Anacortes and the ferry terminal is the Channel House, a 1902 shingled Craftsman bungalow with awe-inspiring views of Guemes Channel and the ferry landing that can be seen from most rooms. Innkeepers Dennis and Patricia McIntyre tell guests all about the 2,500 acres of nearby forest and seven freshwater lakes to explore, regularly scheduled whale-watching trips, and sea kayak rentals all in the vicinity.

The dining room features lush potted plants that stand against dark blue-and-peach wallpaper, white wainscoting, and the original glazed terra-cotta tile floor with cobalt-blue borders. As you breakfast on the house specialty—French toast stuffed with cream cheese, pineapple, and pecans—you can watch the ferries plying Rosario Strait. Ten steps up are the living room, with exposed beams and a 10-ft-high ceiling, and a cozy study. Both rooms display porcelain dolls made by Dennis's mother from antique molds, complete with hand-painted features and hand-sewn costumes.

Each guest room has its own style, but all are spacious and light, with high ceilings, hardwood floors, and Oriental rugs. Grandma's Room is furnished with an antique four-poster bed with Laura Ashley bedding, and a turn-of-the-century Eastlake-type oak dresser; the walls are covered with old family photos and little china collectibles. The more formal Canopy Room has a canopy bed covered with the same antique lace that dresses the window and an early 19th-century fainting couch upholstered in cream-color damask. The walls are covered with a cream and green striped paper with a floral border. In a separate cottage, the Victorian Rose room seems a perfect spot for reverie; its window seat is crowded with soft throw pillows, and the fireplace has cream tiles with hand-painted pink roses that are echoed in the pale-pink walls and ceiling border of roses against a black background. ♙ *4 double rooms with baths, 2 doubles with baths in cottage. Whirlpool bath and fireplace in cottage rooms. Hot tub. $79–$109; full breakfast. AE, D, MC, V. No smoking.*

HASTY PUDDING HOUSE ☞
1312 8th St., Anacortes, WA 98221, tel. 360/293–5773 or 800/368–5588;
www.hastypudding.net/hasty

It wasn't long after banker Mike Hasty arranged for the financing of a bed-and-breakfast for a customer that he and his wife, Melinda, began to search for a B&B of their own. Sunshine streaming through wide windows onto the distinctive fir wainscoting and built-ins of the cheery 1913 Craftsman sold them on this home, and they set to work renovating and remodeling it.

The four charming guest rooms are appointed in walnut or oak antiques (primarily Eastlake and Victorian). Generous swaths of ivory lace and an elaborately carved 7½-ft-high burled walnut headboard from the 1850s make the Queen Anne's Lace Room the romantic choice. Each room has a private bath; two feature deep claw-foot tubs, perfect for a relaxing soak. Sunflowers on hand-painted wallpaper brighten a small room probably originally intended as a nursery adjacent to the Queen Anne's Lace Room.

Mounds of Melinda's hand-stitched pillows fill the home's broad window seats, and an exquisite collection of antique china and silver graces built-in cupboards in the living and dining rooms. Quilts, some made by Melinda and others passed on by generations past, adorn walls and furnishings throughout the house.

The Hastys' smoothies and hazelnut pancakes with homemade toppings help start the day off right. The shops and restaurants of downtown Anacortes are within walking distance, and the ferry landing is just 3 mi away. ♨ *4 double rooms with baths. TV/VCR in 1 room. $75–$89; full breakfast. AE, D, MC, V. No smoking.*

HOTEL PLANTER ☞
715 1st St., La Conner, WA 98257, tel. 360/466–4710 or 800/488–5409,
fax 360/466–1320

In downtown La Conner, the Hotel Planter is a masonry building that was constructed in 1907 of solid concrete blocks made on location. The hotel, whose clientele consisted of lumber-mill and fish-cannery workers, merchants, and tourists from Seattle, was modern for its day, with indoor plumbing—one bathroom for 22 rooms—electricity, and a cement sidewalk. Later the writers, artists, and craftspeople responsible for La Conner's reputation as a cultural center moved in. Today you can enjoy that artistic heritage by stepping right out onto First Street, lined with art galleries, bookstores, crafts shops, and restaurants.

Owners Donald and Cynthia Hoskins bought the building in 1987, opened their street-level Earthenworks Gallery, and then renovated the second-story hotel. Creamy walls, custom-made Southern pine headboards and armoires, and wicker chairs lend a country-French atmosphere. To keep the feeling of the old hotel, the original doors, window moldings, railings, trim, and many of the old light fixtures were restored.

Just beyond the Earthenworks Gallery and buffered from the busyness of First Street lies the hotel's serene and sometimes whimsical garden courtyard. After retail hours, guests are welcome to stroll among the unique garden components, some organic and some not, or to relax in the gazebo-covered hot tub. ♨ *12 double rooms with baths. Phone, TV in rooms. Hot tub. $75–$120; no breakfast. AE, MC, V. No smoking.*

LA CONNER CHANNEL LODGE AND COUNTRY INN ❦

205 N. 1st St. and 107 S. 2nd St., La Conner, WA 98257, tel. 360/466–1500
or 360/466–3101, fax 360/466–1525; www.laconnerlodging.com

A shingled, Northwest contemporary structure with rose-entwined lattice fences, the Channel Lodge is one of few waterside inns in the Puget Sound area. High beamed ceilings add to the spacious country atmosphere of its sister facility, the Country Inn. Both are located a short walk from the many restaurants and boutiques lining the waterfront.

Twig furniture, bark bowls, hand-woven baskets, and dried and fresh flower arrangements bring the Northwest indoors to the Channel Lodge's lobby lounge. A towering stone fireplace and a cozy adjacent library help create a relaxed, homey mood. Weekend evenings, musicians entertain on the grand piano, behind which doors open onto a terraced stone deck leading down to the pier. You can occasionally hear tribal songs and drumming from a Native American gathering across the narrow waterway.

In the Channel Lodge's guest chambers, a marine motif reflects the inn's waterfront location. Extras abound: gas fireplaces, cushioned lounge chairs, coffeemakers, mini-refrigerators, and cable TVs discretely hidden in cabinets, bedside chocolate truffles, soft terry robes, and slate-tile bathrooms with two-person whirlpool tubs. Each of the rooms has a deck or balcony. The Captain's Suite, perfect for families, has a small second bedroom with twin beds, porthole windows, and a nautical door. Couples seeking romance and privacy might opt for the gatehouse with a whirlpool bath in the bedroom (but no view of the channel). Comfortable guest rooms, individual fireplaces and an intimate library at the Country Inn carry travelers back in time to a quiet space. Simple furnishings complemented by earth-tone colors and fabrics add to the country atmosphere.

A Continental breakfast buffet with fruit, fresh-baked goods, and bowls of yogurt and granola is available at each inn. If you prefer, the congenial staff will deliver breakfast to your room. △ *68 double rooms with baths, 12 suites. Phone, cable TV, and refrigerator in rooms. Moorage and charter boats available. $93–254; Continental breakfast, afternoon refreshments. AE, DC, MC, V. No smoking.*

MAJESTIC HOTEL ❦

419 Commercial Ave., Anacortes, WA 98221, tel. 360/293–3355
or 800/588–4780, fax 360/293–5214

Dominating the historical district of Anacortes, the Majestic is one of the Northwest's premier small hotels.

Standing in the two-story lobby filled with 19th-century English leather sofas and wing chairs, an elegant brass chandelier, a white marble mantelpiece flanked by engaged columns, and copious flower arrangements, it's difficult to believe that this space was part of a meat market until 1954. Jeff and Virginia Wetmore, restaurant and inn developers from northern California, discovered this 1889 diamond in the rough. They spent six years stripping away everything except the original framework and restoring it, ultimately opening The Majestic in 1990. Two years later they added a charming English garden, an oasis of greenery and flowers where guests can relax over coffee or play with children.

The Wetmores take particular pride in the Rose & Crown Pub behind the lobby, which serves draft beers from local microbreweries and light meals amid 200-year-old English mahogany wainscoting, a backbar from a Victorian ice-cream parlor, and beveled- and stained-glass doors from a London pub. Fancier environs enhance the fare in The Salmon Run, where compelling cuisine such as clams bordelaise, swordfish, and salmon Caesar salad feature the freshest seasonal ingredients available in the area and a wine selection to match.

Each of the hotel's 23 guest rooms is individually custom-decorated and furnished with art and antiques from around the world. The Scottish Highland Room sports fishing rods, baskets, and old shotguns mounted on the walls, and there is a Scottish military chest from the 1880s. In the Asian Room the walls have been marbleized, and Japanese, Korean, and Chinese furniture and art are featured. An oak-paneled cupola grants a 360-degree view of Puget Sound, the marina, the San Juan Islands, and the Cascade and Olympic mountains. ⚘ *23 double rooms with baths. Phone, cable TV, minibar, and refrigerator in rooms, VCR in most rooms. Restaurant, pub, conference facilities. $98–$225; Continental breakfast. AE, D, MC, V. Smoking on 2nd floor only.*

NORTH GARDEN INN ☙

1014 North Garden St., Bellingham, WA 98225, tel. 360/671–7828 or 800/922–6414; www.northgardeninn.com

High atop a steep residential hillside near Western Washington University, North Garden Inn overlooks Bellingham Bay. The inn is also known as the Robert I. Morse House. The Queen Anne Victorian listed on the National Historic Register celebrated its centennial in 1997.

Music is the most prominent theme at North Garden Inn. A Steinway grand piano is the center of attention in the main-floor parlor and music books and images are displayed throughout the house. Several of the rooms are christened accordingly: Carmen, Rhapsody, Madame Butterfly.

Because of its proximity to the university, the inn attracts a substantial number of parents and job candidates, as well as touring musicians, speakers, and authors. Innkeepers Barbara and Frank DeFreytas, who took on North Garden Inn as a semi-retirement project in the mid-1980s, also welcome children. They create an unpretentious atmosphere in which academicians and musicians mix side-by-side with students' families for conversation and song.

Full breakfasts greet guests each morning. In addition to the standard juice, fruit, and pastries, fare might include fried wontons with sugar, muesli, quiche or omelettes. Barb and Frank have developed dozens of their own recipes and, in addition to being featured in others' cookbooks, have published their own collection. ⚘ *8 double rooms with baths, 2 double rooms share baths. $50–$99; full breakfast. MC, V. No smoking.*

RIDGEWAY FARM ☙

14914 McLean Rd., Box 475, La Conner, WA 98257, tel. 360/428–8068 or 800/428–8068, fax 360/428–8880; www.placestostay.com/lacon-ridgewayfarm

This 1928 brick Dutch Colonial occupies a prime location on Skagit Valley's famous Tulip Route, halfway between Mount Vernon and La Conner. In keeping with its farmstead past, the interior of the home is country comfortable, with a mixture of Early American antiques, lace curtains, and fresh flowers. Bulb flowers and perennials, including 60,000 tulips and daffodils, color the landscaped grounds.

Louise and John Kelly, the hospitable owners, have named the six guest rooms in the main house after their daughters and granddaughters. Cynthia has a claw-foot tub at the foot of the patchwork quilt–covered bed and a commode in a side alcove. The room's soft pink–and–teal color scheme enhances the antique furnishings, which include an Eastlake cherry dresser and night table. At the top of the house on the third floor, Nicole is brightened by skylights and extensive windows offering wide views of nearby farm fields. The Kellys have converted a one-time woodshed and fruit house into a one-bedroom cottage. The namesake of their grandson, Hayden's Hideaway includes a partial kitchen.

Murphy and Paddy O'Kelly, the Kellys' pet felines, are very chummy and enjoy entertaining guests in the living room before the Kellys serve their hearty farm-style breakfast or evening desserts. ♨ *4 double rooms with baths, 2 doubles share bath and shower, cottage. Cable TV in lounge and cottage. $75–$155; full breakfast, evening desserts. D, MC, V. No smoking, 2-night minimum late Mar.–early Apr.*

SCHNAUZER CROSSING ☙

4421 Lakeway Dr., Bellingham, WA 98226, tel. 360/733–0055 or 800/562–2808, fax 360/734–2808; www.schnauzercrossing.com

On a slope above Lake Whatcom this contemporary cedar home dispels the notion that B&Bs in this area mean Victorian. Gracious, sophisticated accommodations entice you to one of three distinct worlds. The Garden Suite, with its tree-framed private entrance, artful and literary appointments, and oversize bath with whirlpool tub and double shower, is a retreat spacious enough even for a family. Through tall cedars and overlooking the lake, The Cottage is an escape, at once sophisticated and subdued. It has the comforts of a partial kitchen and tile bath with Jacuzzi and shower, and inspires contemplation with Japanese-influenced art and furnishings. Original Northwest art and fresh flowers find their way into the Queen Room, with its own lake view and natural setting.

Schnauzer Crossing is surrounded by well-tended gardens, the leisure-time project of Monty McAllister. Flanked by a natural wooded area are several specialty gardens as well as rhododendrons pushing the century mark. If you see something special, Monty may share cuttings and ideas with you.

The unusual name of this B&B derives from innkeeper Donna McAllister's well-behaved schnauzers, Barbel and Marika, the official greeters. Glass doors reach up to a dramatic cathedral ceiling in the main floor great room. Accompanied by classical music and songs from the doves, finches, and canaries in the aviary, breakfast is a special occasion—with individual quiches, rhubarb crisps, and blueberries and raspberries fresh from the garden (you may pick your own). The pampering extends to fruit and cheese baskets, home-baked cookies, fresh flowers, plush robes, and "schnauzer" slippers in every room. The extensive library includes many books signed by their authors, some of whom have enjoyed Schnauzer Crossing themselves. The McAllisters are literate hosts who are glad to share their treasures with you beyond your stay if you'll promise to mail them back. ♨ *1 double room with bath, 1 suite, 1 cottage. CD player and phone in rooms, fireplace, cable TV/VCR, and whirlpool bath in suite and cottage. Hot tub. $120–$200; full breakfast, afternoon refreshments. MC, V. No smoking, 2-night minimum on weekends and holidays.*

SHANNON HOUSE ☙

2615 D Ave., Anacortes, WA 98221, tel. 360/299–3876 or 800/828–1474, fax 360/299–8352; www.anacortes-city.com/shannon

Just a mile from downtown Anacortes and 3 mi from the San Juan Ferry, The Shannon house is framed by flower gardens and a peaceful wooded acreage that gives shelter to deer, rabbits, birds, and other wildlife. Originally built in 1915, the two-story farmhouse was moved to its current location in 1990 and completely restored. Innkeepers Cathy and Al Holiday were attracted to Anacortes by the mild climate and boating opportunities. They relocated from Phoenix in 1997 after working in Arizona's judicial system for a collective 66 years.

Elegant and understated best describe the Holidays' style and hospitality. Luxurious linens with goose down duvets pamper guests in each of the three bedrooms. Soft rose, green, and cream wallpaper, highlighted by lace linen overlays, provide a gentile ambience in Morgan's Room, which shares a spacious bath and oversized whirlpool tub and tile shower with the subtly European Erin's Room. The largest accommodation is the rose and cream Master Bedroom, with a spacious sitting area and private bath.

Guests are invited to make themselves comfortable in the denlike library or the formal living room. Overstuffed leather furnishings and an intricately decorated 200-year-old rolltop desk lend a relaxing atmosphere to the library, complete with a television for those who can't live without it. In contrast, unusual wall coverings, eclectic art, and picture windows overlooking the garden and woods cultivate a gracious living room.

Adjacent to the living room, the dining room offers a sophisticated setting for the full breakfast the Holidays serve each day. Baked egg dishes and French toast are frequent entrées, accompanied by fruit compote, muffins or scones, and plentiful fresh juices and coffee. ♨ *1 double room with bath, 2 doubles with shared baths. $80–110; full breakfast. MC, V. No smoking.*

SOUTH BAY BED & BREAKFAST ☙
4095 S. Bay Dr., Lake Whatcom, Sedro Woolley, WA 98284, tel. 360/595–2086

Perched on a steep hillside across the road from idyllic Lake Whatcom, South Bay is a retreat among retreats. Above the house stretches a forest with old-growth cedars and a creek. Below, South Bay has lake access via the road and a pathway through adjacent undeveloped park reserves. The spectacular view of mountains rising out of the lake and the serene sights and sounds of the woods are calm surroundings for those who lounge in their rooms or on the wraparound porch and deck.

Innkeepers Dan and Sally Moore readily tell the unusual story of how South Bay Bed & Breakfast came to be. A contractor by trade, Dan won a bid to build a new house for the manager of the state fisheries. Part of the project was to remove the existing house, a Craftsman-style Sears home erected in the early 1930s. In lieu of destroying the building, Dan decided in 1995 to recycle it and move it three coves up and across the road. He built a special road up the hillside and enlisted some of the best craftspeople in the area, determined to keep it true to the Craftsman style. The completed house is similar to the original, with the original stairwell and deck, but it has been significantly enhanced and expanded. Recipient of a building industry award for excellence in remodeling, South Bay opened for guests in early 1997.

As distinctive as its legacy is the breakfast menu. Sally draws on local products when possible, including options such as salmon pizza, ostrich sausage, chicken and apple sausage, homemade bread and granola, and ham, apple, and Swiss cheese strata. She also serves afternoon snacks and an evening herbal tea tray.

Outdoors enthusiasts can choose from water sports, hiking, biking, and cross country skiing. ♨ *5 double rooms with baths. CD player in rooms, fireplace in 4* *rooms, whirlpool bath in 3 rooms. Canoeing, kayaking, pedal-boating, fishing, mountain bikes. $125–150; full breakfast. MC, V. No smoking.*

STORYVILLE ☞

18772 Best Rd., Mt. Vernon, WA 98273, tel. 360/466–3207 or 888/373–3207, fax 360/466–3066; www.ncia.com/~vonberry

Between Mt. Vernon and La Conner, and atop Pleasant Ridge, Storyville Bed & Breakfast overlooks expansive Skagit Valley farmlands. Storyville was formerly known as Downey House, named after Art Downey, a founding father of La Conner. James and Francesca Embery purchased the 1904 house with the dream of making it a romantic retreat for couples, intending to pamper guests while assuring privacy and quiet time.

The Emberys have implemented several changes to Storyville since they acquired it in the mid-1990s. Golden walls warm the living and dining rooms and artistic window coverings accent most rooms. While the blue and cream Downey Room, with its sleigh bed and Victorian theme, has been left intact, the Storyville Suite has taken on a European air in shades of sand, yellow, and rosy terra-cotta, furnished with antique vanity, love seat, Queen Anne chairs, and a tea table. The East and West rooms, which share a whirlpool bath, bear the name of the direction they face; one room overlooks the garden and waterfall, the other greets the valley and sunrise. The separate and secluded Bungalow is distinctively furnished with eclectic driftwood furniture in a contemporary color scheme of butter, sand, and black.

James has cultivated a series of gardens surrounding the house. To nearly a thousand tulips and daffodils and extensive flower beds, he has added herb and kitchen gardens, a double waterfall, and nearby putting greens.

James takes special pride in the professional-quality espresso beverages he serves guests at any time, day or night. They also accompany dessert in the evening and gourmet breakfast in the morning, alongside pastries, quiche, crepes, blintzes, and fresh fruits and herbs, many of which James grows himself. ♨ *3 double rooms with baths, 2 double rooms share bath. TV/VCR, CD player in rooms. $90–$125; full breakfast. MC, V. No smoking.*

STRATFORD MANOR BED & BREAKFAST ☞

1416 Van Wyck Rd., Bellingham, WA 98226, tel. 360/715–8441, fax 360/671–0840; www.site-works.com/stratford

An estatelike retreat on 30 pastoral acres, Stratford Manor is a large Tudor-style home that is set back from the road, accessible by its own country lane. One of Stratford Manor's original uses almost 20 years ago was as a private school. Innkeepers Leslie and Jim Lohse bought it in the mid-1990s. It was in such poor repair that it required total renovation, from reconstructing the turret at the entry to refurbishing every room inside. A year and a half later, it was transformed.

All three guest rooms feature beds with down comforters, showers and whirlpool tubs, gas fireplaces, and sitting areas. The Sunrise Room's skylights and blue-accented white wicker furnishings make even cloudy days cheery. The muted tones among the Hillside Room's contemporary oak furnishings and pier bed soften skylight rays to lend a cozy atmosphere. The Garden Room is a favorite for romantics. Decorated in cool colors with a four-poster king-size bed, its main attraction is the elevated, tile-encased, oversize, jetted tub overlooking the garden. A fourth accommodation, the seasonal Room with a View, offers amenities comparable to the Garden Room and takes advantage of summertime's lush, expansive panorama.

A spacious and sumptuously furnished home, Stratford Manor presents several options for relaxation. Various moods and tastes can be accommodated, whether in the library, formal living room, air-conditioned TV-and-games room, parklike grounds, putting green, or outdoor hot tub. Blooming plants and wicker decorate the solarium, surrounded by outdoor decks and leading into an exercise facility complete with Nordic track, Soloflex equipment, a treadmill, a stair stepper, and a TV/VCR. Data ports are available.

Leslie's graceful style extends to breakfast, which follows a room-delivered wake-up tray of coffee and muffins. The menu might include such delights as salmon quiche, Dutch babies with fruit, or veggie hash with poached egg and hollandaise. *▲ 3 double rooms with baths. CD player, fireplace, whirlpool bath in rooms. Outdoor hot tub, exercise room, putting green. $125–$175; full breakfast, snacks and refreshments. MC, V. No smoking. Fourth double room with bath available in summer.*

WHITE SWAN GUEST HOUSE 🐚
15872 Moore Rd., Mt. Vernon, WA 98273, tel. 360/445–6805; www.cnw.com/~wswan

Tucked away along a narrow country road near the Skagit River, just 6 mi from the artistic community of La Conner, is the White Swan Guest House and its 2 acres of English country gardens. In 1898, a Scandinavian farmer, who ran the ferry across the river, built the Queen Anne clapboard farmhouse with a turret from which he could watch for passengers. More than a decade ago, New Yorker Peter Goldfarb fell in love with the house and used his training as an interior designer to make each room colorful and airy, almost like year-round gardens. Public and guest rooms feature distinctively bright walls, white trim, lace curtains, handmade quilts, fresh flowers, and a collection of needlework samplers.

Guest rooms in the main house have king- or queen-size beds with brass and iron headboards and hand-hooked rugs. The Pink Room has a little sitting area in the six-sided turret. A generous assortment of art and garden books and original art invites quiet time in the parlor, while framed words and thoughts displayed around the house offer a glimpse into Peter's well-considered philosophies.

The two-story cottage draws on pine and other light woods, wicker chairs, Pendleton Indian blankets, tile, and stained glass to create a more contemporary environment.

Peter has become almost famous beyond the Skagit Valley on two counts: unrivaled chocolate chip cookies and the acres of breathtaking gardens that themselves have been a subject for numerous magazine writers and photographers. From the familiar to the obscure, there is nearly always something blooming in the ever-expanding gardens, which are well-viewed from rooms throughout the house as well as the brick patio in their midst. *▲ 3 double rooms share 2 baths, 1 cottage. Kitchen in cottage. $80–$150; Continental breakfast. MC, V. No smoking.*

WILD IRIS AND THE HERON INN 🐚
117 Maple Ave., La Conner, WA 98257, tel. 360/466–4626; www.wildiris.com

Two distinguished Victorians side-by-side on La Conner's quiet Maple Avenue adjoin to provide hospitality services collectively yet distinctly.

The Heron Inn is brimming with herons on stained-glass windows, watercolors, prints, and etchings. Even the outside is painted blue-gray. Large windows with lace curtains and a high cove ceiling contribute to the light, airy feel of the lobby-parlor, where you can relax on the Queen Anne–style camelback couch or in wing chairs in front of the fireplace. Guest rooms, all carpeted and featuring a blue-and-rose color scheme, mix modern reproductions, such as wing chairs and beds with oak, walnut, and brass headboards, with antique armoires. All the suites have gas fireplaces.

While coziness is The Heron's appeal, elegance has been the objective for Wild Iris, according to innkeeper Susan Sullivan. Rooms are painstakingly individualized to appeal to a diversity of moods and tastes, drawing on a full spectrum of color and texture combinations as well as furnishing configurations. One person's fantasy might call for the cloud room, with its celestial blue and white walls, white wicker, and lace veil crowning the bed. Another might be drawn to Japanese-theme room, with black roses and dark wicker.

Particular attention is afforded guests of the Victorian duet with special needs or occasions. Each house offers a barrier-free room designed to be easily accessible. Wild Iris creates custom packages for honeymooners and couples celebrating anniversaries and other notable events. Monogrammed champagne flutes and ribbon-bedecked doors are among the memorable touches. Additionally, conference facilities accommodate meetings for 5–30 attendees.

An intimate dining room for breakfast with such delights as eggs *en croute* or quiche is also the setting for a gourmet dinner option for guests. Executive chef Casey Schanen prepares three or four entrée choices, appetizers, pasta, salad and desserts, accompanied by an extensive international and domestic wine list.

♨ *32 double rooms with baths and suites. Phone, TV, clock radio in rooms, 2-person whirlpool bath in some suites. Hot tub. $75–$180; full breakfast. AE, MC, V. No smoking.*

CASCADE MOUNTAINS AND FOOTHILLS

The Cascades form a magnificent snowy spine, stretching from Oregon into Canada, that divides Eastern and Western Washington. The volcanic upheaval that created the massive mountain range also dug the fjordlike Lake Chelan, the country's second deepest lake, and created valleys flanking the foothills—verdant and thick with fir trees on the west side, drier and pine-filled on the east side. The mountains offer spectacular scenery; good skiing in winter; and hiking, camping, fishing, river rafting, and wildlife viewing in summer.

Day trips and longer excursions from Seattle, just west of the range, take visitors into the heart of the Cascades to sample the scenery, a sprinkling of mountain villages—some originally gold- or coal-mining towns from the last century, some simple ski resorts—and a wide range of inns and lodges nestled in valleys or perched on crests.

A variety of mountain experiences are available within two hours of Seattle. Interstate 90, for example, leads east to Snoqualmie Pass, with both downhill and cross-country skiing, and on to the mining towns of Roslyn and Cle Elum. Highway 2 heads northeast across Stevens Pass, another downhill skiing area, to the Bavarian-style village of Leavenworth. Not far from the Canadian border, Highway 20 (closed in winter) cuts through North Cascades National Park, a half-million-acre preserve studded with glaciers and mountain lakes. Heading south out of Seattle, Highways 12, 706, 165, and 410 take you to various entrances of Mt. Rainier National Park.

Drives through the Cascades take you past mountain valleys, alpine meadows, lakes, and waterfalls, but only by hiking the trails can you really experience the beauty and grandeur of the mountains. Not all the trails are rugged; in fact, some are more like alpine walks. The best time to view mountain wildflowers is July to early August.

PLACES TO GO, SIGHTS TO SEE

Lake Chelan. Scenic excursions up the 55-mi-long lake aboard one of the *Lady of the Lake* boats (tel. 509/682–2224) leave from the town of Chelan on the south shore, where the sun shines 300 days a year. The boat takes you to the northern terminus town of Stehekin where you can disembark for a picnic lunch or a short tour in an open bus before returning to Chelan, where you'll find rentals for waterskiing, boating, fishing, and cross-country skiing.

Leavenworth. This former mining and railroading town with a population of about 2,000 is at an elevation of 1,170 ft, surrounded by mountains rising to 8,000 ft. Thirty years ago, Leavenworth was a has-been; when civic leaders turned it into an alpine village, giving every downtown building a Tyrolean-style facade, tourists flocked.

Mt. Rainier National Park (tel. 360/569–2211). Designated in 1899 as the nation's fifth national preserve, the Pierce County park encompasses all of Mt. Rainier, at 14,410 ft the state's highest mountain. Among the park's 240,000-plus acres are forests, alpine meadows, and glaciers (when the weather is cooperative, hiking trails lead right up to the glaciers' edge). Major visitor centers are at Paradise, Sunrise, and Ohanapecosh; some offer slide shows, summer videos, naturalist-guided hikes, and information on hiking trails and the many breathtaking lookouts.

Mt. Rainier Scenic Railroad (tel. 360/569–2588). A vintage steam locomotive takes you on a 14-mi trip across spectacular bridges and through lush, tall forests with views of Mt. Rainier. The train departs from Elbe in season. The trip takes 90 minutes and is accompanied by live banjo and guitar music.

Northwest Trek (near Eatonville, tel. 360/832–6116). This is one of the country's most unusual parks. Through 5½ mi of forest, bog, and pasture, trams take visitors to view North American wildlife—elk, deer, bears, bison, caribou, bighorn sheep, pronghorn antelopes, mountain goats, moose, gray wolves, cougars, lynx, bobcats, birds, waterfowl—in their native habitats.

Puget Sound and Snoqualmie Valley Railroad (tel. 425/746–4025). This steam-locomotive-driven train, operated by volunteers, runs between Snoqualmie and North Bend (just east of Seattle on I–90) from May through September. Tickets can be purchased in the restored 1890 depot in downtown Snoqualmie. The ride takes about 70 minutes and offers views of mountains, forest, and meadowland.

Roslyn. This old mining town, off I–90 near Cle Elum, has mostly fallen into disrepair but manages to support a handful of retail shops, two restaurants (*see* Restaurants, *below*), and a first-run movie theater (in an old mortuary). It has been described as more Alaskan than Alaska by the folks who chose to film the television series "Northern Exposure" here.

Snoqualmie Falls. These 268-ft falls just outside the town of Snoqualmie, in Pierce County, are a crashing spectacle in the spring, when the mountain snows thaw, and when fall rains come thundering down. At the top is an observation deck and a mile-long marked trail down to the base of the falls.

Winthrop. This historic town on Highway 20, the North Cascades Highway, is about a four-hour drive from Seattle. Once a bustling gold-mining town, Winthrop has been returned to its colorful 1890s appearance with barn-board storefronts, hitching posts, and boardwalk-style sidewalks. You can inspect an excellent collection of Old West memorabilia at the *Schafer Historical Museum* (Castle Ave. off Coral St., tel. 509/996–2712) in a 100-year-old log cabin, or rest at *Three-Fingered Jack's* (Hwy. 20 and Bridge St., tel. 509/996–2411), the state's oldest saloon that is now a restaurant.

RESTAURANTS

Alexander's Country Inn (tel. 360/569–2300) in Ashford serves trout fresh from the pond behind the inn, plus seafood, pasta, and delicious desserts. At **The Herb-farm** (tel. 206/784–2222) in Fall City you can tour the farm and watch as nine-course gourmet extravaganzas are prepared (the restaurant was closed at press time due to fire, but the owners plan to have it open again by summer 1999). **Lorraine's Edel House** (tel. 509/548–4412) in Leavenworth offers superlative gourmet meals, including fresh seafood dishes and artful desserts, in a comfortable 1920's house. **Restaurant Osterreich** (tel. 509/548–4031), also in Leavenworth, serves fine Austrian food in a romantically lit spot below street level. **Mama Vallone's Steak House & Inn** (tel. 509/674–5174) in Cle Elum can be counted on for great pasta, steak, and service. The **Roslyn Cafe** (tel. 509/649–2763) offers a jukebox with vintage 78s and good pasta and burgers. The **Salish Lodge** (tel. 425/888–2556 or 800/826–6124), in Snoqualmie, serves gourmet cuisine and a very popular brunch in its dining room, with large windows overlooking Snoqualmie Falls. The restaurant at **Sun Mountain Lodge** (tel. 800/572–0493) offers top-of-the-line dining in a top-of-the-world setting.

TOURIST INFORMATION

Leavenworth Chamber of Commerce (Hwy. 2, Box 327, Leavenworth, WA 98826, tel. 509/548–5807). **Tacoma–Pierce County Visitor & Convention Bureau** (Box 1754, Tacoma, WA 98401-1754, tel. 253/627–2836 or 800/272–2662) provides information about Tacoma B&Bs. **Washington State Tourism** (Box 42500, Olympia, WA 98504-2500, tel. 800/544–1800).

RESERVATION SERVICES

Bedfinders Vacation Rentals (305 8th St., Leavenworth, WA 98826, tel. 800/323–2920). **Pacific Reservation Service** (Box 46894, Seattle, WA 98146, tel. 206/439–7677 or 800/684–2932). **Washington State Bed & Breakfast Guild** (2442 N.W. Market St., Box 355-FD, Seattle, WA 98107, tel. 800/647–2918).

ABENDBLUME PENSION ☞

12570 Ranger Rd., Box 981, Leavenworth, WA 98826, tel. 509/548–4059 or 800/669–7634; www.abendblume.com

Abendblume (an Austrian word for evening flower) sits in the midst of a meadow and mountain setting straight out of *The Sound of Music*. Owners Renee and Randy Sexauer traveled to Austria in 1992 and fell in love with Bavarian-style architecture. They returned to Leavenworth, to the land where Renee was raised, and built an elegant Austrian country chalet that is a romantic destination for adults.

Randy, a former contractor, did much of the handcrafted carving work adorning doors and wood trim. The carved mantel on the living room fireplace is one example. The six guestrooms are individually decorated, and beds have down comforters. The Almrosen and Dornroschen room (which mean "high mountain flower" and "Sleeping Beauty," respectively) has a whirlpool tub and a large marble shower with double shower heads and four body sprays; a wood-burning fireplace; and private balcony overlooking the valley. A therapeutic massage can be arranged in the privacy of your room. An outdoor Grecian-style spa overlooks meadows filled with snow in winter.

The breakfast room has charming Austrian decor, including a cuckoo clock, and breakfast often includes tasty Danish pancakes with homemade apple syrup and French press coffee. A small hut with a grass roof housing a pair of cashmere goats evokes the Austrian countryside. The inn is about a mile from downtown Leavenworth, near Ski Hill and minutes from Haus Rohrbach. ♨ *6 double rooms with baths. Down comforters in rooms, wood-burning fireplace in 1 room, whirlpool bath in 1 room. Hot tub, massage. $77–$159; full breakfast. AE, D, MC, V. No smoking.*

ALEXANDER'S COUNTRY INN ☙

37515 State Rd. 706 E, Ashford, WA 98304, tel. 360/569–2300 or 800/654–7615, fax 360/569–2323

This Victorian-style inn was built in 1912, 1 mi from the southwest Nisqually entrance to Mt. Rainier National Park. Today's owners, Jerry Harnish and Bernadette Ronan, bought it in 1980, but the original builders' presence is still felt through the many old photographs of the family on display.

Beyond the front doors, inset with two 1890 Viennese stained-glass panels of Romeo and Juliet, is the inn's public restaurant. Upstairs is a large parlor for guests, with overstuffed sofas and chairs around a fireplace. In summer you can catch your own dinner in the trout pond and watch hummingbirds from the enclosed hot tub or while having lunch on the new deck overlooking the pond.

The guest rooms, redecorated in 1996, feature floral-print wallpaper; wicker headboards; handmade quilts; Art Deco stained glass; and some fine antiques, such as room 10's New England armoire with fruit-basket designs inlaid in wood and mother-of-pearl. For the Tower Suite, you'll need to be fairly agile to climb a carpeted ladder up from the sitting room to the bedroom, where you'll find a 1920s suite of fan-detailed, bird's-eye maple furniture and stained glass in a fleur-de-lis design.

Breakfast in the dining room includes choices like French toast, blintzes, buttermilk and blueberry pancakes, eggs cooked to order, and fresh fruit. ♨ *8 double rooms with baths, 4 suites, 2 guest houses. Restaurant, hot tub. $95–$129; full breakfast. MC, V. No smoking.*

ALL SEASONS RIVER INN BED & BREAKFAST ☙

8751 Icicle Rd., Box 788, Leavenworth, WA 98826, tel. 509/548–1425 or 800/254–0555

Built as a bed-and-breakfast in 1991 and remodeled in 1998, the All Seasons River Inn in Leavenworth offers antique furnishings in a contemporary setting. Innkeepers Kathy and Jeff Falconer designed the three-story cedar structure, which rests on the terraced banks of the Wenatchee River. As its name implies, the inn affords fishing in the river, sunbathing, and hiking in a variety of scenic areas. The Leavenworth Golf Course, a half mile away, becomes a cross-country skiing destination in winter. Two downhill ski areas, Stevens Pass and Mission Ridge, are less than an hour's drive from the inn.

Five guest rooms each have a whirlpool bath, private deck, river (and some mountain) views, and a spacious indoor seating area; some rooms have fireplaces. The Enchantment Room is aptly named, with its four-poster bed, bay window, and private patio on the river.

Breakfast is served in the airy, antiques-filled dining room and adjacent dining area on the main floor. Gourmet treats include Mexican tamale pancakes, pumpkin muffins, kiwi parfaits, sausage and apples, and applesauce. ♨ *3 dou-*

ble rooms with baths; 3 suites. Cable TV and air-conditioning in rooms. Whirl-pool bath in 5 rooms, fireplace in some rooms. Bicycles, games room. $95–$145; full breakfast. MC, V. No smoking, 2-night minimum stay on weekends, festivals, holidays, and Dec.

FREESTONE INN 🐾

17798 Hwy. 20, Mazama, WA 98833, tel. 509/996–3906 or 800/639–3809, fax 509/996–3907; www.freestoneinn.com

The new Freestone Inn is nestled in the Methow Valley on the grounds of 76-acre Wilson Ranch, west of Mazama, and lies at the edge of the wilderness approach to the North Cascades highway. Owned by R.D. Merrill and Harbor Properties of Seattle, the main inn was built in 1996.

A sprawling log lodge with 21 rooms, it mixes rough-hewn timber, native stone, and wrought iron. The design takes inspiration from the late-19th- and early 20th-century architect, Robert Reamer, who designed Old Faithful Inn at Yellowstone National Park and developed the style known as mountain architecture. The guest rooms and the gourmet dining room—with a soaring native-stone fireplace—overlook Freestone Lake and the forested hills bordering the valley. Two luxurious lakefront lodges, steps from the inn at the edge of the lake, are decorated in rustic tones with sophisticated country-style accessories. Fifteen smaller but equally comfortable cabins are a few minutes' walk from the inn, along Early Winters Creek. The guest rooms in the main inn are spacious, with sophisticated country decor and large native-stone fireplaces.

Jack's Hut, an activities center on the grounds, offers a wide range of activities, including guided nature walks, white-water rafting on the Methow River, fly-fishing, and mountaineering. In the winter there is ice-skating, and you can cross-country ski along the many trails the Methow Valley is known for.

A buffet breakfast of fresh baked muffins and pastries (oatmeal in wintertime), fresh fruits, and fresh-squeezed juices is served in the dining room overlooking the lake. The dining room is open for dinner Tuesday through Sunday; there is no lunch, but you can order a backpacker's lunch of sandwich, fruit, and juice for $8.95. ⚑ *17 double rooms with baths, 4 suites, 15 cabins, 2 lodges. Fireplace in units. Nature walks, fly-fishing, white-water rafting, ice-skating, cross-country skiing, horseback riding, mountain climbing. $115–$325; Continental-plus breakfast (complimentary for main inn guests only), dinner available. AE, D, DC, MC, V. No smoking, minimum-length stay during holidays.*

HAUS LORELEI 🐾

347 Division St., Leavenworth, WA 98826, tel. 509/548–5726 or 800/514–8868, fax 509/548–6548; www.hauslorelei.com

Haus Lorelei is two short blocks from the center of Leavenworth. Yet perched above the Wenatchee River amidst tall evergreens and spectacular mountain scenery, the spacious and rambling lodge-style house (built in 1903 by the town's largest lumber company) feels more like a country cottage. A living room with a large river-rock fireplace and a hot tub overlooking the river promote relaxation. Trails adjacent to the property offer cross-country skiing in winter and hiking in summer. You can also partake of the billiards room, tennis and basketball courts, four mountain bikes, and the large swimming beach at the edge of the property.

All 10 guest rooms are individually decorated with antiques and have private baths. The riverside rooms are slightly more posh, and two have four-poster canopy beds with lace hangings. Three of the upstairs rooms have several beds and lots of extra room and are convenient for families. The inn is a romantic spot—more than 20 weddings are held on the grounds each year.

The German-born owner, Elisabeth Saunders, serves breakfasts of fresh-fruit crepes or Danish pancakes on European china in the bright sunroom-style dining room with river views. Afternoon tea and dessert are served. ♨ *10 rooms with baths, guest house with 3 rooms. Hot tub, tennis court, basketball, hiking, cross-country skiing, billiards. $89–$99; full breakfast (includes afternoon tea and dessert). No credit cards. No smoking.*

HAUS ROHRBACH PENSION ❦

12882 Ranger Rd., Leavenworth, WA 98826, tel. 509/548–7024 or 800/548–4477, fax 509/548–5038

On a hillside a mile outside Leavenworth, this alpine chalet with window boxes full of red geraniums has views of the valley, the village, and the Cascades. It has been owned since 1978 by the Harrilds: Robert, a former phone-company cable splicer, and Kathryn, who comes from a family of resort-motel owners.

With clean lines and dark-pine wainscoting, the house has the look of a small German inn. The comfortable common room, with a large open kitchen, wood-burning stove, sofas, and game tables, looks out to the deck that runs across the front of the house. Guest rooms, some with handcrafted pine bedsteads, are decorated in cream with rose and soft blue accents.

Behind the inn, Tumwater Mountain has hiking trails you can follow for a short walk or a serious hike to reach ever grander views. In winter, there's lots of snow fun, including sledding and snowshoeing in the front yard, or skiing at Ski Hill nearby.

Breakfasts might include sourdough pancakes or Bob's special, Dutch babies. Homemade desserts—such as chocolate peanut-butter pie, ice-cream sundaes, rhubarb crisp, and white chocolate mousse cake—are available for purchase in the evening. Kathryn will pack a picnic for you if you want to explore the countryside. She also prepares dinner on Saturday night upon request. ♨ *5 double rooms with baths, 2 doubles share bath, 3 suites. Air-conditioning in rooms. Hot tub, pool. $75–$160; full breakfast. AE, D, DC, MC, V. No smoking, 2-night minimum on weekends Sept.–mid-Mar. and on festival weekends.*

MAPLE VALLEY BED & BREAKFAST ❦

20020 S.E. 228th St., Maple Valley, WA 98038, tel. 425/432–1409, fax 425/413–1459

Turning their home into a B&B was, for the Hurlbuts, a natural progression. Jayne, who had worked in the travel industry in the San Francisco Bay area, and Clarke, a Northwesterner and retired air traffic controller (now a stonemason), started by taking in Japanese exchange students. Later, the students' families visited. In 1986 they went public and now provide a personable, unfussy refuge with many repeat customers.

This contemporary cedar house set on 5 acres in a wooded area 40 minutes southeast of Seattle has a rustic look—open-beam ceilings, peeled-pole railings, and cedar walls. A large room downstairs has a huge stone fireplace and couches with sheepskin throws. The upstairs sitting room offers games, books, and a field guide and binoculars for spotting wildlife in the pond it overlooks. Jayne is an avid gardener and bird-watcher, and the landscaped yard attracts quail and other the birds that feed right at the window where you eat breakfast. Lace curtains and crystal lamps gracefully accent the two guest rooms whose French doors open onto a deck. One room, with its own sink, has a four-poster bed of hand-hewn logs, topped with a comforter and lacy pillow shams. A fun, thoughtful touch: On cool evenings the Hurlbuts will provide you with a "hot baby," a bed warmer filled with heated sand.

For breakfast, Jayne might serve omelets, waffles, eggs Benedict, or her special baked pancakes with fruit and whipped cream. △ *2 double rooms share bath. $75; full breakfast. No credit cards. No smoking.*

MAZAMA COUNTRY INN ☞
42 Lost River Rd., HCR 74/Box B9, Mazama, WA 98833, tel. 509/996–2681 or, in WA, 800/843–7951, fax 509/996–2646; www.mazama.com

East of the North Cascades National Park, nestled in a valley laced with cross-country skiing trails, is this serenely rural, rustic mountain lodge. Owned by George Turner and Bill Pope, the Mazama is a sprawling 6,000-square-ft, two-story wood-sided building with a front entry of stone and log posts, dormer windows, and a brick-red roof set against a backdrop of pine trees and mountains.

The spacious dining and living room features a massive Russian stone fireplace, vaulted ceiling, peeled-log furniture, and floor-to-ceiling windows that look out at the valley floor and the mountains beyond. Watercolor landscapes by a local artist are displayed throughout. Most guest rooms are comfortable, but certainly not opulent. Some of the rooms on the second floor have two levels, with a queen-size bed on the upper and a child-size bed tucked under the staircase. Four larger rooms have decks. Also available are six cabins (including one cabin that accommodates 12), ideal for families.

The inn attracts guests who want a mountain experience. In summer, the area offers mountain biking, hiking, horseback riding, river rafting, llama trekking, and fishing. In winter, the inn itself provides ski rentals and lessons and arranges for heli-skiing, inn-to-hut ski touring, and dog-sled rides. One of the hedonistic experiences you can enjoy after a day of cross-country skiing is slipping into the outdoor hot tub, surrounded by snowbanks, and gazing at the stars.

Winter breakfasts include hearty oatmeal, eggs, and fruit; in summer, the main dish might be a vegetarian omelet. Makings for sandwiches are set out after breakfast for you to fix your own brown-bag lunches. In winter, dinner is served family style. In summer, dinners are offered from the restaurant menu and may include baby-back ribs. △ *14 double rooms with baths, 6 cabins. Kitchens in cabins. Restaurant, sauna, hot tub, bike rentals, gift shop. $60–$190; full breakfast (not included in summer), lunch and dinner included in winter. D, MC, V. No smoking, 2-night minimum and no meals in cabins.*

MOORE HOUSE BED & BREAKFAST ☞
526 Marie Ave., Box 629, South Cle Elum, WA 98943, tel. 509/674–5939 or, in OR and WA, 800/228–9246

In the town of South Cle Elum, by the old tracks of the Chicago, Milwaukee, St. Paul & Pacific Railroad, is a wood-frame building that once housed railroad employees. Built in 1909, and now on the National Register of Historic Places, it is owned by Eric and Cindy Sherwood.

The inn is crammed with railroad memorabilia, including vintage photographs, model trains, and schedules. The large sitting room has a big wooden train for children to play on. Guest rooms—decorated with calico prints, coordinating colors, and some antiques—include written descriptions of the railroad workers and their lives. A romantic two-room suite features a massive four-poster queen-size bed and a whirlpool tub.

Outside are two caboose cars that have been converted to suites with oversize decks. They have been nicely decorated, for instance one has dark green wallpaper and carpet, bleached-pine wainscoting, rolltop desk, and brass reading lamps. Both cars have cupolas (reached by climbing a ladder) that make a cozy spot to sit and read.

The inn is just steps from the Iron Horse State Park Trail, a 105-mi trail that replaces part of the old Milwaukee Railroad track system. The route is ideal for walking, hiking, and horseback riding; and in the winter for cross-country skiing and snowshoeing. A special feature on the inn's grounds are outdoor horse paddocks that can be reserved for mounts who travel with their owners. For breakfast you can look forward to French toast and sausage, or eggs Benedict, seasonal fruit and sweet rolls. ♠ *3 double rooms with baths, 6 doubles share 2 baths, 3 suites. Mini-refrigerator, coffeemaker, and TV in suites. Hot tub. $50–$125; full breakfast, full meal service for groups by prior arrangement. AE, MC, V. No smoking, 2-night minimum on holiday weekends.*

MOUNTAIN HOME LODGE ☙
Box 687, Leavenworth, WA 98826, tel. 509/548–7077 or 800/414–2378, fax 509/548–5008

Brad and Kathy Schmidt have brought a sense of youthful, relaxed sophistication to their remote mountaintop aerie, 3 mi up a winding, rutted mountain road outside Leavenworth. As you emerge into the lush alpine meadow that surrounds the inn, the views of the Cascades are nothing less than breathtaking. In winter, you can park on Mountain Home Road and be transported to the lodge in a heated Sno-Cat.

The contemporary cedar and redwood inn has broad decks for summer barbecues and dining. An enormous stone fireplace at the center of the dining room is flanked by large sofas crafted from burled redwood and covered with shaggy sheepskins. The comfortable guest rooms are filled with handmade quilts and locally crafted peeled-pine or vine maple furniture, and have binoculars for viewing scenery and wildlife. Robes and port wine await you in your room.

You will find miles of hiking and cross-country ski trails, a fleet of snowmobiles, and a 1,700-ft-long toboggan run, plus a tennis court and swimming pool. Use of cross-country skis and snow shoes is included. Snowmobile rental can be arranged.

Pumpkin pancakes with apple cinnamon sauce, French crepes, or eggs Benedict are the tried-and-true breakfast specialties. Gourmet dinners could include baked apricot Brie in phyllo pastry and roast breast of pheasant. Summer dinners are open to nonguests by reservation. This is an adult retreat, good for families with kids 18 and older. ♠ *10 double rooms with baths. Air-conditioning, pool, hot tub, tennis court. Summer $100–$330; full breakfast (lunch and dinner included in winter). D, MC, V. No smoking, 2-night minimum Dec.–Mar.*

MOUNTAIN MEADOWS INN BED & BREAKFAST AT MT. RAINIER ☙
28912 State Rte. 706 E, Ashford, WA 98304, tel. 360/569–2788, mtmeadow@mashell.com

Owners Harry and Michelle Latimer have freshened up and refurbished this quiet, homey inn 6 mi from the entrance to Mt. Rainier National Park. In parklike grounds, the handsome wood-frame house with an open porch was built in 1910 for the superintendent of what was then the largest sawmill west of the Mississippi.

The Latimers' love of nature and mountaineering is reflected in their collection of John Muir memorabilia gathered over a 20-year period and displayed, along with Northwest Native American baskets, in the antiques-filled common rooms. You can peruse several shelves of Northwest guidebooks and reference materials to enrich your explorations. Guest rooms include queen- and king-size beds, calico prints, and reproduction Early American furnishings. The Mountain Berry room has a claw-foot tub, four-poster bed, and a cloud-painted ceiling.

A modern two-story cottage on the property has three units with kitchen facilities; the largest unit, on the ground floor, has direct access to the spacious backyard and is a good choice for families. In summer the Latimers host evening campfires by the trout pond; in winter, the 90 mi of nearby cross-country ski trails beckon. You are welcome in the kitchen while Michelle prepares country breakfasts, including home-baked muffins and bread, on an 1889 wood-fired cookstove.
△ *3 double rooms with baths, 1 suite, 3 housekeeping units in separate building. Access to sauna and hot tub. $75–$110; full breakfast. MC, V. No smoking.*

RUN OF THE RIVER INN ☜
9308 E. Leavenworth Rd., Box 285, Leavenworth, WA 98826, tel. 800/288–6491, fax 509/548–7547

On the Icicle River 1½ mi from Leavenworth, with a bird refuge on two sides, is this bed-and-breakfast in a classic log structure. It was built in 1979 to take advantage of extraordinary views of the river, Tumwater and Icicle canyons, and the towering Cascades. A second story with cathedral ceilings was added by innkeepers Karen and Monty Turner, who moved here in 1987 from Las Vegas, where they both taught fifth grade. Karen still teaches, while Monty runs the inn and maintains his collection of classic and antique bicycles.

You have the entire wood-burning stove–warmed living area downstairs to yourself because the Turners live in a small house adjacent to the inn. A guest sitting room is at the top of the circular staircase off the entryway; supported by hand-peeled logs fashioned by a local craftsman; the staircase is one of the inn's many hand-hewn log features custom-made for the Turners. Like the rest of the inn, the sitting room has an upscale country look, with handmade willow furniture and a stenciled pine dry sink. Beverages and fresh cookies are set out to make you feel at home.

Three upstairs bedrooms have high cathedral ceilings of pine, hand-hewn log furniture, and locally made hand-embroidered quilts on queen-size beds. Each room has a commanding view of the natural surroundings, along with an old fly rod, ski pole, or snowshoe on one wall as a reminder of the diversions the area offers.

The inn overlooks 70 acres of wetlands, including a small island in the river. The Turners' own landscaping includes a small pond with a log bench, a wildflower meadow with a few trails, and aspen and alpine fir trees. In winter, the area affords the opportunity for sleigh rides and plenty of cross-country skiing and snowmobiling. Summer activities include hiking, white-water rafting, bicycling, horseback riding, fishing, golfing, and harvesting fruit at orchards.

The country breakfast may include yogurt with fruit or a fresh fruit plate, hash browns, cinnamon rolls, and a cheese and sausage strata. △ *4 double rooms with baths, 2 suites. Cable TV in rooms. Hot tub, bicycles. $100–$155; full breakfast. AE, D, MC, V. No smoking, 2-night minimum on weekends and during festivals.*

SALISH LODGE ☞

*6501 Railroad Ave. SE, Box 1109, Snoqualmie, WA 98065, tel. 425/888–2556
or 800/826–6124, fax 425/888–2533; www.salishlodge.com*

At the crest of Snoqualmie Falls is the lodge whose authentic Northwest look and dramatic site made it the choice for exterior shots of the Great Northern Hotel in the old TV series "Twin Peaks." Rebuilt in 1988 to follow the style of the original roadway inn built here in 1916, with dormers, porches, and balconies, the lodge has a stunning new Japanese-style spa where you can relax in hydrotherapy pools and sauna and steam rooms or arrange for a facial or mud wrap.

Run with the professional flair of a small elegant hotel, the entire inn is decorated in a sophisticated Pacific Northwest theme, with warm woods, rusticated stone, and fabrics and wallpapers in rich shades. Northwest art and Native American crafts complement the decor.

The library is an inviting room, with a hardwood floor, hefty maple beams, and rows of maple bookshelves; tea and cookies are set out in the afternoon. Comfortable armchairs, a sofa, and a game table are arranged around the large stone fireplace. Although the lodge is used for meetings and the restaurant is open to the public, access to this room, as well as to the enclosed hydrotherapy and sauna rooms and fitness center, is restricted to overnight guests.

Guest rooms have stone fireplaces, minibars, natural wicker and Shaker-style furniture, either a balcony or a window seat, and goose-down comforters. All baths feature double whirlpool tubs, with French doors that open for fireplace viewing (candles are provided); each comes with thick, hooded terry robes. The four corner suites all offer spectacular views of the waterfalls. Lighted paths leading to the top of the falls make for romantic evening walks. Walking trails wend their way to the bottom of the falls, and bike paths connect with extensive country roads. A sports court (for pickleball, volleyball, and badminton) is across the road.

The dining room serves excellent regional cuisine. The country breakfast is legendary, with course upon course of oatmeal, eggs, bacon, trout, pancakes, hash browns, and fresh fruit. ⚠ *91 double rooms with baths, 4 suites. Air-conditioning, TV, phone, minibar, down comforter, terry-cloth robes, whirlpool bath, and fireplace in rooms. Restaurant, lounge, VCR and video rentals, steam room, sauna, hydrotherapy pools, exercise room, 3 lighted courts for tennis and basketball, bicycles, professional spa services. $180–$575; breakfast extra. AE, D, DC, MC, V. Pets allowed on 1st floor only ($25 charge).*

SLEEPING LADY ☞

*7375 Icicle Rd., Leavenworth, WA 98826, tel. 800/574–2123, fax 509/548–6312;
www.sleepinglady.com*

Sleeping Lady is a unique inn and conference retreat that lies in the foothills of the North Cascade Mountains west of Leavenworth. Spread over 67 acres are clusters of 10 rooms each in cabin complexes. In the middle of the grounds, in a grove of ponderosa pines, is the 200-seat Chapel Theater. Now home to a resident string ensemble and the Icicle Creek Music Center (800/574–2123), it was formerly a chapel when Jesuits ran a youth camp here. The resort is named after a nearby mountain face whose profile looks like a sleeping woman.

Seattle philanthropist, Harriet Bullitt, who spent her summers in a family vacation home across the Icicle River from the inn, bought the property in 1992 when it was in danger of becoming a housing development. The buildings and grounds were completely renovated and she opened the resort in 1995 with the purpose of providing a retreat where nature, arts, outdoor recreation, and healthful dining would inspire reverence for the environment and for creative thinking.

Guest rooms have peeled-log furniture, natural linens, towel warmers, and wrought-iron fixtures by local artisans. There are two separate cabins: The Eyrie, great for honeymooners; and The Rookery, with bunk beds and suitable for groups. Also on the grounds is the Grotto bar, a stone swimming pool, a library cabin, and a sauna, massage, and hot tub spa.

Breakfast in the wild here might include hot oatmeal and fruit, sweet yeast breads, and poached eggs "Sleeping Lady," served on an English muffin with spinach and fresh tomato slices. Gourmet cafeteria-style dinners are served in the Kingfisher Dining Lodge and could include grilled salmon, roast potatoes, and cranberry tart. A glass icicle sculpture by internationally renowned artist, Dale Chihuly, is at the entrance to the dining room; it's especially pretty lighted at night when snow is on the ground. Six of the double rooms sleep four in two sets of bunk beds. ♨ *46 double rooms with baths, 2 cabins. Phone in rooms. $100 per person (includes 3 meals); full breakfast. AE, D, MC, V. No smoking.*

SUN MOUNTAIN LODGE ☜

Patterson Lake Rd., Box 1000, Winthrop, WA 98862, tel. 509/996–2211 or 800/572–0493, fax 509/996–3133

Perched high on a mountaintop above the former gold-mining town of Winthrop, this grand resort offers panoramic vistas of the 3,000 acres of wilderness surrounding the resort, 500,000 acres of national forest, the North Cascades, and the Methow Valley below.

In keeping with its mountain setting, the lodge is constructed from massive timbers and local stone. Lobby sitting areas include hand-hewn furniture, stone floors, and large picture windows. The huge wrought-iron chandelier was created by a local artisan, as were most of the handsome, lodge-style fixtures.

Guest rooms feature hand-hewn birch furniture, original regional art, and, of course, fine views. The best vistas are from the Gardner and the Mt. Robinson wings, actually separate buildings adjacent to the lodge. All rooms in the wings are equipped with gas fireplaces, private decks, and wet bars. (Some main-lodge rooms also feature fireplaces and wet bars.) Housekeeping cabins, with brick fireplaces, are available on Patterson Lake, about a mile from the main lodge.

The restaurant is renowned for its superb cuisine, wines, and expansive views. Dinner might include smoked, autumn-run salmon, or pork with cilantro and red chili butter.

An interpretive center offers nature activities, including slide shows and guided walks. Trail rides, riding lessons, hayrides, and cookouts are available; rowboats, sailboats, canoes, and mountain bikes are for hire. In winter, the lodge offers sleigh rides, ice-skating, ski lessons, and cross-country skiing on the second-largest ski trail system in the United States. ♨ *94 double rooms with baths, 8 suites, 13 cabins. Phone in lodge rooms, wet bar and fireplace in wing rooms and some lodge rooms, kitchen in cabins. Room service, 2 restaurants, 2 heated pools, 3 hot tubs, spa, 2 tennis courts, exercise room, horseback riding, ice-skating rink, gift shop, athletic shop, meeting rooms, 2 playgrounds. $95–$270; breakfast extra. AE, MC, V. No smoking in main dining room.*

SPOKANE AND ENVIRONS
Including Coeur d'Alene

Because of Seattle's moist climate, many think of Washington State as being waterlogged from Idaho all the way to the Pacific Ocean. But poised between the Rocky and Cascade mountains is Spokane, with weather that's both dry and sunny most of the year. Three hundred miles east of Seattle, Spokane is Washington's second-largest city (population 187,700) and, with a plethora of mountains, forests, and lakes in the area, a year-round paradise for outdoors enthusiasts. At the same time, the city's slow pace and dramatic reversals of fortune make it an inviting place for strollers and history buffs to explore.

The fur trade first drew white men to the Spokane River valley, and in the early 19th century they coexisted more or less peacefully with the Spokane Indians and other tribes of the region. By 1858, however, a fierce battle waged against the Northwest tribes had forced the Native Americans onto reservations, and the white settlers began to develop the area aggressively.

The gold, silver, and lead in the nearby Coeur d'Alene Mountains and in British Columbia drew many prospectors who soon began to pour mining money into Spokane, officially founded in 1871. Millionaires were created overnight, and the city attracted gamblers, adventurers, and dance-hall girls. By the turn of the century, the nouveau riches were building elaborate mansions in a neighborhood called Browne's Addition, importing materials and furnishings from Europe at tremendous cost in their game of one-upmanship. Spokane's economic upswing continued as the transcontinental railroad brought more commerce and more settlers to the city. Spokane's fortunes have since waxed and waned with those of the mines, the timber industry, and agriculture.

When the city entered a period of economic decline during the 1960s, civic leaders moved to rejuvenate it in a bid for an international exposition. Expo '74 drew more than 5 million visitors. Riverfront Park, created for the event, remains a popular tourist spot in the heart of downtown.

Its 100 acres feature a century-old carousel, a movie theater with a five-story-high screen, carnival rides, and ducks and swans feeding along a willow-bordered river.

Spokane maintains a gentle hustle-bustle. It has the feel of a small town, with many of its low-rise buildings dating from the early part of the century. These days, the city's livelihood is heavily based on service industries and the wholesale and retail trade, although mining, timber, and agriculture still play an important role in the region's economy. During the past decade, many transplants from California and other parts of the country have added diversity to the city. And its well-earned reputation for a hardworking labor force and good public schools has drawn such corporations as Boeing and Seafirst Bank, which have transferred some of their operations here from Seattle.

One of the biggest advantages of Spokane's compact size is the fact that the countryside can be reached within minutes. The Selkirk and Coeur d'Alene mountains, rising to the north and east, 76 lakes, and four major rivers are all within a 50-mi radius of the city, offering activities ranging from swimming, boating, rafting, hiking, and fishing to downhill and cross-country skiing and snowmobiling.

Just 35 mi from Spokane is Coeur d'Alene, Idaho, site of a pristine lake with 125 mi of shoreline, ringed by richly forested mountains. Coeur d'Alene is Spokane's most popular playground, especially during the summer, when residents and visitors flock to the sandy beach and boardwalk at the edge of the lake. The Coeur d'Alene Resort offers a breathtaking view to those who come to stay and eat. The resort has added to its list of amenities a world-class golf course, complete with a floating green in Lake Coeur d'Alene.

PLACES TO GO, SIGHTS TO SEE

Browne's Addition. Spokane's first residential community was named for lawyer J.J. Browne, who bought its original 160 acres in 1878, when Spokane was a small settlement with fewer than 50 residents. Planned during the early 1880s, this neighborhood in southwest Spokane went on to become one of the most socially correct addresses in the city. During the 1880s, Queen Anne architecture was predominant. As mining money began to pour into the area during the next decade, mansions became more ostentatious, built in historical revival styles that included Greek, Tudor, and Colonial Revival. Today many of the buildings remain, and Browne's Addition is a mixture of trendy and down-at-the-heels. Some of the old homes are now apartments and halfway houses, while others have been lovingly restored. Architecture buffs can stop at the *Cheney Cowles Mu-*

seum bookstore (see below) for a booklet offering a self-guided walking tour of the neighborhood. Along the way, be sure to stop for refreshments at the *Elk* (1931 W. Pacific St., tel. 509/456–0454). A square brick-and-tile building dating from 1940, Elk's still has its original soda fountain. Now a popular restaurant, it serves breakfast, lunch, and a full dinner menu.

Cheney Cowles Museum and Historic Campbell House (2316 W. First Ave., tel. 509/456–3931). In Browne's Addition, the Cheney Cowles Museum has exhibits that trace the history of the Northwest, including the early days of Spokane, and hosts shows featuring nationally known and regional artists. The museum's store features regional art and specialized books available for purchase. Adjacent to the museum is the *Grace Campbell House,* a National Historic Register landmark built in 1898. A Tudor Revival–style home, Campbell House features period rooms that show how a mining tycoon and his family lived during Spokane's "Age of Elegance."

Green Bluff Growers (tel. 509/238–6978). This consortium of fruit and vegetable growers can be found in the foothills 16 mi north of Spokane between Mead and Colbert. They produce many of the apples for which Washington is famous, plus cherries, strawberries, peaches, and other seasonal bounty. Depending on the season, you can pick your own fruit in their orchards. A Cherry Festival is held mid-July, and the Apple Festival runs every weekend from mid-September through October. To locate their farms; produce stands; and antiques and gift shops, which feature locally produced crafts, homemade preserves, and honey, pick up a map at *Spokane Area Convention and Visitors Bureau* (*see* Tourist Information, *below*).

Manito Park (tel. 509/625–6622). South of downtown Spokane, in the midst of residential neighborhoods, Manito Park was designed in 1912 by landscape architects Frederick Law Olmsted (of New York's Central Park fame) and John Charles Olmsted. Today it is a serene, 91-acre oasis for walkers, runners, and bicyclists. Garden aficionados will enjoy the formal Japanese garden; rose garden featuring 180 varieties; Duncan Garden, with its annuals arranged in geometric symmetry around the Davenport fountain; and a greenhouse brimming with warm-weather plants.

Mt. Spokane State Park (off Hwy. 2, tel. 509/238–4258). Thirty miles northwest of downtown on Highway 206, Mt. Spokane State Park is a popular spot for winter recreation, with an alpine ski resort and 35 groomed trails for cross-country skiers. During warm weather it offers hikers scenic trails along mountain ridges and through cool forests.

Riverfront Park. Sprawling across several islands in the Spokane River, one of which contains a spectacular waterfall, this 100-acre park built for the Expo '74 world's fair was developed from old downtown railroad yards. One of the modernist buildings from Expo '74 houses an IMAX theater, a skating rink, and an exhibition space. The stone clock tower of the former *Great Northern Railroad Station* (516 N. Tower Rd.), which was built in 1902, stands in sharp architectural contrast to the Expo '74 building. A children's train chugs around the park in the summertime. At the south edge of the park, a 1909 carousel, hand-carved by master builder Charles I.D. Looff, is a local landmark.

Riverside State Park (tel. 509/456–3964). Just 3 mi northwest of downtown Spokane, Riverside State Park is minimally developed, offering a wild and natural setting on 3,000 acres. Ponderosa pines tower above the Spokane River, which is enjoyed by fishermen and rafters. Venture up *Deep Creek Canyon* to explore the fossil beds of a forest that existed more than 7 million years ago, or view centuries-old Indian rock paintings. *Trailtown Riding Stables* (3402 Aubrey L. White Pkwy., tel. 509/456–8249) charges by the hour for guided horseback trail rides. At the *Spokane House Interpretive Center* (Hwy. 291 at Nine Miles Falls, closed mid-Sept.–early Apr.), site of an early trading post, you can view exhibits about the fur trade during the early 19th century.

Silverwood Theme Park (Hwy. 95, Athol, ID, tel. 208/683–3400). A Victorian theme park 15 mi north of Coeur d'Alene, Silverwood is a popular summer attraction. It offers rides on an old-style locomotive, an antique-airplane museum and air show, plus carnival rides and entertainment.

Skiing. Downhill skiers seeking more challenging slopes than those of Mt. Spokane can find three larger resorts within 90 minutes of Spokane: *49 Degrees North* (Chewelah, WA, tel. 509/935–6649), with eight runs, four double chairlifts, and condominium rentals; *Schweitzer* (Sandpoint, ID, tel. 208/263–9555 or 800/831–8810), with 48 runs, one quad, five chairlifts, a hotel, a day lodge, and restaurants; and *Silver Mountain* (Kellogg, ID, tel. 208/783–1111), with 50 runs, one quad, two triple and two double chairlifts, and a surface lift—but no lodgings. The ski area is accessed by the world's longest single-stage gondola.

Wineries. Tours are offered at wineries near downtown Spokane. *Arbor Crest* (4705 N. Fruit Hill Rd., Spokane, tel. 509/927–9463) invites visitors to tastings at their Cliff House, a national historic site that overlooks the Spokane River. Built in 1924, the Tuscan villa–style house is built in white stucco with a red-tile roof. Most of the house is now reserved for private parties, but its dramatic location, perched on the edge of a cliff, provides visitors with a panoramic view of the Spokane River, Spokane Valley, and Idaho as they enjoy the cool gardens surrounding the house. You can also take part in tours and tastings at *Latah Creek Wine Cellars* (Pines exit off I–90, 13030 E. Indiana, Spokane, tel. 509/926–0164), *Mountain Dome* (16315 E. Temple Rd., Spokane, 99217, tel. 509/928–2788), *Worden* (off I–90 exit 276, 7217 W. 45th, Spokane, tel. 509/455–7835), and *Catarina Winery* (905 N. Washington, Spokane, tel. 509/328–5069).

RESTAURANTS

Any list of Spokane's finest restaurants should include **Milford's Fish House** (tel. 509/326–7251, open dinner only), housed in a century-old building with a tin ceiling. It offers a daily menu focusing on fresh regional fish and shellfish dishes; look for exotic fresh finfish entrées and spicy Cajun crawfish pie. **Patsy Clark's Mansion** (tel. 509/838–8300), the turn-of-the-century residence of gold and silver tycoon Patrick Francis Clark, was built in 1898. Designed by local architect Kirtland Cutter, the project cost a reported $1 million. Its ornate rooms now offer intimate dining areas where you may enjoy seasonal menus featuring such dishes as breast of duck *a l'orange* (sautéed with orange liqueur) and lamb with cabernet juniper-berry sauce. **Beverly's** (tel. 208/765–4000 or 800/688–5253), on the seventh floor of the Coeur d'Alene Resort, is famous for its beautiful view of Lake Coeur d'Alene and its fine seasonal cuisine, which features traditional Northwest dishes prepared with a French influence. Its wine cellar, winner of *Wine Spectator*'s Grand Award, boasts some 9,000 selections. Five nights a week, and by reservation only, travelers in the Coeur d'Alene area can enjoy sumptuous six-course gourmet dinners at **Clark House on Hayden Lake** (tel. 208/772–3470 or 800/765–4593). Succulent entrées typically include beef tenderloin, fresh halibut, or Northwest rack of lamb; the preceding courses are equally rich and imaginatively prepared.

TOURIST INFORMATION

Coeur d'Alene Area Chamber of Commerce (Box 850, Coeur d'Alene, ID 83816, tel. 208/664–3194). **Spokane Area Convention and Visitors Bureau** (801 W. Riverside, Suite 301, Spokane, WA 99201, tel. 509/624–1341 or 800/

248–3230). **Washington State Tourism** (Box 42500, Olympia, WA 98504-2500, tel. 800/544–1800).

RESERVATION SERVICES

Spokane Bed & Breakfast Reservation Service (627 E. 25th Ave., Spokane, WA 99203, tel. 509/624–3776). **Washington State Bed & Breakfast Guild** (2442 N.W. Market St., Box 355-FD, Seattle, WA 98107, tel. 800/647–2918).

CLARK HOUSE ON HAYDEN LAKE ☞

E. 4550 S. Hayden Lake Rd., Hayden Lake, ID 83835, tel. 208/772–3470 or 800/765–4593, fax 208/772–6899; www.clarkhouse.com

If you visit the Clark House on Idaho's Hayden Lake, a 40-minute drive from Spokane, you will most likely be instantly caught up in the history and mystery surrounding the place. A reclusive mining millionaire, F. Lewis Clark had the home built as a copy of a summer palace of Kaiser Wilhelm II of Germany. With 33 rooms and 10 fireplaces, the building, whose construction began in 1895, wasn't completed until 1910. Clark and his wife, Winifred, lived in the house for four years; then he and all of his money disappeared mysteriously. Winifred waited patiently for her husband's return but was forced to sell off the land, furnishings, and eventually the house to pay back taxes.

In 1989 innkeeper Monty Danner and his son Mark bought and restored the mansion, now on the National Register of Historic Places, after it sat empty for 20 years. Monty and his partner Rod Palmer decorated the house in a masterful way; the result is a sumptuously comfortable country inn, set on a secluded 13-acre estate. In the long second-floor gallery, light filters through grand Palladian windows at both ends and murals brighten the walls. The walls of the smaller downstairs dining room are also covered by a mural, this time depicting the artist's interpretation of the house's history. The downstairs library offers a variety of diversions, including a scrapbook chronicling the disappearance of F. Lewis Clark.

The furnishings are both elegant and understated, and even the occasional spectacular decorative flourishes, such as the intricately carved walnut buffet crafted in Connecticut during the 1870s, blend in effortlessly with the overall scheme. Guest rooms are individually decorated and quietly luxurious. Mrs. Clark's Room, done in a tea-rose motif, has a white-and-gold-trimmed Louis XIV–style writing table and high chest. The F. Lewis Clark Room, with its canopied bed, and the Cedar Suite, done in burgundy and deep green, have a masculine, Ralph Lauren look. The Hayden Lake Room, with cream and white brocade and natural wicker furniture, has the best view of the lake. French doors are in every room, some leading outdoors to deck and terrace areas, a lush lawn overlooking Hayden Lake, and a wildflower-filled garden. △ *10 double rooms with baths. TV (on request) and robes in rooms, fireplace in 4 rooms. Refrigerator, hot tub, conference facilities. $85–$200; full breakfast, 6-course gourmet dinner by reservation 5 nights a week. AE, D, DC, MC, V. No smoking; 2-night minimum Memorial Day– Labor Day.*

CRICKET ON THE HEARTH BED AND BREAKFAST INN ☞

1521 Lakeside Ave., Coeur d'Alene, ID 83814, tel. 208/664–6926

Those who are turned on by theater and theme rooms will have their fantasies fueled at the Cricket on the Hearth Bed and Breakfast Inn, 10 minutes from downtown Coeur d'Alene. Actors and hosts Tom and Julie Nash, who met while doing summer stock in 1972 (he played Harold Hill in *The Music Man,* and she was in the orchestra pit), draw on their extensive theater background to create a whimsical bed-and-breakfast experience. These ardent thespians have decorated the guest rooms in their 1920 stucco Craftsman cottage with musical-comedy themes ranging from *Cats* to *Carousel* to *The Unsinkable Molly Brown.* Each of these rooms features original posters from the Broadway productions and remains true to its chosen theme with various props. The Carousel Room has a painted carousel horse, and the Kabuki Room is filled with authentic Japanese prints, wall hangings, and artifacts.

You can relax in the game room, which opens onto a deck equipped for barbecuing. Tom and Julie serve generous breakfasts of fresh fruit, breads or muffins, and a main dish—such as a casserole, French toast, or waffles—in the dining room or on the deck in good weather. ♙ *3 double rooms with baths, 2 doubles share bath. Refrigerator, hot tub, ski packages. $55–$85; full breakfast. No credit cards. No smoking, pets by prior arrangement.*

FOTHERINGHAM HOUSE ☙

2128 W. 2nd Ave., Spokane, WA 99204, tel. 509/838–1891, fax 509/838–1807; www.ior.com/fotheringham

In the heart of historic Browne's Addition in Spokane, Fotheringham House is a century-old Queen Anne home built by the city's first mayor. Among the many decorative features original to the house are ball-and-spindle fretwork separating the entrance hall and living room, an intricately carved oak fireplace with tile faces, an open staircase, and a newel light. The common rooms are furnished with period pieces of the mid- to late-1800s.

Innkeepers Graham and Jackie Johnson's fondness for antique furniture restoration and stained glass is evident throughout the beautifully restored house. What isn't original they have meticulously replaced, such as the tin ceilings in many of the rooms. Each second-floor guest room is also furnished with fine American and European antiques.

Breakfast, including Jackie's hazelnut waffles or huckleberry pancakes, is served on Spode china in the dining room. If you're late to breakfast it is quite possible you'll awaken to the sound of the player piano in the parlor booming away—Graham and Jackie's good-humored version of a wake-up call. Outside, the rebuilt gardens feature Victorian-era cutting flowers, hostas, ferns, and a fountain. Architecture aficionados will enjoy strolling through this Victoriana-filled neighborhood; Coeur d'Alene Park, Spokane's oldest, is across the street. This is not the place for families with children under 12. ♙ *1 double room with bath, 3 doubles share 2 baths. Robes in rooms. Refrigerator, tennis available. $75–$90; full breakfast, afternoon tea. D, MC, V. No smoking.*

GREGORY'S MCFARLAND HOUSE ☙

601 Foster Ave., Coeur d'Alene, ID 83814, tel. 208/667–1232, www.bbhost.com/mcfarlandhouse

At Gregory's McFarland House in Coeur d'Alene, a spacious Classic Revival–Italianate structure, old meets new flawlessly. Built in 1905 for Idaho's second attorney general, the house is a blend of treasures and elegant family heirlooms from other eras and modern comforts and conveniences.

Innkeepers Winifred, Stephen, and Carol Gregory share with guests a home full of family history; many of their 19th-century antiques came from Winifred's ancestral home in England. The carved claw-foot table in the dining room, which once made a journey around Cape Horn, sits on one of several Chinese rugs scattered throughout the house's gleaming bird's-eye maple floors. In one of the common areas, interested guests may play a game of pool on the 1920 regulation Brunswick table.

The guest rooms are large and bright, with rose and pink accents, hand-crocheted bedspreads, and curtains of German lace. One room features an inlaid-wood bedroom suite from the 1860s, with a marble-top table and low dresser. Several rooms have four-poster beds. Breakfast is served in a bright, glassed-in conservatory overlooking the English garden. On a quiet tree-lined street, Gregory's McFarland House provides a soothing atmosphere only six blocks from downtown. △ *5 double rooms with baths. Air-conditioning. $85–$125; full breakfast, afternoon refreshments, high tea (with 48 hrs' notice). MC, V. No smoking, 2-night minimum mid-May–mid-Oct., mid-Nov.–early Jan., and holidays.*

LOVE'S VICTORIAN BED AND BREAKFAST 🐚

31317 N. Cedar Rd., Deer Park, WA 99006, tel. 509/276–6939, www.bbhost.com/lovesvictorian

Forty-five minutes from downtown Spokane, Love's Victorian Bed and Breakfast is a salute to Victoriana. Indeed, the exterior is a veritable encyclopedia of gingerbread. Innkeepers Bill and Leslie Love built this reproduction house in 1986. Working from the plans of an 1886 Queen Anne house, Bill incorporated original Victorian decorative elements: In the sitting room, he fashioned a mantelpiece out of the remains of an 1858 piano; grill- and fretwork in the entrance hall and balusters on the stairway and porch were salvaged from turn-of-the-century houses in Spokane.

The larger guest room, the Turret Suite, boasts a fireplace, balcony, and a sitting area occupying the house's turret. Chintz balloon shades, floral wallpaper, Victorian memorabilia, and breakfast by candlelight give the house an unabashedly romantic air. Amid fields, evergreen forests, and rolling hills, this house is a place where you can get away from it all. Evening walks offer encounters with deer and even moose. Swimming or fishing is available at nearby lakes; cross-country skiing on trails is just five minutes away. The full breakfast buffet, which favors waffles, is served in the dining room amid candles and fine china. △ *2 double rooms with baths. Air-conditioning and robes in rooms, fireplace in 1 room. TV/VCR, indoor hot tub, bicycles, cross-country skis. $85–$110; full breakfast, evening refreshments. MC, V. No smoking, closed 1st weekend in Dec.*

MARIANNA STOLTZ HOUSE 🐚

427 E. Indiana Ave., Spokane, WA 99207, tel. 509/483–4316 or 800/978–6587, fax 509/483–67738; www.aimcomm.com/stoltzhouse

Marianna Stoltz House sits five blocks from Gonzaga University and five minutes from downtown Spokane. Innkeepers Jim and Phyllis Maguire named the classic 1908 American Four-square for Phyllis's mother. The house has a special meaning for Phyllis, who grew up here, moved away, and returned after 28 years to buy it back. Its decor—original dark fir woodwork, leaded-glass china cabinets, and Rococo Revival and Renaissance Revival settees and armchairs in the parlor and sitting room—is well-suited to the architecture and gives the place a solid, comfortable air.

Guests have exclusive use of the spacious parlor and sitting and dining rooms on the main floor. A fax machine is also available in the common area. Upstairs, brass and mahogany beds are covered in quilts that have been in Phyllis's family for decades. One private bathroom has a 7-ft-long claw-foot tub. The largest room has a king-size brass bed; the others have king, queen, or single beds. Tea, coffee, lemonade, and cookies are always available, and breakfast may include specialties such as homemade huckleberry cream cheese on bagels; French toast with strawberry-mandarin orange sauce; homemade granola; muffins with lemon curd; or waffles with homemade Dutch honey sauce. ♨ *2 double rooms with baths, 2 doubles share bath. Air-conditioning, cable TV in rooms. Bicycles. $65–$95; full breakfast, evening refreshments. AE, D, DC, MC, V. No smoking.*

THE PORTICO ℘
502 S. Adams St., Ritzville, WA 99169, tel. 509/659–0800

Travelers between Spokane and Seattle can pull off the freeway and find respite at the Portico, a beautifully restored historic landmark in an unlikely place—Ritzville, a farming town 60 mi southwest of Spokane. At first glance, there seems to be little to see or do here, but this unassuming little town is home to a 1937 Art Deco movie house, a nine-hole golf course, a bowling alley, and a park, which, coupled with Ritzville's clean, safe streets, evoke a simpler time.

The Portico, originally built in 1902, was the home of Nelson H. Greene, a prominent merchant, financier, and wheat broker. When the town burned down in 1889, Greene financed its reconstruction, encouraging the use of brick; hence the Portico's unusual mating of material—buff-color brick—and Queen Anne, Classical Revival, and Craftsman styles.

Innkeepers Bill and Mary Anne Phipps are passionate about architecture and period furnishings, and their attention to detail is evident. The parquet floor in the entrance hall bears a pattern of unstained dark and light oak, bordered with serpentine work in bird's-eye maple. The fireplace in the parlor is framed by oak spindle work supported by Ionic columns. Although the ceiling in the same room resembles pressed tin, it was actually produced by anaglyph, a process favored at the turn of the century for creating a design in relief.

There are two inviting guest rooms. The larger room is decorated with rich paisley wallpaper and mid- to late-19th-century English furniture. A carved walnut canopy bed is adorned with a two-tailed mermaid at its head and an angel protecting a child at its foot, both symbols of good luck. The other room is bright and cheerful, with a white wrought-iron bed topped with a quilt handmade by Mary Anne.

Breakfast is fresh and generous. In season, Mary Anne serves raspberries and blackberries fresh from her garden; homemade cinnamon rolls, delicious yeasty waffles, and homemade granola are often on the menu. ♨ *2 double rooms with baths. Air-conditioning, cable TV. $59–$74; full breakfast. AE, D, MC, V. No smoking.*

WAVERLY PLACE ℘
W. 709 Waverly Pl., Spokane, WA 99205, tel. 509/328–1856, fax 509/326–7059; waverly@ior.com

Waverly Place offers lodgings in a quiet old neighborhood just five minutes from downtown Spokane. The turreted Queen Anne house sits across the street from Corbin Park, whose 11½ acres encompass tennis courts, a running track, a baseball diamond, and a playground. Waverly Place, built in 1902, is one of several turn-of-the-century houses bordering the park; the neighborhood is listed on the state's Register of Historic Places.

Innkeepers Marge and Tammy Arndt are a mother-and-daughter team whose love for rambling Victorian houses led them to buy the building over a decade ago. With distinctive late Victorian pieces—many of them from Marge's mother-in-law's attic—they've created an environment in which the furnishings seem truly at home amid the graceful architecture of the house. Guests have exclusive use of two parlors, where the gleaming fir woodwork includes intricate beading around the mantelpiece and Grecian columns that separate the rooms. Most of the original light fixtures are intact, and Victorian lamps throughout the house sport fringed shades handmade by Tammy. Both women enjoy researching the house; in painting its exterior they consulted old photographs and the builder's grandson in order to remain faithful to the original look.

The guest rooms on the second floor are airy and comfortable, with queen-size reproduction beds and Oriental rugs and dhurrie rugs over shiny hardwood floors. The converted attic is a spacious, cheerful suite.

Breakfast, served in the dining room on Haviland china, reflects the innkeepers' Swedish heritage. Menus feature puffy Swedish pancakes with huckleberry sauce and almond-flavored pastries called *kringla*, as well as egg dishes, sausages, and fresh fruits and juices. ♠ *1 double room with bath, 2 double rooms share 2 baths, 1 3-room suite. Air-conditioning and robes in rooms. Pool, hot tub. $75–$105; full breakfast. AE, D, MC, V. No smoking, 2-night minimum weekends in May and holiday weekends.*

THE PALOUSE

An area of gently rolling hills in southeast Washington, the Palouse—French for "waves of blowing grass"—was named by fur trappers who traveled up the Columbia River from Fort Astoria in present-day Oregon as early as 1811. The Lewis and Clark Expedition had passed through the region in 1805 on its way to the Pacific Ocean, but it was settlers looking for a new life—or, like missionary Marcus Whitman, intending to bring Christianity to the Native Americans—who brought agriculture to the region. They established communities such as Dayton and Walla Walla early in the 19th century; about 90 years later a land-grant college, now Washington State University, was started in Pullman.

Because the northern branch of the Oregon Trail passed just south of Walla Walla, many farmers, finding rich, deep soil, stayed in the Palouse rather than heading on down the raging Snake and Columbia rivers to Fort Astoria and Oregon's Willamette Valley. The farmers quickly built large houses in town, and, as a result, Dayton now boasts more Victorian-era homes than Port Townsend on Puget Sound. Walla Walla, too, has many beautifully restored homes dating from the 19th century.

Agriculture still reigns in this area, but now it's wheat, not grass, for which this farming region is best known; indeed, Whitman County produces more wheat than any other county in the United States. It also bills itself as the lentil capital of the world, and several community celebrations follow the lentil harvest each August. Walla Walla is famous for its sweet onions and throws an onion festival each year in late July. (Walla Walla's other chief industry is the state penitentiary, on a bluff above town.) Some of those not directly involved in farming are employed at the Green Giant canning and labeling plant in Dayton, which processes much of the asparagus grown locally. Dust from plowed fields and nearly constant winds combine to create stunning deep orange and red sunsets.

Although Dayton, Walla Walla, and Pullman are separated by miles of hills, the towns themselves are best seen on foot. Because the region is in a rain shadow, a pocket of land protected from clouds, its climate is less severe than that of Spokane, 158 mi north of Walla Walla. Hence, spring comes earlier in the Palouse; tulips and daffodils burst into bloom in late March. Summer daytime temperatures can reach well into the 90s, however. The best times to visit are spring, when the Palouse is carpeted in green winter wheat, and fall, when the heat has relented and the sun of Indian summer plays off the golden fields.

PLACES TO GO, SIGHTS TO SEE

Dayton. On the main stage route between Walla Walla and northwest Idaho's Lewiston, Dayton profited from an 1861 gold rush in Idaho. Merchants and farmers built lavish houses during the boom years; an impressive 88 Victorian buildings in town are on the National Register of Historic Places. A brochure with two self-guided walking tours is available from the *Chamber of Commerce* (*see* Tourist Information, *below*). One tour encompasses the 73 homes and buildings on the original townsite platted in 1871 (Main Street was formerly the drag used by Native Americans to race horses), while the other explores the many Queen Anne, Italianate, and Gothic homes built in the late 1800s. The 1886 Italianate *Columbia County Courthouse* is the oldest courthouse in the state still in use for county government. Dayton is also home to the oldest family-run hardware store in the state, *Dingle's* (179 E. Main St., tel. 509/382–2581), as well as the state's oldest volunteer fire department and oldest rodeo. One block off Main Street and adjacent to the railroad tracks, the restored *Dayton Railroad Depot*, built in 1881, was in use until 1971.

Juniper Dunes Wilderness. The 7,140-acre Juniper Dunes Wilderness at the western edge of the Palouse includes some of the biggest sand dunes—up to 130 ft high and ¼-mi wide—and the largest natural groves of western juniper in the state; some are 150 years old. This is all that remains of an ecosystem that stretched over nearly 400 square mi south to the Snake and Columbia rivers. The most scenic portion is a 2-mi hike northeast from the parking area where all visitors must leave their cars. Getting to the parking area, 15 mi northeast of Pasco, involves driving some unmarked back roads through farmland; for directions, contact the *Bureau of Land Management* (tel. 509/536–1200). No camping or fires are allowed, and no drinking water is available.

Palouse Falls. Just north of the confluence with the Snake River, the Palouse River gushes over a basalt cliff higher than Niagara Falls and drops 198 ft into a steep-walled basin. Hiking trails at the 105-acre *Palouse Falls State Park* (tel. 509/646–3252) lead to an overlook above the falls and to streams below. The falls are best during spring runoff, starting in late March. Just downstream at the *Marmes Rock Shelter*, remains of some of the earliest known inhabitants of North America, dating back 10,000 years, were discovered by archaeologists. The Marmes site is accessible via a 2½-mi trail from *Lyons Ferry State Park* at the point where the Snake and Palouse rivers meet, and by canoe (there's a boat launch at Lyons Ferry). Much of the actual shelter area is flooded by the backwaters of Lower Monumental Dam, but the area is still popular with canoeists.

Pullman. Although Colfax, 30 mi to the north, is the county seat, Pullman is considered the big town in Whitman County because of *Washington State University,* which anchors the community. Founded in 1890, the university now sprawls across several hills and has some 16,000 students. Tours at the university (tel. 509/335–4527) can keep you busy for a couple of days. National-caliber exhibits, changed monthly, are hung at the WSU *Museum of Fine Art* in the Fine Arts Center. For an impressive insect collection, visit the *Museum of Anthropology and Maurice T. James Entomological Collection* in Johnson Hall. Other campus destinations include the *Marion Ownbey Herbarium* in Herald Hall, the *Beef, Dairy, and Swine Centers*, and the *Jewett Astronomical Observatory* (tel. 509/335–8518 for tours). Pick up a campus map and parking pass from the visitor center adjacent to the fire station (follow signs on Stadium Way).

Skiing. In season, head for the Blue Mountains and *Ski Bluewood* (tel. 509/382–4725), 21 mi southeast of Dayton (52 mi northeast of Walla Walla) for cross-country and downhill skiing. The area, which gets more than 300 inches of snow a year, has two triple chairlifts and two T-bars serving 23 runs. The vertical rise is 1,125 ft, the second-highest base elevation in the state. Ski Bluewood's season usually runs from Thanksgiving through the first week of April.

Steptoe Battlefield and Steptoe Butte. In the Palouse area, Highway 195 offers turnoffs that will satisfy history buffs as well as those who like panoramic views. Following this road, the Steptoe Battlefield, near Rosalia, is 40 mi north of Pullman. As with Little Bighorn later, the U.S. Cavalry lost the battle fought here in 1858 to the Native Americans. Although all you can see now is a wheat field, a marker map on the roadside offers details that help you envision it as a field of action. For a commanding view of the rolling Palouse, take the winding drive 9 mi north of Colfax on Highway 195, to the top of Steptoe Butte. There's a picnic area here, but plan for wind, which is constant.

Walla Walla. A Native American name meaning "many waters" or "small, rapid streams," Walla Walla (population 26,000) dates to 1856, when Colonel Edward Steptoe established a settlement here; Main Street was built on the Nez Percé Indian Trail. Now the streets are tree lined and downtown Walla Walla has 25 historic buildings, many recently renovated. Information about walking and bicycling tours of town can be obtained from the Chamber of Commerce (*see* Tourist Information, *below*). *Whitman College*, a private liberal arts institution, is an excellent place for a stroll; a creek runs through the tree-filled campus. *Pioneer Park* (E. Adler St.), one of the oldest in the state, has an aviary with a fine collection of native and exotic birds. On the western outskirts of town, *Fort Walla Walla Museum* (755 Myra Rd., tel. 509/525–7703) houses most of the heirlooms and artifacts of the town's early families. More interesting, however, is the museum's Pioneer Village, a collection of 14 original settlers' buildings. Seven miles west of present-day Walla Walla, the *Whitman Mission* (Hwy. 12, tel. 509/522–6360) was founded in 1836 by Marcus and Narcissa Whitman. In 1847 a band of Cayuse Indians attacked the settlement and killed the Whitmans and a dozen others; they also took 50 captives, most of whom were later ransomed. The outlines of the mission building foundations are marked; an overlook on an adjacent hill affords a good sense of the vista that the settlers had of the area.

Wineries. Although not as extensive as the wine district near the Tri-Cities in central Washington or the Yakima Valley (*see* Columbia River and Long Beach Peninsula, *below*), the Palouse has its own version of a winery tour. Tourists can stop at *Woodward Canyon Winery* (Hwy. 12, 15 mi west of Walla Walla, tours by appointment, tel. 509/525–4129), which has a small tasting room behind a grain elevator. Housed in the historic old Lowden schoolhouse, *L'Ecole No. 41* (tel. 509/525–0940) offers a dining area and will cater luncheons and dinners on request. In Walla Walla, *Leonetti Cellars* (1321 School Ave., tel. 509/525–1428) has a tiny tasting room open just one weekend a year in September.

RESTAURANTS

Some gastronomes head to Dayton just for **Patit Creek Restaurant** (tel. 509/382–2625), named after the creek that meanders through town, in what was a service station during the 1920s. French-Continental cuisine with a Northwest bent is featured. Call ahead: It's sometimes difficult to get in. If a burger, fries, and a milk shake are more your fancy in Dayton, stop at **Gasoline Alley** (tel. 509/382–2775), another converted service station that rolls up the old garage door and offers dining alfresco in season or in Buddy Holly's tour bus, permanently parked here, where tables have been installed. In Walla Walla, try the salads and pastas at **Jacobi's Café Restaurant & Lounge** (tel. 509/525–2677), a real family spot partially in a former railroad dining car connected to an old railroad depot. It's a hangout for locals, who sit and talk over espresso and beer from local microbreweries. College students in Pullman enjoy similar fare at **Swilly's** (tel. 509/334–3395), in an old brick photo studio perched on the banks of the languid Palouse River. For more formal dining, try the standard American chicken, beef, and pasta dishes at **the Seasons** (tel. 509/332–3638), in a remodeled 1930s clapboard house on a hillside overlooking downtown Pullman.

TOURIST INFORMATION

Dayton Chamber of Commerce (222 E. Commercial St., Dayton, WA 99328, tel. 509/382–4825). **Pullman Chamber of Commerce** (415 N. Grand Ave., Pullman, WA 99163, tel. 509/334–3565). **Walla Walla Valley Chamber of Commerce** (29 E. Sumach, Walla Walla, WA 99362, tel. 509/525–0850). **Washington State Tourism** (Box 42500, Olympia, WA 98504-2500, tel. 800/544–1800).

RESERVATION SERVICES

Washington State Bed & Breakfast Guild (2442 N.W. Market St., Box 355-FD, Seattle, WA 98107, tel. 800/647–2918).

COUNTRY BED & BREAKFAST ℘
Rte. 2, Box 666, Pullman, WA 99163, tel. 509/334–4453, fax 509/332–5163

Set in the stark rolling hills of the Palouse, on a gravel road about 6 mi south of Pullman, Country Bed & Breakfast is not what you'd call fancy. But what it lacks in style is compensated for by the down-home hospitality of its owners, Mary Lee and Bruce Tenwick, who have lived here for 31 years. The farmhouse, surrounded by fragrant junipers and flowering trees, was built in 1893 but has been modernized over the years.

The interior has a practical, suburban look, with lots of cherry-wood paneling. One of the second-floor rooms has white walls, pale carpeting, and a sunken bedroom with a smaller room adjoining it. The Playroom—Bruce's former workshop—is a cavernous dormitorylike room with a fireplace, iron bedsteads, slot and pinball machines, and a pool table. If you've ever wondered what it's like to stay in an RV, the Fifth Wheel, parked away from the house, will satisfy your curiosity. Mary Lee serves a Continental breakfast—typically cereal, rolls, and fruit—and full breakfast and dinner if you reserve in advance. ♙ *1 queen room with bath, 2 doubles share bath, 2 suites. TV in den, TV/VCR in Playroom, hot tub. $50–$100 ($25 for additional beds in playroom); Continental-plus breakfast, full breakfast and dinner by reservation. D, MC, V. No smoking; 2-night minimum stay during college activity weekends.*

GREEN GABLES INN ✿
922 Bonsella St., Walla Walla, WA 99362, tel. 509/525–5501, greengables@wwics.com

In a business where location is often everything, Green Gables Inn has everything. One block from the Whitman College campus, the Arts and Crafts–style mansion is in a picturesque historic district: Trees nearly a century old line the peaceful streets, and most of the homes in the area have been carefully restored.

Rowland H. Smith and Clarinda Green Smith, for whom the house was built in 1909, took the lead in developing the neighborhood. For nearly four decades after 1940, their place housed the nurses and offices of the Walla Walla General Hospital; it didn't return to being a private residence until 1978. Margaret Buchan and her husband, Jim, the sports editor at the local newspaper, bought the mansion in 1990 and converted it into a B&B and reception facility.

A broad porch, tucked under the overhanging eaves, sweeps across the front of the mansion and around one side, an ideal setting for relaxing on a warm afternoon, lemonade and book in hand. The Buchans filled the yard with flowering plants, bulbs, and shrubs. Inside the front vestibule, a large foyer is flanked by two sitting areas, both with fireplaces and one with a TV.

The five guest rooms, whose names are derived from Lucy Maud Montgomery's novel *Anne of Green Gables*, are on the second floor; the hallway between them is lined with floor-to-ceiling bookshelves, and a love seat tucked into a corner creates a cozy library. All of the rooms feature baths with claw-foot tubs. The only room with a fireplace, Idlewild, also has a private deck and a hot tub. Dryad's Bubble is sufficiently spacious to accommodate a reading area with an overstuffed chair and ottoman, a dresser and dressing table, and a king-size bed with striped comforter; French doors open to a small private balcony. The smallest room, Mayflowers, was once the maid's quarters; now the picture of Victorian femininity, with floral wallpaper, an antique quilt, and plenty of pillows with lace shams, it affords lots of privacy.

Margaret serves breakfast, which might include sausage quiche and seasonal fruit, in a formal dining room. An Arts and Crafts–style sideboard displaying her collection of china and serving pieces from the early 1900s runs the length of one wall. Children under 12 are welcome in the carriage house. ♦ *5 double rooms with baths, 2 suites. Fireplace and hot tub in 1 room, kitchen in 1 suite. Cable TV. $75–$160; full breakfast. AE, D, MC, V. No smoking.*

PURPLE HOUSE BED AND BREAKFAST ✿
415 E. Clay St., Dayton, WA 99328, tel. 509/382–3159 or 800/486–2474, fax 509/382–3159

Although only a block off Highway 12—which is also the main street through Dayton—The Purple House Bed and Breakfast is quiet. Perhaps this is because Dayton isn't on the way to anywhere, and traffic is never too bad here. Owner Christine Williscroft spent 12 years remodeling and decorating the Queen Anne Italianate–style home, which is on the National Register of Historical Places. It was built in 1882 by a pioneer physician in what is now one of Dayton's oldest neighborhoods and was opened to guests in 1991.

A native of southern Germany, Christine brought European touches to her B&B. In the main-floor guest room, which she calls the luxurious master bedroom, French doors open to the patio and swimming pool that comprise the entire backyard of the house. Christine's real passion, however, is for things Chinese. Her formal living room is filled with Chinese antiques and appointments: Oriental rugs, an antique screen, a wedding kimono, and a hutch. Two carved wooden temple dogs guard the room's grand piano, and two live shih tzus guard the house.

Privacy was a priority in the design of the guest rooms. The carriage house suite has a freestanding fireplace, a kitchenette, and a sunken Japanese soaking tub. The master bedroom has a pink sunken tub, color-coordinated with the rest of the room, which includes a rose-print bedspread. Two accommodations upstairs share not only a bath with a marble shower, floor, sink, and counter, but also a small sitting area and library at the top of the stairs. An antique oak sleigh bed and tasteful forest-green wallpaper make the smaller of the rooms feel snug. The other room, cheerful and sunny, faces the front yard and has a Victorian feel, with 19th-century mahogany antiques and matching chintz fabrics.

Strudel and huckleberry pancakes often turn up at breakfast along with local bacon or sausage. Christine is a thoughtful host: she packs picnic lunches for her guests, offers afternoon pastries and tea in the parlor, and will accommodate dining restrictions and requests. Dinner, served family style, is available at $25 per person for guests (minimum six people). A typical entrée might be Hungarian goulash, pork roast, or standing rib roast. ◮ *1 double room with bath, 2 doubles share bath, 1 suite. Kitchen in suite. Cable TV in common room, pool, ski equipment, bicycle storage. $85–$125; full breakfast, afternoon refreshments, picnic lunches, and dinner available. MC, V. No smoking, small pets allowed.*

STONE CREEK INN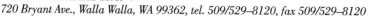
720 Bryant Ave., Walla Walla, WA 99362, tel. 509/529–8120, fax 509/529–8120

When it was built in 1883, the Moore mansion was a home in the country; now it's a 4-acre oasis in a modest residential neighborhood. The house has a distinguished history: Original owner Miles Moore was the last governor of the Washington Territories and later the mayor of Walla Walla. Stone Creek still runs through the estate and century-old trees tower over the lush lawns, punctuated by flower beds near the mansion. The pond in which Moore's three sons splashed has been replaced by a swimming pool, but otherwise the estate has been carefully restored. A thick wall of trees and foliage shields the house and grounds from the street.

Patricia Johnson, an innkeeper from Portland, bought the three-story Queen Anne structure in 1995. Little renovation was required, so Patricia directed her energies toward decorating the first and second floors of the mansion and landscaping the grounds. Her antique furnishings lend an air of graceful sophistication to the enormous rooms (the ceilings on the first floor are 12 ft high). Collecting dolls is an obvious passion for her—a glass-fronted showcase filled with them greets you as you enter the vestibule.

Elements of the Eastlake style are apparent in the abundance of spindle work and ornate bracketing. Governor Moore's lawbooks are still in the bay-window library, which also contains an 1828 Chickering piano. A 1925 Steinway sits in the grandly proportioned living room, where you can relax by the fireplace. There's a parklike view of the grounds from every one of the windows.

The afternoon sun brightens the first-floor Garden Room, which features an opulent bath with a marble counter, gold-plated faucets, and crystal lighting fixtures. A fireplace graces the second-floor Veranda Suite, with sunny yellow wallpaper, turn-of-the-century high oak bed, and access to a private screened porch overlooking Stone Creek and the swimming pool. The Governor's Room, done in terra-cotta and cream with Venetian lace on the windows, opens onto a study and Governor Moore's dressing room. It shares a bath with the Terrace Room, which has a private balcony.

Breakfast—which may include fresh local fruit, home-baked muffins and biscuits, French toast, waffles, or ham and eggs—is served in a formal dining room with a fireplace. ♙ *2 double rooms with baths, 2 doubles share bath. Fireplace in 2 rooms. Pool, hot tub, limousine service from Walla Walla airport. $95–$125; full breakfast. MC, V. No smoking.*

British Columbia

British Columbia

ALASKA
(USA)

37

Hazelton

*Takla
Lake*

*Babine
Lake*

*Stua
Lak*

River

Terrace

16

*NAIKOON
PROVINCIAL
PARK*

Prince
Rupert

16

37

Skeena

Kitimat

Hecate Strait

Tlell
*Graham
Island*

16

Skidegate

Grenville Channel

*Douglas
Channel*

Ootsa Lake

Eutsuk Lake

*TWEEDSMUIR
PARK*

Finlayson Channel

*Moresby
Island*

Fitz Hugh Sound

Queen

Charlotte

COAST

MOU

Cape Scott

Strait

Port
Hardy

19

19

Port
Alice

Vancouver Island

**Camp
R**

N

28

PACIFIC

*STRATH
PAR*

OCEAN

Tofino

Uc

KEY	
——	Rail Lines
⚓	Ferry
🍁	Trans-Canada Hwy.

0   100 miles

0   140 km

VANCOUVER AND ENVIRONS

Bounded by the Pacific Ocean to the west and the U.S. border to the south, the southwestern corner of British Columbia is dramatically beautiful, with verdant forests and rocky spires that look out majestically over fjordlike waterways. This was originally the home of the Coast Salish people, who lived for thousands of years on the area's abundant natural resources.

The face of the land began to change with the influx of miners, trappers, loggers, fishermen, and other settlers who came in the late 18th century, encouraged by the stories of James Cook, George Vancouver, and other explorers. Settlements like New Westminster and Granville (Vancouver's original townsite) sprang up around trading posts and sawmills along the waterfront and continued to grow and develop with the arrival of the Canadian transcontinental railway in the 1880s.

With its deep natural harbor, the town of Vancouver (which had a population of 1,000 by the time of its incorporation in 1886) was destined to become a major shipping terminus. Today it is a dynamic, multifaceted city that comfortably combines cosmopolitan and outdoor attractions. Tourism joins the older shipping, fishing, logging, and mining industries—as well as the newer banking and high-tech businesses—as one of the major sources of revenue for the region. The population's broad spectrum of nationalities—British, Chinese, Japanese, Italian, French, German, Greek, and even American—give Vancouver an exciting international face, as well as some wonderful restaurants.

Many large hotel chains were attracted to Vancouver in the past decades, but when the International Exposition came to town in the summer of 1986, residents began to open up their homes to accommodate the overflow of visitors. Although most of these early B&Bs have since closed, those that remain have become polished, and the trend toward more intimate hospitality continues to make inroads in town.

PLACES TO GO, SIGHTS TO SEE

The Canadian Craft Museum (639 Hornby St., tel. 604/687–8266) showcases traditional and contemporary works in glass, fiber, wood, acrylics, and clay. The Museum Shop has a broad selection of one-of-a-kind, handcrafted objects for sale.

Chinatown. Join the jostling crowds in Vancouver's Chinatown, one of the largest in North America, with its ornate Asian facades, dim sum restaurants, open-front produce stalls, and shops selling noodles, herbs, silks, and souvenirs. Look for the *Sam Kee Building*, only 6 ft wide, at the corner of Pender and Carrall streets.

Gardens. Among the many green spots in Vancouver are two fine Asian gardens and several flower gardens. If time permits, each of the following is worth the trip: *Bloedel Conservatory* (Queen Elizabeth Park, 33rd Ave. and Cambie St., tel. 604/257–8570); *Dr. Sun Yat-Sen Classical Chinese Garden* (578 Carrall St., tel. 604/689–7133); *Nitobe Memorial Garden* (N.W. Marine Dr., 1903 West Mall University of British Columbia, tel. 604/822–9666); *University of British Columbia Botanical Garden* (6804 S.W. Marine Dr., tel. 604/822–9666); and *Van Dusen Botanical Garden* (5251 Oak St., tel. 604/878–9274).

Gastown. Victorian gaslights and false-front shops along the cobbled streets and narrow mews of this restored heritage area make Gastown a favorite site for filming motion pictures. Here you'll find a statue of "Gassy" Jack Deighton, founder of Vancouver's original townsite, and the world's first steam-powered clock, along with antiques stores, clothing boutiques, souvenir shops, pubs, and restaurants.

Granville Island. This revitalized industrial area across the bay from downtown Vancouver is now home to theaters, artisans' studios, a microbrewery, an art college, waterfront restaurants, a kids-only market, a water park, and an enormous public market. The island makes for a good day trip.

Robson Street. No visit to Vancouver is complete without a stroll down Robson Street. You can browse through exclusive clothing boutiques and gift emporiums or stop for espresso at one of the many sidewalk cafés and enjoy the passing parade of people.

Skiing. Three fine ski areas lie within minutes of the Vancouver city center. *Cypress Bowl* (Exit 8 off westbound Hwy. 1, Box 91252, West Vancouver, tel. 604/926–5612); with groomed runs on two lift-serviced mountains, has the longest vertical run of the Vancouver resorts, along with night skiing and a variety of Nordic and backcountry skiing trails. The string of lights visible each night on the North Shore of the city mark the arc-lit runs of *Grouse Mountain* (6400 Nancy Greene Way, North Vancouver, tel. 604/984–0661), offering a variety of runs and lifts, a snowshoe park, sleigh rides, and a mountaintop pub and restaurant. At *Mt. Seymour* (1700 Mt. Seymour Rd., North Vancouver, tel. 604/986–2261) runs are open for night skiing; there are also cross-country trails throughout this provincial park.

Stanley Park. This 1,000-acre green oasis in the heart of Vancouver is home to the renowned *Vancouver Aquarium* (tel. 604/682–1118). There's also a children's petting zoo and miniature train, tennis courts, a miniature golf course, a children's water park, an outdoor pool, rose gardens, totem poles, several sandy beaches, a vast network of forested trails, and a 6-mi seawall promenade for walkers, bikers, and joggers. There are also two fine restaurants.

University of British Columbia Museum of Anthropology (6393 N.W. Marine Dr., tel. 604/822–3825). If your visit to Vancouver will be short, this museum should be on your list of must-sees in town. The incredible collections of Pacific Northwest native artifacts—totems, masks, jewelry, ceremonial costumes, canoes, even longhouses—and of contemporary art are not to be missed.

RESTAURANTS

The palette of international eateries in Vancouver is almost overwhelming. When your taste buds are craving Italian, **Caffè de Medici** (109–1025 Robson St., tel. 604/669–9322), **Piccolo Mondo Ristorante** (850 Thurlow St., tel. 604/688–1633), and **Villa del Lupo** (869 Hamilton St., tel. 604/688–7436) are the best choices. There are numerous excellent Asian eateries in town. For sushi, Vancouverites favor **Tojo's** (202–777 W. Broadway, tel. 604/872–8050); for dim sum, they head to the **Pink Pearl** (1132 E. Hastings St., tel. 604/253–4316). Vancouver chefs are leading the way in defining Pacific Northwest fare. For some of the best, try **Bishop's** (2183 W. 4th Ave., tel. 604/738–2025), or **Diva at the Met** (tel. 604/602–7788).

TOURIST INFORMATION

Tourism B.C. (865 Hornby St., Suite 802, Vancouver, BC V6Z 2G3, tel. 604/660–2861). **Tourism Vancouver Travel Infocentre** (200 Burrard St., Vancouver, BC V6C 3L6, tel. 604/683–2000, fax 604/682–6839).

RESERVATION SERVICES

Best Canadian Bed and Breakfast Network (1064 Balfour Ave., Vancouver, BC V6H 1X1, tel. 604/738–7207, fax 604/732–4998). **British Columbia Bed and Breakfast Association** (Box 593, 101–1001 W. Broadway, Vancouver, BC V6H 4E4, tel. 604/734–3486). **Old English Bed and Breakfast Registry** (1226 Silverwood Crescent, North Vancouver, BC V7P 1J3, tel. 604/986–5069, fax 604/986–8810). **Supernatural British Columbia** (601–1166 Alberni St., Vancouver, BC V6E 3Z3, tel. 800/663–6000). **Town and Country Bed and Breakfast Reservation Service** (2803 W. 4th Ave., Box 74542, Vancouver, BC V6K 1K2, tel. and fax 604/731–5942). **A Travelers Reservation Service** (14716 26th Ave. NE, Seattle, WA 98155, tel. 206/364–5900).

ENGLISH BAY INN ☜

1968 Comox St., Vancouver, BC V6G 1R4, tel. 604/683–8002, fax 604/899–1501

Vancouverite Bob Chapin, a former school administrator, makes innkeeping look easy. His remodeled 1939 modified Tudor is in a prime location just a block from Stanley Park and English Bay and within walking distance of Robson Street. Service is also excellent.

The house, adorned throughout with fresh flowers, has floor-to-ceiling leaded-glass diamond-pane windows and cove ceilings. The sumptuous furnishings include a gilt Louis IV clock and candelabra and an elegant 18th-century Federal sofa in the fireside living room. The equally striking bedrooms are elegantly furnished with Victorian gentlemen's chairs, stained-glass windows, Federal mirrors, and crisply ironed Ralph Lauren bedding on reproduction Louis Philippe sleigh beds. Room 5 is a romantic choice, a suite with a separate sitting room, a whirlpool bath, and a hidden winding staircase leading to a loft bedroom with its own fireplace. Regulars at this much-loved inn will be pleased to hear that Bob has opened two more suites in an equally beautiful Tudor building across the street.

Bob's four-course breakfasts, including fruit, home-baked goods, and entrées such as smoked salmon quiche or shrimp and crab omelets, are served in the elaborately carved Gothic dining room. ▲ *4 double rooms with baths, 3 suites. Phone in rooms; fireplace and whirlpool bath in 1 suite. C$170–C$285; full breakfast. AE, MC, V. No smoking, 2-night minimum on weekends.*

JOHNSON HERITAGE HOUSE 📽

2278 W. 34th Ave., Vancouver, BC V6M 1G6, tel. and fax 604/266–4175;
www.johnsons-inn-vancouver.com

This two-tone gray, 1920 Craftsman sits behind a rock garden overflowing with colorful azaleas and rhododendrons on a quiet, tree-lined avenue a 10-minute drive southwest of downtown Vancouver. Wooden Canadiana furnishings and an intriguing variety of collectibles—gramophones and phonographs, carousel horses, barbershop poles, and antique Chinese statues—illustrate the antiques-dealing past of hosts Sandy and Ron Johnson.

The superb Carousel Suite has a cathedral ceiling; a gas fireplace; mountain views; an Indonesian iron-and-brass four-poster bed decked out in a pretty quilt; and a spacious bathroom with whirlpool tub, pedestal sink, tile shower, bidet, and giant Toledo scale. The other guest rooms also have cathedral ceilings and antique brass beds; the Sunshine Room has a small private deck; the Mountain Room has a claw-foot tub in a private bath across the hall.

Breakfast, served in the sunny dining room with a view of the 20-ft rhododendron bush just outside, is hearty and homey, featuring homemade muffins and jams, fruit, cereal, and hot entrées like apple pancakes or French toast with real maple syrup.

Ron and Sandy are something of a rarity in Vancouver—genuine locals. They're relaxed and friendly hosts and can provide an immense amount of information about the city. They've even created a homemade guidebook for every guest. *⚠ 4 double rooms with bath. Phone and data port in rooms, cable TV in some rooms. Cable TV/VCR in living room. C$110–C$145; full breakfast. No credit cards. No smoking, 2-night minimum may apply.*

LABURNUM COTTAGE 📽

1388 Terrace Ave., North Vancouver, BC V7R 1B4, tel. and fax 604/988–4877
or tel. 888/207–8901; www.ccdesigns.com/laburnumcottage

When you're strolling in the garden at Laburnum Cottage, set next to a forest, it's hard to imagine that you're only 15 minutes from the city center on Vancouver's North Shore.

The English country–style cottage, built in 1945, is near the Capilano Suspension Bridge, numerous hiking and mountain-biking trails, and Vancouver's three ski hills. The biggest treat for many, though, is the award-winning garden, with its formal landscaping, winding paths, and brightly painted footbridges over a meandering creek.

The house, including the lounge where guests can enjoy afternoon tea or sherry, is appointed with fine English antiques, family heirlooms, and an array of collectibles that innkeeper Delphine Masterton picked up on her world travels.

The three second-floor guest rooms in the main house are light and airy; they're furnished with polished antiques, brass beds, Chinese and Persian carpets, and imported linens, and each has a private bath with a shower stall. The English Garden room on the main floor has an electric fireplace, a bath with a tub, and access to a deck in the garden. Amid the roses, dogwoods, and weeping willows in the garden, the romantic little summer house has heirloom wicker furniture, a brass bed near the fireplace, and a kitchenette. The larger Carriage House, popular with families, offers a full kitchen, a fireplace, and a loft sleeping platform above the master bedroom.

The heart of the main house is the spacious kitchen, with yellow-and-white-striped wallpaper and green marble counters. Breakfast, served around the big pine table or in the terra-cotta-tile garden room, is a real event. Delphine and her assistant, European-trained chef Karen Essinger, bustle about the Aga stove preparing strawberry pancakes, Mexican eggs with salsa, or other tasty main dishes accompanied by cinnamon buns or scones and plates of seasonal fruit. △ *4 double rooms with baths, 2 cottages. Cable TV and kitchen in cottages, fireplace in 1 cottage. Piano in public area. C$135–C$275; full breakfast. MC, V. No smoking, 2-night minimum in cottages.*

LOCARNO BEACH BED & BREAKFAST ☞

4550 N.W. Marine Dr., Vancouver, BC V6R 1B8, tel. 604/224–2177, fax 604/224–3141

If you'd rather be on the beach than in the thick of things downtown, Locarno Beach is for you. This contemporary, cedar-and-glass home enjoys spectacular views of the North Shore mountains and English Bay.

Inside is a stunning collection of pottery and tribal artifacts that owner Sigrid Whitman, an art dealer originally from Munich, Germany who speaks some German in the B&B, either crafted or collected on her world travels. Two of the second-floor bedrooms feature handmade Indonesian quilts, modern pine furniture, and double-glazed, floor-to-ceiling windows that take full advantage of the ocean and mountain views. The third is similarly furnished but looks out on the garden instead. One room has an in-suite bath, two have private baths across the hall.

In the downstairs breakfast room you can admire the ocean views, the Asian tribal artifacts, or both, while Sigrid serves up cereal, fresh fruit, baked goods, and traditional breakfast entrées like omelets or sausages and eggs. There's also a private guest kitchen for fixing snacks the rest of the time.

From Locarno Beach Park across the road you can kayak, windsurf, swim, or stroll along the shore, and golf and tennis are within walking distance of the bed-and-breakfast. The famous Museum of Anthropology at the University of British Columbia is just up the hill, and the sights of Granville Island are minutes away by car. △ *1 double room, 2 double rooms with private baths across hall. Cable TV and phone in guest kitchen. C$95-C$110; full breakfast. MC, V. No smoking, 2-night minimum on weekends, closed Oct.–Easter.*

O CANADA HOUSE ☞

1114 Barclay St., Vancouver, BC V6E 1H1, tel. 604/688–0555, fax 604/488–0556; www.vancouver-bc.com/ocanadahouse

This beautifully restored 1897 Victorian within walking distance of downtown is the very house where the first version of "O Canada," the national anthem, was written in 1909. Innkeeper and restoration-fanatic Jim Britten opened the house as a bed-and-breakfast in 1996, after carefully coaxing it back to its 19th-century splendor.

O Canada House, which has since won Vancouver's top heritage restoration award, is furnished throughout with late Victorian antiques. Bathrobes and teddy bears make things cozy, while modern comforts, like TVs and VCRs are tucked away in armoires. The top-floor Penthouse Suite is enormous (about 800 square ft), with two double beds and a private sitting area. A romantic new one-bedroom cottage in the garden has French doors opening onto a private patio.

Guests have the use of a pantry and often gather in the evening near the fireplace in the front parlor. Breakfast, served in the dining room or on the wraparound porch, involves homemade baked goods (raisin scones are a specialty), a fruit dish, and a main course such as salmon crepes or eggs Florentine. ♨ *5 double rooms with baths, 1 cottage. Phone, TV/VCR, and mini-refrigerator in rooms. Guest pantry, free parking. C$125–C$195; full breakfast. MC, V. No smoking, 2-night minimum on weekends.*

PENNY FARTHING ❦

2855 W. 6th Ave., Vancouver, BC V6K 1X2, tel. 604/739–9002, fax 604/739–9004; www.pennyfarthinginn.com

"Enchanted April," was one guest's reaction to the secluded English country garden of this 1912 Craftsman-style home, in the funky Kitsilano neighborhood a few minutes south of downtown Vancouver. Amiable English innkeeper Lyn Hainstock knows how to create a comfortable, relaxed atmosphere for her guests. The house, with its rich turquoise and raspberry exterior, stained-glass windows, lounge fireplace, antique piano, Edwardian furnishings, and hardwood floors, has loads of period charm.

Lyn's sense of humor is evident in guest rooms dubbed Abigail's Attic, Bettina's Boudoir, Lucinda's Lair, and Sophie's Salon, and her sense of romantic style in furnishings such as Victorian lace curtains and big brass beds or oak four-posters. Bettina's Boudoir has a comfy reclining chair in front of a gas fire, and a balcony overlooking the garden. Abigail's Attic is a self-contained suite at the top of the house with a picture window offering views of Vancouver's mountains and skyline.

Copious breakfasts, served in the cozy dining room or, on fine days, on the brick patio surrounded by fragrant gardens behind the house, might include orange pecan muffins, lemon orange scones, stuffed crepes, herbed omelets, and other goodies (don't hesitate to ask for recipes). When it comes to entertaining, Lyn is always assisted by her house cats—Fluffy, Hendrix, Melody, and Frisky, who also plays the piano.

Lyn, who is a great resource for planning your travels around the province, also supplies a guest pantry, and a sort of electronic pantry, with a computer, fax, scanner, and copier for guests traveling on business. ♨ *3 double rooms with baths, 1 suite. Phone, TV/VCR in some rooms and in guest lounge, refrigerator in suite. Book, CD, and video libraries, guest pantry with computer, fax, scanner, and copier. C$110–C$165; full breakfast. No credit cards. No smoking.*

RIVER RUN ❦

4551 River Rd. W, Ladner, BC V4K 1R9, tel. 604/946–7778, fax 604/940–1970; www.cimarron.net/canada/bc/riverrun.html

This unique bed-and-breakfast is part of a charming row of houseboats and riverside houses on the Fraser River, a 30-minute drive south of downtown Vancouver and 10 minutes north of the ferries to Vancouver Island.

River Run, with it serene setting and self-contained units—each with its own cooking facilities, woodstove, and deck—affords plenty of privacy for romantic retreats. Some of the accommodations float on the water, others rest on pylons on the river's edge, and the whole complex is linked with walkways and draped with hanging flower baskets.

The four units include the Water Lily, a little gem of a floating cottage with a loft bed and an interior of beautifully crafted, highly polished wood; and an adorable net loft with a Japanese soaking tub on the deck and a captain's bed tucked away in the rafters. Two other rooms, each with a private deck, share a riverside cottage. The Keepers Quarters has a whirlpool tub, a handmade driftwood bed and a woodstove; The Northwest Room has a fireplace and a bizarre double shower fashioned from slate and river rocks.

The four hosts, Bill and Janice Harkley and Terry and Deborah Millichamp, appear to know a thing or two about romance. They've thought of everything, from welcoming snacks and sherry, to candles, bubble bath, cozy terry robes, CD players, and a list of suggested activities that includes "sleeping in" and "kissing and hugging a lot." Other options are kayaking and cycling (boats and bikes are available); watching the boats, birds, and wildlife go by; or visiting the renowned Reifel Bird Sanctuary just down the road.

Breakfast—including coffee, juices, toast, granola, yogurt, and an imaginative hot entrée—is delivered to your door each morning with a newspaper. You can enjoy it in your room, in bed, or on your private deck overlooking the river.

River Run's waterfront location makes it unsuitable for small children. ♨ *1 double with bath, 2 suites, 1 floating cottage. Refrigerator, microwave, coffeemaker, and phone in units. TV and VCR on request. Barbecue, bicycles, canoes, kayaks. C$140–C$175; full breakfast. MC, V. Pets welcome. No smoking.*

THISTLEDOWN HOUSE ☞
3910 Capilano Rd., North Vancouver, BC V7R 4J2, tel. 604/986–7173 or 888/633–7173, fax 604/980–2939; davidson@helix.net

This 1920 Arts and Crafts house, one of the oldest in North Vancouver, has been extensively and lovingly restored by the new owners. Ruth Crameri, originally from Switzerland, is an interior designer by profession; her historian husband, Rex Davidson, grew up in the Vancouver area. Together they've furnished the house with a low-key, cozy, and eclectic arrangement of antiques, Art Deco touches, and treasures gathered from their travels. The resident Scottish terrier, Talla, helps greet guests.

Each room has its own charm: Under the Apple Tree, with its private patio, fireplace, and whirlpool tub, is a romantic choice; Mulberry Peek has a private balcony overlooking the garden; the Snuggery is small and cozy, with a fireplace.

Breakfasts, served at the long table in the dining room or in the garden, feature yogurt, cereal, fruit, home-baked goods, and such elaborate entrées as ham and asparagus crepes with chantilly sauce, or smoked salmon and herbed cream vol-au-vent. Ruth also whips up homemade goodies for afternoon tea, taken in the sitting room by the wood fire or, in summer, under the apple tree in the garden.

Thistledown House is in North Vancouver, a 15- to 30-minute drive from downtown (depending on the time of day). Though it's on a fairly busy road, the house is almost surrounded by wilderness, with the mountains, rivers, and forests of the north shore all nearby; Capilano Regional Park, with its 16 mi of hiking trails, starts right across the street. ♨ *5 doubles with baths. Fireplace in two rooms. Fax and Internet services. C$110–C$189; full breakfast. MC, V. No smoking.*

WEST END GUEST HOUSE ☞
1362 Haro St., Vancouver, BC V6E 1G2, tel. 604/681–2889, fax 604/688–8812; wegh@idmail.com

The West End Guest House, a 1906 "Painted Lady," done up in bright pink with white trim, is just one block south of Robson Street and within easy reach of Vancouver's best shopping, dining, and entertainment options. Stanley Park is also close by, so leave the car at the inn; complimentary valet parking is available.

Imported door frames, a grand banister, and bathrooms were added during the renovations made before the inn opened in 1986, but the period flavor of the home was preserved, and the addition of many excellent Victorian and Edwardian pieces help re-create the era. The original owner was one of the first professional photographers in Vancouver; his photos chronicling life in the city from 1906 to 1925 now hang in stairwells and hallways.

The current owner, Evan Penner, is an avid collector of antiques. Among his recent acquisitions are the Belgian Art Deco sideboard, hutch, table, and chairs in the dining room where multicourse breakfasts are served. The morning repast includes fresh fruit and home-baked treats, followed by a hot entrée such as smoked salmon Benedict. Evan makes everything from scratch, including the jams.

In the guest rooms, feather mattresses on shiny brass beds and antique armoires and desks are paired with modern amenities, including phones, televisions, and ceiling fans or skylights. Other special touches include thick cotton robes, hand-knit slippers, homemade chocolates, and hors d'oeuvres and sherry served by the fire in the parlor. Number 2, the largest and most romantic room, has sponge-painted walls and a gambrel ceiling; lace curtains around double-sashed windows; a high brass bed, cozy love seat, and gas fireplace; and a long, old-fashioned slipper tub. One large room on the basement level is outfitted with gas fireplace, brass bed, and steam shower. ♨ *8 double rooms with baths. Phone and TV in rooms, fireplace in 2 rooms. Guest pantry, bicycles, free parking. C$150–C$250; full breakfast. AE, D, MC, V. No smoking, 2-night minimum some periods.*

WHISTLER

Whistler Resort, 75 scenic mi northeast of Vancouver, has been a favorite retreat for hunting and fishing since the early 1900s, but it wasn't until the 1960s that skiing became popular here.

Now one of the top-ranked ski resorts in the world, Whistler Resort offers more than 200 marked runs on Blackcomb and Whistler mountains and the longest lift-serviced runs in North America, with a drop of 1 vertical mi. The regular season runs from late November through May and glacier heli-skiing is available throughout the summer. Warm-weather activities, including golf, fishing, mountain biking, hiking, and water sports, make Whistler popular year-round.

The multimillion-dollar European-style Whistler Village, built at the base of Whistler and Blackcomb mountains in 1980, has in the past decade seen the rapid rise of alpine-style pensions in the area. Some are in the thick of the action near the lifts, others are in more rustic lakeside locations.

 PLACES TO GO, SIGHTS TO SEE

Sea to Sky Highway. This stretch of Highway 99, running along Howe Sound and up into the mountains en route to Whistler, takes you past some of the most beautiful scenery on the West Coast. If you're interested in copper mining, heavy machinery, and deep caverns, stop along the way at the *British Columbia Museum of Mining* (Brittania Beach, tel. 604/896–2233, or 604/688–8735 in Vancouver); this is not for the claustrophobic, however. A bit farther up, near the town of Squamish, Shannon Falls, a shimmering ribbon of tumbling water, and the Stawamus Chief, the second-largest granite monolith in the world and a magnet for climbers, are both visible from the highway.

Whistler and Blackcomb Mountains. Both mountains get an average of 360 inches of snow per year and have ski schools to instruct skiers of all levels; contact the *Blackcomb and Whistler Ski and Snowboard* schools (tel. 604/932–3434 or 800/766-0449). Blackcomb is also open from June to August for summer glacier skiing. Whistler is now popular as a year-round resort. Summer visitors enjoy hiking, fishing, mountain biking, tennis, golf (there are five courses in the area), white-water rafting, canoeing, windsurfing, lake swimming, and, increasingly, shopping, dining, and people-watching.

Whistler Village. The heart of the Whistler ski resort, Whistler Village is an ever-expanding, pedestrian-only complex of clock towers, avenues, shops, restaurants, and clubs. Lifts that whisk skiers from the village to the peaks of Blackcomb and Whistler mountains in winter also carry hikers to flower-filled alpine meadows in summer.

RESTAURANTS

In Whistler, you can beat the crowds by leaving the village to dine at **Le Deux Gros** (tel. 604/932–4611), which serves elegantly presented country French fare in relaxed surroundings, or at the **Rim Rock Cafe and Oyster Bar** (tel. 604/932–5565), which offers Continental cuisine and fresh seafood. In Whistler Village (downtown Whistler), best bets are **Sushi Village** (tel. 604/932–3330), **Araxi's** (tel. 604/932–4540) for Northern Mediterranean and Italian cuisine, **Zeuski's** (tel. 604/932–6009) for Greek favorites, and **La Rúa** (tel. 604/932–5011), in Le Chamois hotel (*see below*), for outstanding Continental dishes.

TOURIST INFORMATION

Tourism B.C. (865 Hornby St., Suite 802, Vancouver, BC V6Z 2G3, tel. 604/660–2861). **Vancouver Coast & Mountains Tourism Region** (1755 W. Broadway, Suite 204, Vancouver, BC V6J 4S5, tel. 604/739–9011 or 800/667–3306). **Whistler Resort Association** (4010 Whistler Way, Whistler, BC V0N 1B4, tel. 604/932–4222 or 800/944–7853).

RESERVATION SERVICES

Best Canadian Bed and Breakfast Network (1064 Balfour Ave., Vancouver, BC V6H 1X1, tel. 604/738–7207, fax 604/732–4998). **British Columbia Bed and Breakfast Association** (Box 593, 101–1001 W. Broadway, Vancouver, BC V6H 4E4, tel. 604/734–3486). **Old English Bed and Breakfast Registry** (1226 Silverwood Crescent, North Vancouver, BC, V7P 1J3, tel.604/986–5069, fax 604/986–8810). **Supernatural British Columbia** (601–1166 Alberni St., Vancouver, BC V6E 3Z3, tel. 800/663–6000). **Whistler's Finest Small Inns** (Box 352, Whistler, BC V0N 1B0, tel. 604/938–8007 or 800/665–1892, fax 604/938–8023). **Whistler Resort Association** (4010 Whistler Way, Whistler, BC V0N 1B4, tel. 604/932–4222 or 800/944–7853).

CEDAR SPRINGS LODGE ☞

8106 Cedar Springs Rd., Whistler, BC V0N 1B8, tel. 604/938–8007 or 800/727–7547, fax 604/938–8023; www.whistlerinns.com/cedarsprings

Cedar Springs Lodge, 2 mi north of Whistler Village and easily accessible via the Whistler bus system, is a great place for families—children are most welcome. The exterior of this two-story home is similar to the other West Coast–style Alpine homes in town, but inside, Cedar Springs stands alone in providing creature comforts.

Hostess Jackie Rohde, a lively young Australian with a knack for making you feel right at home, keeps the rooms simple and sweet—plump comforters cover hand-crafted log beds. Some rooms have baths with heated tile floors, others share baths. Two of the rooms are large enough to sleep four, and a family room with a double soaking tub can sleep six. Jackie's husband, Joern, cooks breakfast, served in the fireside dining room or outside on the sunny deck. Homemade breads and preserves (Joern even picks the berries), and hot dishes such as pancakes with strawberries and cream, French toast, or omelets are served along with cereal and fruits.

Cedar Springs is near Meadow Park Sports Centre, which has an indoor pool, ice rink and squash courts, and it's right on the Valley Trail—the resort's main biking and walking route. ♦ *6 double rooms with baths, 1 single and 1 double room share 2 baths. TV/VCR in lounge, library, video library, sauna, outdoor hot tub, ski and bike lockers. C$125–C$189; full breakfast, occasional dinners in winter. AE, MC, V. No smoking.*

CHALET LUISE 🌿

7461 Ambassador Crescent, Box 352, Whistler, BC V0N 1B0, tel. 604/932–4187 or 800/665–1892, fax 604/938–1531; www.whistlerinns.com/chaletluise

When Swiss innkeepers Lisa and Irwin Huber bought Chalet Luise, one of Whistler's oldest European-style pensions, in 1997 they redecorated the guest rooms in a pretty Laura Ashley style, but didn't put a dent in the inn's alpine charm.

In a quiet residential area close to the village, Chalet Luise is also very near the ski slopes and cross-country trails. As traditionally alpine inside as out, the house features carved-wood furnishings and a leather couch set before the gas fireplace in the living/dining room. A hot tub in a gazebo on the patio is also a great place to unwind.

The snug guest rooms have hand-crafted pine furniture and firm mattresses. One of the two romantic rooms with bay windows and gas fireplaces is large enough to sleep three people (but what of romance?). Attention is paid to details: Robes and slippers are on hand for guests, plump rolled towels are piled in a wooden crib above a staircase to the hot tub, and a hallway en route to the sauna is lined with racks for ski clothing to be warmed by a woodstove.

A filling breakfast of cereal, juice, yogurt, muffins, croissants, and a daily hot entrée of pancakes, scrambled eggs, or omelets, is served in the guest lounge, as is afternoon tea, and the occasional ski-season dinners, usually featuring fondues or raclettes. ♦ *8 double rooms with baths. Refrigerator, sauna, hot tub, ski room, ski locker near lifts, ski and summer packages, train and bus pickup. C$140–C$170; full breakfast, occasional dinners. MC, V. No smoking, a minimum stay may apply at peak times.*

DURLACHER HOF 🌿

7055 Nesters Rd., Box 1125, Whistler, BC V0N 1B0, tel. 604/932–1924 or 800/954–8585, ext. 1019, fax 604/938–1980; www.durlacherhof.com

Enthusiastic Erika Durlacher and her husband, Peter, run the most visible château in Whistler—it's on the main highway ½ mi north of the village. Their Tyrolean inn, modeled on the traditional farmhouses in their native Austria, is a favorite among Whistler regulars.

Custom fir woodwork and doors, exposed ceiling beams, a *kachelofen* (a traditional farmhouse fireplace oven), antler chandeliers hung over fir benches and tables, and a basket of slippers (with a pair for each guest), carry out the rustic European theme. The green and maroon guest rooms, all named for European mountains, contain more fine examples of custom-crafted pine furniture, including extra long beds (for tall skiers) covered with goose-down duvets. Four premium rooms on the third floor have such added amenities as refrigerators and double whirlpool tubs. Most rooms have balconies (mountain views are unavoidable here) and, because the idea is to get away from it all, there are no TVs or in-room phones.

For breakfast, platters of fruit salad, granola, sticky buns, French bread, imported cheeses, and Bavarian meats are set out buffet style to supplement the rich Austrian specialties—crepes with apple, cinnamon, yogurt, and fresh blueberries—

served as main courses. Erika also provides a full afternoon tea (and there's no sniffing at the tea from Harrods). Evenings, at the Durlachers' own licensed piano bar, are more civilized than the downtown Whistler party scene, and the Hof's Sunday night guest chef dinners are almost as much of a Whistler institution as Erika's memorable breakfasts. ♨ *7 double rooms with baths, 1 suite. Sauna, outdoor hot tub, massage, ski locker, piano bar; ski, golf, adventure, cooking, and concert packages. C$150–C$255; full breakfast, occasional guest-chef dinners. MC, V. No smoking, 2-night minimum on weekends, 3- to 7-night minimum on holidays, may be closed part of Nov., Apr., or May.*

EDGEWATER ☙

8841 Hwy. 99, Box 369, Whistler, BC V0N 1B0, tel. 604/932–0688, fax 604/932–0686; www.whistler.net/resort/edgewater

In 1965, when Randy Symons bought 45 acres on the edge of Green Lake, Whistler Resort was nothing but a rope tow in the backwoods. A lot has happened since then, including the addition of a long cedar lodge that Randy and his son Jay built on the lakeshore in 1995. The lodge, with its dramatic lake and mountain views, has a rustic family-run feel, but is replete with all the amenities, including a hot tub, conference facilities, and a popular restaurant.

All the rooms overlook the lake and have private entrances, modern furnishings, and window seats nestled into broad windows framing mountain and lake views. A breakfast buffet of homemade croissants and granola, fruit, and yogurt is served in the waterfront dining room. The room, decorated with folk art sculptures tucked into exposed beams, becomes a restaurant in the evening, attracting people from all over Whistler for its highly rated dinners centered around local produce, lamb, venison, or fish.

The adult-oriented Edgewater is a real outdoors retreat. Though it's a few miles from the downhill slopes, it's as close as you can get to all of Whistler's other sporting activities. From here you can enjoy cross-country skiing in winter, or fishing, canoeing, kayaking, bird-watching, hiking, and horseback riding the rest of the year. The nearby Whistler Valley Trail is great for cycling, strolling, or in-line skating in summer, and becomes a day and night cross-country ski trail when the snow falls. Whistler Outdoor Experience (tel. 604/932–3389) runs a summertime activity center on the property, and both the Nicklaus North Golf Course and the Meadow Park Sports Centre are nearby. ♨ *6 double rooms with baths, 6 suites. Phone and TV in rooms. Restaurant, bar, outdoor hot tub, ski storage, meeting rooms, bird-watching gear, hiking, boating, cross-country skiing. C$145–C$225; Continental-plus breakfast, dinners by reservation. AE, MC, V. No smoking.*

LE CHAMOIS ☙

4557 Blackcomb Way, Box 1044, Whistler, BC V0N 1B0, tel. 604/932–8700 or 800/777–0185, fax 604/930–1888; www.powder-properties.com

The multigabled Le Chamois hotel sits across the creek from the bustling heart of Whistler Village, at the foot of the Blackcomb ski runs. This luxurious, intimate property is small enough to ensure personal service but large enough to have all the extras, and its ski-in and ski-out location can't be beat.

The mountain deer from which Le Chamois derives its name is depicted in a beautiful tapestry hung behind the front desk in the lobby. Glass elevators whisk you to apartment-size rooms outfitted with light oak furniture, queen-size beds, kitchenettes, and picture windows overlooking mountain slopes and towering conifers. Naturally, accommodations on the upper floors have the grandest, most expansive views.

The one-bedroom suites with a sofa or Murphy bed in the separate living room and two full baths are well-suited for families. Elegantly appointed three- and four-bedroom suites with gas fireplaces, fully equipped kitchens, and washer-dryers are a good bet for groups on an extended stay.

For those who haven't already gotten enough exercise putting about on one of Whistler's fine golf courses, or hiking, biking, or skiing in the area, the hotel offers a small heated outdoor swimming pool, exercise bikes, and treadmills. The outdoor hot tub might help relax muscles sore from all these activities. Other amenities include a guest laundry and storage room for ski equipment and bicycles in the secured basement garage. La Rúa (*see* Restaurants, *above*), the Continental restaurant on the ground floor of the hotel, is the rising star of the local dining scene. ♠ *47 rooms with baths, 72- to 4-bedroom suites. Kitchenette, phone, cable TV, and air-conditioning in rooms; kitchen in suites. Restaurant, deli, conference facilities. C$225–C$1,160; breakfast not included. AE, DC, MC, V. 5-night minimum during Christmas.*

VANCOUVER ISLAND

Three-hundred-mile-long Vancouver Island lies stretched along the southwestern mainland of British Columbia, with Queen Charlotte Sound to the north, the Strait of Georgia to the east, the Strait of Juan de Fuca and the United States border to the southeast, and open Pacific Ocean to the west. It is an island of intense natural beauty and diversity; the Insular Mountain range runs down its spine, effectively sheltering the valleys and lowlands of the east side from the battering of Pacific rains that the rugged western coastline receives.

Surrounded by the Pacific Ocean and lapped by the warm Japan Current, the island enjoys mild temperatures in both winter and summer. Heavy winter rains feed the lush foliage that carpets its craggy peaks and rolling valleys. Though it has been logged continuously since the late 1800s, the island still hosts huge stands of old-growth Sitka spruce, western red cedar, hemlock, and Douglas fir. Its scenic wind- and water-sculpted coastline and pristine forests draw an increasing number of visitors every year.

Captain James Cook is generally credited with being the first Englishman to set foot on the island; he was met by Kwakiutl and other coastal natives willing to supply the timber, fish, and furs he sought in trade. However, it was Captain George Vancouver who named the island during later explorations of the region. The first white settlement occurred in the mid-1800s with the founding of a Hudson's Bay Company post in what is now Victoria. Abundant natural resources brought in settlers who established new town sites as they slowly fanned up the island to fish, log, and mine coal.

Most of the 500,000 current residents live along the southern half of the east coast, in and between Victoria, in the southern tip, and Nanaimo, midway up the island. The rest of the island is still largely wilderness, dotted with small communities that once thrived on logging and fishing, but are now increasingly turning to tourism for their livelihoods.

PLACES TO GO, SIGHTS TO SEE

British Columbia Forest Museum (R.R. 4, Trans-Canada Hwy., Duncan, tel. 250/715–1313). The highlight of a visit to this enormous indoor-outdoor showcase of logging and milling equipment is a ride on an old steam locomotive across a wooden trestle bridge.

Bungy Zone. If you're of a mind to swan dive off a 140-ft-high bridge over a water-filled chasm—or perhaps just to watch others do it—follow the signs to *Bungy Zone* (Nanaimo, tel. 250/753–5867), the only permanent bungee-jump site in British Columbia. Spectators are welcome to visit any day of the week; call for reservations if you'd like to take the plunge yourself.

Cathedral Grove. Highway 4 takes you into MacMillan Provincial Park and past Cathedral Grove, a corridor of towering old-growth Douglas fir and red cedar. On your way to the West Coast, stop to stretch your legs on the short trail that runs through the grove.

Chemainus. When the local lumber/paper mill announced a shutdown that spelled doom for this little town, the citizens did not sit back and bemoan their fate. Instead they commissioned local artists to adorn buildings and walls with more than two dozen murals depicting events of historical significance to the area. Thus was born the "City of Murals," a worthwhile stop on any tour of the island. The *Arts and Business Council* (9796 Willow St., Chemainus, tel. 250/246–4701) can provide a map and more information.

Cowichan Native Village (200 Cowichan Way, Duncan, tel. 250/746–8119). The history and traditions of Northwest Coast natives come to life through media presentations, interpretive dances, and demonstrations of basket weaving, totem carving, and spinning. You can also sample native foods and purchase handmade Cowichan sweaters.

North Island Wildlife Recovery Association's Museum of Nature (1240 Leffler Rd., Errington, BC V0R 1V0, tel. 250/248–8534) showcases the wildlife typical of Vancouver Island. The recovery center houses an array of injured, ill, or orphaned wildlife, including bears, owls, hawks, and eagles, and has the largest flight cage in Canada (bald eagles are readied for release here). Errington is a 10-minute drive west of Nanoose Bay. The center is open from May to September.

Pacific Rim National Park (Box 280, Ucluelet, tel. 250/726–7721). On Vancouver Island's far western edge, hugging the Pacific Ocean, this rain-forest park is divided into three sections: the Broken Group Islands, reached only by boat; the West Coast Trail, accessible only to very experienced hikers; and Long Beach, the most visited because of its network of easy trails and its fine interpretive center. Birds and wildlife are abundant in this verdant area, and the long shoreline is lined with tidal pools and elevated areas for viewing the whale migration just offshore.

Sooke Region Museum and Travel Infocentre (2070 Phillips Rd., Sooke, tel. 250/642–6351). The fascinating collection of First Nations arts and pioneer artifacts housed in this tiny museum is worth a peek if you're in the neighborhood. A travel infocenter sharing the space provides handy maps for exploring the area.

Strathcona Provincial Park (Hwy. 28, Campbell River, tel. 250/286–3122 or 250/387–5002). The alpine meadows; thick forests; and myriad lakes, waterfalls, and marshy areas of Strathcona, British Columbia's oldest provincial park, are laced with campgrounds, hiking trails, and cross-country ski trails. Crowning all is Golden Hinde, Vancouver Island's highest peak at 7,218 ft.

RESTAURANTS

Over the years, **Sooke Harbour House** (in Sooke, tel. 250/642–3421) has garnered international acclaim for its sophisticated Pacific Northwest cuisine. Other choices for outstanding regional fare emphasizing fresh local ingredients are **Deep Cove Chalet** (tel. 250/656–3541) in Sidney, The **Old House Restaurant** (tel. 250/338–5406) in Courtenay, and **the Mahle House** (tel. 250/722–3621) in Nanaimo. Elegant Continental meals complement the stunning panoramic views at **the Aerie** (tel. 250/743–7115), perched high atop the Malahat. Some of the best dining in British Columbia is to be found overlooking the Pacific surf at **the Pointe Restaurant** (tel. 250/725–3100 or 800/333–4604) in Tofino's Wickaninnish Inn (*see below*).

TOURIST INFORMATION

Tourism B.C. (865 Hornby St., Suite 802, Vancouver, BC V6Z 2G3, tel. 604/660–2861). **Tourism Association of Vancouver Island** (Suite 302, 45 Bastion Sq., Victoria, BC V8W 1J1, tel. 250/382–3551, fax 250/382–3523).

RESERVATION SERVICES

AA Accommodations West Bed and Breakfast Reservations Service (660 Jones Terr., Victoria, BC V8Z 2L7, tel. 250/479–1986, fax 250/479–9999). **All Seasons Bed and Breakfast Agency** (9858 5th St., Sidney, BC V8L 2X7, tel. 250/655–7173). **Best Canadian Bed and Breakfast Network** (1064 Balfour Ave., Vancouver, BC V6H 1X1, tel. 604/738–7207, fax 604/732–4998). **British Columbia Bed and Breakfast Association** (Box 593, 101–1001 W. Broadway, Vancouver, BC V6H 4B1, tel. 604/734–3486). **Supernatural British Columbia** (601–1166 Alberni St., Vancouver, BC V6E 3Z3, tel. 800/663–6000). **The Gourmet Trail** (304–1913 Sooke Rd., Victoria, BC V9B 1V9, tel. 800/970–7722) arranges packages and food- and wine-related tours involving several Vancouver Island country inns. **Town and Country Bed and Breakfast Reservation Service** (2803 W. 4th Ave., Box 74542, Vancouver, BC V6K 1K2, tel. and fax 604/731–5942).

THE AERIE ☞

600 Ebedora La., Box 108, Malahat, BC V0R 2L0, tel. 250/743–7115, fax 250/743–4766; www.aerie.bc.ca

The stunning view over Finalyson Arm and the Gulf Islands persuaded Austrians Leo and Maria Schuster to build their sprawling, Mediterranean-style villa here, high atop the Malahat, about 20 mi north of Victoria. Together they created a luxurious, romantic retreat, small enough to afford plenty of personal attention but replete with every modern convenience—from the stunning dining room, famous for its dinners alone, to the European-style spa treatments added in 1998. There's even a helipad for high-flying guests.

The Schusters brought a great deal of experience to their innkeeping venture: Maria formerly owned an exclusive resort in Eleuthera, and Leo was a master chef at a number of top international hotels. Maria's refined tastes are reflected in the decor, which features billowing taffeta window coverings, lavish Chinese carpets, and Italian antiques. The pale peach, green, and gray color scheme echoes the Mediterranean-style building that Leo designed.

Each of the guest rooms has different layout and amenities, but all are graciously appointed, with custom-crafted furnishings and Christian Dior bed linens. Most have superb views. Some feature whirlpool tubs; others offer vaulted ceilings, fireplaces, or large balconies. The newer wing has plush, multilevel master suites, each at least 900 square ft.

Chef Chris Jones's culinary talents are showcased in the gold leaf–ceiling dining room, where a lavish, European-influenced breakfast competes with the million-dollar view. A breakfast buffet includes fresh fruit, cured meats, cheeses, freshly baked pastries, and a selection of hot entrées such as a smoked salmon and potato latke or eggs Benedict.

The dining room is also open to the public for prix-fixe and à la carte meals each evening; the Pacific Northwest–influenced French cuisine served here is widely considered among the best on the Island. The herb-crusted pheasant breast, and chanterelle-mushroom, potato, and rosemary bisque are alone more than worth the trip. ⌁ *10 double rooms with baths, 19 suites. Fireplace in suites, whirlpool bath in 3 rooms and 13 suites. Restaurant, indoor pool, sauna, spa, indoor and outdoor hot tubs, exercise room, library, conference facilities, tennis court. C$195–C$260; full breakfast. AE, DC, MC, V. Smoking in lounge, closed Jan. 2–Feb. 6.*

BIRD SONG COTTAGE ✿

9909 Maple St., Box 1432, Chemainus, BC V0R 1K0, tel. 250/246–9910, fax 250/246–2909; www.vancouverisland-bc.com/birdsongcottage

Virginia and Larry Blatchford, both professional musicians, have filled their Edwardian cottage with a whimsical collection of antiques and an infectious sense of fun. There's a grand piano and a Celtic harp, an assortment of Victorian hats (all for trying on), and an old-fashioned swing for two on the veranda.

The double rooms, all with fresh flowers, open-air-dried cotton sheets, and window seats that can sleep a third, are imaginatively done. The Nightingale has a claw-foot tub in its bathroom and opens onto a private patio with a goldfish pond. The Bluebird is done in butter and blue under a sloping roof, and the little Hummingbird is tucked under the gables; both have baths with showers.

Breakfasts, served in the glassed-in sun porch (often with piano accompaniment) are also dramatic: Virginia decorates fruit plates with herbs and flowers, and serves up goodies like herbed quiche with smoked Gruyère or scones with strawberries and crème fraîche.

The cottage is a few blocks from the beach and the sites of Chemainus, and Virginia and Larry can arrange (no surprise here) nights out at the local theater. ⌁ *3 double rooms with baths. C$95–C$110; full breakfast. AE, MC. No smoking.*

BORTHWICK COUNTRY MANOR ✿

9750 Ardmore Dr., Sidney, BC V8L 5H5, tel. 250/656–9498, fax 250/655–0715; msiems@sutton.com

Flower boxes and awnings grace this Tudor-style home built in 1974 on Vancouver Island's Saanich Peninsula. It is ideally set in the quiet countryside about 30 minutes from downtown Victoria, and about 10 minutes from Butchart Gardens, the airport, and the Washington and British Columbia ferries.

Pretty flower arrangements with coordinated floral bedspreads, piles of fluffy pillows, and a mixture of antiques and modern furnishings create a bright, cheery tone in guest rooms, each named for a local variety of tree. Sycamore, the largest room, has a second bed tucked in an adjoining alcove room, so it's large enough to accommodate a family of four. The fireplace in the living room is a cozy spot to chat, read, or get acquainted with British hosts Susan and Michael Siems. French doors open onto a covered patio where breakfast is served in summer. Beyond that is a full acre of lawn, with an outdoor hot tub and distant views of Patricia Bay.

The Siems are avid gardeners, as a tour of the acreage will show. Herbs and kiwis grown in their gardens figure prominently in the full breakfast, as do homemade muffins and scones, fresh fruit salads, and filling egg dishes. ⚇ *3 double rooms with baths, 1 2-bedroom room with bath. Cable TV and VCR in common room, library, hot tub, fishing charters, bicycles. C$110–C$150; full breakfast. AE, D, DC, MC, V. No smoking.*

CHESTERMAN'S BEACH BED AND BREAKFAST 🐚
1345 Chesterman Beach Rd., Box 72, Tofino, BC V0R 2Z0, tel. 250/725–3726, fax 250/725–3706; surfsand@island.net

When Joan Dublanko visited Vancouver Island in the early 1970s, she knew immediately that she never wanted to leave. She bought and learned to operate a salmon trawler until she'd saved enough money to purchase oceanfront property and build a home. Now Joan lives on the second floor of this beachfront home she designed and built in 1984. The house sits right on a long sandy beach on the open surf side of the Tofino Peninsula. The rustic house makes great use of local materials, especially driftwood.

The main floor of the home is given over to Ocean Breeze, a rustic two-bedroom suite with a sauna, full kitchen, and fireplace. A charming garden cottage, tucked away in the woods, also has a full kitchen and fireplace. The cozy room above the garage features a private deck and a gas fireplace. All the guest rooms have private entrances.

Just outside, tidal pools, little islands, sea caves, and rocky crevices punctuate the sandy beach. There are no signs directing tourists to this romantic retreat just beyond Pacific Rim National Park, so the peaceful atmosphere remains undisturbed. Breakfast here consists of a tray of freshly baked breads or muffins and a platter of seasonal fruit. ⚇ *1 double room with bath, 1 suite, 1 cottage. Fireplace in units, kitchen in suite and cottage, sauna in suite. C$160–C$195; Continental-plus breakfast. MC, V. No smoking, 2-night minimum June–Sept.*

CLAYOQUOT WILDERNESS RESORT 🐚
Box 728, Tofino, BC V0R 2Z0, tel. 250/725–2688 or 888/333–5405, fax 250/725–2689; www.greatfishing.com

Floating on a barge in Quait Bay, about 30 minutes by water taxi from Tofino, this isolated modern resort provides access to one of the most beautiful parts of the British Columbia hinterland. The 160-ft lodge, moored next to 127 acres of wilderness park, was built for the Expo '86 in Vancouver, floated up here in late '97, and opened in May 1998. The property, part of the pristine wilderness of Clayoquot Sound, includes two lakes, hiking trails, and acres of old growth forest.

Host Randy Goddard, who describes this informal, family-oriented resort as an "adult kids camp" (though children are more than welcome), offers fresh- and saltwater fishing, whale watching, heli-hiking, and nature cruises. Kayaks are on hand for exploring the sound; there's also a waterfall for frolicking and a great stone fireplace to curl up in front of. The small but comfortable rooms all have modern decor, water or forest views (but no phones or TVs), and open onto a wraparound veranda. The in-suite baths are small with showers only.

The chef cooks up three hearty meals and snacks, making good use of the daily catch. In the evening guests can relax at the bar, in the lounge by the fireplace, or outside in the hot tub under the stars. Rates include water taxi pickup from Tofino. ♿ *15 double rooms with baths. Fireplace in lounge, dining room, bar, exercise room, outdoor hot tub, sauna, meeting rooms, 2 lakes, fishing, dock, boating, hiking, helipad. C$249, plus C$85 per person per day for meals. MC, V. 2-night minimum. Closed Nov.–May.*

EAGLE NOOK OCEAN WILDERNESS RESORT 🐾

Box 575, Port Alberni, BC V9Y 7M9, tel. 250/723–1000 or 800/760–2777, fax 250/723–9842; www.alberni.net/~eaglenk/eaglenk.htm

This wilderness country inn, a long two-story modern building reminiscent of an English country inn, sits on a narrow strip of land in Barkley Sound between two sections of the Pacific Rim National Park and is accessible only by sea or air. For all its blissful isolation—the resort is miles from any road and surrounded by water and old growth forest—Eagle Nook offers some highly civilized comforts: It's probably the only place in the world you can watch bears in the wild and eat crepes suzette at the same time.

The guest rooms are enormous, with comfortable modern decor, floral bedding, oak furniture, and deep-green carpets. Some of the rooms have two queen beds, others have one queen bed and a sitting area, and all have water views. The lounge is also of a grand size and, with its clubby leather chairs and great stone fireplace, looks as if it's been transplanted from the English countryside.

The dining room serves fine Pacific Northwest cuisine, which you can enjoy inside, next to the 20-ft-high picture window, or alfresco on the large waterfront deck. Hiking trails lace the woods, and a variety of activities, including fishing, kayaking, whale watching, boat trips, heli-tours, and heli-hiking can all be prebooked. Getting there, by float plane, by water taxi from China Creek near Port Alberni, or by prearrangement on the Lady Rose Ferry from Port Alberni, is a scenic adventure in its own right. There's a two-night minimum stay, prices are per person and include meals and nonguided activities. ♿ *23 double rooms with baths. Dining room, lounge, outdoor hot tub, exercise room, meeting room, hiking, dock, boating, fishing, helipad. C$199 person, includes meals and nonguided activities. AE, MC, V. 2-night minimum, closed Oct.–Apr.*

GREYSTONE MANOR 🐾

4014 Haas Rd., R.R. 6, Site 684–C2, Courtenay, BC V9N 8H9, tel. 250/338–1422; www.bbcanada.com/1334.html

This 1918 cross-gabled house, one of the oldest in the Comox Valley, has exceptionally elaborate and beautifully tended gardens; the acre and a half of flower beds and pathways stretching toward Comox Bay are awash with color all summer.

Inside, the stained-fir paneling in the guest living and dining rooms is the backdrop to a mixture of Victorian and modern furniture brought from England by owners, Mike and Mo Shipton, when they emigrated to British Columbia in 1990. Upstairs, the three plain, sunny bedrooms have queen, double, or twin beds, ruffled curtains on tall windows, and antique furnishings. Two have bathrooms with showers, one has a claw-foot tub in a private bathroom across the hall. The most popular room is the corner room with grand views through windows on three sides.

Leisure options at this adult-oriented bed-and-breakfast include meandering through the gardens; hiking to the pebble beach to watch harbor seals playing in the bay; sipping coffee or tea on the veranda; or curling up with a book in the living room, next to the fire in the wood-burning stove. Hot muffins, scones, pancakes, and eggs are among the breakfast selections. ⚘ *3 double rooms with baths. Piano, nature trails. C$75–C$80; full breakfast. MC, V. No smoking.*

OCEAN WILDERNESS INN AND SPA RETREAT ☙
109 W. Coast Rd., Sooke, BC V0S 1N0, tel. 250/646–2116 or tel. 800/323–2116, fax 250/646–2317; www.sookenet.com/ocean

This large, 1940s log cabin sits on 5 forested, beachfront acres 8 mi west of Sooke. Over the years, owner Marion Rolston has built more guest rooms in a rough cedar addition. An auction buff, Marion furnished her home with a fine collection of Victorian antiques. High beds with canopies and ruffled bed linens dominate the spacious guest rooms, which all have balconies or patios. For romantics, the best room choices are Captain's Quarters and Pacific Panorama, which both have soaker tubs for two in front of windows with views of the Strait of Juan de Fuca and the Olympic Mountains.

In the dining room, a chandelier hangs over a long table set with crystal, china, and silver for Marion's elegant breakfasts. Fresh muffins, potato medallions in dill and butter, and grilled tomato halves with Parmesan and basil feature in the breakfasts. A silver service of tea or coffee is delivered to the room beforehand. Outside, in the beautiful Victorian gardens, stepping-stones lead to a seawater hot tub housed in a gazebo, and a path descends to the pebbly beach cove.

Ocean Wilderness also offers spa treatments, including facial mud treatments, herb and seaweed wraps, and massage, and holds occasional rejuvenation and relaxation workshops on site. Children and pets are welcome at this family-oriented inn. ⚘ *9 double rooms with baths. Mini-refrigerators. Outdoor hot tub, massage and spa treatments, hiking trails, fishing, boating. C$85–C$175; full breakfast. Picnic lunches and dinners available. AE, MC, V. No smoking, pets welcome.*

RED CROW GUEST HOUSE ☙
1084 Pacific Rim Hwy., Box 37, Tofino, BC V0R 2Z0, tel. and fax 250/725–2275

This Cape Cod–style house is set in 17 acres of old growth cedar and hemlock on the sheltered side of the Tofino peninsula, about a mile from the village.

Two rooms underneath the main part of the house open onto a covered veranda and directly onto a private pebble beach. Decorated with family heirlooms and native art, the large, comfortable rooms afford stunning views of tidal waters and the islands in Browning Passage. A smaller room on the top floor is available summers only, and a rustic cedar cottage in the woods has a full kitchen and sleeps six.

Your hostess, friendly American expat Cathy McDiarmid, lives upstairs with her husband Charles, who manages the Wickaninnish Inn nearby (*see below*), and their young son. She can tell you about the bird sanctuary just next door, and the miles of forest trails and beach to explore.

This adult-oriented bed-and-breakfast is great for privacy—all but the small upstairs room have private entrances and their own sitting areas. There's no common room, so Cathy serves breakfast, featuring coffee, tea, and homemade baked goods, in the rooms. ⚘ *3 double rooms with baths, 1 cottage. Refrigerator in rooms. Hiking, beach, boating. C$125–C$135; Continental breakfast. V. No smoking, closed Dec.–Feb.*

SHIPS POINT BEACH HOUSE 🐚

7584 Ships Point Rd., Site 39, C-76, Fanny Bay, BC V0R 1W0, tel. 250/335–2200
or 800/925–1595, fax 250/335–2214; www.shipspoint.com

When Captain George Vancouver sailed into Fanny Bay in 1792 he chose Ships Point as a calm and safe place to anchor. When Vancouverites David and Lorinda Rawlings arrived some 200 years later, they did much the same thing. Luckily for the Rawlings, some earlier settlers had set up a clapboard cottage on the point—they didn't build it there, they just towed it over on a barge from a logging camp up island.

David and Lorinda have transformed this former bunkhouse into one of the more luxurious spots to stay on the North Island. Lorinda's choice of rich colors and her uncluttered blend of antiques, nautical paraphernalia, and native art work well together and create a striking sense of place. Some of the six rooms have fireplaces and all have water views and themed decor, from the nautical Captain Vancouver room to the Asian-style Rose Garden Room, which overlooks some of the inn's 106 rose bushes. A cottage built in 1998 and decorated with a specially commissioned native art mural is completely self contained with two bedrooms, two bathrooms, a full kitchen, and a fireplace.

Breakfast at a Jacobean table overlooking Fanny Bay includes such innovative goodies as poached pears in ice wine, or omelets with the oysters that Fanny Bay is famous for. After that, you can wander down to the seashore just 30 ft away, explore the bay in one of the inn's kayaks, charter the Rawlings' 21-ft boat for a day of salmon fishing, or just admire the bird and wildlife from the veranda or the hot tub.

Ships Point is a good place to break a journey—it's about 2½ hours from Victoria, Tofino on the West Coast, or Port Hardy at the island's northern tip. *♠ 7 double rooms with baths, 1 suite, 1 2-bedroom cottage. Fireplace in some rooms, TV and fireplace in cottage. Outdoor hot tub, exercise room, conference facilities, fishing charters, kayaks. C$135–C$275; full breakfast, evening meals available by reservation. AE, DC, MC, V. No smoking, 2-night minimum may apply, closed weekdays in Jan. and Feb.*

SNUG HARBOUR INN 🐚

460 Marine Dr., Box 367, Ucluelet, BC V0R 3A0, tel. 250/726–2686 or 888/936–5222, fax 250/726–2685; www.ucluelet.com/asnugharbourinn

Seafaring Americans Skip and Denise Rowland sailed around the world looking for a perfect spot to settle. In 1996, they found it here, just south of the Pacific Rim National Park on Vancouver Island's wild West Coast. Their home and B&B makes the most of its dramatic location and offers some of the best ocean views to be had anywhere. From the front, on a side street in tiny Ucluelet, the house looks like an ordinary bungalow; on the ocean side, three stories of balconies, patios, and picture windows are set into a cliff overlooking the Pacific.

The four rooms, all with fireplaces, private balconies or decks, whirlpool tubs, and ocean views, are decorated in a highly individual style. The Sawadee room reflects Skip and Denise's time in Thailand, with a two-side fireplace facing both the bedroom and bathroom, rich carved wood furniture, and Thai artwork and fabrics. The Lighthouse—done in rich greens and natural wood—climbs up three levels and has a private patio with 360° views. The smaller Valhalla room has a nautical theme played out with shades of blue and a hardwood floor. The Atlantis room is, well, unusual: black double whirlpool, black and yellow bedding, naked female statuettes as lamp fixtures and a coffee-table pedestal, large-screen TV, piped in Muzak, and modern pop native Indian art. No expense was spared, but it won't be to everyone's taste.

Breakfasts of coffee, baked goods, and fruit blender drinks are served in what Skip calls the Great Room—a common room with a guest kitchen, a conversation pit around a stone fireplace, and a powerful telescope for looking out to sea or spotting the eagles that nest nearby. There's a lot to do in the area—sport fishing, hiking, beachcombing, kayaking, and even helicopter tours—though many guests prefer to just curl up and watch the crashing waves. This is a couples-oriented retreat and, because of the cliff-side location, not a good place for children. ♠ *4 double rooms with baths. Fireplace and whirlpool bath in rooms. Kitchen, cable TV in lounge, outdoor hot tub, helipad. C$150–C$250; Continental plus breakfast, MC, V. No smoking.*

SOOKE HARBOUR HOUSE ☞

1528 Whiffen Spit Rd., R.R. 4, Sooke, BC V0S 1N0, tel. 250/642–3421, fax 250/642–6988; www.sookenet.com/shh

Highest accolades go to Fredrica and Sinclair Philip's Sooke Harbour House, reputedly among the finest country inns in North America. In the quiet village of Sooke, 23 winding mi west of Victoria, this unassuming 1931 Craftsman inn rests amid lovingly landscaped grounds on an oceanfront bluff that looks out over the Strait of Juan de Fuca and the Olympic Mountains in the distance.

All the guest rooms have fireplaces, handcrafted light-wood furniture, ocean views from decks or balconies, decanters of port, coffeemakers, plates of home-baked cookies, and a profusion of fresh and dried flowers. Of the rooms in the inn, the split-level Blue Heron Room enjoys the best vistas. An oval whirlpool tub sits in the living room across from a stone fireplace and tall picture windows overlooking the sea.

In the 1986 white clapboard addition, the Victor Newman Longhouse Room boasts a grand collection of Northwest native art, including masks, paintings, and a chieftain's bench, along with a cedar pencil-post bed, two-side fireplace, and ocean-view whirlpool bath. The Kingfisher Room has a deck, a greenhouse room with a hot tub, and a claw-foot tub in the spacious bathroom.

Pebbled paths lead through the vegetable, herb, and edible flower gardens whose bounty is used in meals—an imaginative blend of Pacific Northwest, French, and Japanese cuisine—at the inn's restaurant, which has garnered international acclaim. Dinner is an elegant, leisurely affair, enhanced by accompanying wines. The menu, which changes frequently, might include miso seaweed broth with geoduck, crab-crusted rockfish with trout roe and stinging nettle sauce, and pear-lemon-thyme tart with caramel ice.

Mornings start with a huge breakfast tray of elegant gourmet goodies. After polishing this off, you might consider taking a long walk on the beach, because lunch (also included in the tariff) soon follows. ♠ *28 double rooms with baths. Phone, wet bar, fireplace in rooms; whirlpool bath in 6 rooms, hot tub in 8 rooms. Restaurant, massage and spa treatments, meeting rooms, gift shop, beach, fishing and scuba-diving charters, nature tours. C$235–C$350; full breakfast and lunch included. AE, DC, MC, V. No smoking.*

WICKANINNISH INN ☞

Osprey La. at Chesterman Beach, Box 250, Tofino, BC V0R 2Z0,
tel. 250/725–3100 or 800/333–4604, fax 250/725–3110; www.island.net/~wick

Opened in 1996, the Wickaninnish is already the best known luxury inn on Vancouver Island's West Coast. Set on a rocky promontory above Chesterman Beach, with open ocean on three sides and old-growth forest as a backdrop, this three-story weathered cedar building is one of the most comfortable places to enjoy the area's dramatic wilderness scenery, summer or winter.

Every spacious room has a sitting area, an ocean view, and its own balcony, fireplace, and soaking tub. In deference to the elements, closets hold both comfy robes and courtesy rain slickers. Staff here take very good care of their guests; spa services planned for 1999 will add to the pampering.

The inn's Pointe Restaurant has lofty ceilings supported by hand-adzed beams and curved windows prompting panoramic ocean views. Chef Rodney Butters, however, has a mandate to "create food as if there is no view." Butters selects his catch personally at the Tofino docks and serves up Pacific Northwest cuisine that more than does justice to the setting. The seasonal menu features scallops in Rainforest Ale broth, venison and hazelnut pâté, and steamed Dungeness crab. If you can, try the chef's special seven-course dinner, available with 12 hours notice. ♨ *46 double rooms with baths. Phone, cable TV, data port, minibar, and microwave in rooms. Restaurant, lounge, massage, spa, steam room, exercise room, laundry services, conference facilities, helipad, hiking, beach, fishing, whale-watching. C$260–C$300; breakfast extra. AE, D, DC, MC, V. No smoking.*

YELLOW POINT LODGE ☞

Yellow Point Rd., R.R. 3, Ladysmith, BC V0R 2E0, tel. 250/245–7422

A kind of summer-camp vacation for adults, though it's open year-round, Yellow Point Lodge was built in the late 1930s by Gerry Hill. His son, Richard, carries on his simple philosophy of providing a relaxing retreat and satisfying meals at affordable rates. There are no in-room phones or TVs here—just a lot of trails through 165 acres of thick, mossy forest; 1½ mi of waterfront with secluded coves and beaches, a huge saltwater pool; and toys galore—bicycles, boats, and kayaks, to name a few. Everything's included, from the boats and bikes to the basic but filling meals and snacks.

Yellow Point hasn't bothered much with changing its look in the last 50 years. The decor, ambience, meals, and slow pace are all reminiscent of an earlier, more relaxed age. This makes for a friendly atmosphere as guests gather at meals, or around the great stone fireplace in the expansive waterfront lounge. Yellow Point has a special place in many hearts—so many guests have been coming back for so many years some have even started a volunteer group to help preserve the place.

Guest rooms in the main lodge are plain but comfortable. There is also an array of cabins and cottages to choose from. These range from very rustic, with no running water, to comfortably cozy with private bath, kitchenettes, and beds, some made from tree trunks, raised high so you can admire the ocean views without getting up. Yellow Point is loads of fun, but only for grown-ups—it's not recommended for under-16s. ♨ *9 double rooms with baths in the lodge, 25 rustic cabin rooms with no running water, 10 units in shared cabins, 12 private cabins. Hot tub, sauna, pool, 2 tennis courts, volleyball and badminton courts, kayaks, mountain bikes, twice-weekly cutter tours in summer. C$110–C$177; for two, includes all meals, snacks, and activities. AE, MC, V. No smoking in dining and living rooms, 2-night minimum on weekends, 3-night minimum on holiday weekends.*

VICTORIA

Fort Victoria was the first European settlement on Vancouver Island. The Hudson's Bay Company, drawn by the rich fur trade, chose the sheltered southern tip of the island to establish a post in 1843 and named it for the reigning British monarch. Settlers slowly trickled in, but it wasn't until the Cariboo Gold Strike north of Vancouver in the 1850s that the town began to flourish. A steady stream of miners began filtering through to purchase supplies before heading out to the goldfields, and a booming frontier town developed as shops, saloons, and bordellos sprang up around the harbor to meet their demands.

The rough-and-tumble Barbary Coast atmosphere of the inner city was tempered by the more genteel society of British naval men, government officials, and gentlemen farmers who were also attracted to the growing community. By the time the gold supply ran out, Victoria had developed a strong economic and military foothold as a crown colony, and the established political framework stayed in place when British Columbia joined the Canadian Confederation in 1871.

This outpost of the empire has since evolved into an attractive seaside capital of gardens, waterfront walks, and attentively restored 19th-century architecture. Victoria is still lumbered with a reputation as the most British city in Canada, but these days, except for the odd red phone booth, good beer, and well-mannered drivers, the city has shed its tea-cozy image, preferring to celebrate its triple Native, Asian, and European heritage.

To the many visitors who fuel the city's economy, Victoria offers stunning parks and gardens; a thriving dining, music, arts and theater scene; and one of the best museums in Canada. The city also offers some of the most attractive bed-and-breakfasts and small inns in the region.

Victoria is so popular it tends to fill up in the summertime. Many visitors prefer the deep discounts and slower pace of the (by Canadian standards) mild winters.

PLACES TO GO, SIGHTS TO SEE

Antique Row. Stretched between Blanshard and Cook streets on Fort Street are shop upon shop selling furniture, artwork, jewelry, china, crystal, books, and nearly any other collectible you can imagine.

Art Gallery of Greater Victoria (1040 Moss St., tel. 250/384–4101). Housed in a turn-of-the century mansion, this gallery holds one of the finest collections of Asian art in Canada, along with contemporary Canadian pieces and an array of traveling exhibitions. Don't miss the Shinto shrine in the Japanese garden outside.

Bastion Square. Fine boutiques and small restaurants line this cobbled courtyard, which was the site of the original Fort Victoria and of the Hudson's Bay Company's trading post. The *Maritime Museum of British Columbia* (28 Bastion Sq., tel. 250/385–4222), housed in the turreted former courthouse building, chronicles the extensive nautical history of the region.

Beacon Hill Park. A walk through this pretty, 184-acre park east of the Inner Harbour will lead you past abundant gardens, sandy beaches, and scenic views of the Olympic Mountains across the Strait of Juan de Fuca.

Butchart Gardens (800 Benvenuto Dr., tel. 250/652–5256). This world-famous complex on the 130-acre Butchart estate (13 mi north of downtown) offers more than 700 varieties of flowers and includes 50 acres of Japanese, Italian, and English gardens connected by winding paths. There's also a concert lawn, as well as restaurants, a gift shop, and a tea room on the grounds.

Chinatown. The towering red Gate of Harmonious Interest on Fisgard Street marks the entrance to Chinatown, crammed with restaurants and exotic crafts and wicker shops. Narrow Fan Tan Alley was once the gambling center of the area.

Craigdarroch Castle (1050 Joan Crescent, tel. 250/592–5323). This turreted mansion on a hill overlooking Victoria was built for coal magnate Robert Dunsmuir, British Columbia's first millionaire, who died in 1889, just months before the completion of his lavish home. Stained-glass windows, golden-oak paneling and staircase, intricate tile work, period furnishings, and numerous paintings are among the eye-catchers in this lovingly restored, haunted-looking mansion.

Craigflower Manor and Schoolhouse (110 Island Hwy., tel. 250/383–4627). One of four farms established by the Hudson's Bay Company in its effort to colonize Vancouver Island, this Georgian farmhouse dates from 1856 and contains many of the furnishings brought from Scotland by the original overseer. The nearby schoolhouse is also worth a look. It's open May–October.

Crystal Gardens (713 Douglas St., tel. 250/381–1213). This glass-roof structure once housed the largest saltwater swimming pool in the British Empire and now encloses a large tropical garden and aviary. Wallabies, lemurs, and colorful toucans, flamingos, and macaws are among its residents.

Empress Hotel Tea Lobby (721 Government St., tel. 250/384–8111). No visit to Victoria is complete without afternoon tea in the lobby of the stylish Empress Hotel. Guests can linger over fresh fruit, crumpets, scones, tea sandwiches, hazelnut cake, and multiple cups of tea as they gaze out the windows at the Inner Harbour and bustling Government Street. Reservations for daily sittings are a must in summer; a dress code calls for smart casual wear.

Inner Harbour. This picturesque natural harbor is bordered by interesting boutiques and galleries, fine examples of 19th-century industrial architecture, and some of Victoria's kitschier tourist sights, including the *Royal London Wax Museum* (470 Belleville St., tel. 250/388–4461) and the *Pacific Undersea Garden* (490 Belleville St., tel. 250/382–5717).

Market Square (Johnson St. and Pandora Ave.). Over 40 boutiques and specialty shops now fill the restored turn-of-the-century buildings that surround a square bustling with sidewalk vendors and street entertainers.

Parliament Buildings (501 Belleville St., tel. 250/387–3046). A tour of the marbled interior of Victoria's Parliament Buildings provides a good introduction to the provincial legislative process and the history of British Columbia. The buildings are open to the public, and free guided tours are available throughout the year. By night, the complex is outlined with splendid white lights that dance on the harbor.

Royal British Columbia Museum (675 Belleville St., tel. 250/387–3701 or 800/661–5411). You should give yourself at least half a day to take in the 12,000 years of British Columbia's history showcased in this incredible museum, considered one of the best of its kind in the world. Here you can smell the pines in the prehistoric section, walk through the streets of Old Town, experience a submarine voyage in the Open Ocean exhibit, catch a National Geographic film at the six-story-high IMAX theater, or sit in a native longhouse listening to potlatch songs and stories.

RESTAURANTS

Of the many fine restaurants scattered around the city, The **Herald Street Caffe** (546 Herald St., tel. 250/381–1441) never fails to please with its eclectic spin on Pacific Northwest cuisine. Local fish, game, and produce are the core of the menu at the elegant **Empress Room** (Empress Hotel, 721 Government St., tel. 250/384–8111). Another spot for innovative, super-fresh Northwest cuisine is the **Marina Restaurant** (1327 Beach Dr., tel. 250/598–8555). For a romantic evening, best bets are the Pacific Northwest fare at the subterranean, candlelit **Camille's** (45 Bastion Sq., 250/381–3433) or alfresco Italian at **Il Terrazzo** (555 Johnson St., off Waddington Alley, tel. 250/361–0028). A few miles from downtown, **Chez Daniel** (2524 Estevan Ave., 250/361–0028) is widely regarded as Victoria's finest French restaurant. Fun and funky, **Pagliacci's** (1011 Broad St., tel. 250/386–1662) is a more lively option for an Italian meal. The souvlaki, moussaka, and other Mediterranean specialties are good at **Periklis** (531 Yates St., tel. 250/386–3313), one of Victoria's oldest Greek restaurants. There's a fine sushi bar at **Tomoe** (726 Johnson St., tel. 250/381–0223), along with a broad selection of seafood, buckwheat noodle dishes, and Japanese standards such as tempura and teriyaki.

TOURIST INFORMATION

Tourism B.C. (865 Hornby St., Suite 802, Vancouver, BC V6Z 2G3, tel. 604/660–2861). **Tourism Victoria** (812 Wharf St., Victoria, BC V8W 1T3, tel. 250/953–2033, fax 250/382–6539).

RESERVATION SERVICES

AA Accommodations West Bed and Breakfast Reservations Service (660 Jones Terr., Victoria, BC V8Z 2L7, tel. 250/479–1986, fax 250/479–9999). **All Seasons Bed and Breakfast Agency** (9858 5th St., Sidney, BC V8L 2X7, tel. 250/655–7173). **Best Canadian Bed and Breakfast Network** (1064 Balfour Ave., Vancouver, BC V6H 1X1, tel. 604/738–7207, fax 604/732–4998). **British Columbia Bed and Breakfast Association** (Box 593, 101–1001 W. Broadway, Vancouver, BC V6H 4E4, tel. 604/734–3486). **Supernatural British Columbia** (601–1166 Alberni St., Vancouver, BC V6E 3Z3, tel. 800/663–6000). **Town and Country Bed and Breakfast Reservation Service** (2803 W. 4th Ave., Box 74542, Vancouver, BC V6K 1K2, tel. and fax 604/731–5942). **A Travelers Reservation Service** (14716 26th Ave. NE, Seattle, WA 98155, tel. 206/364–5900).

ABIGAIL'S HOTEL

906 McClure St., Victoria, BC V8V 3E7, tel. 250/388–5363 or 800/561–6565, fax 250/388–7787; www.abigailshotel.com

In a quiet cul-de-sac just blocks from the Inner Harbour, this 1930s Tudor-style structure was formerly an apartment building. Frauke and Daniel Behune purchased the romantic little hotel in early 1996 and have been methodically redecorating and upgrading it ever since.

The best rooms in the house are Canterbury Bell and Orchid, named for the triangular stained-glass windows that reach up toward the peaked roof. Each has a chaise lounge beneath the colorful windows, a half-canopied king-size bed tucked into a dormer, wing chairs, an Italian marble fireplace, a minibar, and a hidden mini-refrigerator; the roomy bathrooms feature whirlpool tubs, wicker lounge chairs, and bidets. A canopied four-poster and leather love seat before the fireplace in the bedroom, as well as a whirlpool tub and bidet in the bath, make Foxglove another favorite. Tiffany and Abbey Rose on the top floor have double fireplaces that open onto both the bedroom and the bath. The six large rooms in a 1998 addition are especially romantic, with turn of the century decor, four-poster beds, fireplaces, and marble baths.

In the early evening, you can relax on one of the leather couches in the well-stocked library, play a game of cards, or chat over hors d'oeuvres and sherry in front of the fire. The helpful concierge can make dinner arrangements or offer recommendations on the many things to see and do in Victoria.

The cheerful breakfast room has an open kitchen, so it's possible to watch the chef baking fresh muffins or coffee cakes and whipping up morning specialties such as eggs Abigail with smoked salmon. You can choose between a savory or sweet main course, and there are light "heart smart" options too. The able and accommodating staff is happy to arrange for cozy breakfasts in bed, splits of champagne, and Belgian truffles. ♙ *22 double rooms with baths. Phone in rooms; wet bar, whirlpool bath, and fireplace in some rooms. Library, concierge, gift shop. C$149–C$289; full breakfast. AE, MC, V. No smoking.*

THE BEACONSFIELD

998 Humboldt St., Victoria, BC V8V 2Z8, tel. 250/384–4044, fax 250/384-4052; www.islandnet.com/beaconsfield

This elegant 1905 mansion, with its conservatory and library, rich wood paneling, and mahogany floors, has the look and feel of an Edwardian gentleman's club. The guest rooms are elegantly furnished with period pieces, including some unusual items such as an original Edwardian wooden canopied tub and shower in the Duchess room. Many of the rooms have fireplaces and whirlpool tubs, leaded stained-glass windows, and chandeliers. The Garden Suite downstairs opens onto a private garden patio; the Gatekeepers and Emily Carr suites have whirlpool tubs for two in front of the sitting room fire.

Breakfast is served in the dining room in winter, and by the fountain among the greenery in the conservatory in summer. In the afternoon and early evening, guests gather on the leather sofas in the book-lined library for tea and sherry.

Owners Con and Judi Sollid dropped out of orthodontics and law, respectively, to combine their business acumen in managing the inn; they don't live on the property and leave the day-to-day affairs of running the inn to a live-in innkeeper, but are often around to chat over breakfast.

The Sollids also have a nearby oceanfront beach cottage for two, with a kitchen, two fireplaces, a hot tub, and a double whirlpool bath. *▲ 5 double rooms with baths, 4 suites, 1 cottage. Fireplace and whirlpool bath in some rooms. Refrigerator, library. C$200–C$350; full breakfast. MC, V. No smoking, 2-night minimum on summer weekends.*

CARBERRY GARDENS ☙

1008 Carberry Gardens, Victoria, BC V8S 3R7, tel. 250/595–8906, fax 250/595–8185; www.carberrygardens.com

A 1907 gambrel-roofed, board-and-shingle home tucked away on a quiet tree-lined lane in the historic Rocklands neighborhood, Carberry Gardens is just blocks from Craigdarroch Castle, Antique Row, and the art gallery.

Owners Julie and Lionel Usher have restored the home's original fir floors and intricate moldings, draped the veranda with clematis and honeysuckle, and decorated their bright and airy home with a collection of antiques and pieces crafted by Lionel himself.

A staircase leads up the 30-ft-high entryway to three pretty second-floor rooms, each stocked with sherry, bathrobes, Clinique toiletries, and mounds of pillows. The two front bedrooms catch the morning sun through lace curtains; one has its own fireplace, another has a private balcony with a view of Craigdarroch Castle. One bedroom has a detached bathroom (across the hall) with a shower stall only, but the bathroom's French doors, which open onto a little balcony overlooking the back garden, are compensation.

In the morning, Julie and Lionel, both professional caterers, serve such creative dishes as Southwestern corn-and-spinach flan with roasted-red-pepper sauce on a grated–sweet potato pancake.

The affable dog, a mastiff called Max, is more than happy to get acquainted with all who might give him a rub after breakfast. *▲ 3 double rooms with baths. Fireplace in 1 room. Refrigerator, cable TV/VCR in lounge. C$125; full breakfast. MC, V. No smoking.*

HATERLEIGH HERITAGE INN ☙

243 Kingston St., Victoria, BC V8V 1V5, tel. 250/384–9995, fax 250/384–1935; www.haterleigh.com

This 1901 modified Queen Anne just two blocks from the Inner Harbour is a comfortable base for touring Victoria. After arduous restorations, Paul and Elizabeth Kelly opened the 6,000-square-ft heritage house as an adult-oriented bed-and-breakfast in 1990.

The building's original leaded- and stained-glass windows, ornate plasterwork on 11-ft ceilings, a mantled fireplace, Victorian settees, and complimentary sherry feature in the large living room, which is open to guests until 6 PM. The Victorian theme (with modern plumbing) continues in the guest rooms: Rose-color carpets are coordinated with floral wallpaper, rose-and-plum duvet covers, and creamy lace curtains and valances. Most of the roomy bathrooms have whirlpool tubs or their original claw-foot tubs and charming hand-painted tile work. The smallest room, Rose Gable, is tucked under the roof and has slanted ceilings and a detached bath across the hall. Of the larger rooms, Secret Garden, with its oval whirlpool tub and balcony with a view of the Olympic Mountains, is the romantic choice. Extras, like chocolates delivered to the room on check-in and an Internet newspaper delivered in the morning, are nice touches.

Hearty breakfasts of fresh fruit, warm baked goods, hot entrées, and uncommonly good coffee are served around the big dining room table at 8:30 sharp. One specialty of the house is a cheese scone stuffed with smoked salmon and scrambled egg accompanied by asparagus tips and stuffed mushroom caps. A leisurely walk to the nearby Parliament Buildings or the Royal British Columbia Museum will help you work off the large morning meal. △ *5 double rooms with baths, 1 2-bedroom unit with bath. Whirlpool bath in some rooms. C$180–C$268; full breakfast. MC, V. No smoking. 2-night minimum in July and Aug. and on weekends in June and Sept.*

HOLLAND HOUSE INN ✸

595 Michigan St., Victoria, BC V8V 1S7, tel. 250/384–6644 or 800/335–3466, fax 250/384–6117; www.islandnet.com/~holndhus

A three-story, clematis-covered Italian Renaissance–style structure, Holland House is a refreshing antidote to the many Victorian-theme bed-and-breakfasts in Victoria, and its James Bay location, just two blocks south of the Inner Harbour, can't be beat.

Harry and Margaret Brock, a friendly British and Canadian couple, have decorated their house with vibrant colors, an ever-changing art collection, and a stylish mix of antique and contemporary furniture. Sunflower-color walls pull the design out of paisley bedding in one room; another exhibits a distinctly French feel due to bold black and white Waverly wallpaper. Guest rooms are spacious for the most part. All have sitting areas, and many have fireplaces, balconies, and bed canopies entwined with silk flowers.

A 1998 Arts and Crafts–style addition, linked to the main building through a conservatory, has four large rooms with fireplaces. Guests staying in both sections meet in the sun-flooded conservatory for breakfasts of fruit, baked goods, and hot entrées such as scrambled eggs with lox or German apple pancakes. △ *14 double rooms with baths. Phone, cable TV in rooms. C$145–C$250; full breakfast. AE, MC, V. No smoking.*

HUMBOLDT HOUSE ✸

867 Humboldt St., Victoria, BC V8V 2Z6, tel. 250/383–0152, or 888/383-0327, fax 250/383–6402; www.humboldthouse.com

If you're looking for somewhere to, say, hide an engagement ring in a glass of Champagne, Humboldt House should do the trick. This unabashedly romantic hideaway, in a prettily restored Victorian on a quiet side street, has five rooms, each with elaborate boudoir decor, a wood-burning fireplace, down duvets, a CD player, fresh flowers, candles, and a big round whirlpool tub on a platform by the bed. Still need a hint? The two upstairs rooms overlook the neighboring apple orchard.

Proprietor Mila Werbik, who runs the inn with her daughter and son-in-law, Vlasta and David Booth, has decorated the rooms in individual style. The Oriental room has a magnificent hand carved Chinese headboard, Edward's room has a canopied whirlpool tub set into a bay window, and the Gazebo room has a canopy bed and an orchard view. The elaborate Celebration room (where Rosanna Arquette once slept) has a theatrically celestial look, with clouds of white lace, a crystal chandelier, and sculptures of angels and cherubs dotted about.

There's sherry in the red velvet parlor and champagne and chocolate truffles to greet you in your room, but the real treat arrives in the morning. That's when a picnic basket loaded with breakfast goodies, like seafood crepes, eggs Benedict, fruit, home-baked goods, and yes, champagne again, is delivered to your room by dumbwaiter. ♠ *5 double rooms with baths. Whirlpool bath in rooms. C$245–C$285 (off season discounts up to 50%); full breakfast. V, MC. No smoking, 2-night minimum on holiday weekends.*

JOAN BROWN'S BED AND BREAKFAST ☙
729 Pemberton Rd., Victoria, BC V8S 3R3, tel. 250/592–5929

In the heart of the quiet Rocklands Historic District, this stately Georgian Revival house was built in 1881 for a provincial lieutenant governor. A portico beneath a soaring stained-glass window greets you as you enter the house through the arched entryway. The house, once a meeting place for Victorian high society, still boasts seven fireplaces, hand-painted stained-glass windows, and half an acre of manicured lawns, purple wisteria, and fruit trees secluded behind tall hedges.

Owner Joan Brown has decorated the interior in light shades to soften the sturdy lines of the structure. Bedrooms with Laura Ashley wallpapers and coordinating comforters have large bay windows and Oriental rugs on hardwood floors. Many of the bathrooms have their original tiles and fixtures, and one room has a bed believed to have belonged to Napoléon's sister-in-law. In the largest room on the ground floor, a chandelier hangs from the 14-ft, gold-leaf-trim ceiling above a lovely Italian sleigh daybed and comfortable king-size bed across from the fireplace.

Joan's hospitality also reflects an earlier era. There's no TV, but Mozart and Chopin tunes waft through the house. The sheets are fresh-air dried, and sherry is served each evening by the piano in the lounge. Breakfast, served in the adjoining dining room, features homemade marmalades and muffins along with a sweet or savory hot entrée. ♠ *1 double room with bath, 4 doubles share 2 baths, 1 suite, 1 2-bedroom suite. C$90–C$150; full breakfast. No credit cards. No smoking.*

MULBERRY MANOR ☙

611 Foul Bay Rd., Victoria, BC V8S 1H2, tel. 250/370–1918, fax 250/370–1968; www.mulberrymanor.com

This 1924 Tudor heritage home, in a quiet neighborhood west of downtown Victoria, was the last building renowned Victorian architect Simon McClure designed. The elegant manor has been restored and decorated to magazine-cover perfection with period antiques, crisp linens, and tile baths. Its acre of secluded, terraced grounds, with duck ponds and rose arbors, has the feel of an English country garden.

The Angel Room, named for the cherubs on its wallpaper and in a gilt-framed oil painting, has a sunny balcony overlooking the enormous gardens that wrap around the manor. The Rosewood Room, also overlooking the gardens, has a four-poster bed, an antique damask love seat, and hand-embroidered Indian rugs. Jasmine, in country-French yellow and blue, has a wrought-iron bed facing a fireplace, a sitting room, a large bathroom with a deep soaker tub, and a balcony overlooking a pond.

Delightful hosts, Susan and Tony Temple (originally from York, England), serve gourmet breakfasts at the large Georgian mahogany table, set with silver candelabra and fine china, in their stunning red dining room. The morning repast might include croissants or scones with homemade jam, fresh fruit, Swiss muesli, and eggs Benedict with smoked salmon. ♠ *2 double rooms with baths, 1 suite. Fireplace in suite. Billiards. C$135–C$190; full breakfast. MC, V. No smoking, 2-night minimum in July and Aug.*

PRIOR HOUSE BED & BREAKFAST INN ℘

620 St. Charles St., Victoria, BC V8S 3N7, tel. 250/592–8847, fax 250/592–8223;
www.priorhouse.com

Edward Gauler Prior, one of only two men to serve as both premier and lieutenant governor of British Columbia, built his Tudor Revival mansion in the prestigious Rocklands neighborhood near Government House. Constructed in 1912, this 9,000-square-ft home has a guest library, two parlors, flower decked terraces overlooking beautifully landscaped grounds, and a formal dining room where multicourse breakfasts are served under a Venetian glass chandelier.

The Admiralty owned the home for many years, and it was a boarding house for an exclusive girls' school before Candis Cooperrider and her husband, Ted, purchased it in the 1980s. The couple have lovingly restored the quartersawn oak paneling and moldings, hardwood floors, and large mantled fireplaces.

Guest chambers have a feminine appeal, with pastel walls and romantic canopied beds; all have fireplaces and some have whirlpool tubs and private balconies. The Lieutenant Governor's room is opulent, with a fascinating 1860s "Swedish mother-in-law" bed and other European antiques in the large bedroom; its 400-square-ft bathroom has a crystal chandelier, gold fixtures, and mirrored walls. The boudoir, which makes lavish use of draped Austrian floral fabrics, is the most intimate room. A narrow, winding servant's staircase leads to the two-bedroom Windsor Suite under the gables. The two-bedroom Garden Suite, in the original ballroom on the lower level of the house, features hardwood floors, a fireplace, living room, kitchen, and private entrance.

A big event at the Prior House, besides the full-scale breakfasts, are Candis's elaborate English afternoon teas. Served in the cozy sitting room, the teas (included in the tariff) feature a whole range of fresh baked goodies, from cakes and tarts to unusual savories such as salmon and artichoke scones. △ *4 double rooms with baths, 2 suites. Cable TV in some units, wet bar in some units, kitchen and fireplace in 1 suite. C$180–C$265; full breakfast. MC, V. No smoking, 2-night minimum on weekends and holidays.*

SWANS ℘

506 Pandora Ave., Victoria, BC V8W 1N6, tel. 250/361–3310 or 800/668–7926,
fax 250/361–3491; www.islandnet.com/~swans

When English-born shepherd Michael Williams bought supplies for his kennel at the Buckerfield Company Feed Store in the 1950s, he never dreamed he would one day own the building and turn it into a folksy waterfront hotel. Pretty, flower-filled window grates brighten the brick exterior of the 1913 warehouse; inside, 29 large apartmentlike guest rooms fill the upper floors. A brewery, bistro, and pub occupy the first floor, and there's a jazz bar in the cellar.

Some of the high-ceiling suites have skylights, and every unit has a kitchen, down comforter, and original Pacific Northwest art; the loft units offer sofa beds. Rooms 305 and 307 enjoy the best views of the harbor.

Swans is centrally located on Victoria's Inner Harbour within walking distance of the city's best sights, shops, and restaurants. It's also a top choice for families and groups, though on weekends you'll want to reserve rooms above the third floor to avoid noise from the pub, one of the city's most popular watering holes. △ *5 studios, 11 suites, 13 2-bedroom suites. Phone, cable TV, and kitchen in units. Restaurant, limited room service, pub, coin laundry, free brewery tours and tastings. C$165–C$185; breakfast extra. AE, DC, MC, V. No smoking in some rooms.*

THE GULF ISLANDS

When Captain George Vancouver traveled up the eastern coastline of Vancouver Island in the late 1790s, he dubbed the expansive body of water on which he sailed the Gulf of Georgia, thinking it led out into the open sea. After further exploration revealed that the British Columbia mainland sat to the east, the name of the waterway was changed to the Strait of Georgia, but the islands dotting it continued to be called the Gulf Islands.

Of the hundreds of islands that lie in this strait, the most accessible from Vancouver and Victoria are the Southern Gulf Islands of Galiano, Mayne, North and South Pender, and Salt Spring. A temperate climate, scenic beaches, rolling pasturelands, and virgin forests are common to all, but each has its unique flavor.

Long, skinny Galiano, named for Spanish explorer Dionysio Galiano, was home to Coast Salish natives for centuries before the Spanish, English, and other non-aboriginal settlers arrived to stake claims. The population here is still very small (under 1,000), and the white shell beaches and thick forests remain unspoiled. Activities are generally clustered around the small commercial center of Sturdies Bay.

Middens of clam and oyster shells give evidence that tiny (15-square-mi) Mayne Island was inhabited as early as 5,000 years ago. It later became the stopover point for miners headed from Victoria to the goldfields of Fraser River and Barkerville; by the mid-1800s it had developed into the communal center of the inhabited Gulf Islands, with the first school, post office, police lockup, church, and hotel. Farm tracts and orchards established by early settlers continue to thrive today, and a bustling farmer's market is open each Saturday during harvest season. Many artists now call the island home, and several small galleries here display their work.

Salish natives were probably also the first occupants of Pender, actually two islands divided by a narrow canal dug in 1903 to allow for easier boat passage as more settlers arrived. Largely pastoral in nature, North and South Pender are the southernmost of the Gulf Islands, stretching toward the United States border. And as with many of the other islands, they are populated by artisans, farmers, and fisherfolk; the lack of traffic on the network of winding, hilly roads makes it hard to believe that almost 2,000 people call Pender home.

Named for the saltwater springs at its north end, Salt Spring is the largest and most developed of the Gulf Islands, and the only one with such mainland luxuries as bank machines. Among its first nonnative settlers were black Americans who came here to escape slavery in the 1850s. The agrarian tradition they established, along with Portuguese, English, German, and Japanese immigrants, remains strong, but tourism and art now support the local economy. A government wharf, three marinas, and a waterfront shopping complex at Ganges serve a community of 10,000. Ferry service into Fulford Harbour at the south end, Vesuvius on the west side, and Long Harbour near Ganges in the east connect Salt Spring with Victoria, Vancouver, and the other Southern Gulf Islands.

Quadra Island, one of the Northern Gulf Islands and accessible by ferry from Campbell River on Vancouver Island, is larger and more thinly populated than the Southern Gulf Islands. When Captain Vancouver landed on the island in 1792, he visited an aboriginal village at Cape Mudge. The Cape Mudge band of the Kwagiulth nation is very much in existence today, and its members still make a living fishing for herring and salmon. Quadra was home to canneries and mills by the late 19th century and heavy logging changed much of its face, but several lush wilderness areas remain, hosting such fauna as black-tailed deer, snowy owls, and the seldom-seen peregrine falcon.

PLACES TO GO, SIGHTS TO SEE

Galiano Island. The activities on Galiano are almost exclusively of the outdoor type. The long, unbroken eastern shoreline is perfect for leisurely beach walks, while the numerous coves and inlets along the western coast make it a prime area for kayaking. Montague Provincial Marine Park, with its naturalist's house, walking trails, and white shell beaches, is one of the prettiest parts of the island. The best spots to view Active Pass and surrounding islands are Bluffs Park and Bellhouse Park; these are also good areas for picnicking and bird-watching. Porlier Pass and Active Pass are top locations for scuba diving and fishing.

Mayne Island. Among several noteworthy vintage structures in Miners Bay are St. Mary Magdalene Church (ca. 1897) and the Plumper Pass Lockup (ca. 1896), which now houses a small museum (open July–Aug.) chronicling the island's history. The Active Pass Lighthouse (open daily 10–5) in Georgina Point Heritage Park, originally built in 1855, still signals ships into the busy waterway.

In addition to scenic views of Navy Channel and Active Pass, you're bound to see soaring eagles at Dinner Bay Park, a first-rate, community-built facility south of the ferry dock at Village Bay. The hike to the top of Mount Parke affords the best views, and Campbell Point Park has walking trails and the island's best swimming beach. Mayne, with its compact size and wide roads, is one of the best Gulf Islands for cycling—though you'll need all your gears to get around the hills. Miner's Bay Gas Station rents bikes.

Pender Islands. Bald Cone on North Pender and Mt. Norman on South Pender are the best scenic lookouts. Sights unique to Pender include a native archaeological site at Mortimer Spit near the one-lane trestle bridge that connects the two islands, and, on North Pender, the world's first wilderness disk (Frisbee) golf course. Pender also has a nine-hole golf course, two country pubs, and a long, broken coastline popular with kayakers.

Quadra Island. Topping the list of things to see on Quadra is the *Kwagiulth Museum and Cultural Centre* (tel. 250/285–3733), an attractive modern facility that houses a collection of Kwagiulth potlatch regalia including ceremonial masks, utensils, and headdresses, along with photos of early native villages. There are petroglyphs in the park across from the museum. Pretty Cape Mudge Lighthouse, erected in 1898, stands near the point where Captain Vancouver landed. Of the nine hiking trails on Quadra, the one leading to the summit of China Mountain affords the most rewarding views of the island's lakes and coastline. For swimming and beachcombing, head to Rebecca Spit Provincial Park, north of the ferry landing at Quathiaski Cove. The Village Bay Lake System in the north of the island is popular with swimmers and kayakers.

Salt Spring Island. Ganges, the cultural and commercial center of Salt Spring, is the site of ArtCraft, a summerlong arts and crafts sale, and of the Salt Spring Festival of the Arts, a theater, music, and dance festival held in July. There are bargains aplenty to be had at the Saturday market in Ganges' Centennial Park and artisan shops throughout the island. St. Mary Lake and Cusheon Lake have the best warm-water swimming, and a hike to the summit of Mt. Maxwell affords the best views of the island and surrounding strait. A walk through the church graveyards at St. Paul's and St. Mark's will give you a feel for the island's history.

RESTAURANTS

The best dining in the islands is found at the many fine country inns, which by and large offer innovative Pacific Northwest cuisine featuring local produce, seafood, and lamb. Those that have developed strong reputations include **April Point Lodge** (Quadra Island, tel. 250/285–2222 or 888/334–3474); **Hastings House** (Salt Spring Island, tel. 250/537–2362 or 800/661–9255); **Oceanwood Country Inn** (Mayne Island, tel. 250/539–5074); and **Woodstone Country Inn** (Galiano Island, tel. 250/539–2022 or 888/339–2022). The salmon, venison, and homemade ice cream at **House Piccolo** (Salt Spring Island, tel. 250/537–1844) make it an island favorite. For something really different, try the historical-theme dinners at **Fernhill Lodge** (Mayne Island, tel. 250/539–2544).

TOURIST INFORMATION

Ferry schedules are available from **BC Ferries** (tel. 250/386–3431 or, in BC, 888/223–3779). **Galiano Island Travel Infocentre** (Box 73, Galiano, BC V0N 1P0, tel. 250/539–2233). **Mayne Island Chamber of Commerce** (General Delivery, Mayne Island, BC V0N 2J0, no phone). **Salt Spring Island Travel Infocentre** (121 Lower Ganges Rd., Ganges, BC V8K 2T1, tel. 250/537–5252, fax 250/537–4276). **Tourism Association of Vancouver Island** (Suite 302, 45 Bastion Sq., Victoria, BC V8W 1J1, tel. 250/382–3551, fax 250/382–3523). **Tourism B.C.** (865 Hornby St., Suite 802, Victoria, BC V6Z 2G3, tel. 250/660–2861 or 800/663–6000).

RESERVATION SERVICES

AA Accommodations West Bed and Breakfast Reservations Service (660 Jones Terr., Victoria, BC V8Z 2L7, tel. 250/479–1986, fax 250/479–9999). **Best Canadian Bed and Breakfast Network** (1064 Balfour Ave., Vancouver, BC V6H 1X1, tel. 604/738–7207, fax 604/732–4998). **British Columbia Bed and Breakfast Association** (Box 593, 101–1001 W. Broadway, Vancouver, BC V6H 4E4, tel. 604/734–3486). **Gulf Islands Bed and Breakfast Reservation Service** (637 Southwind Rd., Montague Harbour, Galiano Island, BC V0N 1P0, tel. 250/539–2930 or 888/539–2930). **Supernatural British Columbia** (601–1166 Alberni St., Vancouver, BC V6E 3Z3, tel. 800/663–6000).

ANNE'S OCEANFRONT HIDEAWAY ☞

168 Simson Rd., Salt Spring Island, BC V8K 1E2, tel. 250/537–0851 or 888/474–2663, fax 250/537–0861; www.bcyellowpages.com/advert/a/annes_ocean_hideaway.html

Perched high on a steep slope above the sea, 4 mi north of the Vesuvius ferry terminal, this modern waterfront home shows Salt Spring Island's scenery at its best. The views west from its two wraparound verandas (one has a hot tub) take in magnificent sunsets and the lights of Crofton across the water on Vancouver Island.

Inside there's a cozy library with a fireplace, a sitting room, and, unusual in a bed-and-breakfast, an exercise room. Perhaps it's there to counter the delicious four-course breakfasts that Anne serves in the morning.

Every room has a hydromassage tub and water view; three of the four have private balconies. The Garry Oak is a special occasion room with a canopy bed, a fireplace, a tub for two, and the best views in the house from its private balcony. The Douglas Fir room, also spacious with great views, is fully wheelchair accessible.

Extras like morning coffee in the rooms, robes, down duvets, and a welcoming bottle of wine make this adult-oriented bed-and-breakfast a comfortable place to unwind. Hosts Rick and Ruth-Anne Broad spent over 20 years in the hospitality industry on the prairies before choosing semi-retirement on Salt Spring, and the experience shows in their attention to detail and easy congenialty. Four-course hot breakfasts served at the long dining room table include juice, fruit and yogurt parfaits, homemade baked goodies, and a hot entrée such as salmon Benedict or orange French toast with honey garlic sausage. ♠ *4 double rooms with baths. Air-conditioning and refrigerators in all rooms, fireplace in 1 room. TV/VCR in lounge, outdoor hot tub, exercise room, canoe, bicycles, library. C$145–C$210; full breakfast. MC, V. No smoking.*

APRIL POINT LODGE AND FISHING RESORT ☞

900 April Point Rd., Box 1, Campbell River, Quadra Island, BC V9W 4Z9, tel. 250/285–2222 or 800/663–7090, fax 250/285–2411; www.obmg.com

In 1998, after 50 years as a family business, the venerable April Point Lodge became part of the Oak Bay Marine Group, a chain of luxury Vancouver Island lodges. You can now expect extensively renovated and redecorated accommodations, and something a little more upscale than the fishing lodge of yore. The new owners plan to add, among other things, a sushi bar and adventure eco-tour packages.

April Point is, however, still very much a place to get away from it all. Spread across a point of Quadra Island, a 10-minute ferry ride from Campbell River, the 1944 cedar lodge is surrounded by cabins and guest houses, all newly decorated in a rustic West Coast style. Many of the accommodations have kitchenettes and fireplaces. Some have whirlpool tubs, others have outdoor hot tubs on private decks.

Most people come here to fish the salmon-rich waters of Discovery Passage, but many also come to watch the local birds, whales, and other wildlife, or to hike, bike, and kayak Quadra Island's miles of unspoiled trails and coastline. The lodge is family oriented, and children are most welcome.

The lodge's restaurant and lounge make the most of the local salmon and seafood, and display an impressive collection of Kwagiulth and Haida art. △ *22 double rooms with baths, 5 suites, 11 guest houses and lodges with 1–5 bedrooms. Kitchen in guest houses and 1 suite; fireplace, whirlpool bath and/or hot tub in some units. Restaurant, lounge, gift shop, coin laundry, conference facilities, bicycle and kayak rentals, tennis court, trails, marina, seaplane dock, helipad, airport shuttle, salmon charters, nature tours. C$99–C$395; breakfast not included. AE, DC, MC, V. Some units closed Nov.–Mar.*

BEACH HOUSE ON SUNSET, A BED & BREAKFAST INN ✍

930 Sunset Dr., Salt Spring Island, BC V8K 1E6, tel. 250/537–2879, fax 250/537–4747; www.saltspring.com/beachhouse

Jon and Maureen De West's dream of operating a bed-and-breakfast came to fruition when they purchased this West Coast–Mediterranean-style house on a waterfront slope on Salt Spring Island. From here the sunsets over Stuart Channel and Vancouver Island are stunning.

Three upstairs rooms have ocean views, private entrances, and balconies. A romantic, cedar-lined cottage with a wraparound porch and its own kitchen sits over the boathouse at the water's edge.

The De West's newest offering, a spacious room in earthy browns and siennas, has a cathedral ceiling, a fireplace, a claw-foot tub in the bathroom, French doors framing lovely sea views, a private deck with a tree growing up through the middle, and an outdoor shower. Extra touches in all rooms include down comforters, thick terry robes, slippers, fruit platters, decanters of sherry, and fresh flowers.

In summer you can swim from the pebble beach—the water is warm and clear here—or spend the day on the water: Jon and Maureen can arrange kayak tours and boat charters from here.

Maureen, a Le Cordon Bleu–trained chef, serves a bountiful breakfast of fresh-baked goods with homemade preserves and jams, sliced seasonal fruits, and hot entrées such as seafood crepes. △ *3 doubles with baths, 1 cottage. Kitchen in cottage. C$185–C$225; full breakfast. MC, V. No smoking indoors, closed Dec.–Feb.*

CLIFFSIDE INN ✍

4230 Armadale Rd., Box 50, North Pender Island, BC V0N 2M0, tel. 250/629–6691; www.penderisland.com

British innkeeper Geoff Clydesdale was so struck by the beauty and tranquility of this scenic North Pender Island property that he bought it. He's now the proud proprietor of a charming oceanfront bed and breakfast—a Wedgwood blue board-and-batten contemporary with flowering window boxes under white bay windows. Its outstanding features are a glass solarium dining room and a cliff-hanger deck with a hot tub overlooking Navy Channel.

All the rooms have private entrances and cozy decor, three have sea views, and one overlooks the garden and the forest. The Channel View room has a chintz-covered wing chair near a fireplace, a bay window with ocean views, and a brick patio 9 ft from the edge of the cliff. The Ocean Queen has a private deck and an expansive ocean view.

A full breakfast of fresh baked goods and a hot entrée such as eggs Benedict or omelets is served in the restaurant-style solarium. From its three walls of windows you can gaze out at the sea and islands as you dine. Afterwards, you can gather on the deck to watch Geoff and his staff feed the resident eagles.

Dinners, featuring local bounty such as salmon, beef Wellington, or Cornish game hens, with vegetables from island gardens, are available to guests on Saturday night and by arrangement the rest of the week. ♨ *4 double rooms with baths. Hot tub, kayak platform, boat moorage, seasonal nature cruises and kayak tours, ferry pick up. C$129–C$229; full breakfast, dinner available. V. No smoking, 2-night minimum on weekends.*

CORBETT HOUSE HERITAGE BED AND BREAKFAST ☞
4309 Corbett Rd., R.R. 1, North Pender Island, BC V0N 2M1, tel. 250/629–6305

When convivial innkeepers Linda and John Eckfeldt came to Pender Island in the mid-'80s to go bicycling, they never dreamed they would end up buying the bed-and-breakfast they visited. But they snapped it up when, a little later, it came on the market. Their creamy yellow 1902 farmhouse is named for the Corbetts, a pioneer family who built the general store and started the island's post office.

The interior is a hodgepodge of country-style antiques, John's handcrafted furniture, and locally produced artwork, much of it for sale. The upstairs Red, Blue, and Yellow rooms are simply but comfortably furnished with a mixture of early Canadian and contemporary pieces. Red and Blue have private half-baths and share a shower; Yellow has a full bath and a sundeck.

Edible flowers add a lovely touch to the four-course breakfast served in a dining room that overlooks the orchard. Nearby you can hike, bicycle, fish, sail, or kayak; the less active can gaze at ducks on the summer pond, sheep in the yard, and deer in the meadow. A feeder pond attracts an array of birds, so birdwatching is a favorite pastime here. ♨ *1 double room with bath, 2 doubles with ½ baths share 1 shower. Boots and binoculars for hikes, ferry pickup service. C$95–C$110; full breakfast, evening meal by arrangement. MC. No smoking, 2-night minimum on weekends, closed Nov.–Apr.*

FERNHILL LODGE ☞
610 Fernhill Rd., R.R. 1 C–4, Mayne Island, BC V0N 2J0, tel. and fax 250/539–2544

Built by hand with wood from the property, this weathered 1983 West Coast–style cedar home is host to three fantastical theme rooms—Moroccan, East Indian, and Old English. An authentic 17th-century curtained yeoman's bed in the Old English room and the hand-wrought canopy bed and wood carvings in the Moroccan Room are examples of the attention to detail in the inn. Not strictly historical, but nice all the same, are the outdoor hot tubs on each room's private deck.

Englishman Brian Crumblehulme and his wife, Mary, offer farmhouse dinners most nights for guests and nonguests at this tranquil retreat. By special arrangement, they can also prepare extraordinary historical theme dinners, using fresh herbs and produce from Fernhill's grounds.

Breakfasts are impressive too—you choose from a five-page menu offering such thoughtful creations as Yeoman's Breakfast (apples, sausage, onions, and sage in a white wine sauce) to Love in the Morning (a poached egg with Brie and bacon).

Felines Tippy, Muffin, Cassie, and Champers will happily occupy a lap when you're relaxing in the well-stocked library or soaking in the distant view of Pender Island and Navy Channel from the deck; if you prefer, they'll accompany you on explorations of the medieval "garden of physic" on the 5-acre grounds. ♨ *3 double rooms with baths. Hot tubs, sauna, library, ferry pickup service. C$125–C$150; full breakfast, dinner available. MC, V. No smoking.*

HASTINGS HOUSE 🍍

160 Upper Ganges Rd., Box 1110, Ganges, Salt Spring Island, BC V8K 2S2, tel. 250/537–2362 or 800/661–9255, fax 250/537-5333; www.hastingshouse.com

One of the finest country inns in North America and a member of the prestigious Relais & Châteaux group, Hastings House knows how to pamper its guests. The centerpiece of this luxurious 25-acre seaside resort is a Tudor-style manor built by the Hastings family in 1939 to resemble their home in England. It comes replete with exposed cedar beams and a cowl fireplace constructed from 21 tons of stone quarried on the property.

A broad assortment of accommodations is offered here: rooms in the manor or the farmhouse; garden cottages, and suites in the reconstructed barn. All are plushly furnished with fine antiques (primarily English) and follow an English country theme, with such extras as eiderdowns, fireplaces or woodstoves, stocked bars, covered porches or decks, and idyllic views of gardens, pastures, or the harbor.

Individual service and attention to detail are of prime importance to innkeeper and general manager Mark Gottaas, originally from New South Wales, Australia. He provides many wonderful touches—bountiful flower arrangements, little gifts left on pillows at evening turndown, thermoses of early morning coffee and juice. You can choose to have a deluxe Continental tray delivered to your room in the morning or visit the dining room for a multicourse breakfast.

Elegant dinners in the manor house are a major part of the Hastings House experience, with formal, five-course meals created by Marcel Kauer, an outstanding chef. The menu might include artichoke-and-cassis timbale, marinated sea bass with Digby scallops, and organic pear tarte Tatin. ♨ *3 double rooms with baths, 7 suites. Phone in rooms, TV on request, kitchen in 1 suite. Restaurant, limited room service, massage and spa treatments, croquet, mountain bikes, nature trails. C$365–C$495; full breakfast. AE, MC, V. 2-night minimum on weekends, 3-night minimum on holiday weekends, closed Jan.–early Mar.*

OCEANWOOD COUNTRY INN 🍍

630 Dinner Bay Rd., Mayne Island, BC V0N 2J0, tel. 250/539–5074, fax 250/539–3002; www.gulfislands.com/mayne/oceanwood

The Oceanwood Country Inn on Mayne Island has developed a strong following—no doubt due in large part to its lovely waterfront location overlooking Navy Channel and several Gulf Islands. Originally constructed in 1979, this English country house–style home on 10 quiet, forested acres has been renovated and expanded by owners Marilyn and Jonathan Chilvers.

Guest rooms are airy and inviting; all have cozy down comforters on comfortable beds, and all but one (which overlooks the garden) have grand ocean views from balconies or patios. Some are outfitted with broad French doors, romantic fireplaces, and raised whirlpool tubs. The three rooms in the newer extension are especially spacious, but the top-of-the-line Wisteria Suite, set apart up two flights of stairs, is the grandest. It's on two levels, with a hot tub on a private deck and stunning views across the water.

The numerous common areas include a games room as well as a spacious living room and cozy library, both with fireplaces. Other activities include leisurely strolls with Kelly, the golden Lab, or Rupert, the cat; biking along the rural roads of Mayne Island; and taking afternoon tea in the garden room.

The dining room, with its wall of French doors offering expansive views of the ocean, features some of the best regional cuisine you'll find anywhere on the islands. Reasonably priced four-course prix-fixe dinners featuring fresh, local ingredients, are available to guests and nonguests.

In the morning you'll return to this room for a breakfast of fresh juices, homemade granola, yogurt with fruit purée, and beautifully presented hot entrées such as omelets or orange French toast. *A 12 double rooms with baths. Down comforter, fireplace and whirlpool bath in some rooms. TV/VCR and video library in common room, restaurant, sauna, library, meeting room, bicycles. C$130–$295; full breakfast, afternoon tea. MC, V. No smoking, 2-night minimum on weekends, closed Dec.–Feb.*

OLD FARMHOUSE BED AND BREAKFAST 🐚

1077 Northend Rd., Salt Spring Island, BC V8K 1L9, tel. 250/537–4113, fax 250/537–4969; www.pixsell.pc.ca/bb/1182.htm

Formerly the manager of the popular Umberto's Il Giardino in Vancouver, European-trained chef Gerti Fuss now operates this delightful bed-and-breakfast with her husband, Karl. Their gray-and-white saltbox farmhouse is in a quiet, 3-acre Salt Spring Island meadow edged by towering trees. The architectural style of the main house, a registered historic property built in 1894, is echoed in the four-room wing with private entrance constructed by Karl in 1989.

Sunlight filters through lace curtains in country-comfortable guest rooms with pine bedsteads, down comforters, floral chintz fabrics, wicker chairs, and private patios or balconies. The two upstairs rooms have cathedral ceilings; the bed in one downstairs room is tucked into an alcove beneath stained-glass windows. Gerti's breakfasts, served in the dining room and featuring fresh-daily baked goods, followed by an entrée such as smoked salmon soufflé, are legendary.

The Old Farmhouse is across the road from warm, swimmable St. Mary's Lake, a few minutes from the island's golf course, and a few miles from the ferry terminal and the village of Ganges. *A 4 double rooms with baths. Ferry pickup service, canoe. C$150; full breakfast. MC, V. No smoking, 2-night minimum on holiday weekends.*

SKY VALLEY PLACE 🌿

421 Sky Valley Rd., Salt Spring Island, BC V8K 2C3, tel. 250/537–4210, fax 250/537–4220

Perched on 11 mountain-hugging, forested acres high up in the center of Salt Spring Island, the aptly named Sky Valley Place enjoys spectacular views of the Gulf Islands and of Vancouver's North Shore mountains across the Strait of Georgia. This L-shape West Coast contemporary cedar home has ivy-covered beams and a 20- by 40-ft heated outdoor swimming pool.

Proprietors Pauline and Florian Baumstark, originally from Germany, have created a romantic, sunny, adult-oriented hideaway. Handcrafted pine furniture fills living and dining rooms that seem to have more windows than walls. Clean-lined bedrooms are country elegant, with floral print curtains and coordinated comforters and pillows on cozy wicker chairs. One room has a high, balloon-canopied bed as well.

Fresh berries and herbs from Pauline's gardens are served at breakfast, along with home-baked bread and such glamorous entrées as smoked salmon soufflés or eggs with caviar. After the meal, you can meander through the forest or just admire panoramic scenery from the living room. ♨ *4 double rooms with baths. Robes in rooms, whirlpool bath in 1 room. Pool. C$95–C$120; full breakfast. V. No smoking, 2-night minimum on weekends.*

SUTIL LODGE 🌿

637 Southwind Rd., Montague Harbour, Galiano Island, BC V0N 1P0, tel. 250/539–2930, 888/539–2930, fax 250/539–5390; www.gulfislandreservations.com

Long-time Galiano residents Tom and Ann Hennessy own this 1928 British Colonial bungalow on 20 wooded acres on Montague Harbour—a scenic part of the island known for its white shell beaches, marine park, and full-sky sunsets. Family photos from the 1920s, and decor that Ann describes as "Grandma's House," re-create a sense of lodge life in an earlier era.

The simple guest rooms have a nautical feel, with throw rugs on dark hardwood floors and beds built in under the windows. From the larger, waterside rooms, you can admire the bay views while still tucked up in bed. The shared bathrooms have antique ball-foot tubs and small corner sinks.

Out in the bay, a sleek catamaran waits to take you and skipper Tom on nature-watching trips that include a stop for a lavish salmon barbecue at a secluded sandy beach. The biggest activity at this lodge (besides rusticating and relaxing) is kayaking: Experienced and novice kayakers from around the world come to paddle the still coves of the Gulf Islands; lessons, rentals, and guided trips are available. Sutil's low-season kayaking packages are a great value.

Anne's enormous breakfasts of fresh fruit; home-baked muffins; homemade granola; and a choice of entrées, usually including eggs from Sutil's own chickens, are served at a long table in the lodge's old dance hall. ♨ *2 single and 5 double rooms share 3 baths. Badminton, nature trails, nature-watching and picnic cruises, kayaks and canoes, kayaking trips with guides, ferry pickup service. C$85–C$95; full breakfast. AE, MC, V. No smoking, 2-night minimum on holiday weekends, closed Nov.–Feb.*

TSA-KWA-LUTEN LODGE 🐚
Lighthouse Rd., Box 460, Quathiaski Cove, Quadra Island, BC V0P 1N0,
tel. 250/285–2042 or 800/665–7745, fax 250/285–2532; www.capemudgeresort.bc.ca

Owned and operated by the Cape Mudge band of the Kwagiulth first nation, Tsa-Kwa-Luten Lodge is on a high bluff amid 1,100 acres of forest on Quadra Island; it's a 10-minute ferry ride from Campbell River on Vancouver Island, and a 15-minute drive on a dirt road from the ferry. Authentic Pacific Coast native food and cultural activities are featured here: You are invited to take part in ceremonial dances held occasionally and to visit nearby petroglyphs to make rubbings.

The lodge's centerpiece is a lofty foyer built in the style of a longhouse, with a 45-ft-high peaked ceiling and picture windows overlooking Discovery Passage.

The guest rooms in this modern weathered cedar building are all spacious and uniform in design and decor; all have contemporary oak furnishings, Kwagiulth artwork, large windows with ocean views, and porches or balconies; several have fireplaces or lofts. Four beachfront cabins offer fireplaces, whirlpool tubs, kitchen facilities, and private verandas. △ *29 double rooms with baths, 1 suite, 4 2–4 bedroom cabins. Phone in rooms; fireplace in some rooms; kitchen, fireplace, and whirlpool bath in cabins. Restaurant, lounge, sauna, exercise room, hot tub, rental bicycles, guided salmon fishing charters. C$115–C$460; breakfast extra. AE, DC, MC, V. Closed mid-Oct.–early Apr.*

WESTON LAKE INN 🐚
813 Beaver Point Rd., Salt Spring Island, BC V8K 1X9, tel. 250/653–4311,
fax 250/653–4340; www.bbcanada.com/172.html

Amiable Susan Evans and her partner, Ted Harrison, were drawn to the Gulf Islands for years before they decided to purchase 10 pastoral acres and a home on a hillside on Salt Spring Island.

They've since transformed a 1976 cedar contemporary into a charming English countryside–style cottage, and operate both a bed-and-breakfast and a working farm, producing fresh eggs, vegetables, berries, and flowers for island residents.

Among the many attractions are Susan's beautifully landscaped rhododendron, heather, alpine, flower, and herb gardens; a hot tub on a deck overlooking Weston Lake; 1,200 acres of greenery in nearby Ruckle Provincial Park; and plenty of pets to keep you company. Inside are a spacious living room and a cozy fireside TV lounge.

Canadian art, photos of sailboats, and Ted's fine petit-point embroidery adorn the walls of the guest rooms, which are cheerfully decorated with lace curtains, floral bedspreads, and fresh flowers.

In the large, sunny dining room, Susan serves breakfasts of homemade granola, garden-grown asparagus, herb scrambled eggs, and other tempting dishes featuring the farm's organic produce. Afterwards, you can charter Ted's 36-ft sloop for a day of exploring the islands. △ *3 double rooms with baths. TV/VCR, video library, hot tub, nature trails, sailing charters. C$105–C$120; full breakfast. MC, V. No smoking, 2-night minimum on holiday weekends.*

WOODSTONE COUNTRY INN 🐚

Georgeson Bay Rd., R.R. 1, Galiano Island, BC V0N 1P0, tel. 250/539–2022
or 888/339–2022, fax 250/539–5198; www.gulfislands.com/woodstone

A modern gable building with the look and feel of an English country inn, the Woodstone sits on the edge of a forest overlooking a meadow. Innkeepers Gail and Andrew Nielsen-Pich will loan you gear to scout out birds in the glade just outside.

Stenciled walls and tall windows bring the pastoral setting into spacious bedrooms furnished with a mixture of wicker, antiques, and English country prints. Most of the rooms have fireplaces and patios; and all feature oversize tubs. The Dogwood room has a two-person whirlpool tub, a wet bar, and a whole wall of windows overlooking the meadow.

Works by local artists decorate the walls of the living room, where wing chairs and a couch are grouped around the fireplace. Afternoon tea, served on the patio or by the fire in the lounge, is included in the tariff. Breakfasts, served in the dining room, often feature eggs Escoffier (an egg baked in a croissant with ham) or Belgian waffles with berries and cream.

Woodstone's elegant restaurant is one of the more renowned places to dine on the Gulf Islands. It's open to the public for four-course table d'hôte dinners that can include such French-influenced Pacific Northwest fare as yam soup with toasted almonds and roasted breast of pheasant with pink-peppercorn sauce. △ *13 double rooms with baths. Whirlpool bath and wet bar in 1 room. Restaurant, nature trails, bird-watching platform. C$99–C$185; full breakfast. AE, MC, V. No smoking, 2-night minimum on holiday and summer weekends, closed Jan.*

ALPHABETICAL DIRECTORY

A

Abendblume Pension 180–181

Abigail's Hotel 234

The Aerie 223–224

Albatross 168

Alexander's Country Inn 181

All Seasons River Inn Bed & Breakfast 181–182

Anchorage Inn 141

Anderson's Boarding House 64

Annapurna Inn Massage & Retreat Center 118–119

Anne's Oceanfront Hideaway 242

Ann Starrett Mansion 118

Antique Rose Inn 19

Apple Inn Bed & Breakfast 31

April Point Lodge and Fishing Resort 242–243

Arden Forest Inn 19–20

Astoria Inn 64–65

B

Bacon Mansion/Broadway Guest House 130–131

Bayberry Inn Bed and Breakfast 20

Beach House on Sunset, a Bed & Breakfast Inn 243

The Beaconsfield 234–235

Beckley House 31–32

Bed and Breakfast by the River 87–88

Benjamin Young Inn 65

Beryl House 76

Big Trees Bed & Breakfast 168–169

Bingen Haus 104

Birchfield Manor 104–105

Bird Song Cottage 224

Bombay House 131–132

Borea's Bed & Breakfast Inn 105

Borthwick Country Manor 224–225

Bradley House Bed & Breakfast 105–106

Bridal Veil Lodge 76–77

Brightwood Guest House 77

Brookside Bed & Breakfast 77

C

Campbell House 32

Captain Whidbey Inn 141–142

Carberry Gardens 235

Caswell's on the Bay 106

Cedar Springs Lodge 217–18

Chalet Luise 218

Chambered Nautilus 132

Chamberlain House 78

Chandlers Bed, Bread & Trail Inn 88

Channel House (OR) 169

Channel House (WA) 65–66

Chanticleer Inn 20–21

Chesterman's Beach Bed and Breakfast 225

Chestnut Hill Inn 152–153

Chetco River Inn 8

Chick-a-Dee Inn at Ilwaco 106–107

Clark House on Hayden Lake 193

Clayoquot Wilderness Resort 225–226

Clear Creek Farm Bed-and-Breakfast 88–89

Cliff House 8–9

Cliff House and Sea Cliff Cottage 142

Cliffside Inn 243–244

Clinkerbrick House 53

Coast Watch Bed & Breakfast 107

Colonel Crockett Farm 143

Columbia Gorge Hotel 78

Compass Rose Bed & Breakfast 143–144

Coos Bay Manor 9

Corbett House Heritage Bed & Breakfast 244

Country Bed & Breakfast 201

Country Cottage of Langley 144

Country Willows Bed and Breakfast Inn 21

Cricket on the Hearth Bed and Breakfast Inn 193–194

D

Deer Harbor Inn 153

Domaine Madeleine 119

Doublegate Inn 78–79

Duffy House 153–154

Durlacher Hof 218–219

E

Eagle Nook Ocean Wilderness Resort 226

Eagles Nest Inn 144–145

Edenwild Inn 154

Edgewater 219

Elliott House 89

English Bay Inn 210

Excelsior Inn 32–33

F

Falcon's Crest Inn 79

Farm Bed and Breakfast 107–108

Fernhill Lodge 244–245

Fernwood At Alder Creek 80

Flery Manor 22

Floras Lake House by the Sea 9–10

Flying L Ranch *108*
Flying M Ranch *42*
Fort Casey Inn *145*
Fotheringham House *194*
Franklin St. Station *66*
Freestone Inn *182*
Frenchglen Hotel *89–90*
Friday Harbor House *154–155*

G

Gaslight Inn *132–133*
Geiser Grand Hotel *90*
General Hooker's B&B *53–54*
Georgian House *54*
Gilbert Inn *66–67*
Grandview Bed & Breakfast *67*
Green Gables Inn *202*
Gregory's McFarland House *194–195*
Greystone Manor *226–227*
Guest House Log Cottages *145–146*

H

Hanson Country Inn *33–34*
Harbinger Inn *119–120*
Harrison House *34*
Hastings House *245*
Hasty Pudding House *170*
Haterleigh Heritage Inn *235–236*
Haus Lorelei *182–183*
Haus Rohrbach Pension *183*
Heceta Lighthouse Bed & Breakfast *10*
Heron Haus *54–55*
Hill House *133*
Hillside House *155*
Holland House Inn *236*

Home by the Sea *10–11*
Home by the Sea Cottages *146*
Hood River Hotel *80–81*
Hotel Diamond *90–91*
Hotel Planter *170*
Hotel Vintage Plaza *55*
House of Hunter *34–35*
Howell House *42–43*
Hudson House *67–68*
Humboldt House *236–237*

I

Inn at Harbor Steps *134*
Inn at Langley *146–147*
Inn at Manzanita *68*
Inn at the Market *134–135*
Inn at Nesika Beach *11*
Inn at Penn Cove *147*
Inn at Swifts Bay *155–156*
Inn at White Salmon *108–109*
Ivy House *22*

J

Jacksonville Inn *23*
James House *120*
Joan Brown's Bed and Breakfast *237*
Johnson Heritage House *211*
Johnson House *11–12*

K

Kangaroo House *156*
Kelty Estate *43*
Kittiwake *12*
Kola House Bed & Breakfast *109*

L

Laburnum Cottage *211–212*

La Conner Channel Lodge and Country Inn *171*
Lakecliff Estate Bed & Breakfast *81*
Lake Crescent Lodge *121*
Lake Quinault Lodge *121*
Land's End *109*
Lara House *91*
Le Chamois *219–220*
The Lighthouse *12–13*
Lion and the Rose *56*
Lithia Springs Inn *23–24*
Lizzie's Victorian Bed & Breakfast *122*
Locarno Beach Bed & Breakfast *212*
Log Castle Bed & Breakfast *147–148*
Lone Lake Cottage and Breakfast *148*
Lopez Farm Cottages *156–157*
Love's Victorian Bed and Breakfast *195*

M

MacKaye Harbor Inn *157*
MacMaster House *56–57*
Main Street Bed & Breakfast *43–44*
Majestic Hotel *171–172*
Manor Farm Inn *122*
Maple River *81–82*
Maple Valley Bed & Breakfast *183–184*
Marianna Stoltz House *195–196*
Mariella Inn & Cottages *157–158*
Marquee House *44*
Mattey House *44–45*
Mazama Country Inn *184*
McGillivray's Log Home Bed and Breakfast *35*

McMenamins Edgefield *57*

Moby Dick Hotel and Oyster Farm *110*

Moore House Bed & Breakfast *184–185*

Morical House Garden Inn *24*

Mountain Home Lodge *185*

Mountain Meadows Inn Bed & Breakfast at Mt. Rainer *185–186*

Mt. Ashland Inn *24–25*

Mulberry Manor *237*

M.V. *Challenger* *135*

N

North Garden Inn *172*

Nye Beach Hotel *68–69*

O

O Canada House *212–213*

Ocean Wilderness Inn and Spa Retreat *227*

Oceanwood Country Inn *245–246*

Old Consulate Inn *122–123*

Old Farmhouse Bed and Breakfast *246*

Old Trout Inn *158*

Old Welches Inn *82*

Olympic Lights *158–159*

Orcas Hotel *159*

Orchard View Inn *45*

Oval Door Bed and Breakfast *35–36*

P

Parker House Bed & Breakfast *91–92*

Partridge Farm *45–46*

Peerless Hotel *25*

Penny Farthing *213*

Pine Meadow Inn Bed and Breakfast *25–26*

Pine Valley Lodge and Halfway Supper Club *92*

The Portico *196*

Portland Guest House *58*

Portland's White House *58–59*

Prior House *238*

Purple House Bed and Breakfast *202–203*

Q

Quimper Inn *123–124*

R

Ravenscroft Inn *124*

Red Crow Guest House *227*

Ridgeway Farm *172–173*

RiverPlace Hotel *59–60*

River Run *213–214*

Roberta's Bed & Breakfast *135–136*

Romeo Inn *26*

Run of the River Inn *186*

S

St. Bernards *69*

Salisbury House *136–137*

Salish Lodge *187*

Sand Dollar Inn *160*

Sandlake Country Inn *69–70*

San Juan Inn *160*

Saratoga Inn *148–149*

Sather House Bed-and-Breakfast *92–93*

Scandinavian Gardens Inn *110–111*

Schnauzer Crossing *173*

Sea Quest *13*

Serenity *13–14*

Shaniko Hotel *93–94*

Shannon House *173–174*

Shelburne Inn *111*

Ships Point Beach House *228*

Simone's Groveland Cottage *124–125*

Sky Valley Place *247*

Sleeping Lady *187–188*

Snug Harbour Inn *228–229*

Sooke Harbour House *229*

Sorrento Hotel *137*

South Bay Bed & Breakfast *174–175*

Sou'wester Lodge *111–112*

Spring Bay Inn *160–161*

Springbrook Hazelnut Farm *46*

Stang Manor *94*

State House *46–47*

States Inn *161*

Steamboat Inn *36*

Steens Mountain Inn *94–95*

Steiger Haus *47*

Stephanie Inn *70*

Stone Creek Inn *203–204*

Storyville *175*

Stratford Manor Bed & Breakfast *175–176*

Suite River Bed & Breakfast *82–83*

Sun Mountain Lodge *188*

Sunnyside Inn *112*

Sutil Lodge *247*

Swans *238*

Swantown Inn *125*

Sylvia Beach Hotel *70–71*

T

Thistledown House *214*

Touch of Europe Bed & Breakfast Inn *112–113*

Touvelle House *26–27*

Trout Lake Country Inn *113*

Trumpeter Inn *162*
Tsa-Kwa-Luten Lodge *248*
Tudor House *60*
Tudor Inn *126*
Turtleback Farm Inn *162–163*
Tu Tu Tun Lodge *14*
Tyee Lodge *71–72*

V
Villa Heidelberg *137–138*

W
Wall Street Inn *138*
Waverly Place *196–197*

West End Guest House *214–215*
Westfir Lodge *36–37*
Weston Lake Inn *248*
Wharfside Bed & Breakfast *163*
Whiskey Creek Bed & Breakfast *72*
White Swan Guest House *176*
Wickaninnish Inn *230*
Wild Iris and the Heron Inn *176–177*
Winchester Country Inn *27*
Windsong *163–164*
Wine Country Inn *113–114*

Woods House *27–28*
Woodstone Country Inn *249*

Y
Yellow Point Lodge *230*
Youngberg Hill Vineyard *47–48*

Z
Ziggurat *15*

GEOGRAPHICAL DIRECTORY

OREGON

Arch Cape
St. Bernards 69

Ashland
Antique Rose Inn 19
Arden Forest Inn 19–20
Bayberry Inn Bed and Breakfast 20
Chanticleer Inn 20–21
Country Willows Bed and Breakfast Inn 21
Lithia Springs Inn 23–24
Morical House Garden Inn 24
Mt. Ashland Inn 24–25
Peerless Hotel 25
Romeo Inn 26
Winchester Country Inn 27
Woods House 27–28

Astoria
Astoria Inn 64–65
Benjamin Young Inn 65
Franklin St. Station 66
Grandview Bed & Breakfast 67

Baker City
Geiser Grand Hotel 90

Bandon
The Lighthouse 12–13

Bend
Lara House 91
Sather House Bed-and-Breakfast 92–93

Bridal Veil
Bridal Veil Lodge 76–77

Brightwood
Brightwood Guest House 77
Maple River 81–82

Brookings
Chetco River Inn 8

Cannon Beach
Stephanie Inn 70

Cloverdale
Hudson House 67–68
Sandlake Country Inn 69–70

Coos Bay
Coos Bay Manor 9

Cottage Grove
Apple Inn Bed & Breakfast 31

Corbett
Chamberlain House 78

Corvallis
Hanson Country Inn 33–34
Harrison House 34

Depoe Bay
Channel House 65–66

Diamond
Hotel Diamond 90–91

Elmira
McGillivray's Log Home Bed and Breakfast 35

Eugene
Campbell House 32
Excelsior Inn 32–33
Oval Door Bed and Breakfast 35–36

Florence
Johnson House 12

Forest Grove
Main Street Bed & Breakfast 43–44

Frenchglen
Frenchglen Hotel 89–90
Steens Mountain Inn 94–95

Gold Beach
Inn at Nesika Beach 11
Tu Tu Tun Lodge 14

Government's Camp
Falcon's Crest Inn 79

Grants Pass
Flery Manor 22
Ivy House 22

Halfway
Clear Creek Farm Bed-and-Breakfast 88–89
Pine Valley Lodge and Halfway Supper Club 92

Hood River
Beryl House 76
Columbia Gorge Hotel 78
Hood River Hotel 80–81
Lakecliff Estate Bed & Breakfast 81

Jacksonville
Jacksonville Inn 23
Touvelle House 26–27

Joseph
Chandlers Bed, Bread & Trail Inn 88

Lafayette
Kelty Estate 43

La Grande
Stang Manor 94

Langlois
Floras Lake House by the Sea 9

Manzanita
Inn at Manzanita 68

McMinnville
Mattey House 44–45
Orchard View Inn 45
Steiger Haus 47
Youngberg Hill Vineyard 47–48

Merlin
Pine Meadow Inn Bed and Breakfast 25–26

Monmouth
Howell House 42–43

Newberg
Partridge Farm 45–46
Springbrook Hazelnut Farm 46

Newport
Nye Beach Hotel 68–69

Sylvia Beach Hotel 70–71
Tyee Lodge 71–72

Oakland
Beckley House 31–32

Pendleton
Parker House Bed &
Breakfast 91–92

Portland
Clinkerbrick House 53
General Hooker's B&B
53–54
Georgian House 54
Heron Haus 54–55
Hotel Vintage Plaza 55
The Lion and the Rose 56
MacMaster House 56–57
Portland Guest House 58
Portland's White House
58–59
RiverPlace Hotel 59–60
Tudor House 60

Port Orford
Home by the Sea 10–11

Prairie City
Bed and Breakfast by the
River 87–88

Prineville
Elliott House 89

Roseburg
House of Hunter 34–35

Salem
Marquee House 44
State House 46–47

Sandy
Brookside Bed & Breakfast
77
Fernwood At Alder Creek 80

Seaside
Anderson's Boarding House
64
Gilbert Inn 66–67

Shaniko
Shaniko Hotel 93–94

Steamboat
Steamboat Inn 36

Tillamook
Whiskey Creek Bed &
Breakfast 72

Troutdale
McMenamins Edgefield 57

Waldport
Cliff House 8

Welches
Doublegate Inn 78–79
Old Welches Inn 82
Suite River B&B 82–83

Westfir
Westfir Lodge 36–37

Yachats
Heceta Lighthouse Bed &
Breakfast 10
Kittiwake 12
Sea Quest 13
Serenity 13–14
Ziggurat 15

Yamhill
Flying M Ranch 42

WASHINGTON

Anacortes
Albatross 168
Channel House 169
Hasty Pudding House 170
Majestic Hotel 171–172
Shannon House 173–174

Ashford
Alexander's Country Inn 181
Mountain Meadows Inn Bed
& Breakfast at Mt. Rainer
185–186

Bainbridge Island
Bombay House 131–132

Bellingham
Big Trees Bed & Breakfast
168–169
North Garden Inn 172

Schnauzer Crossing 173
Stratford Manor Bed &
Breakfast 175–176

Bingen
Bingen Haus 104

Cathlamet
Bradley Bed & Breakfast
105–106

Clinton
Home by the Sea Cottages
146

Coeur d'Alene [ID]
Cricket on the Hearth Bed
and Breakfast Inn 193–194
Gregory's McFarland House
194–195

Coupeville
Anchorage Inn 141
Captain Whidbey Inn
141–142
Colonel Crockett Farm 143
Compass Rose Bed &
Breakfast 143–144
Fort Casey Inn 145
Inn at Penn Cove 147

Dayton
Purple House Bed and
Breakfast 202–203

Deer Harbor
Deer Harbor Inn 153

Deer Park
Love's Victorian Bed and
Breakfast 195

Dungeness
Simone's Groveland Cottage
124–125

Eastsound
Kangaroo House 156
Old Trout Inn 158
Turtleback Farm Inn
162–163

Freeland
Cliff House and Sea Cliff
Cottage 142

Friday Harbor
Duffy House *153–154*
Friday Harbor House *154–155*
Hillside House *155*
Mariella Inn & Cottages *157–158*
Olympic Lights *158–159*
San Juan Inn *160*
States Inn *161*
Trumpeter Inn *162*
Wharfside Bed & Breakfast *163*

Glenwood
Flying L Ranch *108*

Greenbank
Guest House Log Cottages *145–146*

Hayden Lake [ID]
Clark House on Hayden Lake *193*

Ilwaco
Chick-a-Dee Inn at Ilwaco *106–107*
Kola House Bed & Breakfast *109*

La Conner
Hotel Planter *170*
La Conner Channel Lodge and Country Inn *171*
Ridgeway Farm *172–173*
Wild Iris and the Heron Inn *176–177*

Langley
Country Cottage of Langley *144*
Eagles Nest Inn *144–145*
Inn at Langley *146–147*
Log Castle Bed & Breakfast *147–148*
Lone Lake Cottage and Breakfast *148*
Saratoga Inn *148–149*

Leavenworth
Abendblume Pension *180–181*
Haus Lorelei *182–183*
Haus Rohrbach Pension *183*
Mountain Home Lodge *185*
Run of the River Inn *186*
Sleeping Lady *187–188*

Long Beach
Borea's Bed & Breakfast Inn *105*
Land's End *109*
Scandinavian Gardens Inn *110–111*

Lopez
Lopez Farm Cottages *156–157*

Lopez Island
Edenwild Inn *154*
Inn at Swifts Bay *155–156*
MacKaye Harbor Inn *157*

Maple Valley
Maple Valley Bed & Breakfast *183–184*

Mazama
Freestone Inn *182*
Mazama Country Inn *184*

Mount Vernon
Storyville *175*
White Swan Guest House *176*

Nahcotta
Moby Dick Hotel and Oyster Farm *110*

Ocean Park
Caswell's on the Bay *106*
Coast Watch Bed & Breakfast *107*

Olga
Sand Dollar Inn *160*
Spring Bay Inn *160–161*

Olympia
Harbinger Inn *119–120*
Swantown Inn *125*

Orcas
Chestnut Hill Inn *152-153*
Orcas Hotel *159*
Windsong *163–164*

Port Angeles
Domaine Madeleine *119*
Lake Crescent Lodge *121*
Tudor Inn *126*

Port Townsend
Annapurna Inn Massage & Retreat Center *118–119*
Ann Starrett Mansion *118*
James House *120*
Lizzie's Victorian Bed & Breakfast *122*
Old Consulate Inn *122–123*
Quimper Inn *123–124*
Ravenscroft Inn *124*

Poulsbo
Manor Farm Inn *122*

Prosser
Wine Country Inn *113–114*

Pullman
Country Bed & Breakfast *201*

Quinault
Lake Quinault Lodge *121*

Ritzville
The Portico *196*

Seattle
Bacon Mansion/Broadway Guest House *130–131*
Chambered Nautilus *132*
Gaslight Inn *132–133*
Hill House *133*
Inn at Harbor Steps *134*
Inn at the Market *134–135*
M.V. *Challenger* *135*
Roberta's Bed & Breakfast *135–136*
Salisbury House *136–137*

Sorrento Hotel *137*
Villa Heidelberg *137–138*
Wall Street Inn *138*
Seaview
Shelburne Inn *111*
Sou'wester Lodge *111–112*
Sedro Wooley
South Bay Bed & Breakfast *174–175*
Snoqualmie
Salish Lodge *187*
South Cle Elum
Moore House Bed & Breakfast *184–185*
Spokane
Fotheringham House *194*
Marianna Stoltz House *195–196*
Waverly Place *196–197*
Sunnyside
Sunnyside Inn *112*
Trout Lake
Farm Bed and Breakfast *107–108*
Trout Lake Country Inn *113*
Walla Walla
Green Gables Inn *202*
Stone Creek Inn *203–204*
White Salmon
Inn at White Salmon *108–109*
Winthrop
Sun Mountain Lodge *188*
Yakima
Birchfield Manor *104–105*
Touch of Europe Bed & Breakfast Inn *112–113*

BRITISH COLUMBIA

Campbell River
April Point Lodge and Fishing Resort *242–243*

Chemainus
Bird Song Cottage *224*
Courtenay
Greystone Manor *226–227*
Fanny Bay
Ships Point Beach House *228*
Galiano Island
Sutil Lodge *247*
Woodstone Country Inn *249*
Ladner
River Run *213–214*
Ladysmith
Yellow Point Lodge *230*
Malahat
The Aerie *223–224*
Mayne Island
Fernhill Lodge *244–245*
Oceanwood Country Inn *245–246*
North Pender Island
Cliffside Inn *243–244*
Corbett House Heritage B&B *244*
Port Alberni
Eagle Nook Ocean Wilderness Resort *226*
Quadra Island
Tsa-Kwa-Luten Lodge *248*
Salt Spring Island
Anne's Oceanfront Hideaway *242*
Beach House on Sunset, a Bed & Breakfast Inn *243*
Hastings House *245*
Old Farmhouse Bed and Breakfast *246*
Sky Valley Place *247*
Weston Lake Inn *248*
Sidney
Borthwick Country Manor *225*

Sooke
Ocean Wilderness Inn and Spa Retreat *226*
Sooke Harbour House *229*
Tofino
Chesterman's Beach Bed and Breakfast *224–225*
Clayoquot Wilderness Resort *225–226*
Red Crow Guest House *227*
Wickaninnish Inn *230*
Vancouver
English Bay Inn *210*
Johnson Heritage House *221*
Laburnum Cottage *211–212*
Locarno Beach Bed & Breakfast *212*
O Canada House *212–213*
Penny Farthing *213*
Thistledown House *214*
West End Guest House *214–215*
Victoria
Abigail's *234*
The Beaconsfield *234–235*
Carberry Gardens *235*
Haterleigh Heritage Inn *235–236*
Holland House Inn *236*
Humboldt House *236–237*
Joan Brown's Bed and Breakfast *237*
Mulberry Manor *237*
Prior House *238*
Swans *238*
Whistler
Cedar Springs Lodge *217–218*
Chalet Luise *218*
Durlacher Hof *218–219*
Edgewater *219*
Le Chamois *219–220*

NOTES

NOTES

NOTES

NOTES

NOTES

NOTES

Looking for a different kind of vacation?

Fodor's makes it easy with a full line of guidebooks to suit a variety of interests—from sports and adventure to romance to family fun.

At bookstores everywhere.
www.fodors.com

Fodor's Travel Publications

Available at bookstores everywhere. For descriptions of all our titles and a key to Fodor's guidebook series, visit www.fodors.com/books

Gold Guides

U.S.

Alaska	Florida	New Orleans	Santa Fe, Taos, Albuquerque
Arizona	Hawai'i	New York City	
Boston	Las Vegas, Reno, Tahoe	Oregon	Seattle & Vancouver
California	Los Angeles	Pacific North Coast	The South
Cape Cod, Martha's Vineyard, Nantucket	Maine, Vermont, New Hampshire	Philadelphia & the Pennsylvania Dutch Country	U.S. & British Virgin Islands
The Carolinas & Georgia	Maui & Lāna'i	The Rockies	USA
Chicago	Miami & the Keys	San Diego	Virginia & Maryland
Colorado	New England	San Francisco	Washington, D.C.

Foreign

Australia	Eastern & Central Europe	London	Scandinavia
Austria	Europe	Madrid & Barcelona	Scotland
The Bahamas	Florence, Tuscany & Umbria	Mexico	Singapore
Belize & Guatemala	France	Montréal & Québec City	South Africa
Bermuda	Germany	Moscow, St. Petersburg, Kiev	South America
Canada	Great Britain	The Netherlands, Belgium & Luxembourg	Southeast Asia
Cancún, Cozumel, Yucatán Peninsula	Greece	New Zealand	Spain
Caribbean	Hong Kong	Norway	Sweden
China	India	Nova Scotia, New Brunswick, Prince Edward Island	Switzerland
Costa Rica	Ireland	Paris	Thailand
Cuba	Israel	Portugal	Toronto
The Czech Republic & Slovakia	Italy	Provence & the Riviera	Turkey
Denmark	Japan		Vienna & the Danube Valley
			Vietnam

Special-Interest Guides

Adventures to Imagine	Fodor's How to Pack	Healthy Escapes	Rock & Roll Traveler USA
Alaska Ports of Call	Great American Learning Vacations	Kodak Guide to Shooting Great Travel Pictures	Sunday in San Francisco
Ballpark Vacations	Great American Sports & Adventure Vacations	National Parks and Seashores of the East	Walt Disney World for Adults
The Best Cruises	Great American Vacations	National Parks of the West	Weekends in New York
Caribbean Ports of Call			
The Complete Guide to America's National Parks	Great American Vacations for Travelers with Disabilities	Nights to Imagine	Wendy Perrin's Secrets Every Smart Traveler Should Know
Europe Ports of Call		Orlando Like a Pro	
Family Adventures	Halliday's New Orleans Food Explorer	Rock & Roll Traveler Great Britain and Ireland	Worlds to Imagine
Fodor's Gay Guide to the USA			

Fodor's Special Series

Fodor's Best Bed & Breakfasts
America
California
The Mid-Atlantic
New England
The Pacific Northwest
The South
The Southwest
The Upper Great Lakes

Compass American Guides
Alaska
Arizona
Boston
Chicago
Coastal California
Colorado
Florida
Hawai'i
Hollywood
Idaho
Las Vegas
Maine
Manhattan
Minnesota
Montana
New Mexico
New Orleans
Oregon
Pacific Northwest
San Francisco
Santa Fe
South Carolina
South Dakota
Southwest
Texas
Underwater Wonders of the National Parks
Utah
Virginia
Washington
Wine Country
Wisconsin
Wyoming

Citypacks
Amsterdam
Atlanta
Berlin
Boston
Chicago
Florence
Hong Kong
London
Los Angeles
Miami
Montréal
New York City
Paris
Prague
Rome
San Francisco
Sydney
Tokyo
Toronto
Venice
Washington, D.C.

Exploring Guides
Australia
Boston & New England
Britain
California
Canada
Caribbean
China
Costa Rica
Cuba
Egypt
Florence & Tuscany
Florida
France
Germany
Greek Islands
Hawai'i
India
Ireland
Israel
Italy
Japan
London
Mexico
Moscow & St. Petersburg
New York City
Paris
Portugal
Prague
Provence
Rome
San Francisco
Scotland
Singapore & Malaysia
South Africa
Spain
Thailand
Turkey
Venice
Vietnam

Flashmaps
Boston
New York
San Francisco
Washington, D.C.

Fodor's Cityguides
Boston
New York
San Francisco

Fodor's Gay Guides
Amsterdam
Los Angeles & Southern California
New York City
Pacific Northwest
San Francisco and the Bay Area
South Florida
USA

Karen Brown Guides
Austria
California
England B&Bs
England, Wales & Scotland
France B&Bs
France Inns
Germany
Ireland
Italy B&Bs
Italy Inns
Portugal
Spain
Switzerland

Languages for Travelers (Cassette & Phrasebook)
French
German
Italian
Spanish

Mobil Travel Guides
America's Best Hotels & Restaurants
Arizona
California and the West
Florida
Great Lakes
Major Cities
Mid-Atlantic
Northeast
Northwest and Great Plains
Southeast
Southern California
Southwest and South Central

Pocket Guides
Acapulco
Aruba
Atlanta
Barbados
Beijing
Berlin
Budapest
Dublin
Honolulu
Jamaica
London
Mexico City
New York City
Paris
Prague
Puerto Rico
Rome
San Francisco
Savannah & Charleston
Shanghai
Sydney
Washington, D.C.

Rivages Guides
Bed and Breakfasts of Character and Charm in France
Hotels and Country Inns of Character and Charm in France
Hotels and Country Inns of Character and Charm in Italy
Hotels of Character and Charm in Paris
Hotels of Character and Charm in Portugal
Hotels of Character and Charm in Spain
Wines & Vineyards of Character and Charm in France

Short Escapes
Britain
France
Near New York City
New England

Fodor's Sports
Golf Digest's Places to Play (USA)
Golf Digest's Places to Play in the Southeast
Golf Digest's Places to Play in the Southwest
Skiing USA
USA Today The Complete Four Sport Stadium Guide

Fodor's upCLOSE Guides
California
Europe
France
Great Britain
Ireland
Italy
London
Los Angeles
Mexico
New York City
Paris
San Francisco

WHEREVER YOU TRAVEL, *H*ELP IS NEVER FAR AWAY.

From planning your trip to

providing travel assistance along

the way, American Express®

Travel Service Offices are

always there to help

you do more.

do more **AMERICAN EXPRESS**

Travel

www.americanexpress.com/travel

American Express Travel Service Offices
are located throughout the Pacific Northwest.
For the office nearest you, call 1-800-AXP-3429.